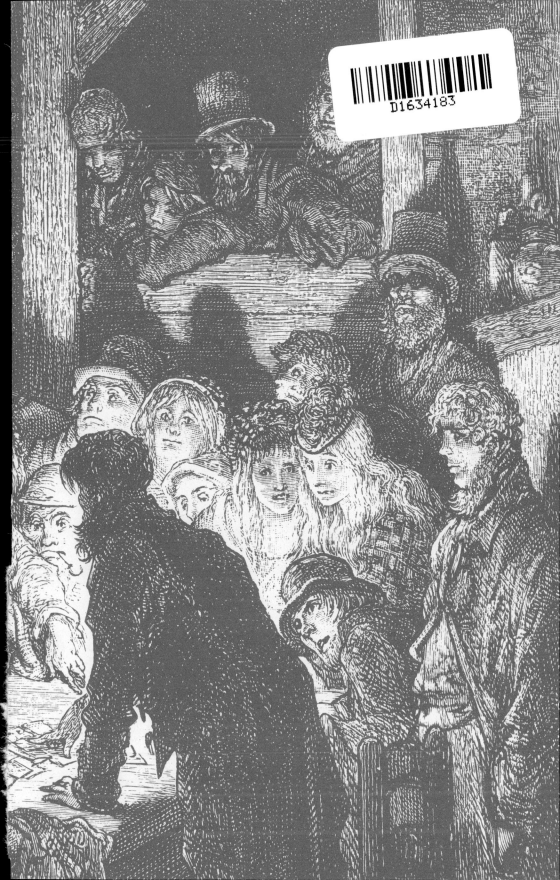

The Victorian Underworld

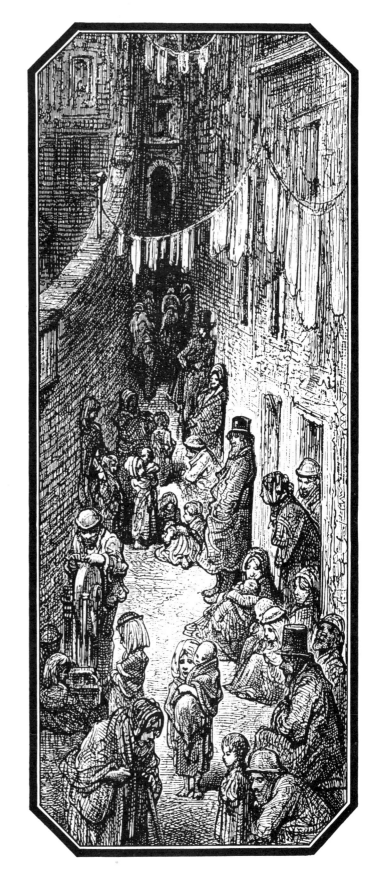

The Victorian Underworld

Kellow Chesney

BOOK CLUB EDITION

© 1970 KELLOW CHESNEY
FIRST PUBLISHED IN GREAT BRITAIN 1970
BY MAURICE TEMPLE SMITH LTD
37 GREAT RUSSELL STREET, LONDON WC1
THIS EDITION PUBLISHED BY
PURNELL BOOK SERVICES LIMITED
P.O. BOX 20, ABINGDON, OXFORDSHIRE OX14 4HE
BY ARRANGEMENT WITH MAURICE TEMPLE SMITH LIMITED
PRINTED IN GREAT BRITAIN BY
REDWOOD BURN LIMITED
TROWBRIDGE AND ESHER

Contents

Plates

For notes on the text illustrations see pages 373–375

All the illustrations by Gustave Doré are taken from *London* (with text by Blanchard Jerrold, 1872). According to Millicent Rose's scholarly *Gustave Doré* (1946) this incomparable portfolio of English types and scenes is the fruit of 'fieldwork carried out in 1869'. Doré's work is not always literal in detail (the arches in the picture of London Bridge on page 36 are incorrect) but he conveys, as does no other artist, not only the brutal and macabre quality of mid-nineteenth-century English low life, but also—uniquely—its vitality and lyricism.

To AMHC

The mid-century

Much of the fascination of the Victorian age derives from its strange familiarity. It is a truism that in many vital ways the human state and prospects have changed more radically during the past three or four generations than during the previous two thousand years: yet compare the common circumstances of the Victorians' daily life with our own, and it is astonishing how *un*remote these people seem. Quite plausibly, a man could wake up in his great-grandfather's house on his great-grandfather's bedstead, breakfast on similar food off the same plates at the same table, and set out past the same stuccoed terrace on his way to work for a firm still trading under his great-grandfather's name. If he were young enough he might even wear some of his ancestor's clothes without attracting particular notice. We are separated by a profound gulf, so narrow we seem able to touch hands.

A modern Londoner who found himself wandering about the horse-redolent metropolis of the mid-nineteenth century would not take very long to grasp the identity of the place. He could hardly miss the line of the river, while the fretted bulk of the Houses of Parliament, though incomplete and partly fuzzed with scaffolding, would be the more striking for the absence of dwarfing blocks along the waterside. Plenty of famous monuments and landmarks (some looking a good deal older and more dilapidated than they do now) would tell him where he stood.

The same thing would be true of some provincial towns, where even today some streets, closes or market squares retain enough of their ancient features to be identifiably the places they were even before Victoria's accession. Moreover the endless files of glum 'industrial dwellings' that are still plentiful round old industrial centres were already a dominant feature of the English townscape more than a century ago. Nor, probably, did many of these sordid streets look very different when they first sprang out of the fields; for they aged quickly, their raw

brickwork became grimy before it was dry and dinginess overtook them with their first tenants.

Nevertheless the lives that go on today in the thousands of
such houses that survive, their roofs bristling with TV aerials,
are as different from those of their original occupants as theirs
were from the lives of mediaeval journeymen. Many of us have
talked with people who recalled what life was like when Victoria
was a bouncing matron. We may have come across bundles of old
correspondence: the ink is rusty, but parts of the chatty family
letter (beginning, not impossibly, 'Dear Mum')[1] might have
been written yesterday instead of the year of Inkerman and
Balaclava. Yet notions of (for example) faith, decency, rank and
decorum have altered so much that the fact that we use the same
terms can itself be a cause of misunderstanding. Indeed it is
infinitely easier to grasp the extent of material change, technical
and social, than to appreciate the shift in ideas and relationships.
It is the persistent paradox, inherent in all attempts to imagine
the past. The very links, physical and intellectual, that connect
us with our forbears—the very properties we have in common
and which enable us, by putting ourselves in their place, to
understand them at all—are themselves sources of error. Time,
like water, refracts the image.

Let us imagine our Londoner translated to a summer morning
near the mid-century. Would he find himself in a congenial city?
Suppose that, disengaging himself from the knot of provincial
visitors who are staring up at Nelson's Column, he begins to
stroll eastward along the Strand. He is now walking down what
Disraeli calls the 'first street in Europe', a broad street lined
with pleasantly proportioned buildings and superior shops,
some of whose square-paned windows catch the sun at a dozen
different angles. Goods of all sorts, some of real excellence, are
being sold by shopmen who now and again run out on to the
pavement in aprons to the doors of important customers' carriages.

Since it is fine the roadway is reasonably clean. There is a
throng of traffic—drays, carts, bright-lettered rattling little
omnibuses, four-wheel and hansom cabs, saddle-horses, broughams and chaises, and once in a while a splendid chariot with the

---

[1] Lord Shaftesbury, the famous evangelical philanthropist and reformer, adopted this
style in addressing his influential mother-in-law, Melbourne's sister and (by a second
marriage) Palmerston's wife.

coachman perched on a brilliant hammercloth and more liveried servants behind. However, especially at the crossings where pedestrians cannot avoid venturing into the roadway, the dung is swept up by a variety of sweepers, of different ages, amongst them an occasional dark-faced, stick-legged Indian. The sweepers are painfully ragged and so are the urchins who, to

earn a few coppers, dart in among the traffic and turn cartwheels almost under the horses' hooves. But here most of the shoppers are well dressed, and some of the women magnificent in heavily flounced crinolined skirts, 'pagoda sleeves' and elaborate mantles. The colours of many of the dress-stuffs are rich, bold and deep. There appear to be more men than women about, most of them in very high, dull-surfaced, black top-hats which produce a repeated vertical motif in the jostling, loitering crowd. Dark frock coats above lighter, narrow trousers and high, dark silk chokers contribute to the dignified, columnar effect favoured by men of the upper, propertied orders—the masters of this assertive masculine civilisation.

As he makes his way along the Strand, through the crush at Temple Bar into the increasingly tight-packed city, and so, close by Newgate Jail, up to the soaring portico of St Paul's and the pleasant bookstalls whose awnings shade the cathedral yard, the time-traveller's appreciation may quicken. The people about him are nowhere devalued by their setting. The scene, now open, now cramped, is varied and lively, with buildings of different styles and epochs and states of preservation jostled together, yet combining to make a congruent, historically intelligible background to the folk who move among them. If he is a reflective man, a comparison between this and the slab-faced inhumanity of his own disproportioned, machine-choked London may well depress him.

Let him turn north from St Paul's and in a minute or two the noise and stench will lead him, if he has stomach enough, to the ground-level opening of an underground slaughter-house, its walls inches thick in putrefying blood and fat, into which sheep are being hurled so that they break their legs before being knifed and flayed by the men below. And these wretches, labouring in horror and filth all a long working week (they need to work long hours, for the London piece-rate for killing and dressing a sheep is about fourpence) lead healthy and fortunate lives compared to many of their fellow-citizens. A stone's throw from the prosperous Strand are courts and passages littered with rubbish and excrement where it is risky for the casual visitor to penetrate even in broad daylight, and above them tenements filled with humanity so degraded that at times (even in the warmest weather) the rotting, uncoffined bodies of the dead remain where they died, day after day, among the close-packed living.

Hideous slums, some of them acres wide, some no more than crannies of obscure misery, make up a substantial part of the metropolis. Because they are so densely occupied they are profitable, and seldom cleared away except to make way for new thoroughfares and frontages. In big, once handsome houses, thirty or more people of all ages may inhabit a single room, squatting, sleeping, copulating on the straw-filled billets or mounds of verminous rags that are the only furniture. There are cellar-homes, dark, foetid and damp with sewage, where women keep watch for the rats that gnaw their infants' faces and fingers.

Everyone knows of the nightmare casbahs, swarming with disease and crime, behind the busy streets; many respectable back-windows command a view over their roofs and yards. Doctors, coroners' officers, missionaries and occasional journalists have penetrated the vilest warrens and made their findings public. But no authority is yet prepared to look the appalling, proliferating problem in the face.

Passing along the Strand our visitor may well have noticed among the crowd knots of gentlemen in twice-about white neck-cloths and subfusc costume. These would be clergymen, mostly of an evangelical persuasion, gathered for a meeting at Exeter Hall, a famous centre for religious and philanthropic endeavour. Among such low church clergy and their prominent lay allies, there are plenty of zealous men who represent the strongest, most pervasive moral influence of the times. For, even if the evangelicals have lost some of their old afflatus, the values they exemplify have permeated the whole upper, articulate part of society during the past two or three generations. Even those who recoil from their uncompromising doctrines and mock their tendency to unctuousness have been deeply affected by the evangelical *ethos*. Indeed the very influences that now threaten the evangelical movement owe much of their vitality to the moral energies it has released.

Certainly there are unabashed cynics in high places. The rakish man of pleasure remains an upper-class institution and plenty of successful men of affairs are blatant materialists. But current manners do not favour their influence; such people do not set the tone. Morality, an explicit sense of moral purpose, is not simply estimable: it has become in the broadest cultural sense *fashionable*, and prudent men with their way to make have learnt to trim their sails accordingly. Even those privileged people who are least attracted by modern earnestness, most indifferent to middle-class pruderies, have been affected by stiffening standards. Aristocratic jobberies and official wanglings of a kind once taken for granted can now raise a storm of protest in an increasingly influential and pontifical press. Domestic scandals that could once have been passed off as peccadilloes can threaten to break a public man. Cynicism, hedonism, irreligion, romantic pessimism in the Byronic vein, all smack of the unregenerate and outmoded Georgian past. The urbanity and sceptical anti-enthusiasm of the last century have come to seem cold and dingy: no English writer is more abominated than Chesterfield. *Earnest, fervent, anxious, faithful, pure* and *true*[1] are key-words. The spokesmen and spirit-movers of the new age—the young and publicity-conscious Court, the great contemporary novelists, *The Times*, Tennyson, Carlyle, Harriet Martineau, Mill, the strenuous disciples of Thomas Arnold, the tractarian high churchmen, a host of writers and compilers of improving and instructive popular works—all in their various ways point to an appetite for moral and spiritual values unmatched since the puritan Commonwealth. And to judge from the satirists, humbug is the besetting weakness of the age.

At the very hub of upper-class London, between the end of the Strand and the elegant Regent Street quadrant, close to Whitehall and the clubs of St James's, lies a flourishing quarter openly dedicated to prostitution. Quiet and shuttered under a Sunday-like calm till past midday, the streets and byways fill, as evening approaches and the gaslights go up, with women and children to suit most tastes and all pockets but the poorest. Starched young swells, awkward provincials, seedy Dick Swivellers, furtive old perverts, all are energetically catered for.

London's anomalies are endless. A few steps from Exeter Hall is Holywell Street, the centre of a lively and well-advertised trade in pornography. Recently another, and particularly virulent, outbreak of cholera has provoked widespread fear; yet still among the packed buildings of the wealthiest city on earth, rises the charnel-stench of grotesquely over-brimming graveyards, protected by an alliance of parish interests and doctrinaire opponents of government interference. Besides the proprietors of slaughter-houses there are fat-boilers, glue-renderers, fell-mongers, tripe-scrapers, dog-skinners and the like, carrying on businesses whose 'mephitic fumes' and effluents are recognised to be a gross public danger. Food and drink made from putrid and diseased ingredients, or adulterated with notoriously toxic substances, are freely sold. In the face of incessant public agitation over the crowds of beggars and the burden of pauperism, manufacturers continue to destroy their workpeople with phosphorus, lead, arsenic and other poisons until they must look

---

[1] 'Earnest', the real talisman-word of the age, seems to have owed its extraordinary ascendancy to Dr Arnold's far-reaching influence. (Cf. *Edinburgh Review*, No. 217.)

either to charity or the workhouse for as long as their rotted bodies survive. As threats to public well-being, even these evils seem trivial compared to the raw faecal filth, often visible and sometimes actually *palpable*, that pollutes a large part of the metropolitan water supplies.

Yet the capital has few abominations that cannot be matched elsewhere, in virulence if not in extent. Indeed London, for all its superannuated system of local administrations, is generally better regulated than the chaotic new urban growths of the industrial north. Nor have the worst of those towns anything viler to offer in the way of human degradation than the unspeakable pest-holes tucked away in tranquil and picturesque old cathedral cities. Some of the most pressing social evils have their roots in the past, old mischiefs persisting and spreading in an expanding society. Practices that were tolerable, even unavoidable, when the economic pace was slower, the population smaller and manners rougher, have been allowed to develop into entrenched, demoralising abuses.

Yet if the administrative apparatus often lags behind social need, it is not just stubbornly unadaptable. The angry dread of social change and the savage repressiveness that characterised authority in the early Jacobin-haunted years of the century have long been waning. By the standards of the past (or of contemporary Europe) the Chartist disturbances of the last decades have mostly been handled with remarkably little vindictiveness, though they threatened a far wider, more concerted proletarian upsurge than any in the heyday of the Jacobin bugbear.[1] The last quarter century has seen an unparalleled tally of reforms. Parliamentary representation, local government, systems of police and poor relief, the machinery of the law and the character of the penal code, have been crucially modified; a series of religious and class disabilities have been abolished; industrial working conditions, public hygiene, popular illiteracy have all been the subjects of official investigation and varying degrees of government action.

And the tide of reform still flows. To progressives what has been achieved is often no better than a beginning, while more reluctant reformers, ready to call a halt, find one thing leading

---

[1] Even Frost, the leader of the armed and bloodily repelled Newport rising—the most violent Chartist outbreak—had his death sentence commuted and was eventually (1854) pardoned. Most striking was the restraint in dealing with provocative literature. According to Sir L. Woodward, 'No chartist newspaper was ever suppressed; no pamphlet or book was confiscated.' (*The Age of Reform*, 2nd edition, p. 141.)

inevitably to the next. The idea of continuous, necessary advance moral and material, is everywhere in the air: the world spins ever faster down the ringing grooves of change and there is little gain in trying to reverse the process. From now on, social stability is to be achieved by accepting and regulating change, rather than by reaction.

Nevertheless progressives are far from agreed on how true progress is best promoted. Freedom and human advance clearly go hand in hand and, to many, a freedom that does not embrace a man's liberty to order his own affairs is double-talk and chicanery. The rightful function of authority is to keep the peace and protect property. Government agencies are traditionally associated with political finangling and ruling-class parasitism and if they set out to regulate everyday activities it can only lead to tax-ridden regimentation and servility. Indeed (so the already classically familiar incantation runs) whatever obscures the stark realities of supply and demand is not only impractical but morally ruinous, discouraging diligence and thrift, and sapping manly self-respect.

Official enquiries have exposed ghastly instances of exploitation of women and children in mills and mines. And prominent free-trade radicals—champions of enslaved negroes, leaders in the struggle against the deadening hand of aristocratic privilege —have fought against laws to mitigate these evils as bitterly as the most obscurantist High Tory coal-owner in the House of Lords. Yet in spite of the obvious interest of such 'Manchester' radicals in cheap food and cheap labour, to see them merely as hypocrites is a pat over-simplification. In an age of unstable political ties, and rampant individualism, the play of moral and material interests produces endless incongruities, not always to the discredit of human nature.

The famous Ten Hours Bill, the most important and strongly resisted Factory Act on the statute book, has recently been levered through Parliament by the efforts of two men, one a conservative nobleman with feudal instincts and a driving evangelical conscience and the other a great northern mill-owner of radical views and formidably autocratic temper. Some of the most rabble-rousing denouncers of class tyranny have been dissident Tories.

The picture is never black-and-white. Restrictions on child-labour can increase the hardships of underpaid textile-workers, while on the other hand the harsh reformed Poor Law is nurturing all sorts of vital developments in public welfare. In one form or another the question confronts reformers of every tint. How far are contemporary miseries and degradations inseparable from progress? Have the material developments that provide the basis of social improvement to be inexorably paid for with dislocation and suffering?

One need not look far to see the problem posed in concrete terms. A profusion of textiles pours out of the mills, bringing great wealth from overseas and providing the means to import food for a soaring population. At the same time it enables the community as a whole to clothe itself better and cheaper than ever before. The benefits are obvious and enormous; yet they are often bitterly denied by those who have felt or seen the hardships that go with them. For years power-made textiles have been driving whole populations of handcraftsmen, whose once-prized skills have become as valueless as the machinery that clutters their cottages, through miseries that have become a national byword down into the degradation of the social sump.

Nor is this the only price to be paid for cheap clothing. Many of the good handsewn garments that gave the crowd along the Strand its prosperous look—from the artisan's solid velveteens to the young swell's braided kerseymere—were put together by the most notoriously sweated labour in the country. And this labour, it appears, remains so abjectly available to the sweater largely because of the effects of technological progress.

The economic and demographic theories of the time do more to justify these miseries, or at least to make them seem inevitable, than they do to indicate remedies.[1]

If society has been getting more elastic, its barriers easier for the enterprising to cross, it is far from becoming egalitarian. In many ways industrialisation has sharpened the divisions between rich and poor—Disraeli's estranged 'two nations'. The rapid rise of new groups to wealth and influence, and the hazardous ups-and-downs of the industrial-commercial hurly-burly, have done surprisingly little to devalue class distinctions, though they have inevitably altered their pattern. The parvenu's zest for all the

---

[1] Current 'Malthusian' and kindred ideas were soon to appear extended, and as it were apotheosised, into a universal natural system of mortal competition for survival in Darwin's *Origin of Species* (1859). The notion that unemployment and its attendant ills were a product of excess population was so widely accepted that 'surplus population' was virtually a standard term for the unemployed, and might be used in this sense even by those who did not subscribe to the theory.

attributes of inherited privilege and the passionate snobberies of a large part of the upper and middling orders are the staple of contemporary satire.

Nowadays few people with any pretensions to gentility would strike a servant (or at any rate care to be caught at it): but the notions of propriety that have made such conduct taboo have done nothing to promote easier intercourse between classes. Less roughness can mean greater stand-offishness, and the coarseness and lewdness of what has recently come to be known as 'the great unwashed' have become increasingly distasteful. The vast industrial working class has grown up largely outside the traditional social order and in conditions that obviously make for sordid and 'impure' habits of life, and though there may be less overt brutality (more genuine sensibility, even) in attitudes towards the lower orders, over-free relations with them are the more liable to seem not just ungenteel but morally contaminating.

At the same time the continuing harshness of the struggle for life, and the repeated collapse of attempts at mass working-class organisation, have not tended to encourage presumption in the underdog. Roughness is to be expected in proletarians and, especially in the industrial north, a certain blunt outspokenness to superiors may even be approved as a mark of the sterling Briton; but by and large the working man knows his place and touches his forelock. It is noticeable that the most notoriously violent sorts of labourers are usually under bosses who are themselves of a low and blackguardly stamp and have no wish to see their employees turn into sober 'respectable operatives'.

At one end, then, of an infinitely graduated social scale are the property-less, voteless millions, for vast numbers of whom, whether resentful or submissive, the social machinery is an instrument of repression. At the other is a shrewdly unexclusive aristocracy, whose social and political prestige has only begun to be undermined by setbacks to the hereditary landed interest.[1] For all the effects of change, this remains a hierarchic and class-conscious society, in important respects more effectively disciplined than its predecessors and marked by a firm spirit of subordination.

Nothing is more typical of the age than the widespread devotion

[1] In the liberal-complexioned administration in power in 1850 nine of the fourteen cabinet ministers were titled noblemen; moreover of the remaining five only one (H. Labouchere, later Lord Taunton) can be fairly said to have come from outside the ranks of the hereditary patriciate. Gladstone's first cabinet in 1868 had seven lords (including a duke and four earls) to eight untitled members—a marked break with the normal pattern.

shown, from the royal couple down, to the cult of the family. To a foreigner, the mystique of the domestic hearthside can seem at once impressive and absurd, but it is at the very heart of the English social ethos. The master of the household is more and more likely to earn his living away from the house,[1] but if the time he spends at home has diminished, his domestic status certainly has not: in some contemporary descriptions there is a sense of something sublime, almost hierophantic, in the role of paterfamilias.

In time to come people whose upbringing was in the strict Victorian tradition will not always report kindly on it. The prosperous Victorian father, back to a comfortable fire under an elaborately fringed mantelpiece, jingling in his pockets the profits of phossy-jaw or industrial phthisis while, with unctuous severity, he dismisses a pregnant maidservant to her ruin on the streets before calling in his trembling children to be thrashed for some nursery peccadillo—this monster, though an ideal figure, is not a purely fictitious one. His shadowy features can be seen behind those of many upright, useful and gifted men, and his principles and prejudices have a direct bearing on the whole character of the society in which he thrives, down to its lowermost strata.

As has been said, this is an age of assertive masculinity. Seldom have the differences in dress and bearing between men and women been so emphatic. 'Manly' and 'womanly' have become the commonest clichés of praise, manly vigour being conventionally contrasted with womanly softness and delicacy. Even in the work of gifted writers a heroine may appear so insipidly ingenuous as to border on the feeble-minded.

Yet the insistent note of romantic submission, when contrasted with the more matter-of-fact acceptance of feminine subordination common in an earlier age, may give rise to suspicion. And in fact one need not look far for signs of a profound change in woman's condition—from the new London Queen's College for ladies to the force of 'respectable female clerks' recruited by the go-ahead Electric Telegraph Company, or the disproportionate

---

[1] The increasing divorce of work from home affected many sections of the community, from the artisan obliged to relinquish his cottage industry to the capitalist who decided it would be more convenient and genteel to reside at a distance from brewery, mill or bank. Obviously both the growing size of some sorts of enterprise and the concentration of businesses in commercial or industrial quarters promoted the tendency. Its incidence was very irregular; but even where there was no physical removal of living from working premises there could still be growing estrangement. The prospering farmer who ceased to live on a familial basis with his hinds and dairy maids but installed a piano in the parlour and kept his daughters in refined seclusion from the midden-yard was a well-established example.

stir aroused by Mrs Bloomer, the American exponent of women's rights and 'rational' pantaloons. It is worth remarking that a woman and a feminist, Harriet Martineau, may claim to have been the most celebrated populariser and popular critic of the socio-economic ideas of the new industrial era. With the Crimean War the astonishing figure of Florence Nightingale streams, comet-like, into view, the only Briton to earn lasting acclaim for a prominent part in that bloodily bungled expedition, and the first of a series of women campaigners who will have an increasing influence on the national scene. Her contemporary, Josephine Butler, the wife of a prominent clergyman, will become the public champion of prostitutes against coercion by masculine officialdom.

At one end of the social scale, the power of great hostesses and other wire-pulling women is as wide as ever. At the other, regiments of women continue to be needed by steam age industry and in some processes technical improvements have increased the proportion of skilled, or semi-skilled, women to men. Women's labour is cheap, and at times its cheapness has meant workless husbands and fathers and bitter hardship for working communities. Nevertheless, exploited though she may be, the 'female operative' who carries away a cash wage on which she can subsist is grasping a potential independence unknown to the boarded servant or shop assistant living in, or to the woman working at the frame in her husband's cottage. Nowhere along the social spectrum has woman's status generally declined, relative to man's; and among the culturally dominant professional classes there are signs that it is rising.[1] By the seventies the slow, shuffling advance of emancipation will be inexorably underway.

All of which is not to deny the general acceptance of woman's inferiority, as prescribed by law and custom. In fact the relations between men and women, like those between the innumerable other groups into which mid-nineteenth-century society can be divided, shift and alter as we look at them.

The closer we try to approach, the more we discount the effects of hindsight, the more contradictory and makeshift does that society appear. However widespread its consciousness of being

[1] It may be straining a point to suggest that the sheer volume of space women have come to occupy is a sign of their greater consequence. Three or four crinolined ladies can practically fill a modest drawing-room, and even the 'neat parlourmaid' covers more floor than a couple of plump men. But certainly one can detect signs of an increased freedom from household tasks in the fact that there are plenty of homes where the mistress, once fully rigged, can hardly squeeze her preposterous flounces down the kitchen stairs.

in the van of progress, of marching in the foremost files of time, it is obvious that for the most part even its leaders have only hazy and conflicting ideas as to where the march is heading. Never before, since God set a firmament in the midst of the waters, have there been industrialised states; and Britain is indisputably the first and greatest and most deeply smoke-grimed. Since the transformation began to overtake them, its inhabitants have been stumbling and groping their way into a new era.

And so, alongside the expansionist bounce, the delight in technical achievement and the earnest faith in moral improvement, there yawn black misgivings. The dislocations and misery that have accompanied great increases in productivity and wealth have produced a sense of helplessness. It is not only the victims who feel that they are living, like a community of sorcerers' apprentices, in the grip of a process beyond control. To many others it seems as if some baneful, arbitrary power (personified by Carlyle's enchanter in *Past and Present* or the tyrant 'King Steam' of the popular ballad-monger) has taken charge of human affairs.

On the one hand the tide of steam age prosperity has been driving through many channels: pouring wealth into the lap of the landowner whose acres sprout smokestacks at other men's initiative, turning the petty builder into a giant contractor, making the engineer into a national hero, bringing golden opportunities for bagmen and brokers, stimulating the energetic, flexible and rapacious in every walk of life. On the other, there are the landscapes of roaring furnaces and smouldering spoil-heaps, stinking waterways, vast miasmic dock-basins, and endless sordid, unhealthy dwellings—the heartlands of the new wealth and power that seem like a panorama of hell.

To the man of 1850 who has seen popular insurrections flaring across Europe from Russia to Ireland, who knows how a short trade recession—even a few weeks of freezing weather—can bring tens of thousands to desperate want, and how, despite the fearful slum mortalities, the packed urban proletariat (recently crammed tighter by hordes of famine-driven Irish) inexorably increases year by year, this may seem a less firm-footed society than it does when looked back on from far beyond the farther side of the Victorian experience.

Nevertheless, with all their record of political disturbance, the past twenty years have seen a striking improvement in the ability of the authorities to maintain public order. The old anarchic mob, swarming out of its warrens to rule the streets and give them over to protracted violence and pillage, has lost much of its former potency.[1] Rapid communications have greatly strengthened the government's hand, while despite the fears roused by huge and growing slum populations, it is plain that the great cities, and above all the metropolis, are far more efficiently policed than they were a short generation ago. No figure is more characteristic of the modern street scene than the solid, calm-pacing, frockcoated 'peeler'.

At this point it may be worth considering, briefly, some of the institutions that most affected the sort of people with whom we are going to be concerned.

By 1840 about six-sevenths of the sixteen million inhabitants of England and Wales lived in areas where the reformed Poor Law was in force. Parishes were grouped into unions which were required to provide workhouses for the destitute. Neither its administrative and financial merits, nor the many benefits traceable to its influence, alter the fact that the 1834 Poor Law Amendment Act—that 'fundamental document of Victorianism'—cast a black shadow over countless lives. It was a harsh measure, designed to inspire fear, and if easygoingness, paternalism, timidity, Christian charity and a hundred other causes often softened its rigour, its provisions were also apt to be distorted and its harshness turned to savage brutality by the cruelty and meanness of those responsible for carrying it out.

Broadly, the framers of the Act intended to remove from circulation those who could not or would not support themselves, by refusing them outdoor relief and admitting them to a workhouse. This in turn was meant to put an end to the force of cheap labour subsidised by the rates, stimulate a rise in wages, and encourage able-bodied men to seek out work wherever it could be found. To bring this about, it was essential that life in the workhouse should be unpleasant enough to make the condition of the average farm or industrial labourer seem attractive. It was no part of the scheme to punish those who through age or sickness were unable to work, but in practice attempts to provide special conditions and premises for them largely miscarried.

---

[1] The 1831 Bristol reform riots, with their sustained looting and destruction, have some claims to be considered the last full Georgian-style English mob boil-over. The fiercest Chartist riots did not show the same persisting fury. However, riots serious enough to involve the use of troops occurred throughout the Victorian era.

Though in fact outside relief not only continued but remained the principal means of dealing with distress, the effect of the 'workhouse test' was very far-reaching. It became the common fate of the destitute, and people would endure desperate cold and hunger before they applied to the dreaded Union.

In the workhouse, husbands and wives were rigorously separated from each other and from their children. Even if, by chance,

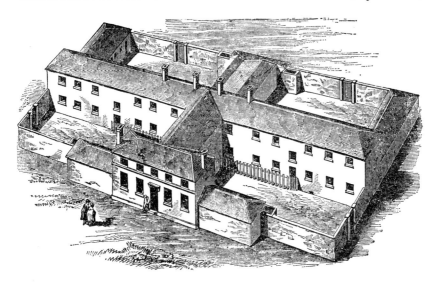

they ate at nearby tables in the hall, they were forbidden to communicate, for all of them, including children still too small to be taken from mothers, were expected to eat their meagre meals—in which gruel or broth, dry bread or potatoes was likely to be the main item—in silence. Once inside the workhouse doors the pauper could see visiting relatives only by special permission, and in the presence of the master or matron. In the bare and sometimes freezing wards, imbeciles, consumptives, syphilitics, expectant mothers, respectable souls driven by starvation, might be indiscriminately lodged; sex and age were the only crucial distinctions. For male paupers, stone-breaking, oakum picking or grinding old bones in hand-mills were suitable occupations. These tasks could also be ordered for punishment, and other ways of enforcing discipline included confinement in cramped closets, penitential dress and a reduced diet. In winter, especially, there were means to bring all but the toughest inmates to heel. On the other hand, elementary schooling for the children was a real benefit, though the teachers, sometimes recruited from among the paupers, were often inefficient as well as brutal. (When the explorer Stanley was a boy in St Asaph's workhouse in the fifties one of his fellows was flogged so severely by the schoolmaster that he died; but the incident seems to have caused no particular scandal.)

Adult paupers, of course, were not prisoners. Any of them could quit the workhouse at will, provided they stayed away. But they had to give proper notice of their intention, and if they stayed in the neighbourhood without visible means of support they could find themselves picked up under the vagrancy laws and sent to jail.

Particularly bad conditions sometimes attracted publicity: at Stockport a man of seventy-two suffering from a bad knee refused to break stones and was taken before a magistrate and ordered fourteen days at the treadmill; at Deptford a child of four was locked three nights in the mortuary, sleeping on coffin covers; at Andover paupers given 'green' (that is still putrefying) bones to grind, struggled for the pieces of meat sticking to them; at the West London Union the attentions of the porter were found to be the cause of venereal disease among girl inmates.

It must be said that the worst workhouses were often old, pre-1834 establishments over which the new Poor Law Commissioners had difficulty in establishing their supervision, but perhaps the most painful exposure of all involved no less than thirteen London parochial Poor Law boards. In January 1849 a number of inquests were held on children who had died as a result of an outbreak of disease at the Infant Pauper Asylum, kept by a man called Drouet, at Tooting.

Drouet's asylum housed some 1,400 children of both sexes, between two and fifteen years old, and the evidence brought out in the coroners' courts showed that, with all allowance for exaggeration, conditions there beggared description. Dirt and fear reigned in this frightful place, from which Drouet apparently made a substantial profit by exploiting his charges' labour. (He was also paid four-and-six a head per week by the workhouse guardians.) The sleeping rooms were crammed; the miserable meals were eaten standing up; there was not even enough drinking water available, and a racket had grown up by which those inmates who controlled a supply levied a toll on others. Complaints to visiting guardians were punished with thrashings, and pauper parents were only allowed to see their children very infrequently and under supervision. One mother was not told of her child's death until after the funeral. A striking feature of the evidence was the attitude of the workhouse authorities: official visitors who were at first outraged by what they saw, subsequently calmed down and 'reported most favourably'. Granted the character of many London local authorities at this time, it seems unlikely that Drouet was able to keep all his profits to himself.

In fairness to the authorities, it must be said that they had at times to cope with difficult inmates. One class of pauper was proverbially intractable. Since a freer movement of labour was a prime objective of the reformed Poor Law, it was laid down that workhouses should provide accommodation for people on the tramp. These 'casuals', taken in for a single night, were often robust and disorderly characters who were not easily intimidated. Though we hear of tramps at Birmingham being locked naked in a black hole under the stairs for more than a week, any attempt to detain and punish a party of tough casuals was likely to involve the authorities in unwelcome difficulty and expense, especially in a small country Union. To deal effectively and legally with really determined troublemakers required a magistrate and constables who might not be readily available. As a result casuals might refuse to do the work allotted to them in exchange for their night's lodging, and workhouse masters, frightened of riot and destruction, would thankfully see them go, leaving filth and confusion behind them.[1]

If it was necessary that the condition of the workhouse pauper should be, as the official phrase went, 'less eligible' than the employed labourer's, it was *a fortiori* necessary that the convict in jail should be still worse off. So indeed he commonly was. But whereas the great Poor Law Amendment Act was in many ways an administrative triumph and produced, by the standards of the time, a remarkable degree of conformity, the prison system was a jobbed-together patchwork, the product of ill-matched and sometimes conflicting penal principles. In spite of the complaints of inspectors and the directives of ministers, it was not till 1865 that a fully effective beginning was made in securing uniform standards of treatment, and not till 1877 that what can be called a coherent national penal system emerged.

[1] See page 63.

In the thirties and early forties there was still great slackness in places. A criminal with good outside contacts who could square the turnkey might well pass his sentence in comparative ease, with supplies of decent food and such comforts as liquor and cigars. But the whole direction of change was towards more efficient administration and supervision, and so in effect towards more rigorous conditions. The same reforming impetus that had swept away the stocks and pillory and roadside gibbets, that had made the flogging of women criminals an intolerable affront to decency and had abolished the 'bloody code' with its innumerable capital offences, also produced jails of great severity. In place of filth, jail-fever and corruption, came the treadmill, the crank and strict regimentation.

It has to be remembered that the notion of the prison as primarily an instrument of punishment, rather than a place to hold criminals awaiting trial or the execution of their sentence, was still growing throughout the first half of the nineteenth century. (Transportation only ceased to be an important method of dealing with major offenders in the early fifties.) Hence there was a lot of experiment. It was obvious that the old-style prisons, with their haphazard arrangements, were truly 'lyceums' and 'academies' of crime, and one object of reform must be to prevent criminals communicating freely inside jail. Solitary confinement was in favour

as a special means of punishment and reform, but it meant spending far too much on accommodation to be generally practicable. However, an alert staff could enforce silence for a good deal of the time, and above all the prisoners could be kept so well occupied that they had little opportunity or energy for corrupting one another. In some prisons these methods were supplemented by making the prisoners wear masks, so that nothing could be conveyed by their features and they might even have difficulty in identifying each other.

Broadly, there were two main types of prison: the local House of Correction, chiefly for men, women and children serving sentences from seven days to a couple of years, and the long-term convict prisons that also provided, increasingly, an alternative to transportation. (In 1853, when transportation for a term of less than fourteen years was discontinued, it was reckoned that four years' penal servitude at home was equivalent to seven years' transportation.) A House of Correction might be a section, or function, of the same common jail that housed suspects awaiting trial and prisoners awaiting execution or transfer. The long-term convict prisons were usually specialised institutions and at the mid-century they included both new-broom penal servitude jails and the decrepit, filthy hulks still floating in the lower Thames.

In one respect at least the severe penal regimes of the time were effective: they left a large number of offenders in a state of enfeebled physical and mental health that can only have made them less efficient criminals. Even a comparatively short spell in a House of Correction like the dreaded 'Steel' (Bastille) in Coldbath Fields could be a highly damaging experience.

Here the treadmills were close compartments in which a prisoner remained for a quarter of an hour at a time, vigorously treading down a wheel of twenty-four steps at a fixed rate. They were arranged in rows which 'gave them somewhat of the appearance of the stalls in a public urinal', the wheels turning a long axle attached to an ingenious apparatus of air-vanes that allowed it to revolve at exactly the right, agonising speed. As a warder explained to the ever curious and compassionate Henry Mayhew, who visited the place in the fifties—'You see the men can get no firm tread like, from the steps always sinking away from under their feet and *that* makes it very tiring. Again the compartments are small, and the air becomes very hot, so that

the heat at the end of a quarter of an hour renders it difficult to breathe.'[1]

Another exercise at the Steel was shot-drill, which was considered so taxing that 'none but the strongest could endure it' and men over forty-five were usually excused. For this the prisoners were formed up in rows round a hollow square with an interval of three yards between each man. To the shouted commands of an officer, each picked up a twenty-four pound cannon ball, carried it as far as his neighbour's place, dumped it, and immediately went back to his original position where the shot supplied by his other neighbour was waiting for him. This drill usually went on for seventy-five minutes.

The 'crank' was an engine of torture consisting of a drum filled with sand or some other resistant matter, with a cupped

[1] Mayhew and Binny *The Criminal Prisons of London*, p. 304. One unpleasant effect of the treadmill is indicated by its cant name among convicts—the 'cockchafer'.

spindle running through it which the prisoner had to turn by a crank-handle. On improved models the revolutions were recorded by a clock mechanism, so that no immediate supervision was necessary. Mayhew was told that at Coldbath Fields the crank was so dreaded that it was used as a punishment for those who shirked at the other forms of labour. Recalcitrant prisoners could also be flogged or birched.

Probably the inmates of the penal servitude convict jails were less tormented—otherwise they would hardly have survived long terms. Certainly they more often spent most of their working hours in the open air and were likely to have better rations.

It has always to be remembered, however, that there were wide differences in treatment even between prisons of the same category in the same part of the country. Sentences also varied wildly: it was possible to find a child of ten in jail for the first time on the charge of having caused a public nuisance by spinning a top—no doubt in most aggravating circumstances—and a blackguard serving a few months in a relatively lax prison for brutal assault.

In 1850 the average number of men, women and children in criminal prisons in England and Wales was claimed to be 17,025; the great majority being, of course, short-term offenders. In addition there were some 'ticket-of-leave' men, released on parole before the end of their sentence and subject to supervision and various restrictions.

Though the ticket-of-leave system did not work very well, the fact that it had become practicable at all was a tribute to an increasingly effective police. The new police were, indeed, the most important innovation to affect the underworld, and the last that needs to be considered here.

The first, crucial step in the formation of a genuinely effective civil police was the creation by Peel's famous Metropolitan Police Act of 1829 of a new London force, responsible for almost the whole metropolis except the City itself. The peelers were headed by two highly capable commissioners and, after some troubles and reorganisation, they proved very effective. They were not popular: the liberties of the common people and their power to influence their betters had in the past owed much to the fact that the country's rulers had had no strong and reliable police at their disposal, and many liberals of different shades, as well as plain upholders of old fashioned ways, shared the hostility of the bulk of the London masses to the peelers. There was a fear that the country would soon be subject to a continental-type gendarmerie, complete with spies and *agents provocateurs*. But the new police could claim that they were essentially 'preventive': their function was, in the first place, to stop crime happening by their conspicuous presence. The case against the old magistrates' runners was that they had looked on the criminal population as something like a crop, to be cultivated and gathered in when the prospect of a worthwhile reward made a criminal ripe for taking. The accusation was almost certainly not true of all the old police agents but the peelers managed, on the whole, to keep themselves remarkably clear of the imputation. Perhaps they were helped by the fact that while the foot patrols of the old metropolitan system were abolished, some at least of the magistrates' runners continued to work as 'criminal officers'.[1]

The lending of detachments of peelers to provincial towns for particular emergencies—they could be specially sworn-in as local constables—helped to increase their reputation and show civic authorities the advantages of having such a force at hand. When, after the 1835 Municipal Reform Act, many towns acquired new regular police forces, they were largely modelled on the metropolitan pattern. An increasing uniformity followed, since the watch committees which controlled the municipal police received subsidies which depended on their forces conforming to standards required by the Home Office.

The marked increase in the efficiency of city law-enforcement seems to have encouraged criminals to shift about the country looking for places where they were not yet known (many were at least seasonally mobile, anyway). Also the growth of urban areas had produced anomalous civic boundaries, so that the authorities of some towns and cities controlled only a fraction of the area over which the town now spread. A man might cross from the territory of a competent city police force into that of a part-time constable belonging to a 'rural' parish without doing more than move out towards the suburbs.

The improvement in county police was slow and irregular. (The Home Office encouraged rather than enforced reform.) In

[1] The metropolitan detective police, under the commissioners at Scotland Yard, dates from 1842 but remained a very small force till the 70s. Divisional police chiefs, however, employed selected men on plainclothes duties.

the forties the Lancashire constabulary could still number among its officers a constable who was largely dependent on shoe-mending for his livelihood. It was not till the mid-fifties that county magistratures were obliged to provide an effective, new-style constabulary in all districts not already covered by another authority.

When speaking broadly of 'England' or 'the English' one hundred and twenty years ago we are apt to have in mind a limited part of the population—that privileged, articulate and more or less informed minority whose tastes and ideas governed what we think of as the culture of the period. Nothing, however, is more characteristic of that minority than the interest it had come to take in the lives of the degraded and obscure.

To a great extent this interest was part and parcel of the moral drive to social reform, the awareness of a land

> . . . full of wrongs and shames,
> Horrible, hateful, monstrous, not to be told.

For two decades an extraordinary amount had been told in the printed reports of the numerous government enquiries into all kinds of horrors and abuses: reports that lit up the underside of society as it had never been lit before, and that not only had a direct impact but inspired journalists, pamphleteers and novelists who carried their message to a far wider public.

The public was ready and eager for such writing, and it is clear that the appetite for accounts of low life went far beyond a moral concern for the unfortunate. It is not hard to understand how descriptions of the jungle-world of the slums appealed to an increasingly prudish and taboo-ridden bourgeoisie. *Oliver Twist*, the greatest fictional presentation of the underworld, relies for much of its appeal on the frankly spine-chilling horror of characters on whom Dickens lavished far more pains than on his insipid hero.[1] Disraeli's *Sybil*, published seven years later, while it incorporates lumps of material from an official report, skilfully exploits the romance of proletarian discontent and degradation.

It is this demand by the reading public for information about the mysterious world so near and so remote from their own, that

[1] Published in 1838, it describes a style of workhouse that was already becoming out-moded by the 1834 Poor Law.

makes a review of the contemporary underworld feasible. Above all the demand produced the unique work of Henry Mayhew and his collaborators—the essential foundation of this book.

In 1851 Mayhew produced the first three volumes of his famous *London Labour and the London Poor*, a vast, shapeless, repetitive and indescribably rich description of the lives of almost every kind of urban underdog, full of records of immediate first-hand encounters and rambling personal narratives, and stretching at times far beyond the London scene. The book, to a great extent composed of material collected for newspaper articles, was the subject of litigation which interrupted its production. Moreover it was perhaps too jumbled as well as too frank to appeal to a very wide public. In the early sixties, however, it was reissued with a crucial fourth volume, also exceedingly long—it is distended by a potted history of whoredom through the ages—but less undisciplined and dealing specifically with the delinquent classes. Here Mayhew's collaborators openly take over: prostitutes and their ways of life are described by Bracebridge Hemyng, beggars by Andrew Halliday, and thieves and cheats are dealt with by John Binny—a perceptive investigator who also shared with Mayhew the authorship of *Criminal Prisons of London*. Taken together these five volumes offer a view of the shadowy proletarian world which for vivid intimacy has no equal in our records, and no parallel until Charles Booth began his very different and more methodical researches towards the end of the century.

Mayhew is not a model guide. His vagaries are endless. At one moment his enthusiasm for statistics will lead him into preposterous figurings; at another he will let his flow of anecdote swirl him away into the eighteenth century without troubling to mention the fact. Those who travel with him need to have a general map of the period firmly in their minds and to be on the alert for landmarks and points of reference.

Nevertheless he and his collaborators and other popular reporters of the time are sometimes more convincing than official sources. These men were moved by curiosity; they followed their noses, sniffing their way through strange territories, and if they were not always above touching up a dull picture, they had little temptation to suppress something paradoxical but revealing for the sake of consistency. Even those reporters who (unlike Mayhew) were firmly *parti pris* and committed to ramming home some particular message, are not necessarily less reliable than more formal enquirers.

For anyone interested in criminality and law enforcement at the beginning of Victoria's reign it is difficult to conceive of a more fascinating document than the 1839 *Report of Commissioners appointed to enquire into . . . an efficient Constabulary Force in the Counties of England and Wales*, the work of Edwin Chadwick, the moving spirit of administrative reform, and Colonel Rowan, the able and intelligent commissioner of Metropolitan Police. Nevertheless, as the vivid, dramatic evidence unfolds it becomes impossible to suppress a creeping unease. There is something amiss. How can this picture be reconciled with the England of writers of letters, memoirs, novels of social life, of clerical jaunts, lonely walking tours, placid spinsters' lives in unpoliced Cranfords? It seems rather a land for blockhouses and fortified manors, where no sensible man would go to a country fair without a primed pistol in his belt. In fact scholarship has shown the report to be a piece of propagandist axe-grinding. This is not to say it is a tissue of false evidence; only that, considered by itself, it can offer a profoundly misleading view. Chadwick and Rowan were not addressing posterity: they were trying to stir up sluggish and obscurantist contemporaries who were well able to provide their own counter arguments.

If we are to get anything like a balanced view, we must make use of as many different sources as possible. We must look back through the eyes of reformers, novelists, government officials, journalists, cranks and scoundrels until the face of a vanished community begins to emerge.

This book is not a history of delinquency between Queen Victoria's accession and death. Its object, merely, is to offer a view of the criminal and submerged classes at a certain period: less a kind of graph plotting the course of change than a group-photograph (as of a school or club) in which a number of related yet diverse types, all unedifying, are to be seen against their own background. The period of exposure must be limited or the figures will shift overmuch and the picture blur. The following pages will be chiefly concerned with the middle years of the nineteenth century.

If we take 1850 as our focal date (the year of Peel's death, of the publication of the last numbers of *David Copperfield* and the

start of work on the Great Exhibition) and allow the field of
vision to stretch some twenty years on either side of this mid-
point, we can hope to have a reasonably firm picture. In spite of
the progress of steam-age engineering, the rate of social change
during these years was not frenetic, especially among the lowest
classes; there was no sudden political or economic upheaval and
the distant Crimean war had little effect on most people's daily
lives. The period is short enough to be coherent, yet long enough
to indicate the direction in which things were moving.

But though this period will dominate the book, it will not be
considered in isolation. For instance, it will hardly be possible
to deal with the question of prostitution without noticing the
events that lead up to the provisions in the Criminal Law
Amendment Act of 1885. Again it may be that a description
of some corner of society, though it belongs to an earlier date,
throws enough indirect light on the state of affairs round the

mid-century to be worth mentioning. In short there will be no rigidly pedantic adhering to a time scheme chosen for the sake of convenience.

There are, of course, many vital questions about the state of society—the growth and movement of population, the distribution of wealth, the shifting bases of power, to name a few—that can only be answered by methods very different from those employed here. If this book does not attempt to grapple with them it is not from any doubt of their importance, but simply that they lie beyond the scope of a work whose aim is portraiture rather than analysis, and which sets out to convey an idea not of processes but of people.

CHAPTER TWO

The borders of the underworld

To define the exact extent of the mid-century underworld would be an impossible task. It had no sharp boundaries but everywhere blurred off into the society around it, and though it was intimately related to poverty and crime its limits cannot be fixed simply in those terms. The miserable west country labourer, half dependent on stolen turnips and poached rabbits, no more belongs than the titled banker jailed for embezzlement; while the Haymarket night-house keeper, rich with earnings the law allowed, qualifies as unquestionably as the pickpocket and the footpad. Yet for all its indefiniteness this underworld remains a clearly recognisable part of the civilisation that produced it— and whose character and values it continually affected.

When respectable people spoke of the *dangerous classes*—a phrase enjoying a good deal of currency—they were not talking about the labouring population as a whole, nor the growing industrial proletariat. Neither were they referring to that minority of politically conscious, mostly 'superior' radical working men on whom any sustained working-class political movement ultimately depended. They meant certain classes of people whose very manner of living seemed a challenge to ordered society and the tissue of laws, moralities and taboos holding it together. These 'unprincipled', 'ruffianly', 'degraded' elements seemed ready to exploit any breakdown in the established order. They roused a natural anxiety among a ruling class conscious of the strains to which rapid economic change was subjecting the whole social organism.

The thieves, cheats, bullies, beggars, touts and tarts with whom this book is chiefly concerned all belonged, more or less, to the dangerous classes. These classes, however, were not limited to professional parasites and delinquents—if they had been they would hardly have seemed such a danger to the established order. What was disturbing was that they included thousands who not only earned a legitimate living when they could, but earned it in ways vital to the prosperity of the society whose stability they seemed to threaten. Among port labourers and street traders, in sections of the iron working and construction industries, were people cut off from the accepted patterns of civilised life: among a good many of them even so fundamental an institution as legal marriage was in general disuse. Society had made itself dependent on a large community of men and women who were estranged from it and hostile to its canons; men and women with no fixed homes or steady livelihood, who looked on the domesticated and respectable with, at best, watchful half-predatory eyes. In trying to come to terms with a subject matter that defies firm definition, it may be worth while to examine some of these groups—the semi-barbarous tribes whose social territories formed, as it were, the marches of the underworld.

Nothing in the Victorian era compared for social impact with the coming of the railways. In two decades a net of what quickly became arterial lines was flung over the land, bringing such transformations that it quickly became difficult to conceive life without it. The elaborate system of cuttings and embankments, bridgings and borings was created, like the pyramids, by concentrations of human muscle. As the creeping railheads drew their trails across the countryside they carried with them armies of navvies and their camp followers.

As their name (land 'navigators' or canal builders) indicates, the navvies were not newcomers to the English scene. For many years villages near canal workings had seen young men go off with the navigator gangs, as lost to home and friends as those who took the King's shilling. Over the years there had grown up a caste of specialised nomad labourers with their own habits and traditions; and although the railway boom vastly increased their numbers and spread them to every region of the country, it did not destroy—though it perhaps began to undermine—their sense of being a race apart. Moreover the huge forces of them now recruited (and not only for railway building) enabled the steam-age navvies to be as much a law to their truculent selves as their eighteenth-century predecessors.

The navvies' manners were rough. One engineer told an official enquiry in 1846[1] that it was dangerous to approach them

---

[1] The Select Committee on Railway Labourers from whose report (*Parliamentary Papers* XIII, 1846) much of what follows has been taken. The engineer was Robert Rawlinson.

when they were not actually at work 'if they were in crowds or at all disposed to be unruly'. Even the contractors and gang bosses, most of whom were exceptionally tough, were often afraid to venture into their encampments.

As for the inhabitants of districts where large-scale works were in hand, they were apt to find themselves living under a sporadic reign of terror, only made supportable by the long hours railway navvies worked. Quiet villages, where the law was represented by a part-time parish constable, would be invaded by a horde of brawny, insolent men in strapped velveteens and spotted neckcloths, inclined to spend their leisure lounging about the lanes, throwing stones at passers, accosting local women, taunting their menfolk and generally spoiling for trouble. On the evening of a Saturday pay-day scenes of wild disorder were likely to break out round the local inns. Ready to bait and ill-treat outsiders, navvies were also given to ferocious fights among themselves, on which they betted freely.

They were no respecters of persons and as willing to stone a lady's carriage as a country cart. Cottagers, farmers and landowners all suffered, for navvies would pillage orchards and henroosts like an army of occupation, and they were ardent poachers. Gamekeepers could not hope to withstand their onslaughts, and landed proprietors (among many of whom game preserving was almost a religion) had to watch while not only fields and coverts but the very park under their windows was denuded of hares and pheasants.

It was not only rural parishes that felt the weight of the navvy's hand. Of an evening, when work on a nearby railroad was over for the day, chance passers through a country town might find the place apparently deserted by all respectable citizens; they had retired indoors leaving the streets to the navvies and their hangers-on. In fact, where they were in strength, the railway navvies seem to have held local authorities in contempt. As a perhaps over-emphatic witness explained to the 1846 committee, 'From being long known to each other they generally act in concert, and put at defiance any local constabulary force; consequently crimes of the most atrocious character are common, and robbery without attempt at concealment an everyday occurrence.'

But there were compensations. Experienced, fully-able navigators might get about twice the current wage of ordinary labourers and, since they were notoriously free spenders, they were not altogether unwelcome to butchers, bakers and brewers.[1] They crammed themselves into cottages, barns, cellars and any other lodging they could find, and for all their destructiveness were likely to be profitable tenants. Where no billets were to be found they simply made bivouacs with whatever materials lay to hand, so that anarchic and insanitary encampments grew up. In the west country there were places where lines of rough and squalid lean-to's followed the high field-banks. When, as happened especially in the north, a railway had to be driven across miles of remote fell and moorland, townships of crude bothies sprang up.

'Some slept in huts constructed of damp turf, cut from the wet grass, too low to stand upright in, while small sticks covered with straw served as rafters. . . . Others formed a room of stones without mortar, placed thatch or flags across the roof, and took possession of it with their families, often making it a source of profit by lodging as many of their fellow workmen as they could crowd into it. . . . In these huts they lived; with man, woman and child mixing in promiscuous guilt; with no possible separation of the sexes; in summer wasted by unwholesome heats, and in winter literally hewing their way to work through the snow. In such places from nine to fifteen hundred were crowded for six years. Living like brutes, they were depraved, degraded and reckless. Drunkenness and dissolution of morals prevailed. There were many women but few wives; loathsome forms of disease were universal. Work often went on on Sundays as well as other days.'[2]

This refers to one of the largest and most permanent of such encampments, but it was in more populous areas, where they were most in contact with local people, that the railway builders left the strongest impression. It was charged against them that they would not only terrorise a neighbourhood but debauch it. By creating a sudden demand for supplies, and by their devotion to gambling and disreputable sports, a large force of navvies encouraged all sorts of shady activity (including a lively market in stolen carcass meat). They also attracted a variety of unsavoury characters. Criminals on the run sometimes went to ground in

[1] A railway building force consisted of several grades of workmen. Unskilled men, often locally recruited, were used for less exacting tasks, and trained miners, who might earn more than the true navigators, were employed in tunnels and deep rock excavations. It was considered that navvies, to be efficient, had to earn enough to buy a generous diet of beef, bread and ale.

[2] J. Francis *History of the English Railway* Vol. 2, p. 71.

their settlements and it was practically impossible to ferret out anyone the navvies chose to protect.

Further, it is clear that the navvies and their ways had a fascination for some of those who came in contact with them. The skill and strength that could sometimes win thirty shillings a week, the hearty eating and swilling and uninhibited sexuality, the bold attitude to authority, were bound to have a certain heroic glamour in the eyes of youths brought up to the parsimony and lock-tugging that were the normal way of the agricultural labourer. Women, too, could be demoralised by the flamboyant invaders. Some threw in their lot with them altogether and took up a mode of life that, in the words of one witness, 'civilised language will hardly admit a description of'. Others simply became more or less openly 'fallen' and disreputable. In these ways railway works were likely to leave behind them a legacy of unrest.

The feebleness of the magistracy in dealing with the little armies of navvies scattered about the country is not hard to understand. Troops were the traditional means of coping with large bodies of peace-breakers, and in many places the only means. But they were a crude instrument: they could be used for suppressing major outbreaks, as when three days of pitched battles between huge gangs of English and Irish navvies interrupted progress on the Chester-Holyhead line, but they were unsuited for continuous, detailed law enforcement. Unlike political rioters, navvies could not simply be dispersed and chivied away to cool down in their separate homes: it was just when they were milling about together at camp or work site that they were most formidable. Also their presence was normally both temporary and, while the work lasted, unavoidable. Any intervention that interrupted the line-building would only prolong the visitation.

Even in places where there was a strong civilian constabulary, a large body of navvies was not easily kept in order. During the mid-forties some four thousand were employed on the ever-expanding Merseyside docks. Every week, from Saturday night till Tuesday, uproar and confusion reigned in the northern quarter of Liverpool where most of them lodged—some in dwellings they had colonised without the proprietors' permission. To arrest one was often a major operation, the more so since they took home with them their short, heavy, sharp-edged excavating spades.

'Even if a man commits a disturbance in a house,' the Commissioner of Liverpool Police told the 1846 Committee, 'it is folly for the police, two or three of them, to attempt to take him in the neighbourhood; there must be a considerable force. I recollect one case where they had a fight among themselves in a court, and one of my men who was near went to see what was the matter; they immediately turned from each other upon him and got him down; in fact they were in the act of butchering him, they were hacking him with their spades and had injured him severely; another of my men came up, and seeing the position bravely took up a spade, stood at the entrance of the court, which was rather narrow at the opening, and threatened to knock any of them to pieces if they interfered; he dragged his comrade out and kept them at bay until assistance came.'

The question presents itself: how far was the navvies' behaviour a result of their employment?

In the early years of the railway age it was usual for construction work to be parcelled out among a host of contractors and sub-contractors. ('The more you dissects it, the better it cuts up' was an accepted adage of the business.) Immediate control of the navvies was, by long tradition, the responsibility of 'gangers', who were nearly always ex-navvies and sometimes actually joined in the pick-and-shovel work. Like so many of the 'butties', 'lumpers', 'strappers' and other boss workmen in different industries, the ganger hired, fired and paid his own men. Sometimes he became in effect a labour contractor on a considerable scale. His status varied widely; according to his resources and the policy of those for whom he worked, a railway ganger might employ from half a dozen to several score workmen. Often he understood more about the business than his employer, who might be a limeburner or brickmaker who had ventured into permanent way building.

It was likely to be to the ganger's advantage to hold back his men's wages as long as he dared, particularly since the 'truck' or 'tommy shop' system flourished at construction sites[1] (it was an entrenched custom going far back into the canal-building era.) Under it, all sorts of supplies and provisions, including his necessary tools, were issued to the workman against his wages, often at exorbitant prices. Various arrangements involving tokens and

---

[1] In theory it was illegal, but the law was openly flouted or evaded in many industries. An Act of 1870 (amended 1887) was more respected.

tickets might be made with local suppliers, but it was the essence of the matter that all dealings were carried out on the authority of the employer who, whether or not he issued the tommy himself, took a heavy profit on each transaction. Obviously the less cash a man had in his pocket and the more tommy he could be induced to take in lieu, the less the real cost of his labour. Gangers and construction contractors alike, profited from this hoary and widespread abuse. It was also by no means unknown for gangers who had received the money for a piece of completed work to bolt, leaving their unpaid gangs without hope of redress.

Navvies worked very long hours. Sixty to seventy hours a week seems to have been considered reasonable, and a longer, seven-day week was no rarity. When after perhaps a month they drew their wages (less, of course, truck debits) they would go off for a day or two, as they said, 'on the randy', and during these sprees they would squander their ready money—so becoming even more dependent on truck during the following weeks.

Railway work, often pushed ahead with desperate urgency, could be highly risky. Lifting gear was for the most part remarkably crude and rickety. In excavating, men undercut masses of earth and rock in a most hazardous way, and blasting powder was casually handled. Those in charge had little inducement to fuss about safety precautions. The law was undemanding. Injured workmen could seldom exact compensation and were easily replaced. Further, the navvies themselves were inclined to display a foolhardy familiarity with danger and were quite capable of adding to their risks by drunken horseplay. (Beer was customarily carted to construction sites and sold in gallons to the sweating men.) Recklessness and violence were woven into a way of life that would have seemed intolerable to men who thought about the future.

With the passage of time there was, as with various sections of the 'dangerous classes', an improvement in the navvies' habits and relations with society at large. They kept a fearsome reputation but it is evident that not very long after the mid-century they were beginning, bit by bit, to be less blackguardly—and at the same time to lose something of their peculiarity as an industrial caste.[1] No doubt the strengthening of provincial, and especially rural, police had its effect, but it was probably developments

[1] Though some of those taken to the Crimea in 1855 to build the famous Balaclava supply railway proved troublesome enough. The Provost Marshal intimidated the more obstreperous with floggings.

inside the industry that did most to bring about the change.

After the frantic boom-and-bust of the forties the whole business of railway-making began to be considered in a cooler light. Small entrepreneurs came more and more under the control of bigger ones, and the influence of men such as Brassey and Peto, the greatest public works contractors of the age, was hostile to the anarchic labour conditions of the early boom: their phenomenal

rise had indeed stemmed from a capacity to impose order on the cut-throat commercial hurly-burly. Morton Peto, already a power in the land, gave evidence before the 1846 enquiry that strongly supported some of the views of reformers like Edwin Chadwick. Unlike them he was able to put his ideas on labour management into practice; he already had some nine thousand men working on his undertakings.

Peto contradicted the standard argument that, as nothing would induce navvies to save money or prevent them indulging in periodic fits of debauchery, it was better to defer pay-days as long as possible. He looked on the truck system with contempt as the practice of men who did not properly understand their own interest, and he was far from sharing the famous Brunel's belief in leaving each operator to go his own way to work.

By his own account, it was Peto's policy to keep the more important jobs for his own workforce, which was supervised by gangers who were simply hired foremen. The labourers' pay was checked by Peto's time-keepers who kept records every man was free to inspect, and any ganger whose gang had not been fully paid by five o'clock on Saturday evening with the coin issued for the purpose 'in convenient change, and in a sealed bag' had for-feited his job. Where there were no adequate billets Peto bar-racked his navvies in standardised bunkhouses, each under the care of a 'well conducted' man and his wife. A shilling a week was charged for this accommodation and the men were also forced to contribute a small sum to retain the services of a local surgeon. As for the minor contractors or independent gangers to whom Peto allotted the rest of his railway work, they were bound by strin-gent agreements and kept under observation by supervisors. Some, Peto observed, resorted to 'all manner of contrivances' to introduce disguised truck dealings, but on detection were 'instantly cashiered'. No liquor was sold at work sites under his control, though the men were allowed to bring their own beer.

Over the matter of accident compensation the great contractor was not liberal-minded; but he made provision for his workmen's souls, paying for a staff of lay missioners whose influence on morals and education he had found conducive to good order. If his views were influenced by his religion (he was a strong dissenter) he made no bones about their severe practicality. There is nothing of cant or soft soap about his downright answers. What he wanted was a steady, manageable labour force and his policy was designed to get it. In his day Peto was probably the ablest and—till the financial scandal of the London, Chatham and Dover Company in the mid-sixties ended his astonishing career—certainly the most influential builder of English railways.

Though better treatment did not automatically turn navvies into law-abiding citizens, there is no reason to doubt that in the long run it made them better neighbours as well as more profitable workmen. The Liverpool police commissioner already referred to stated that, of the 4,000 odd navvies in his area, a group of some 1,800 were, in striking contrast to the rest, remarkably well-behaved and 'tractable'. These men were of the same grades and background as the others but they were directly employed by the Liverpool Dock Committee instead of being at the mercy of contractors and gangers. Anxious to hold their jobs under the Committee (which did not allow misconduct in its employees) these navvies behaved themselves in a way that no fear of jail and treadmill could impose on their fellows.[1]

With the navvies a state of permanent warfare with civil authority was common, but not inevitable; with the London costermongers it was axiomatic.

Navvies occasionally applied to the law in hopes of recovering wages from an absconded ganger. Among costers any resort to the police was considered despicable. A loaded street barrow was not always easy to protect and at nights whatever gear could not be squeezed into the costers' homes had to be left outside in slum courts frequented by thieves; but they would have no dealings with the constable and made it a point of honour not to aid authority against those who wronged them. They relied on mutual assistance and it was their boast that a pilferer would rather take a thrashing from the Billingsgate marketmen—a proverbially unpleasant experience—than suffer the rigours of coster lynch law.

---

[1] A similar pattern among other types of heavy labour suggests that desperation at their manner of employment drove many workers into the 'dangerous' category. Around the mid-century the truck system was at its most virulent in certain Thames-side stevedoring trades which were also notorious for the lawlessness of their workpeople. Many of the contractors were dockland pub-keepers who forced their men to drink away a large part of their earnings in the boss's taproom, reluctant boozers being blacklisted through the trade.

The 'coal whippers' who unloaded the Tyne colliers were particularly badly exploited by petty truck masters and were a byword for their savagery and conflicts with the river police. In 1843 the business was brought under the control of a board of commissioners and the manners of the coal-whippers were transformed. During the great Chartist scare in 1848 they flocked to enlist as special constables.

The costers' animosity towards the police was extreme. To 'serve out a crusher', as they said, was the most admired exploit a young coster could perform, and one who got into trouble for injuring a policeman was usually helped by a whip-round from his fellows' meagre earnings. Often the attacker would lurk in a dark entry until an unsuspecting constable came up, then hurl a brickbat at close range and make off. Sometimes, when he had a grudge against a particular officer, a coster would wait for months for a favourable opportunity to pay off the score. One youth, after nursing his revenge for a long time, saw his enemy involved in a street brawl and, pushing into the crowd, managed to kick the policeman so that he was damaged for life. It was reported that when he learnt what injuries he had inflicted 'his joy was great, and he declared the twelvemonth's imprisonment he was sentenced to for the offence to be "dirty cheap": while his colleagues swore that had he got away they would have furnished him with "a pad or two of dry herrings to send him into the country until the affair had blown over".'

Where there was no threat to property, the criminal law was very lenient towards violence, and the sentences passed on those unlucky enough to get caught for these escapades seem surprisingly light. There were costers who had been jailed a dozen times or more for assaults on policemen. However one may suppose that the police, who returned the costers' feelings, sometimes found means to settle accounts.

In their spare time costermongers constantly mixed with street thieves and other professional delinquents, who often lived in the same courts and tenements: indeed, although the costers are reported to have looked down on such people as poor-spirited creatures, there were evidently close links between the groups.

Mayhew, though he emphasises their dangerous-class status, took a closely sympathetic interest in the costermongers' racy and precarious lives. The oddness of this scattered metropolitan community, set apart by peculiarities of speech, dress and social usage, excited the instinctive ethnologist in him, while their hardships evoked his unsentimental compassion. The picture he gives of the costers in the first volume of his great study of the London poor is remarkable not only for its wealth of detail but for the clarity with which it demonstrates their situation.

Various circumstances tended to weld the costers into a group at loggerheads with authority. There was a contradiction implicit

Wentworth Street, Whitechapel. Gustave Doré

Dock scene—
Friday
night,
Bermondsey.
Gustave
Doré

in their place in the community. On the one hand they performed a vital function. Developments in production and transport had made it possible to supply the urban proletariat with a rapidly increasing range of foodstuffs. These had to be economically distributed and for many important supplies the street trader, mobile and with lower costs than the small shopkeeper, was the most effective agent. (This was officially recognised in so far as no hawker's licence was required for such food trading.) In London and its suburbs the costers were purveyors on a huge scale. In 1850 more than 90,000 tons of herrings[1] are reported to have been taken from Billingsgate by street vendors, besides nearly all the cheapest white fish. A third of the cabbages and more than half the apples and pears reaching Covent Garden and the other metropolitan vegetable markets went the same way. In all (so it was claimed) about two million pounds-worth of food was sold on the London streets yearly, the lion's share of it by fully fledged costermongers.

On the other hand, for all their competitiveness as distributors of cheap food, the costers' trade was in many ways out of joint with the times. They represented no capital interest and operated on a tiny, precarious turnover—a whole coster family might spend the day trying to dispose of a half-sovereign's worth of sprats—and no wholesale dealer in the great markets would give them a penny credit. Disreputable themselves and catering largely for customers without political influence, local or national, they were likely to find themselves in competition with property owners and ratepayers—with the 'shopocracy'.

In a lively passage, Mayhew describes the Saturday night market in the New Cut, Lambeth, the most important retail food market south of the Thames and a focus of coster activity. Lit by a host of lights—intense white carbide lamps, smoky red grease lamps, tallow dips twinkling among the foodstuffs heaped on the stalls, gas flares 'streaming and fluttering in the wind like flags of flames'—so that at a distance the lurid glow above made the street seem afire, the New Cut was packed from wall to wall, road and curb, with chaffering humanity. The hubbub was deafening, the traders all crying their goods with the full force of their

---

[1] These fish were a crucial item in the diet of the urban poor and in London their chief non-starchy nourishment. (In some provincial areas cheese appears to have been the vital source of cheap animal protein.) Save for the very poorest and most ignorant of all, the shellfish sold from street barrows were a favourite 'relish'. Winkles cost a penny a pint: oysters at four-a-penny were a humble luxury.

lungs against the background din of a horde of street musicians.

But by the time Mayhew came to include the description in his book the place had undergone a change. 'The gay stalls have been replaced by deal boards,' he wrote sadly, 'and the bright lights are almost totally superseded by the dim, guttering candle.' The costers, the mainstay of the market, were being harried. They could no longer take up a stand there, under pain of being seized and marched off to the lockup. Those with barrows had somehow to keep them on the move, and even those who sold from the large hawker's tray or 'shallow' had to be careful not to let down the hinged stick underneath that took the weight off the shoulders, for if this was seen to touch the ground the patrolling policeman was 'obliged to intervene'. (This persecution was not the work of the New Cut shopkeepers: their trade was stimulated by the stall-keepers and they suffered from the change. The market's chief enemies were citizens some distance away who resented its power to attract custom.)

Static or mobile, the coster had virtually no rights to his living; he was always liable to be moved on, and could be chivied from his trading places without redress. If he was slow to shift (perhaps because his barrow had broken down) he might not only be taken in custody but have both stock and vehicle—his entire working capital—confiscated. Sometimes, to keep a broken street trader and his family off the rates, a parish authority would put up the few shillings necessary to launch him again in business; but when he tried to re-establish himself he was likely to find the police as actively discouraging as ever. (They faced a never-ending traffic problem and were eager to keep down the horde of road-clutterers.) To costers, who saw all officialdom as a single hydra-headed tyranny, such inconsistencies seemed cruel and fatuous cat-and-mouse play.

Besides the caprice of the law, the coster's trade was desperately exposed to the weather. Unforeseeable changes of temperature could quickly make tempting investments in soft fruit or unfresh fish disastrous, while three days' rain is said to have been enough to bring thousands to the edge of destitution. Again a fluctuation in market prices, putting a few steady lines beyond their customers' reach, might half-ruin a whole sector of the street trade. At every turn the coster's calling required a hardihood, an aggressiveness and a readiness to take risks that were reflected in his whole manner of life.

The coster's appearance, when he could afford it, was thoroughly flash. Since it represents in an emphatic form the characteristic rig of the louche urban proletarian of the period, it is worth inspection. The coster normally wore either a full-skirted velveteen coat, rather like a longish shooting jacket, or else a sort of very long, side-pocketed corduroy waistcoat in the eighteenth-century fashion, with back and sleeves of different stuff. Whatever its style the garment was usually set off with brass, pearl or carved bone buttons. Cord trousers, tight at the knees and somewhat looser below, covered the tops of heavy ankle boots. (Good boots were something all costers liked to be particular about: a smart pair might be ornamented with an elaborate stitched pattern—hearts-and-flowers was a favourite.) For best, he hoped to have a cloth coat with contrasting plush lapels, heavily braided 'calf-clingers' with a line of 'artful buttons at the bottom', and, instead of the usual peaked cap to protect his head from loaded baskets, a beaver-knapped top hat. Workday or gala, a large silk handkerchief known as a 'kingsman' was tied about his throat. Many costers had a stock of these neckcloths and to be seen without one was an almost infallible sign of being in desperate straits.

Though she also habitually wore a kingsman, often a present from her lover and usually displayed over her shoulders, the coster girl was less dressy. Generally her face was framed in a net cap under a somewhat crushed bonnet and she wore the heavy, cotton print dress typical of working class women, cut short enough to show her stout laced boots. If she was lucky she had a bright-coloured shawl or two for cold days and a gaily-ribboned best bonnet.[1]

Woman's subordinate place in coster society was very marked; she shouldered a great share of the labour but (if one excludes brawling) took little part in its recreations. Costers seldom made formal marriages. Most of them had a lively dislike for all kinds of organised and missioning Christianity, and they were reluctant to pay for a superfluous ceremony. Only about one couple in ten, it seems, were legally wedded. A girl of sixteen or so would simply quit her family and go to live with a lad in a hired room: as the boys tended to leave home earlier they were often younger than their companions and according to Mayhew they often set up with their first girl at fourteen. If the few women who were lawful wives felt that their position was more secure, that was the sum of their advantage, for 'no honour attached to the married state and no shame to concubinage'. Unless driven by want to prostitution—which was accepted as a necessary evil in extremity —coster women are said to have been unswervingly constant, and rather than endanger an association that was also a trading partnership would put up with continuous ill-treatment. 'The gals,' a complacent lout is reported as saying, 'axully likes a feller for walloping them.' But the pedestrian fact seems to be that a single woman was at a serious commercial disadvantage. Although young costers left home so soon, costermongering was very much an affair of family-size groups and partnerships. Long hours of noisy selling and tramping necessitated some system of reliefs. Goods that proved hard to sell off a barrow might be successfully

---

[1] The 'traditional' gala pearly costume—gusseted trouser-bottoms, ostrich feather hats on the women, buttons like scale-armour—belongs to the era of the costers' sentimental decline. The later coster cult, associated with the music-hall, belongs with such phenomena as dude cowboys and palm-court gipsies.

hawked in separate basketfuls. To take advantage of the market was vital, and at times costers cured red herrings, prepared shell-fish, jellied eels and even pickled salmon in their slum retreats, activities requiring a division of labour.

Coster children began work young, scarcely ever attending so much as a Sunday ragged school, so that a literate coster was nearly always one who had come to the business fairly late. It was not a closed, hereditary trade—as the growing number of Irish in it emphasised—but it did demand a harsh and thorough train-ing that was best undergone early in life. Established costers were not well disposed to outsiders who tried to compete with them, and in the fierce commercial rivalry of the trade the regu-lars enjoyed many advantages. Indeed for a majority of the unfor-tunate 'underminers', as interlopers were sometimes called, the struggle to wring a living from the streets was, in one old hand's words, 'only another way of starving'.

Whatever his origins, the apprentice coster acquired a training well calculated to impress a sense of group-membership, of belonging to a close-knit craft. Dyed-in-the-wool costers are said to have been able *always* to recognise one another. From the start the beginner learnt to co-operate with other costers as well as to outsmart them, to side with them against the rest of the world, to imitate their appearance and speak their jargon. There were in-numerable things to be learned by working under an experienced trader. Not only had the vagaries of the wholesale markets to be mastered (together with a facility for fast mental reckoning) but all sorts of tricks without which a coster could hardly hope to sur-vive. There were ways of plumping out shrunken fruit; inter-weaving dead eels with live; obtaining 'slang' weights and measures from ironmongers who specialised in such equipment; and so on *ad infinitum*.

Probably the trade attracted, as well as bred, especially tough and sharp-witted boys, for many little costers developed an extra-ordinary acuity and managed while still children to live on the 'bunts' or commission allowed them on their own selling. They could expect plenty of brutality from their masters but little for-mal domineering; the whole atmosphere of the trade was callous, jocular and egalitarian. A lifetime of shouting in the London atmosphere could ruin the voice, and coster boys were often use-ful for their ability to bark their employer's goods. In fact they were notorious for their carrying voices and powers of repartee.

One little creature, twelve years old and 'about three feet high', was not only 'up to the business as clever as a man of thirty' but could 'chaff down a peeler so uncommon severe' that the only way the officer could assert himself was to take the shrimp in charge —the sort of ridicule-rousing act intelligent policemen preferred to avoid.

The costers' elaborate system of backslang was perhaps more an expression of corporate spirit than the secret code they sometimes liked to claim; for the greater part of their trade was in quarters where many of the common terms were widely known (for example, dillo = old, dab = bad, nammo = girl or woman, reeb = beer, escop or esclop = police or policeman) even if few non-costers could use the patter with any fluency. Moreover they were evidently quite prepared to discuss the usage with inquirers.

The coster seldom saved. Neither his way of life nor the character of his chancy trade made it easy for him to put by money, and he considered all savings banks and suchlike institutions to be 'connected with government, and the taxes of the police', part and parcel of a hostile establishment. Many costers did not own their barrows, though they cost only a pound or two, but hired one, year after year, at a high rental. An apparatus worth about twenty shillings would be let out at one-and-six a week. The man who lost his stock money on an unlucky venture and pawned his best coat and kingsman might be saved by a charitable hat passed round his competitors, but otherwise he was usually reduced to borrowing from one of the lenders who advanced costers small sums at enormous charges—twenty to thirty per cent interest weekly. Though the risks were no doubt considerable they did not by any means justify the fantastic usury commonly levied on costers who, if they thought nothing of cheating their customers, were not unscrupulous about their debts. Further, those who gave them credit specialised in the trade, they could pick and choose their clients, and constantly saw their outlays repaid many times over. The costers, cut off from ordinary sources of credit, had to turn to those they knew and who were willing to deal with them. They accepted the charges they had to pay, and indeed when they lent to one another they were likely, for all their generosity, to exact similar rates.

It was a vicious circle. If the costers' disorderliness was largely a result of a desperately precarious livelihood harshened by the hostility of the police, equally their lives were made more precarious and the face of authority more unfriendly by their own mistrustful disreputability. Even a prosperous coster could not greatly extend the scope of his business—or rather, if he extended it, he ceased to be a true coster. The rough, egalitarian trade can have been no better suited to the ambitious than to the weak and unaggressive; and the man who meant to rise in the world was likely to move away from it, perhaps to become a regular greengrocer or to branch out into the kindling and small-coals line. He would get decently married, possibly to a respectable servant who could help him with her small savings and knowledge of middle-class ways—in which case he had already come far, for no domestic in her senses would consider accepting a coster.[1]

The figure of fifteen shillings a week quoted by Mayhew as the average profit earned by a coster family plainly cannot be more than a knowledgeable guess; but their earnings cannot have been much higher if one considers the trade as a whole, including those 'underminers' who sold the same lines and followed more or less the same methods as the established costers. Men, women and children, there were reckoned to be some 15,000 unquestionable coster folk, and perhaps roughly the same number of interlopers and miscellaneous hawkers of food.[2] Some of these hawkers, however, only made their appearance at certain times of year, chiefly in winter when many industries laid off labour. Whatever their numbers and earnings, it is painfully clear that far too many followed the trade for them all to maintain themselves by it, and that in general costers endured such hardship that one can only marvel at their resilience and satirical spirits.

Whichever way the economic weather veered it was apt to blow chill on the street trader. In bad times when his customers starved he was likely to starve with them; but better days did not necessarily bring him prosperity. For a brief time he might benefit, but in the long run a rising standard of living meant a greater demand for meat and groceries, which costers could not supply, and a correspondingly decreased appetite for herrings and other very cheap fish which were the backbone of their trade. More purchasing power in poor districts meant more shops; and when

---

[1] There were, obviously, gradations of acceptability. Such servant-maids 'as wouldn't marry a rag-and-bottle shop,' Mayhew was once told, 'don't object to a coal shed.'

[2] The distinction between costers and other street traders is hard to make. Costers always sold food (in London a street trader could not officially sell anything else without a licence) but finally the difference between costers and others is a matter of their style of life.

employment slumped for a time the wretchedest little tripe-and-cowheel shop had resources beyond the average coster's command. Most importantly the shopkeeper could often allow steady customers credit in a way impossible to the hand-to-mouth barrow man.

The best-off costers seem to have been the dealers in fruit and garden stuff (still pretty much of a luxury among the mass of the people) and more especially those in the 'aristocratic' line who catered for the sort of customers who would buy delicacies like new peas and asparagus. With a pony worth five pounds or more, a light rattle trap and a good middle-class suburban connection, a coster probably stood at the apex of his profession. According to one who was experienced in the high-class trade, the customers who would pay the highest prices were the kept mistresses living in detached suburban villas.

The more mobile of the pony and donkey-keeping costers were also prepared to go far beyond the outermost suburbs in search of trade and, on occasion, to make themselves scarce after a brush with the police. Sometimes they would stay away for weeks, buying and selling about the countryside. Since the costers had long established connections with the trade in poached game, it is reasonable to think that some of their excursions were connected with this valuable sideline.

In some ways, even the costers' reputation was better than that of the chimney-sweeps. Not all sweeps, of course, were blackguards but the trade had a most unenviable name.

It was a career in which men were apt to start early in life. Some still began as climbing boys and it is easy to see how the conditions under which young sweeps lived might affect those who were tough enough to survive and continue in the trade. (There was probably a fair amount of human wastage; besides the risk of serious accident, respiratory disease and cancer of the groin were occupational ailments among climbing boys.) Apprenticeships were not sought-after openings and from 1840 the indenturing of child sweeps was forbidden by law, so that masters often had to recruit small boys whom no one cared to protect. Breaking boys in to the work was not always easy and sometimes scared children were driven up tight flues by pricking or scorching the soles of their feet. Moreover the narrowing of domestic chimneys and the growing number of high industrial smokestacks must have added to the rigours of a system which, though prohibited and fast declining, lingered long enough to remain a scandal up till the last quarter of the century.

Many masters must have been under strong pressure to ignore a feebly enforced law; for it was perfectly obvious that broad old-fashioned flues with their ledges and recesses could be far more effectively cleaned by a scrambling urchin than by a remotely manipulated 'patent machine'. Nor are the masters to be blamed for the behaviour of customers who would not inconvenience themselves by putting out their fires in time for chimneys to be cool and clear of fumes before a boy had to climb them. Chimney-sweeping was a highly competitive business.

It seems unlikely that sweeps deliberately starved their lads to keep them undersized, as propagandists claimed. It is true that

the boys had to be slight and wiry, but the work also demanded great energy, and a quick, strong boy was a valuable asset. On the other hand boys no doubt often went hungry in lean times and it is not difficult to believe that they drank gin and smoked and sometimes slept among soot-sacks in foul cellars. One may suppose that much the same sort of brutish life went on in sweeps' households as among other ill-conditioned but not always unhearty folk on the barbarous fringe of society.

Yet the trade certainly had a well-maintained tradition of misconduct and brutality—and not merely in the way its apprentices were treated. About the best known mid-century sweep was James Cannon, the Walworth Terror, a ruffian whose outrages led to seventeen convictions for assault in ten years and culminated in a turn-up in which a couple of policemen suffered a terrible mauling at his hands. This last feat proved a mistake. At Quarter Sessions he received the unusually heavy sentence of two years imprisonment for the injuries inflicted on one policeman: but higher authority was now aroused and at the instance of the Treasury Solicitor the case was transferred to the Old Bailey where, partly maybe because of the general odium attaching to his profession, a jury found Cannon guilty on the capital charge of attempting to murder the other officer. He was condemned to hang. According to an eye-witness 'the sweep seemed astonished at the verdict'—as well he might, considering the leniency with which such offences were often treated. In the upshot, however, the penalty was commuted to penal servitude.[1]

So far as crimes against property are concerned, chimney-sweeps whose thoughts turned to housebreaking had some important advantages. A climbing boy's training was a first-rate preparation for cat-burglary, and the most sensationally agile thief of the century was a runaway sweep's apprentice. Further, to a degree quite unique among the disreputable classes, sweeps had opportunities to enter premises worth robbing and study their lay-out and potentialities. Even if they did not want to attempt a robbery on their own account they were often in an excellent position to provide professional criminals with inside information— a very saleable commodity.

By far the commonest method of heating for houses, offices,

---

[1] Cannon was tried in 1852 and though hanging for attempted murder was now very rare his sentence was no mere formality. The last execution for attempted murder took place in Chester in 1861.
For further remarks on connections between sweeps and crime see page 161.

shops and even warehouses, was by open grates which were mostly inefficient and deposited huge quantities of soot. There had necessarily to be a great deal of chimney-sweeping, so that, if only a small fraction of the sweeps ever had dealings with criminals, their influence on the pattern of crime would still have been considerable.

Compared to the ordinary sedentary citizen, the people with whom this chapter has been concerned were a restless, shifting crowd. Even when they lived among ordinary people they remained to a great extent cut off from them by their way of life and by their own view of themselves as outsiders.

Yet navvies, sweeps or costers seem stay-at-homes compared with those other border-dwellers of the underworld who did not have even so settled a home as a railway encampment but passed their whole lives on the road. It is they—the true wanderers—who now move onto the scene.

CHAPTER THREE

The wanderers

In the first half of the Victorian era, poor people in the great cities were less cut off from the country than the already endless miles of bricks and mortar might suggest. The contacts were (and remained) closer in the industrial north and midlands than within the vast metropolitan complex; yet, in the sixties, East End slum dwellers north and south of the river went out to work as field labourers in market gardens, and what would in time be considered quaintly rustic crafts—basket weaving and the like— were carried on in the slum courts of Bethnal Green with materials gathered on Essex marshes and farmland.

Animal husbandry was a common urban pursuit:[1] besides innumerable draught animals, dairy cattle were kept in the biggest cities, and at the mid-century one could find grimy pigs rootling about alleys in the City of London as well as among the middens of inner Manchester. Until the livestock market was moved in 1855, a considerable area in the heart of the capital had, with its leather-gaitered, flat-hatted dealers and drovers, much of the air of a busy—but exceptionally unpleasant—country town.

A variety of poor people were constantly shifting in and out of the main centres of population, some leaving the towns to make long, slow foot-journeys through the countryside. (Perhaps the fact that a good proportion of the urban proletariat had been born and raised as countrymen helped to encourage this movement.) Paradoxically, as the century went on the improvement in communications, especially the increase in rail transport, tended to promote the estrangement of town from countryside by reducing the number of people—waggoners, drovers, wandering traders, showmen, craftsmen and labourers—who lived more or less amphibiously between the two.

Much of the mobile population was thoroughly disreputable,

---

[1] Admittedly of a limited kind. London cow-keepers commonly bought animals in milk and kept them for one lactation only. Urban horse dealers and liverymen often had a second establishment in the country. Horse dealing was of course an enormous and vitally important trade, generating an endless complex of urban-rural relationships.

and its shuttlings had a significant bearing on the economy of the underworld. Altogether, any attempt to survey the seamy underside of mid-nineteenth-century life would be futile without some look at the various migrants dotting the white metalled highroads —now almost deserted by the stage-coaches, post-chaises and great ship-like long distance carriers' waggons that recently had passed along them. In sharp contrast to the settled inhabitants of the countryside, these nomads were the least charted section of contemporary society. Many familiar wayside types remained more mysterious than the occupants of the darkest urban warren. About the only certain characteristic of this floating, heterogeneous population was that it was never constant. Not only was it to a great extent seasonal, but its numbers and composition were affected by the state of trade, the incidence of public works, the tides of immigration, the activities of police and poor law officials, and a whole host of agencies, local and national.

One important, ever-fluctuating class of wanderers consisted of men in search of some particular type of work. The end of a large job might release hundreds of navvies: in a district of big arable farms the harvest would attract scores of migrant field workers. At such times large gangs of labourers, which might include some women and children, would drift through an area, coalescing and dispersing as they went. When a regional industry suffered prolonged depression, considerable parties might set off on the trek together, drawn by reports of a demand for labour somewhere else.

Less conspicuous, and less troublesome to residents in the neighbourhoods through which they passed, were the men who moved around on their own or with one or two occasional companions, trying their luck at place after place. At times there were numbers of trained artisans roving about in this fashion, journeymen who visited their trade's particular 'house of call' in each town in turn in hopes of discovering an opening. The house of call was usually a public house accredited to a particular trade or trades, for which it served as a local centre and a kind of employment agency: it might well provide sleeping accommodation, and trade union meetings were likely to be held on the premises. Going off on the tramp was a recognised means of avoiding a local slump at home and improving one's prospects, even in better paid crafts. Trade unions in areas where too many applicants for jobs weakened their bargaining power actively encouraged it, giving their members documents that would enable them to get help and even financial credit from distant branches or allied organisations. 'If it had not been in our power to keep up our tramping support,' declared the General Union of Carpenters in 1846, '. . . a general reduction of wages would have taken place.'[1] And in the labour troubles of the sixties almost every major organised trade apparently worked some such system to help members on the tramp.

Nevertheless life on the tramp was likely to tell hard on the artisan who was used to a settled life, and it could be morally disorientating as well as physically weakening. Among journeymen engineers it was not only considered despicable to subject a man fresh off the road to the crude 'horsing' normally meted out to newcomers in an engineering shop, but common practice to do a share of his work for him till he had settled in. It was accepted that he was bound to be more or less seriously knocked up and, without help, in danger of losing his new job. The engineers were a notably close-knit, craft-conscious body of skilled men, who in 1857 organised the most effective national union in the country. For others in less prosperous and cohesive trades a spell on the road might well be ruinous.[2]

To reputable workmen, resort to any kind of begging was hatefully degrading. Moreover among the first generation of Victorians this feeling seems to have grown stronger. In its report of 1860 the Society for the Suppression of Mendicity—and a less complaisant witness would be hard to cite—noted with 'astonishment' that a horde of London building trade workers had suffered through a protracted series of strikes and lock-outs without 'recourse to mendicity'. But the unsuccessful tramping workman could come to a stage when begging was scarcely avoidable. He was far away from anyone who would help him—or in whose eyes he had some status to maintain—and so ragged and wretched that he was more likely to be offered a charitable shilling than a job by any prospective employer. It must sometimes have been fearfully easy for him to slip past the imperceptible point when begging became the ordinary, inevitable manner of life. In a society where deaths from want of food and shelter were accepted events, mouching and cadging[3] were the down-and-out's obvious means

---

[1] Quoted in *The Tramping Artisan* by E. J. Hobsbawn, *Economic History Review*, 2nd Series, Vol. III, 3.

[2] Cf. Thomas Wright ('The Journeyman Engineer') *The Great Unwashed*.

[3] *Mouching* here means (as with Richard Jefferies) habitual rural vagrancy and the shifts such a life necessitated. In the last century *cadging* often had a more specific meaning than now. The description 'cadger' occurs in official communications, indicating a delinquent beggar and cheat of the lowest class, but not necessarily a tramp.

of survival; and in wayside beershops and low lodging houses, perhaps in the very houses of call to which his trade took him, the wanderer fell in with adepts in these arts. For their part, because they often liked to follow circuits they knew and needed fresh faces to help them put over their tricks, skilled cadgers were sometimes glad enough to take new acquaintances into partnership.

Once he had fallen into vagrancy his sense of failure and degradation must often have helped fix a formerly respectable man in the life. Moreover the change did not always mean a fall in living standards. If he survived the first hardships, a man was unlikely to be worse off scrounging his way along the open road than he would have been as a tailor in a Whitechapel sweatshop where a dozen unfortunates worked seventeen hours daily, seldom issuing from one stifling, stinking little room where they ate their bread-and-scrape at the worktables they slept under, always in debt to a proprietor who might confiscate their coats as security to prevent them cutting loose. In the late forties an ex-handweaver told a correspondent of the *People's Journal* that he picked up a better living on the pad, hawking sham nostrums, than his trade could ever bring him.

The poor law organisation did little to preserve the migrant workman's good intentions and self-respect. The framers of the reformed poor law had intended the workhouse casual wards to provide brief shelter and subsistence for penniless working folk on the trek, so helping the redistribution of labour, and no destitute traveller who applied to a relieving officer was supposed to be turned away. Unfortunately the aura of disgrace that attached to any form of indoor workhouse relief strongly discouraged bona fide seekers of employment and left the casual wards largely to delinquents who had no sense of dignity to lose.

Theoretically, 'casuals' were supposed to be lodged in separate, secure premises, kept under firm control and made to pay for their night's hospitality by putting in a stint of workhouse labour before going on their way. In practice there was often neither proper accommodation nor adequate means of disciplining the men, and there was a real danger that a pack of roughs, having burned the oakum they had been set to pick and smashed every window within reach, would come swarming, filthy and verminous, into the body of the establishment and set the whole place in an uproar. The master of a rural or small-town workhouse might be largely dependent on a staff of more or less decrepit paupers promoted to the job: it was small wonder if he was sometimes only too glad to let regulations go by the board and leave his visitors free to misconduct themselves together much as they liked, so long as they left peaceably when they had swallowed their morning gruel.

One way in which local poor law boards resolved the problem of casuals was simply to ignore the obligation to admit them, and for a decade from 1848 that solution was more or less endorsed by the central authority. Alternatively, where they had the means, they might enforce measures to cow any troublemakers and deter all but the most desperate from applying. What each board had to guard against was the reputation of being less rigorous than others in the region, for news of the conditions at different workhouses passed through 'the whole corps of tramps' with 'telegraphic despatch' (as one official put it) and any Union erring on the side of laxity or humanity was in danger of attracting undesirable vagrants from far and wide.

The itinerants who most consistently gave trouble both to local authorities and to country people in general were what may be called the regular mouchers. Sometimes alone or with a single female companion, sometimes in quite formidable parties, padding along the dusty verges of the summer roads, they were a common and universally unwelcome sight, and a prime reason, or pretext, for the shutting of casual wards.

Ragged and usually filthy, the moucher did not necessarily present the physically collapsed appearance that a later age came to associate with tramps. Indeed the number of young, sturdy men, confirmed in a life of wandering idleness and fully prepared to resist attempts at coercion, was in official eyes a most disturbing feature of the vagrancy problem. Though the life demanded a good deal of cunning and endurance, most mouchers were evidently of limited abilities—or they would have graduated to more sophisticated and profitable levels of mendicancy and imposture. Scrounging, pilfering, wheedling, all the humbler kinds of 'monkry'[1] including a fair amount of half-threatening begging— these seem to have been their normal resources, while the more spirited occasionally went in for the downright terrorisation of lonely people or isolated cottage households. Cash or goods, a pair of old boots, a scrag of cold mutton from a back door meat-

---

[1] The general art of wandering mendicancy, embracing a vast variety of dodges, some of them of great antiquity. An account of beggars and begging methods is given in Chapter 7.

Barnet Fair, showing dancing booth, cheap jack, circus menagerie (in middle distance) and stage players. From an oil painting by Charles Green (Mansell Collection)

Interior of a gipsy tent on Mitcham Common, late 1870s (Mansell Collection)

safe, a rabbit in a trap, almost anything usable or consumable was grist for the moucher's mill. Constables who saw his fire twinkling chased him away and kicked it out, farmers and gamekeepers threatened him with a peppering of small shot. His best nights were spent with noise and beer in some verminous road-side

tramps' lodging, where the proprietor was often ready to buy any trifle he might have picked up. His worst were passed hunched in a wet hedge or snuggled for warmth against a fuming midden. No matter how practised he might be, the life was scarcely supportable in winter and mouchers were a seasonal phenomenon, mostly disappearing into city tenements and doss-houses until spring returned.

A report in 1848 suggests that the number of troublesome

tramps about the countryside was increased by the strengthening municipal police forces, whose activities drove some of the urban cadgers and street thieves to leave the towns and take to periodic mouching. The fact remains that London, with its pre-eminent police, notoriously absorbed hordes of vagrants each autumn. Some of the less adroit mouchers certainly survived by going into workhouses for parts of the winter, while a few found a roof by deliberately getting themselves committed to jail. On the face of it, it seems probable that vagrants resorted chiefly to big urban Unions where there were less likely to be awkward questions about their 'settlement' (that is their status as genuine inhabitants) and the authorities had less reason to be nervous of unruly elements. Certainly it seems clear from Mayhew's account that around 1849–50 metropolitan Unions could be very lax.

Obviously, despite the English workman's fear and loathing of the workhouse, it was not only confirmed tramps and beggars who went to it for casual relief. According to one workhouse master, honest 'destitute mechanics' on the pad sometimes turned up so weak from starvation that they could barely crawl to the gates and had to be kept for days in the infirmary before they were strong enough to continue on their way. And in fact there was a large body of poor folk, for the most part desperately eager for employment, who shared so little of the native English horror of the poor law 'bastilles' that they were glad to take advantage of the free shelter and skilly even when they had the means to lodge outside. These were the poor Irish, who had their own standards of misery and hardship.

When the immigrant stream from across the Irish sea burst into flood in the late forties, the results in certain areas were so startling that some observers fatuously claimed that virtually *all* vagrants were Irish, those who didn't superficially conform to type being in reality Irishmen in disguise. But for years these invaders had been an important part of the migrant population— and an increasingly significant influence on the whole social scene.

The wild Milesian features, looking false ingenuity, restlessness, unreason, misery and mockery, salute you on all highways and by ways [declared Carlyle in his *Chartism* at the end of the thirties]. The English coachman, as he whirls past, lashes the Milesian with his whip, curses him with his tongue; the

Milesian is holding out his hat to beg. He is the sorest evil this country has to contend with. In his rags and laughing savagery, he is there to undertake all work that can be done by mere strength of hand and back; for wages that will purchase his potatoes. He needs only salt for his condiment; he lodges to his mind in any pighutch or doghutch, roosts in outhouses; and wears a suit of tatters, the getting on or off of which is said to be a difficult operation, transacted only in festivals and the hightides of the calendar. The Saxon man if he cannot work on these terms, finds no work . . . the uncivilised Irishman, not by his strength but by the opposite of strength, drives out the Saxon native, takes possession of his room. There he abides, in his squalour and unreason, in his falsity and drunken violence, as the ready-made nucleus of degradation and disorder.

It was not true that Irish immigrants were generally bad workers and they certainly had no monopoly of drunkenness. Although they were so numerous in poorhouse casual wards they were not conspicuous troublemakers, while those who became navvies and street-traders—as many did—seem to have behaved no worse than their 'Saxon' mates (though a natural tendency to support each other easily led to a dangerous picking-up of sides). But for the most part they arrived in England primitive peasants, uprooted by pressure of want from a poor and inefficient rural society untouched by industrialism and with a long tradition of oppression and violence. Ill-equipped for more sophisticated work,[1] desperate to seize whatever means of life a strange and unfriendly environment offered, they were bound to depress living standards and harshen the struggle for survival among the lowest strata of the population. Beggars and strike breakers, with alien habits and values, they were apt to be despised by people of every class. Inevitably some of them, including some of the most energetic and adaptable, became confirmed enemies of ordered society and a powerful recruitment to the criminal underworld.

During the period of famine, disease and social breakdown that followed the failure of the potato crops in 1845 and 1846, Irish emigration became less a matter of groups and individuals who hoped to make good overseas than a great flight of refugees

---

[1] Nothing is more striking than the frequency with which contemporary newspaper advertisements for the better sort of household servant stipulate that no Irish need apply. This was only partly crude prejudice: the poor Irish were often almost unbelievably ignorant of the simplest domestic conventions.

escaping from a nightmare homeland where their countrymen perished by the hundred thousand—where, in the worst-struck districts, the puffed bodies of the dead and half-dead littered the villages and roadsides.

A great many, perhaps nearly all those who could manage it, took passage on to America, some in murderous 'coffin ships' which were often ill-found old sailing vessels and in which the emigrants were crammed in the holds almost like slaves on the old 'middle passage'.

But the majority came ashore destitute, and for thousands of them the only hope was to find some sort of charitable relief before they died of want. Their crossings from Ireland were often paid for them—they might cost no more than a few shillings and there was every motive for their better-off countrymen to speed them on their way—and all kinds of craft engaged in the traffic. Some, not the unhappiest, went all the way to London in the pig-boats that sailed round Land's End, stowed among the filth and warmth of the squealing cargo. Most refugees, naturally, reached western ports. The greatest single point of entry (and also of re-embarkation for America) was Liverpool where, in spite of great efforts to help them, combined want, disease and muddle took a frightful toll. Here, however, a large part of the influx consisted of 'lusty young men, willing to work and unencumbered' who, once on their feet, stood a fair chance of making their way in the vast, still growing industrial community on whose door-step they had landed.[1]

Most terrible of all was the situation in South Wales, where families poured in from the poorest Irish provinces, among them an 'incredible number of widows with three or four small children'. For all their misery, they had good reasons to set off at once on the tramp, for if they fell into the hands of local officials they were likely to be sent back to Ireland. Some were dumped clandestinely, perhaps at night, to stumble away inland as best they could. Other shipmasters acted on a different principle and actually relied on their human cargoes being rounded up by the authorities: in this way they did not need to trouble how little

---

[1] Their priests, many of whom followed the emigrants from Ireland and stood by them through the worst, played a vital role in organising their affairs. In fact, his priest, often born a peasant like himself, was often the only educated person an emigrant could turn to with any hope of being sympathetically understood. From this came, in part, the extra-ordinary authority wielded by the priesthood in Irish slum areas in Liverpool, Manchester, London and elsewhere, though with succeeding generations of settled Irish this influence tended to decline.

they were paid for bringing the deluded wretches over as they could reckon on satisfactory payment for carrying them back.

Many who landed, especially children in winter, can have been in no condition to walk a step. The evidence of Harriet Huxtable the manageress of an official asylum for vagrants at Newport Monmouthshire, provides a telling vignette: 'There is hardly a family that have come over and applied to me but we have found a member or two of it ill. They are chiefly troubled with dysentery. . . . They don't live long with it, there is a sort of dropsy attends it. They are very remarkable; they will eat salt by the basins' full and drink a great quantity of water after. I have frequently known them, who have been stopping with us and could not have been hungry, eat cabbage leaves and other refuse from the ash-heap.'

In 1848, looking back over the dreadful peak of the famine exodus, a senior officer of the Cardiff police stated that to the best of his knowledge every healthy emigrant who had applied for relief during the last two years had been repatriated.[1] In the broad, such efforts probably had little effect. North and south the refugees flooded in and—many of them—tramped away in search of some means of staying alive.

Long before the great famine the Irish had been the most conspicuous non-native element on the roads, but they were far from being the only one. Another set of peasant exiles were the uprooted Highland crofters who, together with other poor Scots, continued to follow the traditional route south. However these northerners were not only few in comparison with the Irish but more easily absorbed. They came from a country where the standard of education was generally higher than in England, they were normally Protestant and there was no national stigma on them—indeed Scotsmen had a reputation for conscientiousness and self-improvement that might well help them in their search for work.

Foreigners of various nationalities were to be found among the innumerable strolling exhibitionists—street acrobats, fire-eaters, sword-swallowers, strongmen, jugglers, rope-walkers, contortionists, stilt-dancers, owners of performing dogs, mice and fleas, and so on—who wandered about singly or in family groups.

[1] The quotations and much of the matter in these remarks on the Irish famine emigration originate in *Reports and Communications on Vagrancy*. *Parliamentary Papers* 1847–8, III.

Foreign itinerant musicians were very common, especially the ubiquitous German bands which, ranging from sorry little parties of near-beggars to large, well-organised combinations in fancy uniforms, not only thumped and tootled through the streets but turned up at nearly every sort of popular open air occasion. These bands were mostly summer migrants, Bavarians who returned home to their normal callings in autumn, and though in time the expression 'German band' came to mean almost any collection of street musicians, authentic Germans continued to come over till 1914.

The Italian organ-grinder, too, was a familiar figure, often with his hurdy-gurdy slung from one shoulder and a monkey perched on the other, and the *fantoccini* or Italian marionette players were famous. (Punch and Judy—that uninhibited drama so much to the taste of children and other oppressed classes—was Italian in origin.) A great many travelling show people were Jews though this did not necessarily mean that they were immigrants. And needless to say there were also plenty of performers, from hairy ladies to trapeze artists, who posed as exotic characters though they were actually as English as suet pudding.

Many people looked on all fairground folk as vagabonds. In fact there were great differences of standing and reputation among them, though these were not always easy to see at a glance. Some circus-menageries were considerable businesses, with quantities of stock and equipment loaded on their long, lumbering waggon trains, and while the family that ran one might be seen cooking their dinner in black pots outside their caravans like so many gypsies, the gaffer's name on a bill could well be good for a very substantial sum.

Besides the circuses there were travelling stage companies who instead of relying on halls and theatres, carried their own elaborate wood and canvas structures about with them. These could sometimes hold a larger audience than any available local building, but could still be assembled or packed up in a few hours, so that the companies could take full advantage of the ephemeral fair-crowds. But great or small, solid or shifty, the show folk were a rough and ready tribe. Their way of life did not make for delicacy and, moving about a countryside that was still not adequately policed, they had to stand up for themselves.

In his memoirs, Lord George Sanger,[1] the greatest of Victorian circus impresarios, recalls a number of lively scenes. In 1849, at the Whitsun fair at Walsall, a 'very superior' mobile theatre company managed to occupy a site coveted by Wombwell's big circus. To dislodge this rival attraction the circus people crashed their heavy waggons into their competitors' vehicles, packed with valuable sets and properties. The victims, who had already suffered from Wombwell's aggression at another fair, were deter-

---

[1] *Seventy Years a Showman.* Sanger (1825–1911) was brought up on the road, the son of a modest peepshow proprietor who had been pressed for a sailor and wounded in the Napoleonic wars. He adopted the prefix 'Lord' as a half ironic stunt because his rival Buffalo Bill called himself the Hon. William Cody; but it so suited Sanger's panache that it stuck for good.

mined to put up with no more of it. Armed with picks and crow-bars, a crowd of actors suddenly came swarming round the backs of the great animal vans and began breaking in the panels so as to set free the animals inside, some of which were highly dangerous. The roaring and trumpeting and general alarm can be imagined: Sanger himself, who was a very cool hand, was badly frightened. The manoeuvre was totally successful. Seeing that their enemies were in full earnest, the menagerie men—whose chief had been killed only the previous day by an irritated exhibit—made no attempt to pursue the argument but pulled out their vehicles before any of the beasts had got free. The victors were left in full possession of the pitch. It is a comment on showmen's *mores* that, despite the danger to which they and their families had been exposed, all the smaller fry who had collected for the fair applauded the victory and drank the healths of the theatre people for having so sportingly resisted the overweening circus.

When big concerns came in collision their various satellites and camp followers would sometimes rush to their support with a sort of feudal loyalty. On one occasion when Wombwell's was on the march it became entangled with another circus. A whole host of minor show people bound for the same destination weighed in, and a tremendous battle broke out along the road. Even the freaks were seized with a spirit of partisanship and in the general *mêlée* a weird duel took place between a professional fat man armed with a door-hook and an emaciated American known as 'The Living Skeleton' who attempted to batter the other's head with a peg-mallet. Before the contest ended many caravans had been wrecked, at least one set on fire, and two elephants had escaped from an overturned pantechnicon. It is not difficult to understand why magistrates disliked show people as a class and were very prone to harry the majority who lacked the means of legal protection.

But undoubtedly it was the blackguards who appeared almost wherever stalls and booths sprang up who were the most impor-tant cause of official hostility. Many of them were not show folk nor even itinerants. Every big fair and sporting meeting attracted a miscellany of roughs; and among these there were likely to be a number who were simply the dregs of the local population, sometimes as bad as the worst of the professional fairground ruffians and a great deal more numerous. In some districts these local troublemakers were far the most dangerous element present. They had no interest in the prosperity of the fair and did not care whom they frightened away, and they could be the chief perpetrators of the disgusting brutalities—bludgeonings, eye-gougings, thumb-bitings—which were a commonplace of the worse sort of fairground fracas.[1] The Lancashire wakes had an outstandingly bad reputation on this score: it was not unknown for a gang of roughs from some iron foundry or colliery township to beat down a victim and then hack him to death with their iron-shod clogs.

One way and another show people themselves seem to have been the worst sufferers from the ruffianism that clung about their trade, putting them in perpetual bad odour with the law which was for a long time better able to harass than protect them. For all but the biggest, wealthiest concerns great care was essential. The only way of making sure of a pitch might be to arrive the day before a fair opened and camp overnight on the ground, but that might also invite arrest and imprisonment on a technical charge of vagabondage if the municipality was a strict

[1] Crushing an opponent's thumb between the teeth, so paralysing him with pain, was a favourite trick around this period. Before antiseptic surgery such an injury, requiring amputation, might prove fatal, as it did for one victim during the footpadding scare of the early 1860s.

one or its officers had not been adequately bribed. Again, the booth keeper who was slow packing up and getting clear of the course after a race meeting might find himself set-on and pillaged by the riff-raff who used, notoriously, to remain skulking about such places, seeing what they could scavenge and hopeful of pulling down some tipsy straggler with a pocketful of winnings. Occasionally these hyena-like characters would band together to attack even a substantial proprietor with a number of able-bodied helpers. Even on a regular fairground, showmen were at times unable to save themselves from wholesale looting and outrage.

Some ten years before the incident at Walsall, Sanger, then a boy of about thirteen, was on the road with the family peepshow. Migrating from fair to fair in their twelve-foot caravan, the Sangers arrived in due course at the yearly sheep and cattle fair on Lansdown Hill, a mile or so outside Bath. At that date (and till comparatively recent times) Bath concealed behind its graceful terraces some of the most revolting slums in Europe.

Though they were an important event, the Lansdown sales lasted only one day. At dusk, when business was over in the cattle ring that formed the centre of the encampment, dips and flares were lit on the hundreds of stalls, swings, merry-go-rounds and other diversions which covered the hillside and the whole assembly gave itself over to jollification. As night closed down, however, and the countless smoky lights showed more vividly, the nature of the crowd began to change. Farmers and dealers took themselves off, rowdiness increased, fights broke out: from the crowded dance and drinking booths, above the yells and swearing, came the sound of raucous choruses. All this, no doubt, was to be expected. But at about ten, just as Sanger's father had decided that their show was no longer drawing and they might as well shut up shop, a new uproar rose from lower down the hill where the fairground bordered the Bath road. Soon the family were frantically dismantling and packing away their gear, everything breakable or removable being either stowed inside the caravan or made fast beneath it, and all secured with chains and bolts.

The cause of the din and panic was the arrival of a small army of slum dwellers who had come swarming out of the stinking recesses of the city to claim their share in the fun of the fair. Brutalised and poverty-stricken, they had not come to lay out money on peaceable recreation: hence their appearance *en masse* after dark. Apparently they had some sort of crude organisation, their captain being a woman—a gigantic, red-haired virago, 'strong as a navvy', called Carrotty Kate, who was well known and feared about Bath, where she lived in an almost impenetrably disgusting and dangerous hole known as Bull Paunch Alley.

What few constables were available round Lansdown were incapable of dealing with Kate and her myrmidons. 'Half stripped, with her red hair flying wildly behind her, she incited the gang of ruffians with her to wreck the fair. The drinking booths were the first to suffer. The mob took possession of them, half killed some of the unfortunate owners, and then set to work to drink themselves into a state of frenzy more acute than before. The scenes that followed are almost indescribable. Not content with drinking all they could, the ruffians turned on the taps, staved in barrels, smashed up bottles, and let the liquor run to waste. Then they started to wreck the booths. Canvas was torn to shreds, platforms were smashed and made bonfires of, waggons were battered and overturned, show-fronts that had cost some of their poor owners small fortunes were battered to fragments. Everywhere was riot, ruin and destruction.'

In fact the destruction did not spread all over the fairground. It was mainly concentrated in the lower section and the Sangers were not themselves attacked. It is worth noticing that Mr Sanger, the father, though he was evidently a brave and firm-minded man and something of a leader among the small showmen, made no move to help his friends and competitors. When they had finished loading and securing their caravan he ordered his wife and children to be ready to escape up the hill as soon as the rioters approached, while he himself stood ready to defend his property to the end. From the whole tenor of his son's account it is perfectly clear that there was nothing in any way discreditable or contrary to showmen's ethics about this; and one may infer that the other showmen also held aloof till they were directly attacked. Their highly individualist, self-reliant way of life and over-riding concern for their own equipment seems to have made combined defence psychologically impossible.

However, they could cooperate for revenge. At dawn the mob straggled noisily away towards the city and the showmen began to collect in groups, licking their wounds and bitterly comparing

notes. In the upshot a number of the draught horses were collected and about thirty stalwarts, mounted and armed with clubs,
set off after the enemy. Catching up with them, they succeeded
in capturing Kate herself and a dozen or so men whom they
believed to have been particularly forward in the wrecking. They
brought them all back to the camp where everybody turned out
to enjoy the spectacle.

At the bottom of Lansdown Hill was a wide, deep pond, and
the male prisoners, fastened in a row by their hands to a long
rope, were hauled back and forth through the muddy water by
two teams of eager volunteers until some of them were insensible
and the less savage among the haulers feared they had died. The
victims were allowed to lie on the ground 'to drain' and recover
a little before they were dragged up the slope to the waggon
lines, followed by a jeering crowd. Here they were tied to
wheels, two at a time, and hideously thrashed with whalebone
whips. The question of how many blows each was to receive had
been referred to Mr Sanger, who at first had decided on twenty-
four apiece; but an old woman whose living-waggon had been
wrecked cried out 'Make it three dozen for all my beautiful
chaney ornaments' and he increased the sentence accordingly.

Everything considered, the treatment of Carroty Kate seems
relatively chivalrous. She was not ducked and remained fastened
to a cart-wheel until the flogging of the men was done: then she
was seized by six stout women and caned by two more till their
rage was exhausted. She was still bravely and villainously
cursing as she crawled away.

Meantime not all the other raiders had got safely back to the
city's sinks. Although there had been no useful intervention
during the night-long riot, a force of police equipped with heavy
staves successfully intercepted the returning mob, now weakened
with drink and fatigue. The result was a bloody fight in which
many of the rioters were severely injured, many arrested,
and a police officer crippled for life. Surprisingly enough no
one seems to have been actually killed during any of these
events.

Nothing emerges more clearly from Lord George's descriptions of his early days than the precariousness of the life. For
many show people the 'tenting' season was short and winter
employment a desperate problem. It was not very unusual for
some of the most unfortunate to die of want before the Easter

fair time came round. Sanger retained a vivid picture of a huge, once magnificent-looking man, known to the fairgrounds as 'The Wonderful Scotch Giant' and advertised as 'the finest specimen of humanity ever brought before the public', lying stretched 'a pitiful bag of bones, dead of starvation, on the floor of his stripped and empty caravan'.

Yet, despite the cruel hardships and insecurity, there is a sense in which the mid-century was something like a golden age for wandering show people. There were, no doubt, plenty of barnstormers beside whom Crummles' seedy crew in *Nicholas Nickleby* seem almost affluent. ('If we are doing bad business and we pass a field of swedes,' Mayhew quotes one as saying, 'there's a general rush for the pull. The best judges of turnips is strolling professionals.') Yet in the tenting season the opportunities for finding a succession of pitches were almost unlimited. It is true that during the course of the nineteenth century fairs and wakes lost much of their economic importance and by the end of it many of them had disappeared, including some of the most famous; but the earlier part of Victoria's reign was a boom-tide for the fairground entertainer. This was true even of London where there was severe competition from a host of rival attractions. The Queen's coronation was marked by a tremendous, almost unprecedented, nine-day fair in Hyde Park; and in the following decade or so, in addition to the many long-established and exceedingly popular fixtures,[1] a series of 'new fairs' flourished around the metropolis. The growing number of race meetings provided new openings up and down the country, and indeed almost any sort of large public gathering could serve as a focus for showmen.

As for the law, though the authorities were generally ill-disposed, they were not anxious to suppress traditional celebrations or meddle with the rights of landowners and ground lessees. Both private proprietors and corporations stood to profit from well-packed amusement grounds.[2] In general, the great social stir-up of the steam age stimulated the demand for cheap popular

[1] Wandsworth, Greenwich, Deptford, Blackheath and Clapham fairs, were amongst the best known. Stepney fair was then the showmen's Mecca, bigger than any of the great northern wakes. The Great Exhibition of 1851 was accompanied by a large fair in Knightsbridge. On the other hand some particularly inconvenient or disorderly fairs were being closed—notably St Bartholomew's, Smithfield, shut down in 1853.

[2] At Bristol fair, according to Sanger, a guinea per foot of frontage was charged for booths and stalls. At Epsom in the early forties even thimble-riggers were paying from five to ten shillings to come on the racecourse, sticking their receipts in their hats to show they were entitled to practise there. Parliament and local magistrates did however make some efforts to control the more scandalous manifestations of fairs and 'revels', and public bullbaitings and kindred atrocities were put down.

entertainment, and the travelling showmen, traditional entertainers of the poor, were—at first—among the chief beneficiaries.

The appeal of the wandering life was not just that it offered some sort of a livelihood. In a world increasingly dominated by the sound of factory bells and steam whistles, punctuating long days of dull machine-regulated labour, men hankered, as they said, 'to shake a loose leg' and follow, for a time at least, a changing, bohemian existence.

There were close links between itinerant showmanship and itinerant trading, and travelling traders and cheapjacks seem to have lived in much the same way as showmen. Those who had a good business moved about in quite elaborate covered carts or vans—sometimes fitted with a little safety fire-place like those on ships—in which the proprietor and his wife slept, surrounded by their stock-in-trade. Often there was also a lad who besides minding the horse knew how to act as 'sweetener' and start a sticky crowd buying. Such folk dealt in dry-goods, crockery and all sorts of wares from the most rubbishy trinkets to inferior sporting guns, buying from the cheap 'swag' warehouses in great towns and trading wherever there was hope of custom. Fair-grounds provided their liveliest pitches; but they would turn up at any season at remote places where they were probably as much welcomed for the distraction and gossip they provided as for their goods which they now and then bartered with farmwives for eggs, bacon and other produce.

Not surprisingly, their behaviour varied a good deal. The 'han-seller' was usually, at least on the surface, an orderly, pro-estab-lishment character. Anxious to stand well with farmers and people of influence, he was normally careful about gates, fires and fences, though he had a liking for poached game. Since his life was passed in grinding about lonely roads with his cargo of stores, it was natural for him to approve of authorities who stood for the pro-tection of property.

But at fairs and street markets he found himself on the other side of the fence. Frequently he had no fixed stall but sold, with-out licence, from his cart's tail, his horse between the shafts ready for a quick move. In towns he was almost inevitably at logger-heads with the shopkeeping interest, and as he shouted his wares he kept an eye skinned for the head-piece of a constable or beadle advancing through the crowd. Often he increased his risks and entertained his public by making rude remarks about local traders, naming names and comparing their skinflint avarice with his own generous offers.

In many ways the flow of patter conformed to a traditional style that still survives: it is not hard to put a voice, harsh yet fruity, to samples noted down over a century ago.

'Here I am, the original Cheap John from Sheffield. I've not come to get money. Not I. I've come for the good of the public and to let you know you've been imposed on by a parcel of pompous shopkeepers. They got up a petition—which I haven't time to read to you just now—offering me a large sum of money to keep away. And here I am, Cheap John, born without a shirt—one day while my mother was out—in a haystack—consequently I've no parish for the cows ate up mine, and therefore I've no fears of going to the workhouse. I've more money than the parson of the parish. Nobody *can* sell as cheap as me, seeing that I gets all my goods on credit and never means to pay. . . .

'*This* is the original teapot [producing one] formerly invented by the Chinese; the first that was ever exported by those celebrated people—only two came over in three ships. If I do not sell this today, I intend presenting it to the British Museum and the Great Exhibition. It is mostly used for making tea—sometimes by ladies for keeping a little drop on the sly. It is an article constructed upon scientific principles, considered to require a lesser quantity of tea to manufacture the largest quantity of tea-water, than any other teapot now in use—largely patronised by the teetotallers. . . .'[1]

It is not always easy to distinguish between the less prosperous cheapjacks and the army of miscellaneous hawkers who peddled every sort of oddment from boot varnish to ballad sheets, quack aperients to stolen umbrellas. The huckster with a well-stocked van, selling several pounds worth of stuff a day, had very likely worked his way up from a far more disreputable start; and the substantial hanseller was simply an outstandingly successful and mobile practitioner of a trade that involved all sorts of shifts, honest, half-honest, and fraudulent, and at its lowest levels shaded away into a mere pretext for begging.

God-fearing men and women lived between four walls: the best-behaved of the wanderers with whom we have so far been concerned were to some extent suspect. But even the shadiest and most rootless of them remained, essentially, limbs of the settled society from which, one way or another, they got their living. The state of the true Ishmaelites, the gipsies and their kin, was different; for them the roving life was orthodox and ordained, and hostile relations with ordinary people were a part of an immemorial dispensation.

Aloof and secretive, the Romanies had kept their racial and cultural identity for centuries, nursing their separateness through long periods of persecution. They had long memories and returned with interest the suspicions of the *gorgiki*,[2] and inevitably the division between the gipsies and the rest of the wayfaring people

---

[1] See Mayhew, Vol. I, p. 356 et seq.

[2] Non-gipsy. According to W. I. Knapp (George Borrow's learned biographer and editor) the noun *gorgio* signifies, revealingly enough, non-gipsy, stranger or *policeman*.

was keenly felt on both sides. Gipsies regarded the poor *gorgio* on the pad with contemptuous dislike: the moucher who showed too familiar an interest in their encampment had the dogs set on him (rangy beasts whose bite was likely to be a lot worse than their bark). At fairs the other showpeople tended to look askance at the gipsies who were usually relegated to their own separate quarter of the ground. Nevertheless the gipsies and the others had all sorts of material interests in common which willy-nilly kept bringing them into contact with each other. It is easy to underestimate the gipsies' influence on those among whom they pursued their aloof and secretive lives.

It has to be remembered that when Victoria came to the throne England was still a predominantly rural, agricultural society and the gipsies' way of life harmonised with it as it could not do with the life of an industrial, urbanised state. In course of time they had established themselves in various activities, of which much the most important was horse-coping. They were pastmasters at this and were far from dealing only in petty sums and fourth-rate animals. Indeed as long as the horse remained a chief prop of our civilisation they retained some economic importance.

On almost every sort of showground gipsies were conspicuous. As showmen they preferred the simpler sort of attractions and went in for such things as fortune-telling, lucky dips and shies at which customers had to knock down prizes with short heavy staves known as 'livetts'. (In case of disturbance these livetts made useful weapons.) At these public occasions the more prosperous of them — and prosperous gipsies were not very rare — liked to show off a wealth of ornaments: the women paraded with jewelled rings on their fingers and in their ears and heavy gold bangles loading their wrists; the men with gold and silver buttons on their velveteen coats, glittering buckles on their clogs and gold loops under their oily hair. Like the costers, they had a mania for large silk handkerchiefs, and sometimes girls appeared entirely swathed in them, from neck to ankle. A number of the girls were exceptionally good-looking, and no doubt their striking appearances helped to attract the public when their shows met growing competition from the organs and roundabouts of their more machine-minded rivals. Rather surprisingly, some gipsies are reported to have kept big dancing and drinking booths.

There were certain fixtures to which gipsies were especially attracted, and when they gathered in large numbers they could be troublesome. Sanger once watched a column of gipsy vehicles at least a mile long stream away in the course of a few minutes from Moulsey Races. The trouble had started when a posse of constables broke up a fist fight that had been arranged between two

gipsies, the champions of their clans. The contest had aroused strong tribal enthusiasms and the gipsies, who had been greatly looking forward to it, were so enraged that they fell on the police in a body, flailing their livetts 'beneath which men went down like pole-axed oxen'. They drove everybody in their path towards the nearby river where boats overburdened with fugitives foundered in scenes of panic confusion. Then, before anyone else knew of it, word that strong reinforcements of police were approaching reached the gipsies. Suddenly, 'as if by magic', they broke off their attack, and making for their booths like one man, packed up and rattled away.[1]

It is no great paradox that the gipsies' divorce from organised society had for centuries encouraged ties between them and other outlawed and disreputable people, and it is often hard to guess how far their influence on sections of the Victorian underworld was a legacy of the past. To take a minor instance, there existed a system of conventional signs used by cadgers and tramps for each other's guidance—marks left on walls and roadsides to indicate danger, easy pickings, and so on. These signs had a marked affinity to the gipsy *patteran* or trailcode, but they may well have been first adopted by the wandering beggars whom Tudor officials hanged alongside gipsy companions in misfortune. What is plain is that, in however desultory a fashion, the gipsies remained 'men at war with the law',[2] and that they did not prosecute their warfare without allies.

A strong link between gipsies and others was an interest in sport. Gipsies were greatly drawn to horse-racing and prize-fighting, both of which had strong criminal connections. Racing was an increasingly popular sport and, since it was often scandalously ill-regulated, it offered opportunities for just the sort of tricks that the gipsies, with their talent for manipulating horseflesh, were best qualified to play.[3]

Horse stealing was in fact the most serious crime that the public was inclined to pin on the gipsies; and if the idea owed more to tradition and rumour than solid evidence, it was certainly not without some foundation. It is true that gipsies were probably not very well placed for actually stealing horses: if a horse disappeared any gipsies in the neighbourhood would be automatically suspect and they were very unlikely to own premises where it could be well hidden. Moreover it was not hard for suspicious authorities to make life very uncomfortable for them. But when it came to trading in animals of doubtful origin, who was better placed than the mobile, taciturn gipsy coper with his network of contacts among his own people? Such men bought and sold for spot cash and, being illiterate, kept no books.

[1] Sanger, Chapter XIV.
[2] G. E. Leyland *The English Gypsies*.
[3] It may have been largely through sporting contacts that certain Romany words gained wider currency. 'Pal' was already sporty middle-class slang in mid-Victorian times. 'Chiv' (in the sense of knife or razor), a word that came to be particularly associated with racecourse gangs, remains principally an underworld usage.

Another offence that brought the gipsies into contact with non-gipsy criminals was passing off forged coin—essentially a product of urban craftsmanship. Some of them must have been well established in the business, for one reads of gipsy 'smashers'[1] who took in batches of unfinished counterfeits with unmilled edges and over-bright surfaces and worked them up into passable coins (quite a skilled process). And needless to say the gipsies' mastery of every sort of device for living off the countryside made them an object lesson in efficiency to poachers, poultry thieves and other rural wrong-doers.

Both before and after their mysterious migrations into this island, the gipsies had been influenced by the people among whom they pitched their camps. There had also been, through the generations, a certain number of mixed marriages, so that they were nothing like so homogeneous a race as they seemed to outsiders. In reality there were a variety of ethnic shadings, from the more conservative septs with their traditional matrilineal structure and ritual taboos to the *diddiki* and *poshrats* of mixed descent. Presumably it was chiefly from these last that the gipsy beggars, hawkers and pickpockets to be seen in city streets were recruited.

Perhaps the most important single bond between the English gipsies was the Romany speech. At the period we are concerned with, this was less a language than a kind of jargon or cant, vulgar-English in form but loaded with words taken from the languages of countries the gipsy people had passed through in their wanderings from India to the Atlantic. Its great virtue as a cultural tie, lay, of course, in the fact that it was unintelligible to outsiders.

For all his quirks, extravagances and limitations George Borrow was a keen amateur philologist who knew the gipsies of his time as did no other English writer. Although he did not take the words down verbatim but worked the thing up from prose jottings, the ballad or *gillie* of 'Drabbing the Baulo' from *The Romany Rye* may serve as a sample of Romany as it was spoken around this time. It is also evidence, from a friendly witness, of the sort of practice that could make gipsies unwelcome neighbours. The first six stanzas run as follows:[2]

---

[1] Utterers of forged money. For coining etc. see Chapter 8.
[2] The text given is not exactly as printed in Chapter VII of *The Romany Rye* but follows Professor Knapp's notes to Murray's Definitive Edition (London 1905). The rough line-by-line translation has been made in the light of the same editorial source, Borrow's own admittedly 'lady's album' rendering being sometimes misleading.

To mande shoon ye Rommany chale,	*Listen to me ye Gipsy lads,*
Who besh in the pus about the yag,	*Who sit in the straw about the fire,*
I'll pen how we drab the baulo,	*I'll tell how we poison the pig,*
I'll pen how we drab the baulo.	*I'll tell how we poison the pig.*
We jaws to the drag-engro ker,	*We goes to the poison-monger's*
	(apothecary's) house,
Trin hors-worth there of drab we lels,	*Three pennyworth there of poison we*
	buys,
And when to the swety back we wels,	*And when to the (Gipsy) folk back we*
	goes
We pens we'll drab the baulo,	*We says we'll poison the pig,*
We'll have a drab at the baulo.	*We'll have a go at poisoning the pig.*
And then we kairs the drab opre,	*And then we makes the poison up,*
And then we jaws to the farming ker	*And then we goes to the farmhouse*
To mang a beti habben	*To beg a bit of victuals,*
A beti poggado habben.	*A bit of broken victuals.*
A rikeno baulo there we dick,	*A fine pig there we see,*
And then we pens in Rommany chib;	*And then we says in Gipsy talk:*
'Chiv lis odoy opre the chik,	*'Throw it there on the dirt,*
The baulo he will lel lis,	*The pig he will take it,*
The baulo he will lel lis.'	*The pig he will take it.'*
Coliko, coliko sorlo we	*Next day, next day in the morning we*
Apopli to the farming ker	*Once more to the farmhouse*
Will wel and mang him mullo	*Will go and beg for him dead,*
Will wel and mang his truppo.	*Will go and beg his carcass.*
And so we kairs, and so we kairs;	*And so we does, and so we does;*
The baulo in the rarde mers;	*The pig in the night-time dies;*
We mang him on the sorlo,	*We beg him in the morning,*
And rig to the tan the baulo.	*And carry the pig to the camp.*

And the song goes on to tell how, having meticulously washed the animal's entrails so that no trace of poison remains, the gipsies celebrate their feast with beer from the alehouse, fiddle-music and song.

Besides the Romany-speakers of varying strengths of gipsyness, there was another, lesser race of wanderers who were apt to be confused with them. 'Tinker' is a title of baffling vagueness that could be applied to any mender of pots and pans but actually often referred to a particular class of nomad. Typically, tinkers were gipsy-like in their habits and, while not necessarily dark-skinned, rather like gipsies in appearance, though their manner of life was more squalid and their dirtiness literally proverbial. In addition to their aptitude for rough metal work they had their own lore and customs, such as marriage by 'jumping the budget'—the bride and groom hopping over a string or some other symbolic obstacle. The gipsies, for their part, looked down on them and much resented any ignorant identification: and in fact it would seem that the tinkers were never, or very seldom, as well off as the better-to-do gipsies and that, despite the tendency to confuse the two, the general inferiority of the tinkers was well recognised. When some dignified gipsy elder caused a stir by appearing in his best clothes in a metropolitan law court, a distinguished figure in a complete, handsome eighteenth-century outfit, no one would have described him as a tinker.

There is one strong clue as to where the tinkers came from. Their characteristic talk among themselves was Shelta, a complex jargon that took in a number of Irish Gaelic words and corruptions.[1] Broadly speaking the role that the gipsies played in many western countries was, in Ireland, largely taken by tribes of tinkers. Their origins are lost in obscurity but students have held them to be descended from a caste of itinerant smiths who, in the course of ages, sank from their original hieratic status to a condition of wretchedness painful even in comparison with that of the peasantry. Some of these Shelta-using nomads crossed into England with other immigrants, and few of the Irish can have been more rigorously adapted to survive the change of country or to dodge repatriation in the bitter days of the late forties.

Fairly clearly in Victorian times these people of Irish origin formed at least the hard core of the vagrant tinkers. For some years after the mid-century Shelta is said to have been so common that it was virtually impossible to take a walk through the London slums without hearing it spoken—though one may doubt if many literate observers could have distinguished it from ordinary Erse.

Almost the only thing that is quite unambiguous about the tinkers is that they are to be counted among the very lowest and roughest of the wanderers. Indeed those who tried to investigate them could find it a risky as well as perplexing task. There is a revealing little anecdote of a scholarly observer earnestly taking down notes of Shelta in a low pub when, suddenly, he catches the actual gist of the speakers' intentions and, ramming the table

---

[1] Shelta is reported to be full of the inversions and cryptic devices typical of the jargons of outcast, oppressed and delinquent groups—though these have also been enthusiastically ascribed to its sacred pagan origins. It is still spoken by Irish tinkers.

against their legs, bolts for his life before they can cut off his escape.

Before leaving the wayfaring people, something should be said about an activity that probably affected most of them at one time or other. Commercial poaching (taking game for sale, not for the cottager's pot) was a flourishing trade, especially in countrysides within easy reach of the biggest cities.

Until 1831 virtually all sale of game was forbidden, but in fact all who could pay could eat it. Pheasants, partridges, hares, grouse and other delicacies that could only have been obtained illegally were openly served in places patronised by the ruling classes, and notably by the landed gentry for whose benefit the grossly inequitable game laws existed. At Mansion House banquets and other official functions ministers of the crown, judges and bishops were publicly feasted on what they, and everybody else, perfectly well knew must be poached game. Thus the matter was on a different footing to ordinary law-breaking: poachers might be criminals but the most conventional people could accept their wares without qualms.

After the reform of the game laws, the poaching trade lost its monopoly but gained in other ways. More intensive preserving led to larger stocks of birds for which the competitive and pretentious hospitalities of the bourgeoisie helped to provide a bigger market than the lawful trade could satisfy.[1] Furthermore poached game could now find open outlets alongside legitimate supplies.

Partridges and ground game were chiefly taken by methods requiring expertise, stealth and intelligent study of the terrain, at all of which gipsies excelled. Nets and snares were the usual ways, and partridges were netted by taking advantage of the way a gently disturbed covey would follow an habitual track along the ground—a wonderfully skilful art. These methods did not bring in great quantities of game at a time, and it was the nineteenth-century landowners' growing enthusiasm for the pheasant that was the great boon to commercial poachers. Where it was intensively cultivated this saleable bird, with its habit of roosting

---

[1] Though some sporting proprietors evidently did sell dead game in quantity, the practice was still looked at askance. Game was a potent status symbol and its distribution to tenants and friends a traditional means of maintaining a magnate's influence. Also it was only later in the century, in the era of the breech-loading gun, that huge bags of driven birds became common.

nightly at no great height and staying put while its fellows were removed from adjoining perches, lent itself to cruder, more wholesale operations.

On a night when moon and weather were favourable, a gang a dozen or twenty strong would descend on a covert. Perhaps they began by pulling down the easiest birds with hooks or wire loops on poles, perhaps they immediately opened up with short-barrelled guns. The keeper, whose cottage was likely to be some distance from its nearest neighbour—and who, if he was con-scientious, was probably the best hated man in the place—knew when he heard the fusillade that he could do little against such raiders without help. If a party was mustered in time to intercept them it was still likely to be outnumbered by men ready to resist with clubs and scatter shot and, at a pinch, risk close-range murder. Sometimes the big gangs would split up into squads, one section first banging away noisily in one direction while the rest prepared to set about serious work in another.

Where they met alert opposition these forays could lead to maimings and killings on both sides. What seems remarkable is that encounters in isolated places between angry men with guns did not lead to more fatal bloodshed than they did. Some credit, perhaps, may go to the game preservers. Poaching was no longer held to be a crime like housebreaking, against which almost any means of protecting one's property was legitimate; and English landowners and justices of the peace, whatever their sins, were not as a class the men to relish homicide on their home ground or encourage trigger-happy servants. (Which is not to say that unlawful spring-guns and man-traps were not secretly set, or that a keeper never fired a charge of swanshot from cover without warning. A wounded, escaped poacher was not going to advertise his injuries.)[1]

Raids of this sort were known to be chiefly the work of urban toughs who often came from considerable distances. But if they plainly did not demand the same skill and experience as secret poaching, it is equally plain that they cannot have been organised and carried through without some knowledge of local conditions.

---

[1] By soon after the mid-century this style of open, warlike poaching seems to have declined, or at least become much less ferocious. Richard Jefferies, writing of the south in the seventies, speaks of it as of a long past, half-forgotten evil, though in the north and near great cities the tendency to violence seems to have been stronger and more persistent. The 1862 Game Act, stimulating the newly strengthened rural police, no doubt helped to curb poaching generally; but it is also reasonable to think the business was becoming less attrac-tive commercially.

A bunch of roughs with their horses and traps, rattling through the night in blind hopes of lighting on a woodful of half-tame pheasants, would have had little chance of success.

It cannot have been easy for a gang either to survey a countryside or to investigate a particular preserve: strangers prowling about quiet rural parishes quickly attracted attention and countrymen were notoriously suspicious of outsiders. It is hard to imagine how the more ambitious long-distance expeditions can have been managed without the help of someone who had a house or cottage within a few miles of the scene; but for the essential role of spy, guide and contact man, the obvious candidate—disreputable but unremarkable—is the professional wayfarer.

To quote Dr Watts, with whose improving verse so many Victorians became familiar almost as soon as they could toddle:

> Though I am but poor and mean,
> I will move the rich to love me,
> If I'm modest, neat and clean,
> And submit when they reprove me.[1]

The people we have been concerned with conspicuously rejected this ideal. Different as some of them were in their origins and ways of life, their attitude to authority—and authority's attitude to them—gave them a common bond. Costers, navvies, itinerants, they were all axiomatically disreputable and even among the best of them it might take very little (perhaps a short, all too readily earned spell of jail) for a man to pass permanently into the ranks of regular, professional crime.

Surveyed from the vantage point of the mid-nineteenth century most of these people belong, as groups, more to the past than the future. In the long run the times were against them. Throughout the second half of the century the growth of communications and the pressures of an ever more industrialised society were gradually eroding many of the peculiarities of behaviour and costume that had marked various minor divisions of the labouring population and kept alive a sense of separateness and group identity.[2] Moreover, if the lower classes in general

---

[1] Quoted in *The Victorian Tragedy* by E. Wingfield-Stratford. Besides his famous hymns, Watts' best known lines include 'Let dogs delight' and 'How doth the busy little bee'. A contemporary of Swift's, he anticipated in some ways the spirit of a later age.

[2] The new style trade unions, by fostering wider solidarities, probably quickened the process. In the second half of Victoria's reign their influence was strong for respectability, and broadly favourable to a decent chapel-going Sunday-suit conformity.

were not becoming more submissive, they were certainly growing more orderly—partly, no doubt, because they were no longer
subject to so many brutal social injustices. By 1900, 'navvy', its
original meaning forgotten, was a loose term that could be quite
well applied to a quiet local road mender; while to speak (as
Mayhew had done) of the costers as a body posing a threat to
public safety would have been ridiculous.

The wayfarers were inevitably affected by the current of
change. The number of tramps continued to fluctuate with the
ups and downs of the economy, and the badgered remnants of the
Romany are still with us, even today. Nevertheless, much of the
old migratory society, or anti-society, of the countryside was
already on the verge of becoming an anachronism over a hundred
years ago. Once the railway age is fully under way a whole long
dusty procession of caravanners and foot-padders—showmen,
mountebanks, gipsies, tinkers, hawkers, drovers—become diminishing figures on the English highway.

CHAPTER FOUR

Citadels of the underworld

'Those members of the "surplus population" who—goaded by their misery—summon up enough courage to revolt openly against society become thieves and murderers. They wage open warfare against the middle classes who have for so long waged secret warfare against them.'[1] So wrote the young Engels, outraged at what he saw about him in industrial Lancashire during the early forties.

Events in modern communities hardly favour the idea that crime is a simple product of poverty and class-conflict. But in the England Engels was writing of, where hundreds of thousands grew up in the 'undrained, unpoliced, ungoverned and unschooled'[2] urban jungles, where lawlessness flourished as naturally as disease, what motive was there to look for sophisticated explanations? People held widely different views about responsibility for the situation, about the natural turpitude of the poor or the conduct of their employers; but that pauperism, filth, overcrowding and crime were intimately connected, and slums the major breeding grounds of criminals, seemed too obvious to be denied.

Chartist riots and recurrent cholera epidemics sharpened people's awareness of the wretchedness that existed down side-alleys and behind the fronts of superficially orderly streets. The problems of the ever-growing slums, inseparable from every project of social reform, were earnestly discussed in novels and pamphlets and became the subject of more and more official inquiries. The 'police intelligence' columns of the press were enough to make plain the frightening barbarism of the lowest levels of industrial society—especially since it was obvious from the very nature of these people's lives that only occasional samples of their lawlessness and brutality could ever be publicised. To take

[1] F. Engels *Conditions of the working class in England in 1844* (translated by W. O. Henderson and W. H. Chaloner) p. 100.
[2] G. M. Young *Early Victorian England*, p. 432.

an unsensationalised, cursorily reported instance: in 1849 four young men were tried for cooperatively raping a girl at Willenhall in Staffordshire (the model of Disraeli's hideous Wodgate in *Sybil*, where there was 'not a single sight or sound that could soften the heart or humanise the mind'). The crime is not in itself a very remarkable one and no doubt could have been paralleled in many a decent-seeming rural parish: what gives it significance is that it took place on an open space in a populous township before a crowd of both sexes and various ages gathered to enjoy the spectacle.

Willenhall, like many urban areas outside municipal boundaries, was still almost unpoliced at the mid-century. But even where properly organised new-model constabularies patrolled the open streets, the solidarity of the poor against those they considered their professional oppressors, the vagaries of the law, and the dense-packed buildings of many poor districts often made it impossible for them to keep any real control over the swarming back quarters. The rule of law was apt to stop at the alley-corners, beyond which the police appeared less as custodians of public order than as raiders in hostile territory.

By the time Victoria was crowned, it is true, many of the cruellest and most absurd features of the old criminal law had been abolished. The life-cheapening lottery of the 'bloody code', which encouraged minor offenders to acts of desperation, was virtually over. Nevertheless, the system remained full of quirks and abuses. It had a strong, though inconsistent, bias in favour of property and a corresponding unconcern for personal violence (short of murder) where property rights were not involved. Inevitably this increased the dangers and difficulties of keeping order. As we have seen, a costermonger who attacked a policeman from behind and disabled him for life was imprisoned for a year—at a time when the penalty for stealing a few pounds worth of goods might well be ten years transportation. Assaults involving concussion and broken bones were commonly met with a fine or a week or two's jail, less severe treatment than might be meted out for accidentally breaking a window, hawking without a licence, unlawfully removing rubbish (the property of the dust-contractor), obstructing the road with a barrow and a host of other trifling offences. Low public houses were often the scenes of all sorts of brutality, including savage and illegal sports, carried on under the open patronage of the landlords who clearly had no fear of losing their licences. Yet in 1840 a publican found guilty of stealing a 'piece of honeycomb tripe and a cow-heel, worth ninepence' was not only jailed but, as a convicted felon, sentenced to forfeit his whole property.[1] On the other side there was the case of a man who so belaboured a girl that he destroyed one of her eyes, broke her nose and induced concussion of the brain, then after violently kicking her prostrate body seized her legs and hurled her over a parapet to a ten-foot drop. His victim survived and he was sentenced in the absence of any extenuating circumstances to twelve months hard labour. This happened 'near Gloucester': in the heart of a slum area he would have been unlucky not to escape prosecution.[2]

It is little wonder if the police, confronted with this scale of legal values and often kept shamefully short-handed by parsimonious authorities, were inclined to spend more time on protecting the rights of the well-to-do than on intervening in the internal ferocities of the slum jungle. In this way the slum dwellers were to a great extent left to their own brutal devices. Edwin Chadwick was perhaps over-pessimistic in believing that 11,000 Britons died yearly from acts of violence;[3] but he was a man used to supporting his statements with evidence and well placed to make the estimate.

Naturally, as the new police grew more numerous and efficient, they were able to move into the swarming back courts and bring them under more direct control. The metropolitan force—exceptionally strong, with an officer to every four or five hundred citizens[4]—was certainly something more than a mere agency of repression. Indeed it is hardly possible to read much about the mid-century police, particularly those in London, and doubt that on the whole they behaved with more disinterested goodwill and devotion to order for its own sake than could reasonably be expected of them. But in essence, of course, the problems of the slums was not one of law enforcement—something that is a good

[1] His judge appears to have felt that it was a hard case. See *The Times*, 30 November 1840.

[2] Cited by J. C. Symons, an experienced circuit barrister and editor of the *Law Magazine* in *Tactics for the Times* (1849). The point that the often trifling penalties for assaulting the police cannot have inclined them to restraint and strict regularity in their dealings with dangerous criminals is emphasised by W. Hoyle, *Crime in England and Wales*.

[3] S. E. Finer, *The Life and Times of Sir Edwin Chadwick*, p. 148. Chadwick apparently put forward this opinion in the late 1830s.

[4] In 1848 the ratio in Warrington appears to have been one policeman to every 3,600 inhabitants, in Bolton 1:2,400. Metropolitan constables, better paid than the average, got just under a pound a week wages, without rights to a disability pension or widow's compensation.

deal more obvious to us than to contemporaries. It was not till the seventies that the housing reform movement began to have any perceptible effect on a problem that had been exercising social reformers for forty years.

In many spreading factory towns a familiar pattern of housing had already been long established. The prosperous had moved away from the source of their wealth to new suburbs, preferably on rising ground. Nearer in came belt after belt of houses, each less pleasant than the last, until the nucleus of the old pre-industrial town was reached. Here, in an irregular ring around a busy, grimy city centre, close to the smoke-stacks and gantries of mills and warehouses, and often to a black stinking waterway thick with sewage and industrial effluent, might be found decayed houses that had once stood on the edge of a market town and that were now enmeshed in a growth of courts and annexes. In big long-established cities the pattern of development was often too broken up to be easily recognisable; but wherever the economic current washed up great numbers of workpeople round existing centres the same process of ingrowth and cramming was almost inevitable. In practice there were few restrictions on what the

owners of property could do with it and, where sites were already hemmed in by older but still highly profitable buildings, the natural course was to squeeze new dwellings into any open ground still left and pack the old ones tighter. Yards and gardens were built over, passages and landings colonised and windowless cabins boarded off. Especially if there were good sized old houses with cellars and attics, a maze of human nests and burrows could soon come into being where the most lawless and disreputable tended to gather.

This, then, was the archetypal Victorian rookery, an accretion of newer buildings around an earlier core, developed under the pressure of industrial concentration into a shameful, dangerous warren. Different local circumstances produced an almost endless range of variations but roughly the same sort of life went on in them.

Slums are as old as townships, and a number of notorious rookeries in London and elsewhere were legacies from the past, traditional strongholds of crime that seem to have kept much the same character for generations. If their inhabitants had become more crowded, they were probably neither filthier nor more depraved than their eighteenth-century predecessors, and certainly a good deal less ready to sally out *en masse* and terrorise their respectable neighbours.

Other plague spots, on the other hand, were of wholly recent construction. Even on new land, working class housing was not only built low for cheapness but also laid out so as to take up as little space as possible. In the worst developments, lines of back-to-backs might be run up with a passage way only four or five feet wide between the double rows in which rubbish dumps, a water point, latrines and other 'conveniences' all had to be accommodated. Sometimes, as in a case noticed at Preston at the middle of the century, the builder might solve the sanitary problem by simply running an open cess-trench down the middle, leaving only ledge-like paths on either side. Where dwellings were arranged round a rectangular court, the inhabitants were likely to congest it with water-barrels, pigsties, and lean-to sheds. If adjoining courts were not linked in the builders' plan connecting runways could soon be established. It is not hard to see how a system of such 'entries', linked to each other, often opening into streets just wide enough to allow for the movements of builders' carts, and tenanted by a degraded and disorderly population, could provide formidable slum-nexuses almost ready-made.[1]

Many of the worst criminal slums lay conveniently close to their denizens' hunting ground. The port districts of Liverpool, Newcastle, Cardiff, Rotherhythe and Stepney, for instance, enjoyed a particularly bad reputation, with their contingents of whores, pandars, crimps, bullies and catamites, inhabitants of the runways behind the shining gin palaces and dance saloons.

Rookeries almost ringed the landward boundary of the City of London and lay close to the commercial hearts of Birmingham and Manchester. In West London the fact that packed tenements could be highly profitable helped to bring the wretchedest members of society into grotesque proximity with the richest and most powerful. In St James's, in Marylebone, and in the affluent parish of St George's, Hanover Square, there were disease-ridden warrens almost in the shadows of great people's mansions. (This meant easy opportunities for spoil—even poor puss, whisked up at the mews corner, his miaows stifled in a greasy bag, might fetch a half sovereign ransom instead of the few coppers an East End dealer would pay for his pelt—but it also brought its own dangers since the police were particularly watchful in these areas. The majority of thieves and cadgers working 'polite' residential streets seem to have been invaders who disappeared eastwards as soon as the job was done.)

In favourable circumstances a landlord might lease a ten-room house for between twenty and forty pounds a year and let out the rooms at from five to ten shillings a week each, while maintenance costs were limited to preventing the structure subsiding into the roadway. However the financial picture was seldom quite as attractive as these figures suggest. For one thing profits were often divided between a number of people (when a building did in fact collapse or the sanitary authorities tried to clear up some centre of infection, their efforts were constantly held up by the difficulty of discovering where, among a tangle of tenancies, responsibility could be fixed). Collecting rent, too, was a troublesome and sometimes dangerous business, the more so since to be a payment or two in arrears was often the only security against being slung out in favour of a tenant offering a

---

[1] Such slum clearance as did occur usually occurred more or less by chance, often as the result of driving a road or railway through a poor district. As no thought was given to resettling the evicted people, it commonly led to the neighbouring tenements becoming even more closely crammed.

View from Brewery Bridge over tenement roofs
to St Paul's. Gustave Doré

The Devil's Acre, Westminster.
Notice the three descending layers of increasingly
squalid development. Gustave Doré

few pence more for the same place. Some landlords countered by employing the biggest blackguard on the property to collect the rents of the others in exchange for a remission of his own, but that system plainly offered endless possibilities for extortion and fraud.

Many of the poor could not afford even two or three shillings a week rent, and in the worst slums the regular tenants of a room often shared it with a number of lodgers who might pay them from twopence to fourpence a head daily. One London Irishman was found to be paying ten shillings a week for a front room (probably in a small Georgian terrace-house) in which he also lodged three couples, each at sixpence a night, so that he lived rent free and made a weekly profit of sixpence. In addition, he expected at least an occasional share in his sub-tenants' meals.

This sort of rack-rented tenement was one typical way for the most wretched to live, but it was not the only way. One cannot give a picture of the rookeries—or indeed of the organisation of the underworld as a whole—without looking at that key institution, the low lodging house. There were many variations of arrangement and management, and many gradations of decency even amongst the cheapest, but the characteristic features of the common slum dosshouse or 'nethersken' were well enough described at the time to allow a general description.

The main room, and the focus of the whole place, was the kitchen, where, except in the very poorest houses, a fire blazed away winter and summer. Before it the lodgers warmed themselves, dried out their clothes, and toasted their food. Their cooking might be helped by a meagre selection of pots and pans that could be borrowed from the management against small pledges. Benches and a bare table or two were likely to be the chief furniture, unless there were removable cots or bunk-boxes round the wall. In towns where there was a gas supply a single jet on a bracket by the chimney-breast half-lit the place after dark. Apart from *graffiti* and some crude prints pasted to the wall, decoration was sparse. In the sleeping rooms, usually the most offensive part of the place, there would be beds or palliasses jammed close and equipped sometimes with blankets, sometimes with a single heavy coverlet. They were often shared and usually verminous. Sometimes there were old four-posters in which a whole party, perhaps a family, slept together. When the place was crowded— and in some of the rougher houses as a general practice—people stretched themselves out at night on the floor wherever they could, the strongest or most favoured by the fire, the worst-off along passages or under leaking garret slates. The sanitary habits of most of the lodgers were disgusting, but washing might be possible under a tap or pump in the stinking back yard where there was also some kind of privy—a collection of buckets or a hole over a cess-pit. Payment was by the night and customarily entitled the lodger to hang about the kitchen till the following evening. Threepence seems to have been the usual fee in the forties and fifties.

There were, naturally, great differences in the kind of custom these houses attracted. Many, especially in minor provincial towns along the main roads, were almost exclusively 'padding-kens' where wayfarers on the pad put up. In such places, where the sleeping space might be one or two rooms or a shed attached to a mean beer shop, tramping journeymen on their uppers fell in with professional beggars and mouchers who initiated them into the arts by which they scrounged a living from the unfriendly world. (A new face, unfamiliar along the routes they worked, could be useful to a party of cadgers.) The paddingken proprietor, who in country places was often a woman, might be very helpful to her customers. It was part of her business to keep in with the local constable and when necessary 'gammon' him on their behalf. Often she was able to help them dispose of begged or stolen goods. Above all she was an up-to-date informant on local conditions, and some enterprising proprietors actually kept a list of charitable, gullible or easily intimidated local residents which was available to trusted customers for a small payment.

In the slums of great cities there were much larger netherskens, some taking a hundred and more lodgers, with a less transitory clientele. (In many it was the practice to encourage people to remain a week at a time by not charging those who had been there since Monday for their Sunday night's entertainment.) Here were to be found specimens of all the types of the social sump. A big rookery nethersken might harbour a shifting collection of casual labourers, hawkers, beggars, thieves, low night-stand prostitutes, petty touts and sharpers, road-sweepers, street per-formers, broken servants and more or less unspecifiable riff-raff. Nevertheless, as with most places where people gather together, there was a tendency for those who shared the same interests to favour particular houses. Some were literally thieves' kitchens, chiefly frequented by pickpockets, house robbers and their confederates, while others were largely tenanted by beggars. Others again enjoyed a special reputation as 'servants' lurks' where out of work servants of bad character congregated, often ready to make plans for robbing their employers. There was a good deal of club spirit about some of the smaller lodging house kitchens, a sense of membership that encouraged sharing and conviviality when someone had a stroke of luck, and that made them specially dangerous to intruders.

Among the inhabitants of these places there was a sprinkling of educated people—broken-down clerks and businessmen, an occasional derelict clergyman or lawyer. Men of this type, who were often confirmed soaks, sometimes built up practices as 'screevers' or drafters of bogus testimonials and similar documents. (The job seems to have been at least as well paid as much publisher's hackwork.) A lodging house frequented by beggars and criminals was obviously a good site for commissions of this kind, and that may partly explain why people one might have expected to prefer any sort of misery to the communal brutishness and turmoil of a nethersken kitchen seem actually to have been drawn to them. (Though one educated lodger who, according to Mayhew, had formerly 'moved in good society' gave a different explanation, observing that 'when a man's lost caste . . . he may as well go the whole hog, bristles and all, and a low lodging house is the entire pig.')

Perhaps the worst feature of these places in which so much human debris collected was that they often swarmed with children of all ages. Indeed the condition of some of the most filthy was, as in other slums, largely due to the numbers of untended infants who relieved themselves all over the stairs and passages. Many of them were of course the children of adult lodgers, and others were kept by resident beggars and thief masters who trained them and used them for their own ends; but precocious independence was a leading underworld characteristic and a number of these child lodgers, down to eleven years old and less, were making their own way. There were numerous stray urchins living about the streets as best they could, dodging the terrors of the Union and the House of Correction and keeping clear of authorities who in turn were often willing enough to avert their eyes from further charges on the rates. Many of these children found shelter in lodging houses. They might get in at a reduced charge by piling four or five into a single sleeping space, and they could prove useful by bringing in stolen food for cheap sale. Nowhere were they more likely to be debauched or to receive a thorough grounding for a life of crime. Some lodging house keepers maintained gangs of professional child thieves and even ran schools for pickpockets in their kitchens. But though these children might be brutally treated they were not usually kept in bondage: little delinquents drifted easily from one lodging to another, accepting tutelage as it seemed to their advantage, and then disappearing into the maze of slums they knew so well—or into the hands of the law.

In some houses a certain amount of privacy might be possible. One hears of couples securing a room and a bed to themselves for half-a-crown a week, or three-and-six if they had children with them. Some houses took only men. But, in general, huggermugger promiscuity seems to have been the thing. Often several couples slept in the same room and might vary their entertainment by changing partners during the night. In hot weather the parasites in their clothes and bedding, and the stifling atmosphere, made lodgers of both sexes lie on top of the beds entirely naked— a powerful indication of how far they had abandoned all standards if one considers contemporary notions about nakedness, which were common to every class.

In certain houses, young lodgers, children and adolescents, were bundled in together. 'There was very wicked carryings on,' said a girl who had experienced this. 'The boys, if any difference, was the worst. We lay packed on a full night, a dozen boys and girls squeezed into one bed . . . some at the foot and some at the top—boys and girls all mixed. I can't go into all the particulars, but whatever could take place in words or acts between boys and girls did take place.'[1] Even these scenes were preferable to what could happen where people of all ages were indiscrimately mixed, or where (as also happened in some workhouse casual wards) all males were herded together and small boys had little chance of escaping the attentions of mature perverts.

Lodging house keepers did not conform to any clearly marked type. In big cities as in country towns, many of the smaller places were run by women, often in conjunction with a modest pot-house or coffee shop. These 'mots'—often most formidable characters —were specially given to egging on young lodgers to bring in

[1] Mayhew, Vol. I, p. 459.

stolen food. Some houses were kept by major fences who did a regular trade in burgled goods and actually melted down gold and silver on the premises, though most of the stolen stuff brought, into netherskens seems to have been of modest value— food, silk handkerchiefs, clothing sneaked from outside shops, and the like. Lodging house proprietors were notoriously shady characters.

Some, all the same, were substantial citizens: a house with eight or so rooms might accommodate a hundred lodgers and there were men who owned three or four such places as well as a public house, perhaps, and half a dozen cabs. One prominent proprietor of lodging houses in the St Giles rookery in London also owned a number of genteel properties in Hampstead. Where the business was on this scale the daily running of each house was normally confided to a sharp tough known as 'the deputy', whom his employer might control by planting a spy among the lodgers. Altogether the management of lodging houses demanded shrewd judgement and a sharp eye. One speculator furnished a small chain of houses with articles from the condemned Small Pox Hospital at Kings Cross, which—there being no other takers— went very cheap. There were employers, notably petty truck masters in the Port of London, who improved their profits by insisting that the labourers on their books must lodge (or at least have their pay debited for lodging) in the boss's dosshouse.

Not all very cheap lodging houses were of this kind, even in disreputable quarters and even before serious efforts at reform began. Here and there philanthropic associations or individuals, sometimes justices of the peace concerned at the evidence constantly before them, set up 'model' establishments. In the 1840s the Society for the Improvement of the Conditions of the Labouring Classes, a very active evangelical charity, already had two model houses in London slums—one in St Giles and the other among the squalors of Drury Lane. A place owned by Lord Kinnaird in the worst part of Westminster had a detached, shut-off kitchen, public rooms, strictly regulated sleeping arrangements, and individual lockers. But such places hardly scratched the surface of the problem; moreover it was the common trouble with model lodging houses (as with so many Victorian charities) that an over-rigid system of improvement was apt to defeat its own ends. Even characters not beyond reform might feel more at home by a squalid kitchen hearth than listening to a clergyman's exhortation in a scrubbed day-room; while an insistence on early hours kept out the many street sellers whose best hope of custom was with the late public house and theatre crowds. Perhaps the best casual lodging was provided by commercially-run houses whose proprietors, though catering for a very poor trade, maintained a fair standard of order and cleanliness. There were such places, even in sinister districts, and in fact some of the reputable 'houses of call' connected with particular trades and used by card-carrying artisans seem to have been simply decent workmen's lodging houses. Yet cheap as they might be, something had to be charged for the extra space and gear required for the elementary decencies, and an additional copper or two a night was a serious barrier to those for whom a sixpenny 'tightener' was a rare feast. Furthermore the cadged and pilfered 'scran' (food) often sold in penny and halfpenny-worths by fellow lodgers in the more disreputable kitchens must have been a great attraction.

During times of seasonal unemployment or trade recession lodging houses were the scenes of a ghastly want that is itself a commentary on the workings of the Poor Law. Mayhew took a particular interest in one house in the London dock area, a very wretched place but not especially tough or criminal.[1] It was situated off a fairly wide slum court, cluttered with coster carts, where a number of prostitutes of the poorest sort lay asleep. Large green entrance doors, like those of a stable yard, led to a kitchen filled with a fog of smoke through which sunlight from a hole in the roof cut a narrow shaft.

> The flue of the chimney stood out from the bare brick wall like a buttress, and was black all the way up with smoke; the beams, which hung down from the roof and ran from wall to wall were of the same colour; and in the centre to light the room was a rude iron gas pipe. . . . The floor was unboarded, and a wooden seat projected from the wall all round the room. In front of this was ranged a series of tables on which lolled dozing men. A number of the inmates were grouped round the fire; some kneeling toasting herrings, of which the place smelt strongly; others without shirts seated on the ground close beside it for warmth; and others drying the ends of cigars they had picked up in the streets. As we entered the men rose and never was so motley and so ragged an assemblage seen. Their

[1] Mayhew, Vol. III, p. 313 et seq. He seems to have visited it some time in the latter forties.

hair was matted like flocks of wool and their chins were grimy with their unshorn beards. Some were in dirty smock-frocks; others in long red plush waistcoats with long sleeves. One was dressed in an old shooting jacket with wooden buttons; a second in a blue flannel sailor's shirt. . . . On the form at the end of the kitchen was one whose squalor and wretchedness produced a feeling approaching awe. His eyes were sunk deep in his head, his cheeks were drawn in, and his nostrils pinched with evident want, while his dark stubbly beard gave a grimness to his appearance that was almost demoniac; and yet there was a patience in his look that was almost pitiable. His clothes were black and shiny at every fold with grease, and his coarse shirt was so brown with wearing, that it was only with long inspection you could see it had once been a checked one; on his feet he had a pair of lady's lace-sided boots, the toes of which had been cut off so that he might get them on. . . . I never beheld so gaunt a picture of famine. To this day the figure of the man haunts me.

Mayhew planned to give these people a good dinner, made arrangements with the keeper of the place, and ordered 'enough beef, potatoes and materials for a suet pudding' to be sent from a nearby market. Naturally he supervised the affair himself.

The dinner had been provided for thirty but the news of the treat had spread, and there was a muster of fifty. We hardly knew how to act. It was however left to those whose names had been taken down as present on the previous evening to say what should be done; and the answer from one and all was that the newcomers were to share the feast with them. The dinner was then half-portioned out in an adjoining outhouse into twenty-five platefuls—the entire stock of crockery belonging to the establishment numbering no more—and afterwards handed into the kitchen through a small window to each party, as his name was called out. As he hurried to the seat behind the bare table, he commenced tearing the meat asunder with his fingers, for knives and forks were unknown here. Some, it is true, used bits of wood like skewers, but this seemed almost like an affectation in such a place; others sat on the ground with the plate of meat and pudding on their legs; while the beggar boy, immediately on receiving his portion, danced along the room, whirling the plate round on his thumb as he went, and then, dipping his nose in the plate, seized a potato in his mouth.

The charge at this house was twopence a night, which could be paid up till eleven p.m. when those who had not paid were turned out and no further applicants admitted. Mayhew learnt that about half the lodgers were thieves, up to a quarter dock labourers, and a sixth regular street beggars; in addition some collected old bones and dogs' faeces (for tanners) while there were one or two aged wretches who managed to survive partly by parish relief and partly by charity. It is worth noticing that his chief informant (who acted as a kind of Virgil in this inferno) was a man of 'good education and superior attainments' who had lived there four months.

Even that place was not the absolute nadir of lodging houses. The poorest people were often desperate for shelter of any sort and conditions in many provincial cities seem to have been as bad as they were in London. Workhouse casual wards, when they functioned at all, usually allowed only one or perhaps two nights shelter, and such charitable night-refuges as existed also had to rebuff attempts to use them as permanent quarters. Bad weather and the vagrancy laws drove the poorest of all into 'packs' which might be no more than bare rooms or sheds, furnitureless and fireless, where lodging meant no more than the right to struggle for a body-space on the filthy floor.

Here, in the words of the Town Clerk of Macclesfield is a description of premises visited by officials of the new local Board of Health one night in the early 1850s:

> In four small cottages, with two bedrooms each and with two rooms on the ground floor, there was an average of 188 persons lodged; they had a small yard, and the remains only of what had been two privies, all the ordure being in the open yard. In this yard was also a building, in a loathsome condition, occupied by a man, his wife and child, and one female lodger, the dimensions of the room on the ground floor being 6ft 2in. long, by 4ft 4in. wide, and 5ft 4in. high; and the bedroom 9ft 8in. long, 4ft 4in. wide, and 5ft 4in. high. This had been a nailer's shop and the walls and the floor were jet black. In the same yard, in one bedroom, 8ft 9in. by 9ft and 7ft high, lived a husband, and a wife, and six children. In another lodging house near, there were three small rooms upstairs:

in the first were 16 men, women and children, lying together
on the floor; in the second there were twelve, also on the
floor; and a third room upstairs was used as a privy, the
boarded floor being literally covered with human ordure. In
the same yard at the same time, but in another lodging-house,
in worse condition than the last, there was a bed in the house-
place, on which lay a woman in the pains of labour; by her
side lay a man apparently asleep, and ten other men, women
and children were in the same room. This was at 2 a.m. In a
back place, with the window out, and used as a receptacle for
the filth of the house, lay three little children in some shavings.
In the room over this lay six women and children on the floor,
and in the front room were four beds on the floor, filled with
men, women and children, varying from 2 to 6 in a bed.[1]

In seaports there were (and long remained) 'penny hangs'—
cellars chiefly patronised by drunken sailors where the keeper
suspended ropes breast high from wall to wall so that his clients
could drape the upper part of their bodies over them until, in the
morning, he unfastened the ends and the company collapsed on
the swimming floor.

Up till the middle of the century the low lodging trade boomed
and proliferated unchecked. A moderate sized provincial town
might well support a hundred or more netherskens while in
London they abounded in almost every squalid neighbourhood.
They were so numerous as to be a conspicuous scandal. Ob-
noxious alike on grounds of public health, law enforcement and
morals (and a matter of financial indifference to the big ground
landlords who got their rents just the same from ordinary slum
tenements) they were an obvious target for reformers. The
Common Lodging House Act of 1851 began a serious drive to
bring them under control. They became liable to regular police
supervision and could be forcibly shut down if they failed to reach
elementary standards of decency, while fines were inflicted for
various irregularities including failure to keep a proper register
of lodgers.

So far as public order was concerned the Act was a useful
measure, stimulating police authorities and providing them with
a lever. To the poor it brought benefits as well as some increased
hardship. Certainly hundreds of the vilest pest-holes up and

[1] *Parliamentary Papers* 1857 (2nd Session) XLI. Reports on Common Lodging Houses,
23.

down the country were ferreted out during the next decade. In Bristol, a city of widespread and abominable slums, the inspector appointed under the Act closed some sixty houses, while Macclesfield announced the suppression of over 150. Surprisingly, even after so many lodging houses had been shut down, the surviving ones were sometimes reported to be half empty. This may partly have been because increased employment, rising wages (and possibly also dearer food) diminished the tramping population during the war years of the middle fifties; but the other explanation is that, as supply and demand adjusted themselves, the increased costs of complying with the new Act were passed on to the lodgers, and some of them could not afford to pay. The pressure on Union casual wards and the outbreak of footpadding in the hard times of the early sixties may very well have had some connection with the disappearance of the worst and cheapest paddingkens on which reformers had congratulated themselves a few years earlier.

Of course the Act did not make a universal clean sweep. In London the state of the registered houses seems to have been very greatly improved: after about 1860 references to entirely foul and disorderly places of the old type are strikingly absent and, though there were still lodgings full of delinquents, one no longer hears of the hordes of child lodgers. In the country as a whole, however, the enforcement of social legislation of this sort was often weak, and a responsibility that fell on borough magistrates to be paid for as 'part of the General Expenses of the Constablewick of the Place' was unlikely to be carried out vigorously if it was against local interests. (The licensed victuallers, who had close connections with lodging house keeping, were scandalously influential on watch committees.) In fact, though the lodging house trade was curbed, it seems to have adapted itself and remained fairly prosperous. Taine, touring the Manchester slums with a police guide at some time in the sixties, found himself peering into what appears to have been a series of typical thieves' kitchens,[1] until the suffocating atmosphere and the predatory faces in the gaslight made him feel as if he were involved in some nightmare fantasy of Edgar Allen Poe's. In the seventies and eighties the old complaints against the corrupting influence of vagrant's lodgings could still be

---

[1] Taine refers to them as 'cabarets'. His description does not suggest a tour of criminals' flash-houses though some of the premises he saw may well have been poor 'beer shops'. See *Notes sur Angleterre*, p. 323.

heard—and no doubt remain true of dosshouses down to the present day.

The immediate effect of the reform can only have been that many people who had been living in lodging houses packed themselves into rented rooms as sub and sub-sub-tenants, giving up the communal kitchen hearth which was the nethersken's greatest boon to its inmates. These dispersals helped to break up some of the large associations of poor delinquents, and in doing so they accelerated a process that was already underway. In the past, for example, there had been highly organised companies of beggars who based themselves on the lodging house headquarters of their organising 'captains' and parcelled out the profitable territories of Westminster and St James's, chivying away any competition. By the forties they had vanished, and even the feasts of steak and hot gin with which turns of good fortune had been traditionally celebrated in the cadgers' kitchens were probably little more than a memory.

With the first and best regular police in the country, London had also by far the largest and most diverse underworld for them to cope with. Metropolitan criminals, on the run or in search of easier pickings, made their way to cities up and down Britain— and indeed to Europe and across the Atlantic—while London also sucked in and schooled delinquents of every kind from elsewhere. In London, too, there were examples of almost every kind of criminal refuge and breeding ground, from crazy, piled-up tenements that had been villainous under Queen Anne to the squalid new warrens of the industrial age.

As in every great city, the criminal community, for all its diversity, remained firmly attached to its citadels. The master cracksman or swell pickpocket might live in a respectable suburb like Camden Town or New Cross, but it was through contacts in Snow Hill, Whitechapel or the Old Mint that he found his associates and the means of carrying on his trade. In lodging house kitchens, in the taprooms of flash pubs, in coffee shops and eating houses, among festoons of second hand clothes in little grotto-like shops off the reeking hubbub of Rosemary Lane, was carried on the essential traffic of the underworld. Here robberies were hatched, the disposal of stolen property arranged, packets of counterfeit money marketed, forged documents commissioned, and above all information bought and exchanged. Deep inside the rookery the coiner carried on his elaborate craft in relative security and the hunted thief went to ground.

Walking westward from where High Holborn approaches Shaftesbury Avenue, near the old Palace Theatre, one finds oneself in a scrappy townscape of bulky but unimpressive blocks. Among them are the untidy remains of some older streets, dwarfed by the later buildings, and the baroque tower of St Giles-in-the-Fields. The general effect is depressing, an oddly devitalised little piece of London so lacking identity that once quitted its features can hardly be recalled. Here, straddling New Oxford Street and extending from Great Russell Street to St Giles High Street, is the central site of the infamous 'Holy Land', the great St Giles rookery. At the moment of writing the passer-by can still see houses that were once part of the most notorious criminal slum in Britain.

Even if the less dense and squalid outlying stretches towards Seven Dials are included, the Holy Land was not the largest criminal quarter in London. It was less dangerous to walk through than the lanes behind the Ratcliffe Highway and a good deal less pestilential than Jacob's Island, the Bermondsey 'Venice of Drains'. What gave it its evil celebrity was the fact that such a menacing stronghold of the underworld stood in such a strategic situation. It could be reached from the dives and run-ways round Leicester Square and the Haymarket, and from the shady turnings off Regent Street, almost without crossing an honest thoroughfare, so that it was a convenient asylum for the offscourings of the night-world of theatres, gaming rooms, supper cellars, brothels and houses of assignation. It was also a natural habitat for beggars and sneak thieves working the rich fields of west London. Once safely inside, a wanted man could often only be winkled out—if at all—by a long and expert process.

From the seventeenth century to the mid-nineteenth, the strength of the place lay in the sheer congestion of the 'back settlements'—the net-work of yards and passages behind the miserable lanes that traversed the area—crammed with a desperate outcast humanity who knew they could only look to each other and the intricacy of their warren to save their skins from the unending oppression of the law. Charles Knight, the author of the most celebrated guide to Victorian London, first knew the rookery when its recesses were virtually inviolable. He compares it rather rhetorically to the fastnesses of the Scotch

Covenanters whom persecution made more and more intransigent. 'Favoured by natural position,' he observes, 'the blackguardism of St Giles was only increased by harsh treatment—it was pounded into tougher consistency.'

As with most such areas, there were no precise bounds to the rookery. As Knight puts it, it blended into 'the more civilised districts in its vicinity, by insensible degrees, like the hues of a rainbow'. But at the beginning of the Victorian era the heart of it covered some six to ten acres—

a dense mass of houses 'so olde they only seem not to fall' through which narrow and tortuous lanes curve and wind. There is no privacy here for any of the overcrowding population, every apartment in the place is accessible from any other.

... Whoever ventures here, finds the streets, by courtesy so called, thronged with loiterers, and sees, through half-glazed windows rooms crowded to suffocation. The stagnant gutters in the middle of the lanes, the filth choking up the dark passages which open upon the highways, all these scarce leave so dispiriting an impression on the passenger as the condition of the houses. Walls the colour of bleached soot, doors falling from their hinges, door-posts worm-eaten, windows where shivered panes of glass alternate with wisps of straw, old hats and lumps of bed-ticken or brown paper, bespeak the last and frailest shelter than can be interposed between man and the elements.

Against the incursions of the law, however, there were remarkable defences. Over the years the whole mass of yards and tenements had become threaded by an elaborate complex of runways, traps and bolt-holes. In places cellar had been connected with cellar so that a fugitive could pass under a series of houses and emerge in another part of the rookery. In others, long established escape routes ran up from the maze of inner courts and over the huddled roofs: high on a back wall was a double row of iron spikes, 'one row to hold by, and another for the feet to rest on,' connecting the windows of adjacent buildings. To venture into the passage mouths that led into the back settlements was risky; to chase a wanted man through the escape ways could be really dangerous, even for a party of armed police. According to a senior police officer who became inspector of lodging houses in the district, a pursuer would find himself 'creeping on his hands and knees through a hole two feet square in a dark cellar entirely in the power of dangerous characters' who might be waiting on the other side; while at one point a 'large cesspool, covered in such a way that a stranger would likely step into it' was ready to swallow him up.

East of the Holy Land lay a timber yard into which there was a secret entry, running through an appalling brothel. Through this entry criminals were able to pass in and out of the rookery unobserved even when the surrounding streets were under watch, and it was so carefully hidden that it was only discovered by the police when the brothel was demolished.

At the corner of a lane lined with disreputable netherskins stood the celebrated Hare and Hounds public house, kept by 'Stunning' Joe Banks, an amiable-mannered rogue who was a powerful influence in the affairs of the prize ring. Here might be seen fashionable sporting bloods with their imitators and hangers on, often in the company of pugilists. There were also swell criminals, vagrants, whores and old scrubbing women. At night there was sometimes dancing and young gentlemen would gratify a taste for low life by drunken horseplay with rough, hilarious tarts. So long as they stayed on the premises they were likely to be fairly safe, for Stunning Joe inspired great respect in the underworld and successfully guarded his reputation as a host and for seeing fair play.

Although it lay between the two churches of St Giles and St George's, Bloomsbury (the latter is said to have been built because respectable bourgeois families could not traverse the slum) and although there was a good deal of mission work in the neighbourhood, the core of the rookery remained stony ground for the evangelist. A great number of Irish lived in it, but they had become so rootless and degraded that—unlike the Irish colonies in east London—they seem to have largely lost their religious connection along with almost every other social tie. Protestant missioners who ventured in were likely to be severely discouraged. One man from the City Mission, perhaps the most energetic of all slum missions, is reported to have made his way into the kitchen of a lodging house, where, after listening for a while, some harpies set on him and tore at his clothes, leaving him indecently exposed. After this the men in the place hauled him into the yard outside, stuffed his mouth with powdered mustard and submerged him in the water-butt before letting him escape.

From their foundation, the peelers took a more repressive line with rookery dwellers than the old magistrates' officers, who were concerned only with catching particular offenders. Nevertheless for some time they had to be extremely cautious in their dealings with the Holy Land.

In November 1840, as a result of a tip-off from an informer, an inspector with more than half a dozen officers, all armed and in plain clothes, broke into a house in Carrier Street, one of the narrow thoroughfares through the rookery. According to *The Times* the raid was managed 'with every precaution', and although it happened at about half past two in the afternoon the party must have gathered outside the door without exciting enough suspicion to rouse an alarm. They burst in together and, knowing the lay-out, made directly for a back room where they surprised three coiners busy at work 'in a kind of closet'. There was a fire with a pot of molten metal on it, various tools and pieces of equipment lying about and a supply of white metal spoons ready to hand. The raiders seized and handcuffed the 'bit-fakers', took possession of a quantity of material evidence and made ready to leave.

Unlike nearly all such places, this coiners' workshop was not hidden away up a back court but was in a house fronting a public street. The street was a narrow and disreputable one but even so one would think that a fairly strong party of determined police-men would have been able to bring their prisoners away without too much difficulty. But during the short time they had been in the house the news had spread and a crowd gathered. The hand-cuffed criminals were greeted with yells of 'Rescue! Rescue!', stones began to fly, and several of the officers were hit. This possibility had been foreseen and soon a squad of police from another division appeared on the scene and succeeded in joining up with the original party. Then the combined force, with the coiners in the middle, began to struggle out of the rookery, not towards the St Giles station house which lay a dangerous hundred yards or so to the south, but north towards the nearest open space in Bloomsbury Square. They reached the square, where a section of the mob made a final rush; but the attack was driven off and its leader, who came on desperately with a knife, was tackled and disarmed by an officer called Restiaux. Some four wheel cabs were standing by—no doubt by arrangement—and before further trouble could arise the prisoners, who now included the leader of the rescue party, were bundled in and rattled away to a lock up.

During the next decade the grip of the police tightened.

As is usually the case when authority is confronted with criminal casbahs, a great deal depended on particular officers who cultivated connections inside the rookeries and made them-selves familiar with the terrain. Restiaux was such an officer and a specialist in the Holy Land.[1] On one occasion in 1844, according to Inspector Hunt, he went with a sergeant into a nethersken

[1] I have failed to trace his career, but it is likely that this 'well-known criminal officer' (Binny) was either an ex-runner who joined the peelers or else a magistrate's officer out-side the new metropolitan force. He was not drafted into the new central detective force in 1842; but divisional superintendents continued to employ a number of their abler men as plainclothes detectives. These quasi-official plainclothes men were for some reason often known simply as 'active officers'.

Mayhew's dinner for the inmates of the twopenny lodging house. '. . . the beggar boy, immediately on receiving his portion, danced around the room, whirling the plate round on his thumb as he went, and then, dipping his nose in the plate, seized a potato in his mouth.' From *London Labour and the London Poor*

'Taken by the police in a threepenny lodginghouse.'

buried in the rookery in search of a thief who was known to have connections with some of the lodgers and whom Restiaux believed was on the premises. In the kitchen 'seven male and five female thieves were seated, along with several cadgers, of the most cunning class,' but not the wanted man. One of the cadgers, however, made a sign indicating that someone had that moment slipped out, which sent the two officers scrambling over a wall at the back and on a hectic chase through the yards and back premises of eleven houses into a yard known as Jones Court, connected 'by roof, yard and cellar' with other parts of the rookery, and long famous for its guardian bull terrier. Here, where he might well have thought himself safe, they overtook and arrested their man while about twenty people looked on without interfering. As Hunt remarks, 'It would have been a different matter had he been apprehended by strangers.'

During the second half of the forties the task of the police was eased by the disappearance of a section of the rookery. The clearance was not of course made for that reason, nor because of the filth and misery the buildings harboured. London's perennial traffic problem had become particularly serious at this time and property rights had to yield to the pressing need for new commercial arteries. The focus of these arterial roads was the Thames-side zone of docks and industry, and their construction led to the breaching of several big rookery areas, the most important being the one demolished by the cutting of the great road junction at Aldgate East. New Oxford Street was a part of this arterial system and it cut a great swathe through the Holy Land. Some of the worst of the back settlements, including Jones Court and many other fastnesses, disappeared in rubble.

But the coming of the prosperous thoroughfare did not improve the character of the district behind its glittering new plate glass frontage. Many of the ousted Holy Landers crammed themselves into the remainder of the slum, where they were quickly reinforced by some of the famine-flood of Irish refugees. There was also a migration towards Seven Dials, which became yet more depressed and notoriously criminal. Taken as a whole the St Giles slums were probably as horrible at the mid-century as at any time in their history; but for all their congestion they could not offer the same resistance to outsiders as the old solid acres-wide rookery had done. Compared to their state ten years

before, they were already—like many other underworld citadels
—effectively cowed.

One night towards the end of 1850 Dickens made a tour of
several dangerous slums. Probably none of them were entirely
unfamiliar to him, at any rate in their outskirts. On this occasion
his guide was Inspector Field, the formidable chief detective at
Scotland Yard, for whom the novelist seems to have taken a
marked fancy. He describes him at this period as 'a middle-aged
man of portly presence, with a large, moist, knowing eye, a
husky voice, and a habit of emphasising his conversation with a
corpulent fore-finger'.[1] The tour set off from the police station,
by St Giles High Street, the party consisting of Dickens, an
Assistant Commissioner of Police, Field, a detective sergeant,
and Rogers, a local constable with a bull's-eye lamp strapped to
his belt. It was a dull, wet, windy night when the street lamps
looked 'blurred as if we saw them through tears'. With Rogers
and his lamp leading they plunged into the notorious and long
surviving block known as Rats' Castle.

How many people may there be in London, who, if we had
brought them deviously and blindfold, to this street, fifty paces
from the Station House, and within call of Saint Giles's church,
would know it for a not remote part of the city in which their
lives are passed? How many, who amidst this compound of
sickening smells, these heaps of filth, these tumbling houses,
with all their vile contents, slimily overflowing into the black
road, would believe that they breathe *this* air? How much Red
Tape may there be, that could look round on the faces which
now hem us in—for our appearance here has caused a rush
from all points to a common centre—the lowering foreheads,
the sallow cheeks, the brutal eyes, the matted hair, the infected,
vermin-haunted heaps of rags—and say 'I have thought of
this. I have not dismissed the thing. I have neither blustered
it away, nor frozen it away, nor tied it up and put it away?'

This is not what Rogers wants to know, however. What
Rogers wants to know, is, whether you *will* clear the way
here, some of you, or whether you won't; because if you
don't do it right on end, he'll lock you up! What! *You* are
there, are you, Bob Miles? You haven't had enough of it
yet, haven't you? You want three months more, do you?

---

[1] In 'The Detective Police' where he appears under the transparent pseudonym 'Inspector Wield'. (*Reprinted Pieces*, 1858.) He is also the model for Bucket in *Bleak House*.

Come away from that gentleman! What are you creeping round there for?

'What am I a doing, thinn, Mr Rogers?' says Bob Miles, appearing villainous, at the end of a lane of light, made by the lantern.

'I'll let you know pretty quick, if you don't hook it. Will you hook it?'

A sycophantic murmur rises from the crowd. 'Hook it, Bob, when Mr Rogers and Mr Field tells you! Why don't you hook it, when you are told to?'

The most importunate of the voices strikes familiarly on Mr Rogers' ear. He suddenly turns his lantern on the owner.

'What! *You* are there, are you, Mister Click? You hook it too—come?'

'What for?' says Mr Click, discomfited.

'You hook it, will you!' says Mr Rogers with stern emphasis.

Both Click and Miles *do* 'hook it', without another word, or, in plainer English, sneak away.

'Close up there, my men!' says Inspector Field to two constables on duty who have followed. 'Keep together, gentlemen; we are going down here. Heads!'

Saint Giles's church strikes half-past ten. We stoop low, and creep down a precipitous flight of steps into a dark close cellar. There is a fire. There is a long deal table. There are benches. The cellar is full of company, chiefly very young men in various conditions of dirt and raggedness. Some are eating supper. There are no women or girls present. Welcome to Rats' Castle, gentlemen, and to this company of noted thieves!

'Well, my lads! How are you, my lads? What have you been doing today? Here's some company come to see you, my lads! *There's* a plate of beef-steak, Sir, for the supper of a fine young man! And there is a mouth for a steak, Sir! Why, I should be too proud of such a mouth as that, if I had it to myself! Stand up and show it, sir! Take off your cap. There's a fine young man for a nice little party, Sir! An't he?'

Inspector Field is the bustling speaker. Inspector Field's eye is the roving eye that searches every corner of the cellar as he talks. Inspector Field's hand is the well-known hand that has collared half the people here, and motioned their brothers, sisters, fathers, mothers, male and female friends, inexorably to New South Wales. Every thief here, cowers before him, like a schoolboy before his schoolmaster. All watch him, all answer when addressed, all laugh at his jokes, all seek to propitiate him. This cellar-company alone—to say nothing of the crowd surrounding the entrance from the street above, and making the steps shine with eyes—is strong enough to murder us all, and willing enough to do it; but, let Inspector Field have a mind to pick out one thief here, and take him; let him produce that ghostly truncheon from his pocket, and say, with his business-air, 'My lad, I want you!' and all Rats' Castle shall be stricken with paralysis.

Where's the Earl of Warwick?—Here he is, Mr Field! Here's the Earl of Warwick, Mr Field!—O there you are, my Lord. Come for'ard. There's a chest, Sir, not to have a clean shirt on. An't it. Take your hat off, my Lord. Why, I should be ashamed if I was you—and an Earl too,—to show myself to a gentleman with my hat on!—The Earl of Warwick laughs and uncovers. All the company laugh. One pickpocket, especially, laughs with great enthusiasm.

So, *you* are here, too, are you, you tall, grey, soldierly-looking, grave man, standing by the fire?—Yes, Sir. Good evening, Mr Field!—Let us see. You lived servant to a nobleman once? Yes, Mr Field.—And what is it you do now; I forget? Well, Mr Field, I job about as well as I can. I left my employment on account of delicate health. The family is still kind to me. I get a trifle from them occasionally, and rub on as well as I can, Mr Field. Mr Field's eye rolls enjoyingly, for this man is a notorious begging-letter writer—Good night, my lads!—Good night, Mr Field, and thank'ee Sir!

Clear the streets here, half a thousand of you! Cut it, Mrs Stalker—none of that—we don't want you! Rogers of the flaming eye, lead on to the tramps' lodging-house!

A dream of baleful faces attend to the door. Now, stand back all of you! In the rear Detective Sergeant plants himself, composedly whistling, with his right arm across the narrow passage. Mrs Stalker, I am something'd that need not be written here, if you won't get yourself into trouble, in about half a minute, if I see that face of yours again!

Saint Giles's church clock, striking eleven, hums through our hand from the dilapidated door of a dark outhouse as we open it, and are stricken back by the pestilent breath that issues from within. Rogers to the front with the light, and let us look!

Ten, twenty, thirty—who can count them! Men, women, children, for the most part naked, heaped upon the floor like maggots in a cheese! Ho! In that dark corner yonder! Does any body lie there? Me Sir, Irish me, with my wife and eight poor babes. And to the left there? Me Sir, Irish me, along with two more Irish boys as is me friends. And to the right there? Me Sir and the Murphy fam'ly, numbering five blessed souls. And what's this, coiling, now, about my foot? Another Irish me, whom I have awakened from sleep—and across my other foot lies his wife—and by the shoes of Inspector Field lie their three eldest—and their three youngest are at present squeezed between the open door and the wall. And why is there no one on that little mat before the sullen fire? Because O'Donovan, with his wife and daughter, is not come in from selling Lucifers! Wheresoever Mr Rogers turns the flaming eye, there is a spectral figure rising, unshrouded, from a grave of rags. Who is the landlord here?—I am, Mr Field! says a bundle of ribs and parchment against the wall, scratching itself—Will you spend this money fairly, in the morning, to buy coffee for 'em all?—Yes Sir, I will!—O he'll do it Sir, he'll do it fair. He's honest! cry the spectres. And with thanks and Good Night sink into their graves again.

Thus, we make our New Oxford Streets, and our other new streets, never heeding, never asking, where the wretches whom we clear out, crowd.

Intelligence of the coffee money has got abroad. The yard is full, and Rogers of the flaming eye is beleaguered with entreaties to show other Lodging Houses. Mine next! Mine! Mine! Rogers, military, obdurate, stiff-necked, immovable, replies not, but leads away; all falling back before him. Inspector Field follows. Detective Sergeant, with his barrier of arm across the little passage, deliberately waits to close the procession. He sees behind him without any effort, and exceedingly disturbs one individual far in the rear by coolly calling out, 'It won't do Mr Michael! Don't try it!'

After council holden in the street, we enter other lodging houses, public-houses, many lairs and holes; all noisome and offensive; none so filthy and so crowded as where Irish are.

In one, The Ethiopian party are expected home presently—
were in Oxford Street when last heard of—shall be fetched,
for our delight, within ten minutes. In another, one of the
two or three Professors who draw Napoleon Buonaparte and
a couple of mackerel, on the pavement, and then let the work
of art out to a speculator, is refreshing after his labors. In
another, the vested interest of the profitable nuisance has
been in one family for a hundred years, and the landlord drives
in comfortably from the country to his snug little stew in town.
In all, Inspector Field is received with warmth. Coiners and
smashers droop before him; pickpockets defer to him. Half-
drunken hags check themselves in the midst of pots of beer, or
pints of gin, to drink to Mr Field, and pressingly to ask the
honor of his finishing the draught. One beldame in rusty black
runs a whole street's length to shake him by the hand; tumbling into a heap of mud by the way, and still pressing her
attentions when her very form has ceased to be distinguish-
able. Before the power of the law, the power of superior sense
—for common thieves are fools beside these men—and the
power of a perfect mastery of their character, the garrison of
Rats' Castle and the adjacent Fortresses make but a skulking
show indeed when reviewed by Inspector Field.

   Saint Giles's clock says it will be midnight in half-an-hour,
and Inspector Field says we must hurry to the Old Mint in the
Borough. The cab-driver is low-spirited. Now, what's your
fare, my lad? O *you* know, Inspector Field, what's the good of
asking *me!*[1]

The excursion lasted into the dawn and eventually brought them
to worse places than St Giles. In the Old Mint they visited the
famous farmhouse buried in an accretion of slums, and kept
remarkably clean and orderly by a landlady whom Field treated
with careful civility. After that they came back across the 'creeping, black and silent Thames' to the garish sailors' haunts along
the Ratcliffe Highway and then home by way of the abominable
rookery east of Petticoat Lane. Here in a lodging house among
the labyrinth of narrow streets and yards, for the first and only
time that night, Field was defied. Dickens describes the proprietor of the place, a notorious fence he calls Bark, leaning over

---

[1] 'On Duty with Inspector Field' (*Reprinted Pieces*. First published in *Household Words*
14 June 1851.) The extract is here somewhat abridged.

the half-door of a kind of hutch where he sleeps, yelling obscenities and swearing to rip up his visitors. Leaving two constables
to keep an eye on Bark the rest of the party descends into a
basement kitchen 'crammed full of thieves, holding a conversa-
zione by lamplight. It is by far the most dangerous assembly we
have yet seen. Stimulated by the ravings of Bark above their
looks are sullen but not a man speaks.'

When they return to the floor above Bark blocks the way to
the upper staircase and shouts down to the men below, inciting
them to come up and deal with the intruders.

> 'If the adjective coves in the kitchen was men, they'd come
> up now and do for you! Shut me that there door!' says Bark,
> and suddenly we are enclosed in the passage. 'They'd come up
> and do you!' cries Bark, and waits. Not a sound in the kitchen!
> 'They'd come up and do for you' cries Bark again, and waits.
> Not a sound in the kitchen! We are shut up, half-a-dozen of us,
> in Bark's house in the innermost recesses of the worst part of
> London, and in the dead of night—the house is crammed with
> notorious robbers and ruffians—and not a man stirs. No,
> Bark. They know the weight of the Law and they know
> Inspector Field and Co. too well.

That five police officers, several of them almost certainly carrying
firearms and conducted by the most feared detective in the
metropolis—officers whose whereabouts would certainly be
known to the local police and who were likely to have reinforcements at hand—should be able to visit such a place without being
lynched may seem a less than triumphant demonstration of the
Law's ascendancy. It certainly impressed Dickens very deeply,
and his standards derived from a long and intelligent interest in
the affairs of the underworld.

The police were just then being stimulated to fresh efforts by
the imminence of the Great Exhibition of 1851. A few months
later they successfully confounded the pessimists who had been
arguing that the whole project would be disorganised and dis-
credited by the horde of criminal riff-raff it would inevitably
attract. In fact, although the exhibition did provide splendid
opportunities for smart criminals, it left the police strengthened
in numbers and reputation and gaining popularity among such
people as small shopkeepers and artisans.

The St Giles back-settlements were a survival, not a product of the times. All the same, they were not an anachronism for, in their time-elaborated intricacy, they were matched by many contemporary slums. Despite their dilapidation, they embodied many durable old structures and they were typical, on an extended scale, of many rookeries hidden away behind cathedral closes and bustling high streets. About fifteen minutes walk north from the lodging house where we left Dickens and Inspector Field, past Spitalfields vegetable market and the whistling and clanking of Shoreditch railway terminus, was a small acclivity called Friar's Mount. This was the core of a different type of abscess, still in process of development.

At the time of the Napoleonic Wars, Bethnal Green[1] had been a modest suburb, with beds of flowers round porched cottages, wide stretches of market garden and rows of cheap and sometimes squalid housing. (Many of them were old clapboard buildings of the common country pattern.) Though the neighbourhood now contained acre on acre of poisonous congestion, it still carried the marks of its earlier sprawling, open-spaced character. Like people in many industrial towns, some of the inhabitants retained a strong rural tradition and were given to poaching, fishing, withy-cutting and bird-nesting in the Essex farmland and among the Lea marshes. They must have been a long-standing bane to farmers, for the district had a poor reputation for honesty. In the early thirties, when dingy dwellings had already devoured most of the fields and allotments, its bad character was firmly established: it was at premises not far from Friar's Mount that Bishop and Williams, the Bethnal Green burkers, butchered their victims before hawking the corpses round the anatomy schools.

As the mid-century approached, with more and more people packing themselves in, the remaining open spaces became a doubtful asset.

> I found [wrote a sanitarian who studied Bethnal Green in the forties] that all the space enclosed between a hoarding on either side of the Eastern Counties Railway . . . a distance of

---

[1] The region's old divisions make too involved a jigsaw for exact nomenclature. 'Bethnal Green' commonly meant (and means here) an area stretching east from Shoreditch High Street to Old Ford Road, and particularly the more densely populated western parts of it. In fact the Friar's Mount complex—the Bethnal Green slum area *par excellence*—lay largely inside the Bethnal Green Union, though the Shoreditch parochial boundary cut through it. Because the silk industry stretched into the area, and also perhaps because of the closeness of the Spitalfields workhouse, it was sometimes simply referred to as Spitalfields.

about 230 feet, and from 40 to 60 feet in width, was one enormous ditch or stagnant lake of thickened putrefying matter; in this Pandora's box dead cats and dogs were profusely scattered, exhibiting every stage of disgusting decomposition. Leading into this lake was a foul streamlet, very slowly flowing, and from it another which widened and expanded into a large ditch before it disappeared in the open end of a sewer. Bubbles of pestilential exhalation resulting from putrefaction, were being most abundantly given off from the ditches and the lake. The ripples on the surface of water occasioned by a shower of rain are not more numerous than those produced by the bursting of the bubbles. What must be the effect of this lake on the health and lives of those who shall inhabit the houses that are rapidly springing up all round it? A row of 22 new houses of two flats, with cesspools in front, are being built parallel to, and within ten feet of this disgusting scene. A ditch has been dug on either side of the Railway to prevent the foundations of the arches being endangered. The double privies attached to the new houses on the south side are constructed so that the night soil shall drain into it. . . . It appears therefore that after the public have laid down a sewer, in order that this lake of putrescence might be drained, it is intended that the ditches shall be retained, and rendered if possible still more deadly and abominable by the copious addition of night soil. The solution of this apparently inexplicable problem is to be found in the immunity which attaches to the perpetration of such outrages.[1]

Not far off the same investigator found an equally disgusting place. 'On the western side of Spitalfields workhouse is a night-man's yard. A heap of dung and refuse, about the size of a pretty large house, lies piled to the left; to the right is an artificial pond, into which the contents of cesspools are thrown. The contents are allowed to desiccate in the open air; and they are frequently stirred up for that purpose.' On two sides of this horrid collection of filth was a patent manure factory.

These features lay to the east and south of the Friar's Mount area—or 'The Nichol' as it came to be called from local street names. On its northern fringe were Nova Scotia Gardens, where the burkers' house was. These gardens had now become the site

---

[1] Hector Gavin *Sanitary Ramblings*, p. 19.

of an immense rubbish pile. By the later fifties this dump had reached such a size that, in the mind of one Scottish sanitarian, it was 'not to be thought of without astonishment and fear'. At the same time he found a kind of appalling picturesqueness in the monstrous crag of refuse, towering up above the roofs like a sort of Arthur's Seat, its stinking miasma overhanging the entire neighbourhood.

The Nichol's fifteen or so acres never became a thieves' stronghold, although the many arched passage-openings lent themselves to ambush and it was no place for a stranger to wander about, especially after dusk. The rubbish-filled streets were not particularly narrow, and though a few of the low two-storey houses had cellars, no complex of bolt-holes was evolved. When Thomas Archer came here in 1863, looking for copy,[1] it was the dull, crushing misery rather than the villainy that most struck him, as it had earlier visitors—even if prudence or a weak stomach stopped him penetrating to the Mount itself.

It was a damp district, hopelessly ill-drained, and the skimped foundations and rotting floors of the houses rested on soil that had absorbed every sort of soluble filth till it had become a putrid sponge. By Archer's time the streets were obstructed at intervals by beams, put there to buttress the sagging walls. The alleys leading to the yards where most of the population were hidden away—twenty or thirty souls in a four-room tenement—were sometimes so narrow that a really broad shouldered man might only be able to negotiate them crabwise, while the little square yards within were each 'a foetid tank with a bottom of mud and slime'. Here, besides one or two unspeakable latrines, there might be a solitary tap from which water could be drawn for an hour or so daily when it was 'besieged by haggard looking women and prematurely old children, bearing every possible variety of vessel'. In the blackened, moistly crumbling walls the doorways often gaped emptily, for doors were wrenched off for firewood. In fine weather, some of the inmates would squat outside, preferring the stinking yard to the stench and vermin indoors. In summer many windows showed all night the gleam of lights kept burning to discourage bugs.

Although there were respectable working and even middle class households not far away, the Nichol was not a distinct social

---

[1] See his *The Pauper, the Thief and the Convict* to which is owed a large part of what follows.

entity, cut off from the people who lived round about it. Nor was its development a matter of chance. Rather, it was the most grossly obvious instance of social morbidity affecting a whole urban zone; and its rapid development was as much in keeping with the times and as firmly linked to the zone's economy as that of any colliery village, sprung up by a pithead.

It lay within an area with many sources of irregular and poorly paid employment. Brickyards and market gardens, pushed ever further out by the spreading streets, needed seasonal supplies of low-skilled labour, laid off at just those times when the struggle for life was hardest. Also it was within walking distance of the huge, ever-fluctuating market for casual labour in and around the docks and shipyards. The long tramps to work meant more effort for less reward, but rents in Bethnal Green (inconveniently far from the river for industry) were perhaps the lowest in London. Round the mid-century, slum cottages rented by speculators for a couple of pounds a year would bring in half-a-crown a week from sub-tenants. The neighbourhood was a natural, if inconvenient, home for the most helpless and exploited manual workers.[1]

Nothing about the district was more characteristic than the way it housed the decaying remains of a once important domestic industry. Families of the famous Spitalfield silk weavers continued for a long time to struggle for survival. In the sixties some could still be found clinging to their Huguenot decencies, though their wide-casemented cottages had become embedded in the Nichol's slums. They kept the interiors clean enough to protect the silk and preserved an occasional relic ('a silver-keyed flute, a scrap or two of old point lace') left over from a happier past. In a different category, but similarly bound by their specialised skill and equipment to a depressed trade, were the independent makers and upholsterers of cheap furniture. These 'garret' or 'chamber masters'[2] worked up to seventeen hours a

---

[1] When the prolonged freeze-up early in 1861 threw 'nearly the whole of the labourers in and about the London docks, and along the banks of the river' out of work (besides interfering with market gardening) Bethnal Green was among the five worst afflicted Poor Law districts and the *only* one away from the commercial river side. (*Parliamentary Papers* 1864, IX. Report on Administration of Relief to the Poor, p. 189 et seq.)

[2] The term, also applied to makers of clothing and footwear, often meant small subcontractors who were at once sweated and themselves the sweaters of a few miserable hirelings (in addition to their own families). Mayhew describes the furniture chamber masters as utterly cowed by the conditions of trade. One 'pale, feeble-looking man' whom he 'met on a Saturday evening at the west end, carrying a mahogany chiffonier' told him: 'I have dragged this chiffonier with me from Spitalfields, and have been told to call again in two hours. (It was then half past seven.) I am too tired to drag it to another linen draper's, and

day in cramped rooms making gimcrack pieces for the 'slaughter-house-men' as the cutprice furniture dealers were called. Their whole families, down to withered brats of five and six, worked with them. Sixty little writing desks, cut, pinned, veneered, glued together and delivered could bring in a fourteen shilling profit on this market. Since they had to manhandle their bulky articles out of their premises before humping them round the dealers' warehouses, these tradesmen can seldom have lived inside the rookery courts; but they abounded all about the neighbourhood and their starveling households, like the silk weavers', were an object lesson in the futility of learning and trusting to an honourable trade.

Many poor Bethnal Green families—most of the women and children perhaps, at one time or another—carried on some miserable domestic craft involving little outlay and earning infinitesimal returns. Some took in stitchwork for the White-chapel sweaters; others wove cages and baskets from cane or withies, or made bandboxes, matchboxes, clothes-pegs, fly-papers, and the like. Work of this kind, offered to highly com-petitive traders by people always on the brink of destitution, might fetch ninepence on a long day's toil.

There seems to have been a good deal of small trading in food and animal products. The closeness of Spitalfields Market favoured costermongering, but besides barrow donkeys there were numbers of pigs and even some tubercular cows—main-tained in revolting conditions and presumably fed on the vege-table refuse that cluttered parts of the streets and alleys. Like most of the area along the east side of the city, the place har-boured dried fish vendors (who cleaned and hung out their fish 'like bats asleep') and a ghastly commerce in the skins of strayed and stolen cats, sometimes flayed alive to get a better priced pelt. Cage-birds, pigeons, rats, guinea-pigs, ferrets and other small creatures were offered for sale at the local Club Row market (which still exists today).

A district like the Nichol, in which unlucky, shiftless, exploited proletarians had accumulated, was less a criminal retreat than a breeding ground for future jail bait. On fine Sunday afternoons, Club Row, which ran into the very heart of the Nichol, served as a promenade for the young bloods of the place—the most vigorous,

indeed I shouldn't have so good a chance there; for if we go late the manager considers we've been at other places and he'll say, "You needn't bring me what others have refused."'
(Vol. III, p. 223 et seq.)

least resigned of the local population. Archer, marking the knots of 'shambling, tight trousered, sleek haired, artful but yet hulking youths of seventeen or eighteen,' their faces framed with carefully curled and oiled side-whiskers known as 'Newgate knockers', felt he was looking at an alarming phenomenon. Many of them, if not professional criminals, belonged to 'that dangerous class which is found occupying a position between pauper and convict' and were (he thought) likely to prove a greater social nuisance than either in the long run. If there was work to fill their bellies, most of them were probably willing enough to do it; but when there was not, they had 'too little moral restraint' to starve, or half-starve, in their foul homes. Unlike many of their elders, who were often glad enough of any chance of outdoor relief in hard times and would even, in the last extremity, face the workhouse, nothing would induce them to have any truck with the Poor Law and its officials. They were not tamed and—as one who well remembered the childhood taste of workhouse gruel told Archer —they knew 'a trick worth two of that'.

The boast was not idle. The mere fact that, among people of whom only a minority survived childhood, they had lived and grown into 'hulking youths' rather than rickety dwarfs, argued vitality and some natural advantages. In such districts most children either went out to scavenge and pilfer what they could about the streets or were put to some miserable, often vitiating, employment. No doubt some of these lads had attended the shameful twice-weekly hiring mart, held under the nearby White Street railway viaduct, where boys and girls from about ten up offered themselves to unsavoury employers. Many must have had their experience of life enlarged—and received some formal education —in the workhouse, during short spells in jail, or for longer terms at a reformatory or in one of those industrial schools (or 'refuges') where the sinister expression stamped on the children's faces so disturbed Taine. But whatever his outside educators, the child of the Nichol began to learn its fundamental lesson from the moment he started to crawl about the courts and alleys—that the means of life were desperately scarce and that the race went to the toughest. Here was a fully competitive society without disguise, where all could see that strength, cunning, quick response to opportunity and danger, courage and freedom from scruple were the keys to survival. The fly barrow boy with his slang weights made a living while the drudging chamber carpenter went under.

The woman who hawked herself in Kingsland Road, or enticed fools to the passageway where her man waited with a cosh in his sleeve, was better able to feed herself and her children than the one who stitched gunny sacks night and day—her bloody-fingered children stitching with her. Wherever casual labour was taken on (notably among the thousands at the dock gates) the child could see his elders fight and trick one another for work as they did for every other advantage. In five lucky minutes a gang of urchins could take goods off a badly loaded dray worth as much as one of their fathers earned in as many days labouring. To believe the virtuous precepts handed out by authority, whether magistrate, missioner, workhouse schoolmaster, ragged school teacher or whoever, and whether emphasised by the jailer's birch or dispensed with a bowl of soup and a yard of Christmas flannel, was simply to be duped. Authority, whose commonest face was the constable's, was something to be countered either by defiance or feigning.

The remarkable thing is not that the ramping slum jungles nurtured criminals, but that they did not, in the end, produce anything like such a dangerous crop as those who first investigated them dreaded. By the mid-seventies, less than fifteen years after the great garotting panic and other alarms of the early 1860s, a serious writer could assert that there was no known country or period 'in which life and property were so secure as they are at present in England,'[1] and for many years to come the consensus of official and popular opinion shared this complacency. One sign of how much the underworld had declined, by the end of the century, as a threat to respectable society is the reduction in the array of shutters, bars, bolts and chains fitted to the homes of the better off. The armament became sparser and feebler with each new row of suburban houses.

One factor in this was obviously the removal of some of the worst and densest nests of delinquency. Besides such incidental clearances as the arterial roads driven through St Giles and Aldgate, a philanthropic campaign against the rookeries developed during the second half of the century. At first this was piecemeal and haphazard. Blocks of model dwellings for 'the deserving poor'—some of the earliest of them surprisingly solid and airy—

[1] L. O. Pike *A History of Crime in England* (1867) p. 480. He was well-informed, if not unprejudiced.

started to rise here and there in the worst districts. Slum rehabilitation programmes (after the ingenious pattern promoted by Octavia Hill)[1] began to spread from the sixties onwards, though the crucial difficulty in rehousing the poor is illustrated by the troubles of the Peabody Trust which, in Shadwell in 1867, could not find tenants able to pay five shillings a week for their model family flats.

There were private benefactions on a very considerable scale. Even by the time Archer visited the Nichol the great rubbish mountain dominating its northern approaches had disappeared to make way for a complex of new buildings, including a huge market designed to make a current of trade flow through the whole area.[2]

In the eighties a greatly publicised Royal Commission, loaded with notables, focused interest on the horrors of the back courts and led to a series of municipal clearances, including the core of the warren round Friar's Mount. Grown even viler with the passage of time, it was eventually dragged down almost about the ears of its angrily swarming inhabitants.

Despite all this, it would be wrong to attribute the general decline in crime and disorder solely or chiefly to slum clearances. It was already well under way before most of them were so much as thought of and from first to last the Victorian clearances hardly did more than scratch out a few of the most villainous pest-holes. There were undoubtedly more—and probably proportionately more—slum dwellers at the end of the Queen's reign than at the beginning. Yet it is astonishing how little trouble this great submerged population gave. A minimum of repressive force kept in check an underworld which had lost much of its old desperation and aggressive spirit. There was a lot of agitation about slum conditions and racking landlords, but the menace of the rookeries, the old fear of the dangerous classes murmuring in their horrible hives behind the prosperous streets, had vanished from respectable minds.

---

[1] 1838–1912, active from 1865 onwards. She was a crucial pioneer of housing reform and management and her methods and example had a lasting effect on concepts of social welfare and slum improvement.

[2] The benefactress was Angela Burdett-Coutts who spent huge sums on the district, some to good effect though the market turned out an enduring white elephant.

CHAPTER FIVE

Gonophs, footpads and the swell mob

If one accepts Engels' view of Victorian criminals as placeless men, driven by desperation into a state of 'open warfare' with a cruel society, it is important to remember that no one suffered more from them than the poor themselves. Nowhere was the war waged so openly as in the impoverished districts of great cities and against those whom society was least concerned to protect.

A good place to study professional thieves at work was a great port thoroughfare. Streets like Jamaica Road or the Ratcliffe Highway were infested with thieves, and in the crowded disorder they behaved with a blatancy that would soon have landed them in jail if they had tried it in Regent Street or the Strand. In such places the police had other things to do than watch the movements of every 'gonoph'.[1] These thieves were on their home ground, they were close to their hide-outs, and above all they were unlikely to trouble many influential people. This is not to say that the police could afford to ignore them; but in Shadwell and Rotherhythe authority could assert itself in ways that would hardly have passed muster in more respectable places.

Some time in the early sixties (probably at the time he was investigating the Nichol) Thomas Archer watched an odd scene in the Highway. Attracted by a public house shindy, he peered into the fracas round the bar but wisely stayed in the road outside talking to a voluble, cleanly dressed Irishwoman who had just emerged and who with some humour showed him her bleeding scalp, laid wide open in the free-for-all.

As they talk Archer becomes conscious of several lean, shabby youngsters among the crowd that has gathered. It is a seedy group, mostly poor women, among whom he can notice no one 'it would seem worthwhile to rob, although there are one or two sailors inside the house'. All the same, there can be no doubt

---

[1] A cant word meaning thief and more particularly common street thief and pickpocket. It usually implied youthfulness and (in England not America) carried an undertone of contempt. It was of Yiddish provenance and perhaps achieved underworld currency from Jewish traders, fences and showmen; but it did not imply that the thief was himself Jewish.

about the youths or what they are at. Their appearance and bearing is hardly mistakable, and as for the poverty of their potential
victims, such thieves 'would snatch the half-pence from a child
looking hungrily into a cook-shop window'.

The excitement inside quietens and as the crowd on the pavement begins to thin the youths seem to drift away. However
Archer soon spots a little knot of them over the road, lounging on
the cellar flap of a beer house, apparently looking at the people
around with casual disinterest. And in a moment he notices
another relaxed figure, a man of vulgarly sporting appearance
'wearing a billycock hat, and with the fag end of a cigar in his
mouth and a short piece of rattan cane swinging in his hand'. The
link between this newcomer and the party on the cellar flap soon
becomes obvious.

> He is their Nemesis, and carelessly as they have seemed to
> watch the crowd, just so indifferently has he been watching
> them. Before the warning whistle of the sharpest of the party
> can save them he is across the road and in their very midst,
> dealing smart cuts to two or three of their number, who dart
> away each with a stinging souvenir but, except in one instance,
> without a word or a cry. The truth is that this lounging obser-
> ver is a detective officer, known, it would seem, to every man,
> woman and child in that neighbourhood. . . . It is evident that
> the Highway and all the terrible neighbourhood around it is
> now under a control which may be far from the best influence
> that might be brought to bear upon it, but is very effectual in
> preventing the sort of impunity which would render this a
> worse district than the old Alsatia. The police are not 'out of
> the way', here, at all events, and though their appearance is not
> too apparent they can easily be summoned, and the sound of
> their rattles will bring speedy aid from their comrades.

And Archer goes on to illustrate how far the police have brought
the area under control: when the row in the bar flared up again, a
uniformed officer disappeared for a few moments among the mob
inside and quieted it without much more than moral support from
Billycock Hat and 'an acute looking young man in a peaked cap'
who turned out to be his colleague.

Street thieves like these are generally reported to have had a
hungry, shabby look. Even when they managed to put a better
face on things, they led pinched, anxious lives, mistrusting each

other, always shifting from one slum roost to another, despised by the costers and others with whom they associated.

Clearly, one of the chief reasons for the general miserableness of these men was that their profession was badly overcrowded. The commonest type—or at least the one most commonly complained of—was the half-swaggering, half-furtive youth in his teens or early twenties, sometimes in flash clothes, often threadbare though not absolutely ragged, perhaps made all the more conspicuous by his jail-cropped head. Most of them were pickpockets and there were numbers of them in the less reputable districts of all the largest towns and cities. In London, as well as working the dock areas, they clustered round the railway termini and the great wholesale food markets, which were thronged

with well-to-do people and also conveniently near the slums into which a thief could disappear. Sometimes they made a nuisance of themselves in upper-class residential streets; but these were usually planned excursions into alien territory rather than the sharp-eyed hanging about that was their normal way of hunting. Whether in London, Liverpool, Manchester or Birmingham the gonoph was a creature of poor, crowded districts, and the further away from them one went the rarer he became and the more untypical his behaviour. He liked to be near some friendly slum, not just from anxiety about the police but from fear of the general pursuit that might start with a shout of *Stop Thief!* (or *Hot Beef!*).

It is not hard to see why, for all its risks and its generally meagre returns, street thieving remained such a common type of crime. The brat who grew up begging and pilfering, who learned

when he saw a badly loaded dray to yell '*The fat's runnin'!*' and
bring his fellows swarming round the tailboard even before he
himself was old enough to dart in under the carter's whip, came
to regard the streets as a natural hunting ground. It was easy to
get rid of stolen goods—there were poor districts where the
police declared every little chandlery shop was a receiver's—and
on crowded pavements a child thief had advantages that encouraged him to graduate early from casual filching to regular
pocket-picking. The restless, loitering, vivid existence of the
juvenile street thief easily became a fixed way of life.

The youths Archer watched in the Highway were indubitable
'buzzers' (pickpockets) but one cannot assume that this was their
only resource or that they would continue at it for many more
years. Pickpocketing was characteristically a crime for the young.
To get any sort of a living by it, even a poor one, required acute
responses. Jail-labour, drink and the wear and tear of an impoverished life could soon fatally blunt one's dexterity and speed.
Even the élite among street thieves, the most skilful of the swell
mob,[1] seldom kept their full powers very long. For the crude
majority, the period during which they could command the necessary adroitness was likely to be short indeed.

Street stealing, however, included an almost endless variety of
lays and dodges, suited to a wide range of abilities. Even wresting
small sums from children was so common as to be a well recognised routine, sometimes known as the 'kinchin lay'. Dickens
makes Fagin describe it thus:

> 'The kinchins, my dear, is the young children that's sent on
> errands by their mothers, with sixpences and shillings; and
> the lay is just to take their money away—they've always got it
> ready in their hands—then knock them into the kennel and
> walk off very slow as if there's nothing else the matter but a
> child fallen down and hurt itself.'

Subtle operators might invest in a bun or a paper of sweets and
lure the child up a passage. Very young maid servants and
apprentices, carrying an empty jug that showed they were on
their way to the public house or dairy, were sometimes enticed in
this way. Knocking the child down, of course, had the merit of
making it temporarily incoherent. Some thieves worked the lay

[1] A term almost wholly confined at this period to the upper crust of well dressed and
highly skilled pickpockets. They were themselves 'swells' and preyed on a 'swell' public.
'Mobsman' in Victorian slang carried no implication of violence.

by seizing packets from shop messengers—little milliners' apprentices with parcels of silk being especially worthwhile victims.

Another trick of the street thieves was stealing laundry. Fine linen and lace were expensive, and the skilled gofferers and clear starchers who enjoyed the cream of the west London trade lived in the outer suburbs for the sake of drying grounds away from the all-pervading metropolitan soot. They might be by Earls Court ponds, at Peckham or even Uxbridge. Because of this the washerwoman herself, or some helper, would have to trundle the hampers on a hand-barrow or donkey cart over a long route. A small gang would waylay it and make off with the laundry basket. Though fairly safe and easy, this needed some organisation. 'Snowing', or simply running off with things from drying lines, needed nothing but an ability to run. Though largely a child's practice, snowing was not despised by experienced gonophs. There was a huge second-hand clothes trade.

A slightly less degraded class of theft was what Mayhew's collaborator Binny calls 'area diving'. Here the basic procedure was very simple; one merely crept down basement areas or round suburban back doors, tried the handles and got away with whatever could be instantly lifted. However there were refinements. The most promising time was obviously when the servants were busy above stairs—for instance for morning bed-making—and the scientific diver would keep watch and get to know daily timetables. If cook was alone in the kitchen, a ring at the front door brought her up from her basement while the diver slipped down and tried his luck.

Thieves of this school who could command the clothes and the histrionic ability would pass themselves off as workmen or clerks, sent round to measure for a carpet or with some question over an account. They would be allowed to wait inside while a servant went up to the drawing room to enquire, and they could then grab some silver, or anything else that was easily picked up, and bolt. Some of them made a speciality of clearing coats, umbrellas and silver-knobbed sticks from ground floor lobbies— but not apparently hats, which were too bulky. Always the essential problem was to circumvent servants.

A man who regularly worked such lays usually had a confederate waiting round a quiet corner, perhaps with a barrow ready loaded with old clothes. The loot would be quickly passed over and the thief would make off on his own. He might very well never set eyes again on objects that could be in a dealer's back shop within an hour or two of leaving their owners. It was a golden rule of professional thieving, from this humble level upwards, that the thief himself should get rid of the stolen property as soon as he possibly could.

Among the commonest and most useful accomplices of street thieves were their women. Like so many other inhabitants of the underworld, the young gonoph often set up with a girl a year or two older than himself, perhaps when he was about fourteen or fifteen, and in the course of his life he was likely to make a series of these quasi-permanent liaisons, none of them involving legal marriage. (Spells in jail were a common cause of separation.) Thieves often lived with prostitutes, and certainly there were a number of prostitutes who not only robbed their clients in collusion with men but were themselves practised thieves. Nevertheless, contrary to what has sometimes been maintained, there is little reason for thinking of the typical thief's woman as inevitably a professional street walker. Broadly, the more a woman devoted her energies to theft the less likely she was to be making a major part of her living as a prostitute. If she was quick-witted and adroit but not specially attractive, and if she did not have a temperamental bent towards prostitution, she might well find regular thieving both more rewarding and more congenial.

Though women could be involved in pretty well every kind of robbery, it was among the street thieves that they most often played a leading part. A woman could act as a spy or decoy, or she could take stolen things off the men she worked with. There were also plenty of situations where a woman's touch was best for making the theft itself. She could usually get a child's confidence better than a man, and women sometimes worked the kinchins with great success. There was one odd variation of the lay which seems to have been entirely a feminine speciality. This was 'skinning', or luring small well-clad children into some deserted corner where they could be stripped of their boots and clothes. (It was best done in cold weather when they had most on.) The child was terrorised into silence and immobility until the thief had got well away with her bundle. Skinners usually went out of their own district to find victims and some worked on a large scale and over a wide area.

About Christmas 1850 (according to the *Household Narrative*) a certain Susan Nunn of St George's-in-the-East, a 'showily dressed young woman of thirty,' was brought before a magistrate. A 'swarm of little boys and girls, estimated by the gaoler to be nearly fifty in number' turned up with their parents, to testify to having been stripped by her. At an identification parade many of them picked her out without hesitation and she was sent to the Old Bailey. More typically, skinners were elderly women who found that the game suited their years and infirmities.

Some of the chief limitations and advantages of the woman thief had to do with her clothes. Even in the relatively short skirts that only an openly disreputable young woman would wear, it was difficult to run far or fast; to pass as respectable she had to wear a full, heavily petticoated skirt, covering the ankles. Plainly, women's clothes were hopelessly ill-adapted for area diving or making a dash over backyard walls. On the other hand, stolen objects could be handily tucked into shawls, mantles and muffs, and the great bell-shaped skirt made an excellent hiding place for all but the largest and heaviest things. Skirts of the period frequently had a pocket, usually on the right side and opening under a flounce. Among professional thieves this was modified so that the opening led into a huge pouch sometimes extending all round in a sort of double petticoat. The weakness of this almost perfect hiding place was, of course, that once something had been stowed away it was not easily jettisoned or slipped to an accomplice in emergency.

Finally, the sheer size of a crinolined, shawled, puff-sleeved woman could make her a useful screen for thieves working in public places.

The problem of hiding objects about themselves was often a troublesome one for male thieves. Smock frocks had once been freely worn even in London; by now they might pass at fairs and race meetings but they invited suspicion in a city crowd. Long, deep-pocketed jackets of the kind sometimes called shooting-coats were common enough but any coat could be easily searched. Sometimes a stolen watch or other valuable would be carried down the trouser-leg, hung on a thread, but this only served with very small items. Once the police had collared a man and run their hands over him the game was likely to be up. A woman accomplice was not only less apt to be suspected in the first place but much more of a nuisance to deal with if she was. Victorians of all ranks could be very touchy about the treatment of women: feminine modesty was a sensitive topic, and a constable needed to be sure of his grounds before taking an apparently decent woman into custody and carting her off to a station house where she could be searched by a matron. (If she broke down she would have to be removed in a cab for which, if there was no conviction, the officer was likely to have to pay.)

As one might expect, stealing from shops was a crime at which women were outstanding, though it was not a feminine preserve. Indeed, then as now, it seems to have been a favourite game for a wide range of crooks. Circumstances, however, were different. Not only was more retailing done from stalls, but shopkeepers were much more given to displaying goods in the open. In poor districts one often found narrow streets almost like oriental bazaars, lined with shops that were little more than open-fronted caves, their stock festooned about the entry or laid on trestles. These conditions encouraged street prowlers. Urchins, naturally, were a particular bane to food sellers, who commonly thrashed out of hand those they caught. On foggy, twilit London evenings, gangs of youths would work their way through a poor shopping district, marking suitable plunder; then one lad would whip away a chosen object and disappear into the murk while others of the gang, idling in the road, acted as 'stalls' to obstruct and misdirect any pursuit.

There was a class of bold female thieves who went in for stealing large things like rolls of carpet and calico put on the pavement in front of dealers' doors. They would examine the goods like desultory shoppers, perhaps during a dinner hour when there was only a dozy lad minding the place, and at the right moment signal to one or two male confederates—said to have usually looked like costermongers. With their help they would 'quickly and dextrously' get the spoils out of sight and onto a waiting cart. The success of these manoeuvres no doubt depended partly on the way the woman masked the theft with her body, but also on the fact that ponderous stuff of this kind was often hardly watched.

Stealing from behind shop windows was more difficult. Many young crooks learned the art of 'star-glazing' (much used by housebreakers) while robbing shops with a street gang. The majority of shop windows were made up of many panes set in small square wooden frames. Several lads would gather at a window, flattening admiring noses against the glass, while one in the middle inserted the point of a strong knife at the edge of the frame directly in front of whatever they had decided to steal. Careful pressure splintered the pane without dislodging it; then a large brown paper sticking plaster was quickly applied and pulled away with the pieces of broken glass sticking to it. The thief reached in, handed the prize to a sprinter waiting behind, and in an instant the group had scattered. Tobacco—one of the few articles of common consumption worth smuggling—was a favourite 'pull'. The technique could not be applied to the plate-glass sheets of up-to-date establishments, and straightforward noisy smash-and-grab raids on these seem to have been rare, presumably because of the difficulty of making a clear getaway from the hue-and-cry.

In better class shops there was a lot of occasional thieving by many different types of women. Some of them were driven by want, but according to Binny 'ladies in respectable positions' were not immune to the temptation to pick up what caught their fancy. However, conditions hardly favoured the amateur. The art of commercial display was steadily developing—especially in the somewhat vulgar new 'show shops'—but most of the things a modern thief finds laid out within reach were stowed away in shelves and drawers behind a broad wooden counter. Assurance and expertise were needed for a worthwhile pull.

Two or three professional 'palmers'—they were apt to be female pickpockets working an alternative lay—would walk into a large London draper's and haberdasher's. Shops of this type were often long and narrowish with a limited frontage, somewhat warehouse-like but glittering with gas globes and dangerous mirrors. Two young women might enter together and a third follow separately, apparently unconnected with them. Very probably they looked like superior ladies-maids or respectable dressmakers. The classical procedure was for one palmer to play the exacting customer, demanding to see a range of goods, determined to match this with that, till the counter was piled and jumbled. While she kept the shopman busy, hopping up his steps to bring down more samples from the shelves behind, her companion idly looked over the heap of stuff and at the right moment snaffled some expensive, compact item (for instance a packet of French gloves). Meantime the third thief, keeping an eye on the rest of the shop, tried to post herself so as to shield the first two. After a pull or two the principal shopper would become dissatisfied with the assistant's efforts, and, leaving the poor man to put his stock back in order, walk out of the shop with her friend. By this time the stolen goods might well have been removed by the third of the trio.

The only kind of shoplifting, apparently, at which men equalled women was taking rings and brooches from jewellers— a refined and dangerous art calling for sleight-of-hand adroitness. It meant bamboozling the salesman into laying out a quantity of stock and then lifting something from it, so that a well dressed and gentlemanly male thief was best suited to the job. A man of this sort often worked alone, and the moment he had sauntered out through the jeweller's door lost no time in making himself scarce.

The higher-powered shoplifters of both sexes, however, usually belonged to the swell mob and were altogether more polished than the inferior street criminals with whom we are still chiefly concerned.

The most frightening street crimes were those that took place at night. One common nuisance was the robbing of luggage on the highway, which was normally a night-time or twilight affair. A four-wheel 'growler', its top piled with baggage, would be followed through the quiet streets by a light cart with two or three coster-looking figures aboard. The cart jogged sedately after its quarry until, in a deserted stretch, one of the men leapt out, tore after the cab, and jumped onto a rear spring. He slashed any cords that were holding the luggage, pulled down a piece or two and let them fall in the road. The coster cart pulled up, the cases were pitched on, the pony's head dragged round, and in a few moments the stolen load was rattling away breakneck down a turning. At other times 'dragsmen' (as these thieves were called) waited on foot at a suitable spot, probably on a hill, darting out when a likely cab came past and disappearing up some narrow by-way with whatever baggage they could easily carry off.

Dragsmen were helped by the fact that the approaches to big railway stations were often through shady, socially run-down districts. Also, the lurching and clatter of a cab grinding over cobbles might easily prevent a passenger grasping what was up. But the chances of a robbery of this sort succeeding must have been very doubtful without the connivance of the cabbie, perched up with his long-handled whip at his hand. In fact hackney drivers as a class were a rough set with a doubtful reputation for honesty, and it is plain that some of them were useful allies of the criminal underworld. It was just those of the worst type who most often worked at night—when criminals from burglars to dragsmen had most need of their services. Respectable cab owners did not generally like letting their cabs work late, and the less reputable ones whose vehicles plied through the small hours followed a bad system whereby their drivers undertook longer turns of duty than they could work at a stretch. As the driver usually paid the proprietor a fixed sum for each turn of duty, there was every inducement for him to work the wretched animal in his charge as hard as possible, and he did this by handing over the cab for a spell to an unlicensed deputy. These irregular or 'buck' cabbies were drawn from the dubious characters who often hung about cab ranks, especially near the railway terminuses, helping with watering and feeding and picking up a living no one quite knew how. Since they had little to lose, they lent themselves readily to shady jobs, some keeping false licence plates for the purpose.

The most sinister style of robbery in the night-time streets was known by those who practised it as 'propping' or 'swinging the stick'. Not unnaturally various sorts of delinquent now and again resorted to footpadding. Beggars mouching along a lonely lane might decide it was more profitable to assault a chance stroller than beg from him; the gambling cheats and toughs who frequented race meetings sometimes trailed and beat up a racegoer who had had a profitable day. But aside from this opportunist banditry there was a certain amount of violence and street robbery by bullies with whom it was something like a regular business. Such attacks could become numerous and ferocious enough to start a minor national panic.

These 'rampsmen'[1] were less often violent adolescents than men around middle life of limited abilities and brutal temper, too dull or lazy to adopt a more sophisticated lay. Discharged or deserted soldiers and run-down prize fighters were likely types. In normal times they mostly haunted poor districts, where their outrages were not apt to provoke any great stir; in the dingy outskirts of great cities, among the dust-heaps and brickyards, it was often wise, after dusk, to be on guard for the lurking propper.

The essential thing for the footpad was to be quiet, quick and unrecognised. Ideally, what he wanted was a solitary stranger

[1] Rough, crude, street and fairground thieves.

off his guard in a lonely place. But when he simply skulked by some unfrequented corner, on the chance someone suitable would pass, he was likely to have a long vigil; while if he followed a man away from the lighted street, the victim might well take alarm, raise a commotion, show a turn of speed or even an under-estimated capacity for self-defence. A favourite solution to these difficulties was the hoary old device which at this period was known as 'bearing up'.

In this the footpad got a woman to entice his victims. She might be a professional street walker, though very often she was not. She would pick up a dupe in a pub or at a street corner (tipsy men were best) and get him to go with her to some secluded place. Once his interest was roused it was usually easy to detach him from companions. When they got to a dark archway she would make sure he was preoccupied enough to be unaware of his danger when her confederate—or perhaps confederates—'bore up'. Sometimes the bearer-up pretended to be an outraged husband and allowed a scared wretch, caught at a hopeless psychological disadvantage, to buy him off with whatever he had in his pockets. Alternatively the victim was set on, beaten into half paralysed submission, and stripped of everything worth taking.

Firearms were not the rampsman's weapons. His object was to overcome the capacity to resist or escape as quickly and quietly as possible and he wanted something that could deal a quick, disabling blow. The 'neddy' might be a small weighted cudgel, a short metal bar with a welded knob which could be carried in the sleeve, a sausage like length of sand stuffed canvas (rather like an old fashioned draught excluder and sometimes referred to as an 'eel-skin') or a two pound spherical iron shot in a stout stocking or piece of cloth. One device, useful for surprising a man encountered face on, was a shot of this sort attached to a length of cord; the ball was held concealed in the hand and suddenly flung at the victim's head like a horrible yo-yo. Partly, perhaps, from fear of killing him—though the wearing of stiff hats may have had something to do with it—the victim was less usually stunned outright by a knock on the skull than incapacitated by strokes on the upper arm, shoulder or thigh. After one or two blows he was unlikely to give any trouble. This sort of attack required no great skill or nerve—especially when, as often happened, two or more bullies teamed up.

Bearing up was perhaps the most dependable tactic, and also

the least risky one since a good number of sufferers must have been reluctant to report the circumstances in which they had been attacked. Nevertheless it was fairly slow work, and since it was largely limited to the kind of victim ready to follow a cheap night-stand tart it cannot have paid very well. Usually propping was a dullard's crime: the younger, spryer sort of rampsman as a rule preferred grabbing watches from drunks in pub-yards and urinals, snatching reticules from women in the street and suchlike brisk, scuffle-and-run encounters.

It is not easy to account for the curious outbreak of foot-padding in the early 1860s. Economic distress must have played a part, though it can hardly have been the whole explanation, and the discharge of troops after the Crimea and the Indian Mutiny no doubt had a temporarily toughening effect on sections of the underworld. At the time many people blamed changes in the penal system, particularly the stopping of transportation and the im-prudent release of ticket-of-leave convicts. It is not even clear just how sudden, novel or widespread the outbreak in fact was, for the subject lent itself to exaggeration. What is certain is that between 1861 and 1864 there was an unexpected number of street robberies using the method of attack known as 'garotting', and that a series of these attacks, chiefly in London, roused consider-able alarm.

Garotting, in this sense, was by no means a new thing: Chokee Bill, the rampsman who grabbed his prey by the neck, was already a well established underworld type. However, some time in 1861 or early '62, and probably in east London, the special merits of the method began to be more fully appreciated. Possibly it was the successes of a single well-drilled gang that set the ball rolling.

Unlike the run of crude proppers, the more efficient garotters showed marked skill and daring. The lay required a team of at least three—two to do the hold-up while the third kept watch. The choker himself either lurked in ambush at a corner with his assistant or, strolling openly down the road, let his prey pass and then sprang at him. He attacked from behind and without warning, slipping a rope, a cloth or simply a powerful arm about the victim's neck, and with vigorous strangling pressure forced him to bend back. Meanwhile his partner quelled any attempt to struggle by blows against the helpless man's exposed front as he rifled his pockets. He was likely to carry a neddy. Leaving the victim slumped on the pavement in no condition to cry out, the party bolted. With a well organised team the whole affair was over in a few almost silent moments.

Sometimes the lookout, who might be at a little distance from the others, was a woman—a less suspicious figure than a loitering man. A woman could, of course, also be used as bait; but the whole merit of the system lay in a speed and silence that allowed garotters to extend their activities well beyond the scope of the slum archway bearer-up.

During the summer of 1862 the boldness and brutality of footpad attacks caused growing alarm. Once dark had fallen no one, it seemed, was safe; after so many years of gas lighting and peelers the underworld was gradually reasserting its old ascendancy over the night time streets. In the middle of July Mr Pilkington, M.P., walking from Parliament to his club in Pall Mall, was savagely garotted and robbed in an 'open well-lighted place'; none of the five officers patrolling nearby beats heard anything. The same night the distinguished octogenarian antiquary Edward Hawkins was assaulted between St James's and Bond Street. Further east such attacks were becoming frequent and disquiet grew as the season of long nights and fogs approached. In November a jeweller was stopped by a 'respectable looking female' and garotted with such energy that his throat was crushed in, though in fact he survived several days. Another victim, a gunsmith, had his hand so mangled in a struggle that it had to be amputated and he too died.

It seems probable that what lay behind the great garotting scare was less any astonishing increase in the total of street banditries than the fact that they were now carried out in ways that brought them wide publicity. Respectable people identified themselves with respectable victims. From the nature of their sinister method, it was plain that garotters could not stop to argue; they had to seize their prey unsuspecting, and the more ferocious the assault the safer for the assailants. Moreover there was a strong flavour of thugee and other exotic villainies, popular among the contemporary reading public, about the mysterious night-stranglers. All this made garotting excellent copy; cases that would normally have gone unnoticed were reported, and when news was thin there was a tendency to include all sorts of violence under the title.

Not surprisingly, there were outbreaks of footpadding in the depressed north during the winter of 1862–3, and these were well publicised. Cases of garotting, some genuine, some distorted, were reported in Lancashire, Yorkshire, Nottingham and Cheshire. Further, there were signs that, as a result of the publicity, not only thieves but roughs with a grudge to pay were resorting to this form of violence.

So the garotter, lurking in the shadow of the wall, quickening step behind one on the lonely footpath, became something like a national bogey. For a while, as in a war time spy-scare, credulity became a social obligation. Decent householders took their own letters to post in the evening rather than let a maidservant venture into the dusk: even in daylight, nervous people baulked at the sight of a rough fellow with a loose scarf. An element of farce began to come into it. Men of coarse appearance but blameless intentions were attacked—indeed sometimes fell on each other—under suspicion of being garotters. Innocent people were dragged to police stations and the police hampered by misinformation. Anti-garotting societies flourished. Early in December 1862 the *Weekly Dispatch*, which had itself been fomenting excitement, piously declared: 'The manner in which anti-garotters armed to the teeth proceed along the streets at night, clinking their sword canes and ready to draw at a moment's notice, is calculated to strike terror into the breasts of others as well as those of the great enemy.'

The panic also had its effect in the courts. More people were hanged in 1863 than in any year since the end of the bloody code, the programme including a quadruple event at Liverpool. In July, after the troubles that provoked it had largely died down, the measure known as the 'Garotting Act' was passed. It provided for the flogging of offenders and those who fell within its terms were often treated with great rigour. In Lancashire, where the cutting of cotton supplies by the American Civil War brought severe suffering and social dislocation, a number of brutal robberies were punished in a fashion that certainly inspired terror. A police officer who stood by them in the Manchester court long recalled the kind of horrified collapse with which men in the dock heard their sentences. An atrocious feature of the punishment was that it could be inflicted in instalments, with intervals for recovery and anticipation.

Whether, as was widely believed, the act of 1863 and a policy of fierce retribution stamped out garotting remains an open question. It is true that there was no serious recurrence and that footpads in general became less of a menace. It is also true that at the very time of the outbreak the efficiency of the police was being widely improved, and there is good reason to think that in the long run criminals are more deterred by the probability of being caught than by a ferocious code. From their surprising initial successes it is clear that the London gangs, or gang, who started the panic caught the authorities bending. They never answered for their worst outrages. The police, depending as always on carefully accumulated knowledge of criminals' habits and an established web of contacts, were faced with an innovation to which they took some time to adjust themselves. But in view of their excellent record of increasing competence and authority it is reasonable to guess that they would have mastered the garotter with no severer sanctions than were already provided in treadwill, crank, stoneyard and solitary cell. The real significance of the garotting scare is that the excitement and publicity it provoked made citizens readier to accept the need (and expense) of efficient, nation-wide law enforcement and so speeded the general improvement of public order.

Among the many speculations (some wild enough) about the cause of the garotting epidemic was a theory relating it to a very different style of street thieving. The outbreak occurred at a time when the professional pickpockets who plagued the business and shopping districts of every large city were becoming noticeably less active. One influential penologist believed that the chief credit for this belonged to the reformatories to which for several years a growing number of young offenders had been committed. In these establishments, he claimed, children were set to tasks that in twelve months 'ruined for ever the delicacy of touch necessary for a pickpocket'.[1] The supply of recruits was therefore being cut at source and some frustrated pickpockets may for a time have resorted to rougher methods; hence the wave of thuggery. This was distressing but—so runs Lloyd Baker's implication—it was not altogether a bad thing if it meant that a very troublesome crime was replaced by one which might be more dramatic but which was a far less widespread and persistent mischief.

Whatever the effect on garotting, there is no reason to doubt that, in the end, the spread of reformatories and industrial schools helped the decline of 'dipping' as a fine art. In the short term, however, Lloyd Baker may have overestimated the results of the reformatory movement (he was a pioneer in it and actually set up a model institution on his own estate) and he was certainly much too sanguine in foreseeing the rapid disappearance of the skilled pickpocket.

The growing wealth of the middle classes, the improvement and cheapening of communications, the great increase in shop-trading and entertainments, the ready circulation of gold currency, the fashion for prominent personal ornaments, the growth of rookery populations and the gradual suppression of cruder ways of stealing, all helped to promote highly skilled pickpocketing. For a while the very improvements in urban policing may have stimulated it. Expert evidence before the Constabulary Commission of 1839 offered the opinion that pickpockets were thriving because 'people think they are safe under the eye of the new police, and will take large sums of money in their pockets'.

The pickpockets who most successfully lifted these large sums under the eye of the law were not, it need scarcely be said, shabby gonophs. The swell mobsmen were experts who mingled incon-

---

[1] T. B. Lloyd Baker *War with Crime*, p. 23. Though the concept was not new, the juvenile reformatory movement only got properly under way—through philanthropic agitation and funds—from 1849. Legislation in the fifties greatly extended the scope of reformatories and industrial schools, enabled magistrates to commit many young offenders to these institutions, and generally improved the provision for delinquents and vagrant children. (Though an idiotic regulation still obliged the courts to sentence most juvenile thieves to a preliminary spell in a jail.) Thereafter the movement grew apace. Manual crafts and agricultural labour coarsened the hands as the crank and treadmill could not.

spicuously with the well-to-do people they robbed. Prosperous looking, often 'square rigged' (dressed in a decorously conservative style), easy and leisurely in their bearing, these virtuosos, who might take twenty or thirty pounds in a good afternoon, were far removed from the squalid urchins who slipped out from slum courts on 'tailing'[1] expeditions, and perhaps varied their approach by begging and turning cart-wheels in the street. Yet, almost without exception, this was the swell mobsman's apprenticeship—and many a swell 'tooler' was too young to have long emerged from it. It was the belief among police and mobsmen alike that the lad who had not mastered the grammar of his art by the time his voice broke seldom achieved excellence.

The converse, of course, was not true. Many children were called to become pickpockets, but few were chosen to graduate beyond the impoverished ruck. Of all the wretched gonophs who disgraced the streets only a fraction can ever have attained the eminence of the swell mob; and of that fraction the majority were probably the victims—or beneficiaries—of careful schooling and exploitation.

The open-minded reader of *Oliver Twist* may find himself thinking that there is something to be said for Fagin and his establishment. It is not till he is brought to the dreadful house in the Field Lane rookery that, for the first time in his life, the workhouse boy finds himself with enough food, cheerful companions and a fair chance of not being wantonly flogged. Certainly he gets a better welcome there than he could have expected if he had been taken up at his begging by a constable or resorted to the Mendicity Society's charitable refuge. (In either case he would probably have been sent back to the parish which it had almost cost him his life to escape.)

Fagin was what was known in the underworld as a 'kidsman', and these managers of child thieves did in fact train them in the way described in this most documentary of Dicken's novels. In the scene concerned, the old monster, having loaded his pockets, stuck a brooch in his shirt, and buttoned up his coat, potters round the room like an elderly gentleman sauntering down a street, continually stopping to stare in shop windows.

> At such times he would constantly look about him, for fear of thieves, and would keep slapping all his pockets in turn in

---

[1] Stealing, usually handkerchiefs, from coat-tail pockets. This was a relatively easy lay for children in a moving throng.

such a very funny and natural manner, that Oliver laughed till the tears ran down his face. All this time the boys followed him closely about: getting out of his sight, so nimbly, every time he turned round, that it was impossible to follow their motions. At last the Dodger trod under his toes, or ran upon his boot accidentally, while Charley Bates stumbled up against him behind: and in that one moment they took from him with extraordinary rapidity, snuff box, note-case, watchguard, chain, shirt-pin, pocket handkerchief, even the spectacle case. If the old gentleman felt a hand in one of his pockets, he cried out where it was; and then the game began all over again.

The Dodger and Bates were an unprepossessing pair to look at (though they liked their boots well polished) but it is clear that the Dodger at any rate was a larval swell mobsman, and if bad luck had not ended his career he would have become the 'great man' Fagin foresaw, perhaps with furnished rooms in Camden Town and a smart dolly to share them.

Some trainers worked in a harsher fashion than the old Jew. In the winter of 1850–51 the deputy of a nethersken off Grays Inn Lane appeared on a pickpocketing charge at Middlesex Sessions. A police officer gave evidence that he had managed to peep through a window into a lodging house where he saw the prisoner surrounded by a group of small boys. From a line stretched across the room a coat was hanging, with a number of handkerchiefs tucked into its pockets. Each child 'in turn tried his skill in removing a handkerchief without moving the coat or shaking the line'. Those who 'performed the manoeuvre with skill and dexterity . . . received the congratulations of the prisoner,' but bunglers were punished and the watcher saw two boys 'knocked down and kicked for not having exhibited the requisite amount of tact and ingenuity'.[1] Other teachers used tailors' dummies, and there was an exacting method in which the clothes used for practice were sewn all over with little bells that tinkled at the slightest vibration.

Besides being nippy and inconspicuous, child dippers had another advantage. When they were caught they were usually tried summarily and, unless they made repeated appearances in the same police court, they were likely to be treated relatively leniently. Young criminals often claimed to be younger than they

---

[1] *The Household Narrative*, 28 January 1851.

were and of course gave different names on different occasions. In this way they could sometimes avoid being committed to higher courts even after several convictions, and this was especially true in London where there was a profusion of magistrates' courts which often passed sentence in ignorance of a prisoner's record in other districts.

In general pickpocketing was considered a less serious offence than stealing from premises. Both police and magistrates were apt to be embarrassed by little offenders who would sometimes try to lie down in the gutter on their way to the police station, weeping and howling and protesting their innocence to passersby, and whose heads, when they appeared in court, were barely visible over the edge of the dock. Birching was a quick and convenient way of disposing of these unpalatable cases, though a child taken in the act of stealing could very well find himself given a month or two in the House of Correction for a first offence—after which he might be recovered by a kidsman and put back on the lay. Where there was nobody to acknowledge responsibility for a child, the court might order him to be admitted to 'a place of occupation' in the care of the poor law authorities. The children dreaded that worse than a spell in jail, and this no doubt helped bind them to exploiters who would arrange for somebody to put in an appearance on their behalf.

High-class pickpockets usually worked in gangs of three or four. The rest of the party acted as protectors to the thief who made the dip, and there seem to have been quite a number of minor swell mobsmen who normally played only these secondary —but often crucial—roles. Sometimes a gang trained up a likely child who would do all the actual dipping under their instructions. A clean, quiet, well-dressed little boy looking as if he belonged to some nearby family party was ideally suited to work a prosperous crowd. At a Christmas theatre, for instance, he could sidle through the throng without rousing suspicion even in that pickpocket-conscious age. The plan also had the great merit that the child could not insist on the lion's share of the takings, as an expert adult would inevitably do.

Among the innumerable criminals interviewed by Mayhew and Binny was one whose story throws a good deal of light on this practice, and on the pickpocket's life in general. He was an intelligent man who had been given only a little elementary schooling but had read a lot in a desultory way and evidently had an intellectual bent. At the time of his meeting with Binny, in 1861 or '62, he was by his own account thirty-one, but plainly washed-up as a swell mobsman and very down on his luck. (It is unlikely that he would have been available for interview otherwise.) He was a shabby, middle-sized man, already battered by hardship; his sallow, bearded features occasionally betrayed a lively temperament, though his normal expression was composed. He lived in a low lodging house and his livelihood, he said, was pattering—that is, reciting and selling broadsheets in the streets.

He had been what would nowadays be called a 'disturbed' child in the straitly pious family of a nonconformist preacher in rural Shropshire. At the age of nine he had run away from home and made his way by coach to London.[1] He had taken a few pounds in his pocket and he found lodging first at an East End coffee shop and then in a slum nethersken in Field Lane—a perfect place for making criminal acquaintances—where the good-natured landlady let him stay on for a little after his money was all gone. Finally he took refuge with a gang of boys whose headquarters were in the wheel-less hulk of an old prison van abandoned under the arches of the Adelphi. There was a man here known as Larry

who bought silk handkerchiefs the boys stole, paying them ninepence apiece though they might be worth as much as four or five shillings. Larry had established a monopoly: boys who did not bring him their wipes were not allowed to sleep in the van or steal from the passengers at Adelphi Stairs, where the busy Thames steamboats put in to the quay and which was the gang's special reserve. Poachers were driven away, and Larry's authority over

[1] Various inconsistencies in this painful part of his story suggest falsifications or omissions. It seems likely that the narrator understated by a year or two the age at which he quit home and launched on a criminal career and that someone originally brought him to London. In general, however, his story is coherent and convincing.

his boys maintained, by fear of being informed against and arrested. Constables on the beat can hardly have been unaware of his organisation.

The boys were kind to the little newcomer, sharing their food with him. In the end, encouraged by their advice and example and ashamed of being parasitic, he plucked up courage and succeeded in removing a handsome green kingsman from the coat tail of a gentleman preoccupied with a little dog on a lead. Soon he became quite bold and accomplished; in fact he began to show such outstanding natural ability that Larry invited several men to come and witness his prowess, meaning no doubt to sell him. These discreet characters watched the boy and tipped him but otherwise kept their thoughts to themselves. However he had not been very long at the game when an alert ferry passenger grabbed him with a handkerchief in his paw and he was hauled off to Bow Street. The magistrate sent him for two months to the newly rebuilt Westminster Bridewell, a prison in which a lot of women and children were confined.

When he came out his life changed. Waiting with a cab near the jail gates were two smart young men who had come to inspect him at the Adelphi. He went with them willingly enough and was taken to a house in Flower-and-Dean Street, Whitechapel, where each of the men occupied a floor with his mistress. Here he was given a good scrubbing, clean new clothes, ample meals and a short spell of careful training. He was destined to become a 'tooler' or picker of ladies pockets—a much more genteel and profitable lay than 'smatter hauling' (handkerchief stealing) — and while one of the young women acted as mark the child practised extracting a purse and other things from her skirt pocket, his movements always shielded by the screening bodies of the men. It was not long before he learnt that he had been brought in as a replacement for a lad who had been sentenced to transportation.

After three days he was judged fit to start work. Dressed in a close-fitting black frock coat, black trousers, black cravat and a little beaver hat (full mourning was common wear for children and eminently respectable) he set out with three young mobsmen all got up 'in fashionable style'. They went to St Paul's Churchyard, and, going into a pastry-cook's, ordered some refreshment while they studied the women passing in and out for a promising victim. It was about half past two in the afternoon and the Churchyard was a centre for good, old-fashioned, rather expensive shops.

At last they followed a customer out of the confectioner's, all of them, naturally, rather nervous at this first essay by a new hand. However the boy's skill did not fail him, and while the lady was gazing at a hosier's window he took her purse, which had the best part of two pounds in it. The gang examined their takings in a friendly house nearby (very likely in the back room of a coffee or cigar shop) and then strolled along Newgate to Cheapside where the boy took four more 'pogues' before they returned to White-chapel at five o'clock.

The tactics followed by this team evidently followed an ortho-dox pattern. When a quarry had been chosen they would follow her in formation, one stall going ahead alone, another walking alongside the tooler and on his right, and a third bringing up the rear. Since the pocket was normally on the right side of a woman's dress it was necessary for the tooler to approach her on that side and stand close to her—but not quite level—when she came to a halt. First he would gently 'fan'[1] the surface of her skirt to make sure her pocket was loaded, then insert his fingers and delicately fish out her purse, which was often a small embroidery or net-work porte-monnaie, easily concealed though apt to chink. This was normally done with the right hand, the thief's arms being loosely crossed so that his right hand and wrist passed under his left elbow. This boy took to carrying an overcoat over his left arm to help conceal the movement, and it seems that like other experts he could, if necessary, do the business 'on the fly', that is while the victim was moving. While the tooler went to work, the stalls placed themselves so as to mask him from passers by. Obviously the clothes women wore, the armour-like stays and above all the voluminous stiffened petticoats that held their skirts away from their bodies, greatly diminished the risk of the dip being noticed. A smartly dressed woman in a crinoline must have been perpetually brushing and pressing against people and objects.

The instant a purse was in his hand the pickpocket's first thought was to pass it to the 'stickman' next to him who might in turn pass it on to another stall. It was the stalls' duty to keep a sharp look out for the police or anyone likely to recognise the gang and, if the dipper was detected, do everything possible to confuse and obstruct pursuit. After a successful 'pull' the gang

---

[1] This is one of various nineteenth-century cant words (*stir, racket, plant* are others) that emigrated to America and then, apparently, returned via crime fiction to England where they had ceased to be current.

would stroll, separately, to an agreed rendezvous to check their takings, since it was important for all of them to be satisfied that the share-outs were fair. Unless they were really valuable, empty purses and any other easily identifiable objects were thrown away.

The Flower-and-Dean Street kidsmen, none of whom were skilled toolers, treated the boy well, always giving him an equal share in the takings and protecting him with care. When, after a few weeks, he was caught in a situation from which all their efforts could not extricate him and landed for three months in the Blackfriars Bridewell, their interest with the staff in this rather lax prison was so effective that his jailers provided him with meat, butter, tea, pastries and even cigars, for which he first acquired a taste during this confinement. On his release he rejoined the gang, and kept out of the hands of the police for some three or four prosperous years. They would go out once or twice a week— sometimes less often—and rob women at churches, open air gatherings, theatres (where mothers taking distracting children to the pantomime were a special boon), Madame Tussaud's, and so on; but most often in shopping streets. One Derby day they drove to Epsom course where, against his better judgement, the young tooler was induced to try and steal from some ladies as they were getting into a carriage. He was detected, a shout went up, and he was only saved by the quickness of his three stalls, one of them interposing himself so blatantly that he was arrested and spent four months in prison.

In his thirteenth year (by his not very reliable reckoning) he took a mistress, a 'tall, thin, genteel girl about fifteen years of age and very good looking'. He lived with her in a couple of furnished rooms, wore smart clothes and a gold watch and chain and was never with less than twenty pounds in his pocket. He seems to have kept the girl well supplied with money but he beat and abused her until she finally ran away from him.

Then—he believed his luck changed with the girl's departure —he was seized for an attempt in the street and given a six months sentence, part of which he served in the Westminster Bridewell and part in the more relaxed atmosphere of the Black-friars one. The silent system was now being enforced and as he behaved in a 'very wilful' manner his stretch was far more dis-agreeable than before, though he managed to spend the last weeks of it in the prison infirmary. When he came out he quarrelled with his old companions, whom he believed to have swindled him over the legal expenses of his trial, and eventually took up with a couple of Ratcliffe Highway characters in whose company he worked various East End localities, tooling women as before.

No doubt he changed to these inferior hunting grounds partly in the hope of being less easily recognised; but in six weeks he was once again in a police court and this time was sent for three months to Coldbath Fields, the dreaded 'Steel'. When he came out he found himself, perhaps five years after his arrival in London, once more without refuge or regular associates. During the next fifteen months he lived badly, lodging for a spell in the slum nethersken where he had stayed before joining Larry's little myrmidons, and cohabiting with a stout young woman ten years his senior, presumably a prostitute. He seems to have been afraid of her and she exploited him with considerable success. In this needy period he stole on his own, chiefly taking men's watches and stick pins—a type of buzzing where team work was less essential than in picking skirt or coat pockets. His miseries were made worse by another short spell in the Steel (he must once again have appeared before a magistrate ignorant of his long record) but after about six months he joined forces with 'some of the swell mob at the Seven Dials' and once more found himself in the money. He followed his old speciality, working with the gang at theatres, the Zoo, Surrey Gardens and other places of entertainment. Meanwhile he had taken up with the mistress who was still with him when he related his adventures, a girl a year or two older than himself who in due course became (against his will, he said) a skilled 'maltooler' or omnibus pickpocket.

He was now running into the pickpocket's chronic trouble—becoming a familiar face to the plainclothes men who watched the best hunting places. In 1847 he was caught with two companions robbing a woman in the old Colosseum (a celebrated exhibition hall in Regent's Park) and for the first time committed for trial before a jury. Fantastically enough, his earlier convictions were not brought up before sentence was passed and, though his associates got stiff terms of penal servitude, he escaped with a year's imprisonment. His faithful girl was waiting when he emerged and he was soon back in harness.

It was the spring of 1848, and a few days after his release he and three stalls attended the famous Chartist rally at Kennington. There were a number of well-off people among the great gathering listening to the harangues on the common, and he lifted 'several ladies' purses, there, amounting to three or four pounds'. Then he had the good luck to notice a foolish man putting his pocket book back in his coat tail pocket. That kind of dipping was no longer in his line (and probably not very easy for a grown youth who would have to stoop) but he decided the opportunity was too good to miss and soon relieved the man of his 'reader'. It proved to contain £135 worth of bank notes.

This prize was too dangerous for the thieves to handle and they had to take it to a fence. The five pound notes fetched £4 10s each and the ten pound notes £8 10s, while for the two of twenty pounds they received, rather surprisingly, £36.[1] It seems likely that the man who lost this money was a stranger to London, unaware that, like fires and other excitement, any prospect of political disturbance always brought out the pickpockets in droves.

In this period of his life the youth had various strokes of bad luck, including an illness that affected his legs and involved heavy doctors' bills. (It was while he was out of action that his girl took to maltooling.) But despite all this and despite his twelve months in jail, the half dozen years he spent with this gang were the most prosperous of his career. He and his girl spent four or five pounds a week on their domestic expenses, ate well and went to theatres and other places of amusement for pleasure as well as profit— including now and then famous Bohemian song-and-supper resorts like The Coal Hole. Like most thieves of the time he was a keen gambler and when he had the money played cribbage at two or three pounds a game.

The rich opportunities of the Great Exhibition marked the zenith of his fortunes. His girl had been jailed for six months for her omnibus thefts and when she came out she found he had a couple of hundred pounds in hand. From then on, the permanent decline set in. The Exhibition stimulated Scotland Yard as well as the criminals and it was no doubt because he was being dogged by the police that he next made an ill-judged attempt to change his lay altogether. He joined up with a pair of burglars, under the mistaken impression that they were pastmasters in their art. In fact, though he was apparently acquainted with plenty of cracksmen, he knew little of cracksmanship and his new colleagues

[1] Normally, the larger a note's denomination the heavier the receiver's discount. But notes circulated by provincial banks-of-issue might be bought at a different rate from Bank of England money.

proved prize bunglers. The gang's third venture was a daytime
raid on a building in the City which they wrongly thought was
deserted for the afternoon. It totally miscarried. The alarm was
given, the criminals tried to bolt, and the unlucky novice had
managed to run some distance from the building when a passing
pedestrian, alerted by the cries of 'Stop Thief', felled him with an
umbrella. All three burglars were taken and soon found themselves in Newgate awaiting trial. Once again—and this time it
is inconceivable that the information was not deliberately withheld—the police did not bring his record before the court, so that
he received only eighteen months for the attempted burglary.
The other two, old lags, got seven and ten years apiece.

In Holloway prison he was put in solitary confinement—then
much in vogue—and was discharged in a state of nervous debility.
For the first time since running away as a little boy he went
home to Shropshire where he stayed seven weeks with his
widowed mother before returning to London and his mistress,
sufficiently recovered to resume pickpocketing. However, his
vital professional standing in the swell mob was lost, and he
had to go back to buzzing men's watches and shirt pins on his
own. He contrived to keep at liberty for a year before another
summary conviction—presumably for a not very serious offence
—sent him back to Coldbath Fields for six months. The sentence
marked the end of his career as a high grade thief. During the
seven years that had elapsed between his release from 'the Steel'
and the time Binny heard his story he had existed on sporadic
thieving and by pattering in the streets. Sometimes he acted as
stall to his mistress when she worked the omnibuses. He was in
terror of the law and had escaped further conviction, though he
had been held in jail for a period on remand while the police
waited for an accuser to come forward. His woman, like himself,
had been changed by adversity and imprisonment. She had taken
for a time to shoplifting, but had become prone to drunkenness—
a fatal weakness in thieves who relied on quickness of hand and
eye. Both of them, in the phrase he used to describe a common
fate of pickpockets, had 'had the steel taken out of them'.

This man had been taken up at an early age by the Flower-
and-Dean Street gang and passed the peak of his career rather
sooner than most swell mobsmen. He was certainly lucky to
escape being either 'boated' to Australia or condemned to a
long term of penal servitude at home. But in general there is little

in his story that is out-of-the-way. Not only was any swell mobsman's career likely to be brief, but superior tooling was a particularly tricky speciality. The well-pursed women for whom the tooler was looking were not much found in the jostling places all pickpockets preferred. They did not gather at executions, or crowd round in a street fracas, or wander about casually tipsy at sporting events. They had to be sought in genteel shopping streets and, worse, inside buildings like theatres and exhibition-rooms which, if the alarm went up, became traps. The detectives who hunted the swell mob could easily be lurking there and they only needed to spot a member of a gang without themselves being spotted. Further, it has to be remembered that the number of pickpockets in circulation made the public alert to the danger of being robbed and quick to seize any thief who blundered.

Some toolers used instruments. There was one rather like the little whisks used to flatten sparkling drinks which, when a catch is moved, blossom out at the end into a sort of minute besom. Appliances of similar design, but ending in three little grapnels that clutched instead of expanding when the catch was worked, were made and sold (at about ten shillings each) to gadget-minded pickpockets. They could be slipped into a narrow pocket and would effectively hook an embroidery or open-work porte-monnaie. Skilful purse thieves were sometimes known as 'fine-wirers' and it may be that both this expression and the word 'tooler' are related to the same device. A crude technique, favoured by maltoolers, was simply to slash the pocket from outside with a small blade.

Women, like children, were well suited to stealing from women. They were oftener of the right height than a man, had smaller, more pliable hands and could press close to a woman without rousing the same awareness of their presence. Buses gave them excellent opportunities. In the fifties and sixties they were still too dear to be freely used by the poor, and though in theory it was not completely ladylike to travel in one, sensible women at most social levels made few bones about it. It was the easiest, cheapest way for the middle-class suburban housewife to come into town. Women always sat inside, and the passengers, facing each other across the narrow little saloon, were often pressed so close together that billowing dresses and mantles overlapped. Moreover the jolting of the badly sprung vehicle helped to cover up the maltooler's moves. Sometimes two thieves got on together and sandwiched a victim between them in a confusion of flounces, fringes, reticules and muffs; then one would engage her attention while the other emptied her pocket. Once the pull was made, the maltooler got out of the bus as quickly as possible, even at the risk of attracting attention: it was too close a trap for delay. Sometimes she had the help of a male stall who stationed himself next to the narrow door at the back to help her escape. The conductor, or 'cad', whose usual place was outside on the rear step, might also be in collusion with thieves who regularly worked his vehicle.

It was the stealing of coins that made tooling so attractive. Almost everything else a pickpocket might take had to go to the fence, usually for a fraction of its value. Further, pickpockets were naturally afraid of being picked up with traceable valuables on them, and if they took, say, a good watch and chain at a race-meeting they might break off rather than run any further risk, even if there were other tempting opportunities. There might be more cash in men's pockets than women's but it was often less accessible. Trouser pockets were cut rather high and too much to the front to be convenient. Generally speaking, the pick-pocket's interest was likely to focus on the watch and chain in a man's waistcoat—there might be coin there too—the pin in his shirt, and the snuff box and handkerchief in his coat. A pocketbook like the one taken at Kennington was, of course, a magnificent haul; but gold was commoner everyday currency than paper money and an elaborate, dangerous pull from an inside pocket could easily produce nothing better than a few visiting cards.

This does not mean, however, that all the most talented and best organised mobsmen usually stole from women. On the contrary, it is clear that parties of highly proficient operators made a practice of touring race-meetings, prize fights, political rallies, military reviews and other gatherings where there were far richer opportunities for robbing male than female spectators.

Mobsmen on this lay would adopt rather freer methods than were used for tooling women. A gang, picking on a promising looking spectator at a sporting meeting, will work through the crowd, keeping discreetly apart, till they are in position around him. The thief who is about to make the pull comes up close on the right of his prey, apparently squeezed against him by the throng: in fact the pressure is being increased by his associates.

First he lets the back of his hand brush against the front of his neighbour's buttoned coat; then, folding his arms, he waits till the man's interest is fully engaged by the spectacle in front. Then he slides his long fingers under the flap of his coat till they feel the chain attached to the watch.[1] He has now to ease the watch from its pocket with a strong, deft movement of his thumb, snap or prise open the gold fastening by which it is held, withdraw it smoothly and immediately pass it to a confederate. To free a watch in this manner requires a powerful, sensitive and highly practised touch and is reckoned one of a first-class pickpocket's most valuable accomplishments. The moment the theft is completed, the gang melts away.

But sometimes a different approach is best. Among the drifting crowd near the refreshment tents, towards the end of the day, the gang mark a slightly flushed and unsteady gentleman in an open coat, exposing a tempting breast pin and perhaps a set of seals dangling by his watch pocket. Now the pickpocket will manoeuvre so as to face or half-face his man and then violently collide with him. The best way of producing a collision is for the thief to stand still while one of the gang gets behind the victim and, at a signal, barges into him so that he lurches forward —when the thief, very naturally, throws up protesting hands against the other's chest to hold him off. Another drunk blunders into them and during the brief entanglement the victim's watch, pin and other valuables disappear. This rifling of a groggy subject allows the pickpocket to use more force and steal more things than the stealthy sideways dip, but it demands discrimination and perfect timing.

Whatever the method, or type of victim, good team work and team spirit were essential for really successful pickpocketing. Its advantages were so obvious that the most talented dippers normally preferred to split their profits rather than work alone, whilst among the less talented, intelligent cooperation sometimes made up for lack of technical virtuosity.

Sometimes gangs devised quite elaborate charades. A man walking down a narrow street might be annoyed to find himself spattered with flour from a sack thoughtlessly shaken at the roadside. At once a good natured stranger takes his part, commiserates, draws him into the open doorway of a nearby coffee

---

[1] A variety of watch-guards were worn. Thin, tough chains or cords (often woven of a beloved's hair) which passed round the neck were common and apparently considered a good protection. But there was always a chance of a weak gold connection.

shop. Several other parties appear, all sympathetically concerned. One dashes to borrow a clothes brush and sets energetically to work with it, others crowd round, dusting the bemused man's lapels and flapping his coat-tails. In a few moments the bustle reaches crescendo, but almost before he can make an irritated protest his hat is jammed over his eyes, the door slams and they have all vanished, nobody knows where, leaving him frantically slapping his empty pockets.

A similar drama was staged in public houses. In this the dupe would fall foul of a fellow customer and get knocked down. While the bully-boy sulkily withdrew on the barman's orders, a couple of sympathetic girls would fan the sufferer's face, loosen his neckcloth, dust the sand off his coat, and comb his pockets.

This last trick was often played by 'bug-hunters'—a broad description covering the various criminals who hung round pubs robbing drunks. Many bug-hunters were women who accosted men in the streets. A couple of girls, flighty and 'dollymopish' but not with the air of professional prostitutes, would pertly invite a tipsy-looking man to treat them in a nearby saloon. Inside, all standing agreeably close together at the bar, one girl would engage the dupe's fuddled attention while the other picked his pocket. A difficulty here was getting the takings away quickly; unless the victim was almost paralysed with drink he was liable to tumble to what had happened before the girls could get clear, and they would find themselves trapped. One safeguard was for them to be followed into the pub by a male accomplice. If the drunk proved too quick in the uptake, this man would push into the agitated knot at the bar, side with the victim against the girls and, having had the booty slipped to him, rush off to fetch a constable. Of course he was not seen again, and the women, without a shred of tangible evidence about them, could happily face a search.

In early Victorian times no kind of thieving approached pick-pocketing as a serious, endemic pest, at least in towns. The dipper was the bane of nearly every kind of public gathering from church services to executions, ship launchings to subscription dances. Distance was little bar: when the crowds of visitors went off to seasonal watering places, the pickpockets followed on their heels like wolves after migrating game; while the famous Eglintoun Tournament (a Gothic-revival jousting spree) brought members of the London swell mob streaking hundreds of miles northward into Ayrshire. To townspeople 'thief', unqualified, normally meant 'pickpocket'.

By the sixties the plague was noticeably diminishing. In some places dippers remained a great nuisance for generations—indeed they extended their activities to new fields, finding excellent opportunities in the new London Underground, for instance—but the old ubiquitous menace was fading. Above all, the virtuoso élite who boldly rubbed shoulders with all sorts of respectable company had begun to decline to the point where they could hardly be differentiated in the public mind from the general run of pickpockets. Before the end of the century the swell mob, as a conspicuous entity, had passed into history.

Various explanations, none conclusive, suggest themselves. It is natural to think that a continually strengthening police were most interested in catching those street thieves who stole the largest sums and robbed people who were able to make their influence felt. The swell mobsmen were the most easily identified and detected. They concentrated on a particular method and type of victim and frequented a limited number of hunting grounds, even in London. Again, if Binny's acquaintance had started on his career as a child thief fifteen years later he would probably have been sent to some sort of reformatory and perhaps permanently spoilt for skilled finger-work. Almost certainly, if he had persisted, he would not have escaped hearing his long record of convictions brought up in a higher court and being sentenced to a swingeing term of penal servitude.

It seems likely, too, that the decay of the swell mob had a discouraging effect on lesser pickpockets. Young delinquents are as prone to admire and imitate as other youths, and in their heyday the mobsmen, elegant, affluent, free with their money, were among the most conspicuous of the criminal aristocracy. With their fine clothes and glittering watch chains, lolling in the best places at some backyard prize-fight or badger-bait, they must have been an inspiration to the young idea.

Finally there was the influence of fashion. For a long time much the commonest lay for young pickpockets was stealing silk handkerchiefs from men's coats—usually from the coat-tail pockets. Small boys were admirably suited to it and it made a sound training for more ambitious thieving. 'Stock-buzzing' was profitable because, as the name suggests, large silk handkerchiefs found a ready market as neckerchiefs. Good specimens in the colours currently favoured by costers and the like could fetch several shillings each in Petticoat Lane and the Minories where swags of assorted kingsmen, all identification marks carefully removed, could be seen hanging in the clothes dealers' dens.[1] After the mid-century however the exuberance of Englishmen's town clothes fell away; moreover snuff-taking, the functional reason for very large coloured handkerchiefs, was going out. Gentlemen continued to use large handkerchiefs, but the enormous bandana, flourished and stuffed back in the pocket, sometimes with a corner picturesquely trailing, was on the way to becoming the half-comic property of an outmoded age. At the same time, of course, the snuff box itself, often a valuable and easily lifted prize, was disappearing from coat pockets. Further, little by little, the number of suitable coat tails diminished. Even in the fifties smart young men of the upper classes could be seen in the streets of London wearing fairly short buttoned-up jackets; and these unaccommodating clothes became even commoner at railway stations, sporting meetings and other jostling places where pickpockets looked for their easiest prey.

For the purse-lifter the passing of the crinoline must also have been a cruel blow. In the seventies well made skirts, though often very voluminous in the rear, hung almost straight down in front; after generations, fashion had once again brought the front of a woman's dress close to her legs. The forward-swelling skirt, with a pocket almost as convenient to the pickpocket as the wearer, vanished virtually for ever.

[1] A whole cant vocabulary grew up about this trade. A blue silk handkerchief was a 'watersman', a green-and-white a 'randlesman', a yellow-and-white a 'fancy yellow'. By the fifties black fogles—bought by their original owners for mourning—were the most sought after.

CHAPTER SIX

Cracksmen and fences

Though the commonest way of exploiting little thieves was to set them stealing in the streets, it was by no means the only kind of robbery in which children could be useful. A cool-headed, undersized boy, supple enough to wriggle in between window bars or through a small unprotected back window, was sometimes the best means of cracking a tight crib, and once inside he could open a barred door or shutter for his elders. Such a child was known professionally as a 'snakesman'.

This was the role in which little Oliver Twist was to assist Sikes. That any housebreaker in his senses who had met Oliver should have employed him in that way must be put down to the demands of the plot. But it is Dickens' relish for authentic detail that makes him show how using a boy at all was a second-best expedient (only adopted because no servant in the house could be got at) and then portray Sikes lamenting the absence of 'that young boy of Ned's, the chimbley-sweeper's' whose master used to 'let him out by the job'.

A sweep's climbing boy, indeed, was the natural choice for such work. If they survived uncrippled, young sweeps sometimes gained astonishing agility from their apprenticeship and became well known criminals on that account. There were many underworld legends about a housebreaker called (variously) Williams or Whitehead, who had been a climbing boy and who made perhaps the most remarkable English prison break of the century.

In 1836 he was in Newgate sentenced to death for burglary. There was an exercise yard for the condemned surrounded by sheer granite walls, near the top of which, fifty feet from the ground, was a chevaux-de-frise of revolving iron spikes, supported by a horizontal bar embellished with additional points. It was impossible for a human body to pass between the chevaux-de-frise and the masonry, and there was a further barrier above it—a row of long, sharp, inward-projecting spikes guarding the top of the wall. Above the corner of the yard, however, a water cistern stuck out from the blank side just below the revolving spikes. The turnkeys did not trouble to keep a continual watch on the place and Williams seized his chance. With his back and feet braced against the rough stone like a rock climber he worked his way up the angle of the wall, reached the cistern, and clambered on top if it. From there he got to the bar holding the chevaux-de-frise and painfully made his way along it, crabwise, round three sides of the yard until, badly lacerated, he came to a spot opposite and rather below the top of the Press Yard buildings. He then leapt some eight or nine feet to the roof and clambered over the leads of the prison and the adjacent buildings till he got above a nearby street. Seeing a woman hanging out her washing on a roof, he hid by a chimney stack, then followed her down into the house. The people inside were alarmed at his wild and bloody appearance, but when he pleaded with them they raised no alarm. (By this time, feeling was running strongly against the barbarity of hanging people for property offences.) He went out into the street and got clear away.

According to Williams' old master, even this feat was less notable than his boyhood escape from apprenticeship: he had been sent up the chimney of a sugar refinery and when he came out of the top he swarmed down the *outside* of the bare brick stack thirty or forty feet to where he could reach an attic window and freedom.

Besides their climbing talents, chimney sweeps had many chances of getting to know the layout of households worth robbing. Also they had the advantage that in their trade it was quite usual to be on the move during the hours of darkness. Nevertheless, it seems doubtful if many sweeps or ex-sweeps were to be found in the higher flights of cracksmanship.[1] For here, as in pickpocketing, obvious brutality and a rough manner were the marks of the inferior exponent. Suavity was what mattered, and that was about the last quality associated with chimney sweeps. A burglar might be agile and intrepid and an expert safebreaker and still be no great hand at his trade, for these were not—or very seldom— the first essentials. Before anything else a worthwhile haul had to be located and arrangements made to get at it; and it was in carrying out these preliminaries that more sophisticated and pre-

---

[1] There was a technical distinction between 'cracking' or 'busting' which denoted the breaking of a lock or fastening by the application of force, and 'screwing' which implied the use of keys, picklocks, etc. Unless it was necessary to emphasise his speciality, however, a screwsman was often referred to as a cracksman.

sentable cracksmen showed their superiority. Moreover, sensible robbers naturally preferred to avoid dangerous feats and go in and out by the door.

Broadly, the most satisfactory sort of housebreak was the inside job. That is, it was one that involved the servants.

To us the sheer profusion of servants on the nineteenth century scene is striking. In 1851 between seven and eight per cent of the entire population of the country were servants, if we ignore children under ten. For women and girls the figure was over thirteen per cent and for them 'service' was so much the commonest job that it accounted for nearly twice the number employed in the whole textile industry—by far the most important group of manufactures and one in which the majority of workers were female.[1] It can almost be said that every family able to feed and clothe some sort of servant kept one. Within this vast and heterogeneous army conditions varied from the miserable child-of-all-work, sleeping on a sack under the stairs, in bondage for a few coppers a week and her wretched keep, to the great magnate's house steward, a prosperous member of the middle class.

There were various ways in which the servants' manner of life helped the underworld. One was their mobility. It was an age of financial ups-and-downs, in which households of servants were assembled or disbanded; and for the parvenu who wanted to show off his new prosperity there was no more obvious way than by getting together a collection of footmen in rich livery, gold braided and swagged, with buckled pumps and larded, powdered hair.[2] A number of well trained and impressive-looking servants of this kind could move from job to job with great ease. There were men who declared it 'lowering' to stay overlong in one situation, and there were pairs of footmen so well matched that they found it profitable to insist on being engaged together, their imposing appearance side by side behind a chariot being as gratifying as a spanking team of matched

[1] Sir J. Clapham *Free Trade and Steel*, Chapter 2. I have included charwomen and indoor farm maidservants with the servants, lace and hosiery makers with the textile workers. The figures originate from the report on the 1851 census. *Parliamentary Papers* 1852–3, LXXXVIII, Ages and Occupations, Parts I & II.

[2] The effrontery and misconduct of great people's coachmen and footmen, apt from the nature of their duties to spend much time idly hanging about, was traditional. Early in the Queen's reign a disgraceful brawl of peers' servants outside the House of Lords resulted in serious damage to Lord Galloway's coach and legal proceedings against men in the service of Lord Melbourne and three other prominent noblemen. The police were so reluctant to interfere that they did nothing to break up the rumpus.

hackneys in front. More important, perhaps, was the practice of making a temporary, or seasonal, splash by taking over a house for a short time and filling it with servants of all sorts. Many of them could expect to be dismissed at the end of a few months, and this sort of coming and going made it far easier for criminals to plant a contact inside a house.

Again, there was the fact that most servants were poor. Apart from a small upper hierarchy, they were often ill-paid and squeezed into wretched accommodation. This became particularly important when 'the family' were away. Those servants who were left behind would often be put on an inclusive 'board wage' rather than being given their meals in addition to their pay. This probably meant that they fed less well, and at the same time there was likely to be a serious falling off in their perquisites. James Yellowplush in the hall relied more on tips than on his wages of a pound or two a month—hence the well-known lack of cordiality to less wealthy callers. Hare and rabbit skins, feathers, fat, bones, old clothes, bottles, corks, scrap metal were often sold at back doors and the money went into the servants' pockets. Some of the more important members of a large staff, especially the cook, were squared by tradesmen in proportion to the household's expenditure. All this meant that a staff of servants might face a sharp drop in their living standard just when they were left pretty much to their own devices. It was obviously a situation in which a free-spending casual acquaintance had an unusually good chance of being welcomed in. Even if the family plate was at the bank, he could still make vital contacts and carry out reconnaissance.

In general, however, well-to-do people kept a remarkably sharp eye on their dependents' lives. For all the contemporary love of display the evangelical ethos was strong and, besides the moral satisfaction, it was obviously safer and more economical to have a strictly regulated, God-fearing establishment where family devotions were rigorous and temptations few, 'followers' discouraged and cold remainders scrutinised. It is true that menservants were given more latitude than women, and in a large, departmentalised household, where two six-foot men escorted a plate of muffins upstairs, even the most rigorous housekeeping could hardly forestall every irregularity. But in the middling sort of household, small enough to allow close personal control, the mistress had power to enforce a very strict standard. A home with conscientious and solid employers was a highly desirable thing, and the supply of recruits for such places—at any rate female recruits—exceeded demand. The strictest propriety of conduct, decorous submission, long irregular hours of duty, and acceptance of an endless supervision that left no going-out or coming-in unaccounted for, could be (and were) exacted.

Yet strictness might defeat its purpose by fostering secretive habits or outright deception. And if a girl did get herself dismissed, what was she to do when she found herself dumped in the street with a few shillings and a flimsy hamper of possessions? Without a reference she had little chance of finding a respectable situation: unless she had family or friends who were able and ready to help her, she was thrown, at a severe disadvantage, on a glutted labour market. Especially if she was a provincial brought into a city where she had no connections (as many servants were) she was likely to drift towards prostitution and the underworld.

In the underworld, perhaps in a lodging house that had the reputation of being a 'servants' lurk', a sharp young woman might find means to put her misfortune to account. If the house from which she had been ejected was worth burgling, a first-hand knowledge of it was an asset that she could sell, while if she wanted to get back into service the underworld could supply the references she lacked. Scrupulous housewives mistrusted written evidence and went to the pains of calling personally on the servant's previous mistress, but this was not always possible. For girls who knew the ropes, there were screevers who could produce the most plausible testimonials and answers to enquiries. Thus the disgraced servant's best chance of survival might lie in striking up a connection with criminals.

There is little evidence about methods of planting an accomplice where an elaborate robbery was planned. This may be simply because it was an efficient system which, then as now, was used by careful organisers who seldom came up for prosecution. But the servants who were planted must have been presentable and competent at the job, as well as singularly cool customers. When the burglary had been committed they did not as a rule give themselves away by promptly disappearing: they stayed on until they could leave in regular fashion, though the police, who knew all about the system, must have taken a strong interest in anyone who had recently been engaged.

The other way of arranging an inside job was to reach an understanding with a member of the existing staff. This was probably the commonest method and there were many ways of making the contact. Back-door buyers and hawkers, loungers and touts in pubs used by footmen, waiters hired for a night—all of these were possible tempters. The light-fingered housemaid, anxious to sell some small valuable before her belongings were searched, might be a valuable contact, or the discharged one with friends left behind. Above all, most domestic servants were women and, except in big houses, they were usually short of male company: for the house thief who hoped to have his way smoothed nothing was more useful than 'a captivating address'.

Thieves who struck up an acquaintance with the servants did not necessarily have to turn them into conscious accomplices. If they could arrange to get in at a suitable time they could rob the house without the staff having any idea of what was in the wind until it was too late.

Binny gives an example. A London cook, employed at a house in a fashionable square, went out for a walk with a smartly dressed young man who had got to know her. The family were away and the cook presumably was in charge, so she invited him in to tea. He came bringing a friend, a Frenchman, who tactfully applied himself to the housemaid who was also of the party. Indeed he proved so fascinating that he persuaded the girl to let him take her upstairs. The cook's boyfriend was less gallant; saying that he felt unwell and needed some fresh air he went out into the back garden, where he no doubt made some signal to an accomplice. In due course the couple upstairs decided that further refreshment would be a good idea, so the Frenchman went off alone to buy some liquor, letting himself out by the front door, while his companion went down to rejoin the cook in the basement. The Frenchman soon returned with the drink, but in the meantime he had left the front door unfastened for another member of the gang who slipped in unseen and went to work in the upper part of the house while the party enjoyed themselves below. When the robber upstairs had made a thorough haul he left as he had come, signalling that he had finished the job by a tug on the door bell. This interruption broke up the party in the basement; the visitors took their leave while one of the servants, going up to answer the bell and finding no one, locked up for the night, thinking no harm.

On this occasion the servants discovered the loss quickly and reported it, making something like a clean breast of the affair. The two criminals they could describe were identified as members of a gang and picked up and sent to penal servitude, though the unseen thief seems to have escaped. As a result, the method by which the trick was worked was exposed in some detail. But it is not hard to see what temptation there must often have been for servants who had been duped in this sort of way to do everything they could to disguise the real nature of the robberies. Perhaps very unwillingly, they would cover up the criminals' tracks, and many of the improbable exploits of thieves like Spring Heel Jack may have begun with servants hard pressed for a story. (Jack himself was a pure legend.)

Any servant who had let a criminal tempt her into compromising conduct was to some extent in his power. It was also possible to make use of servants who were quite unaware that they were doing anything wrong. Menservants especially, gossiping in the taproom at the mews corner, were apt to let fall information about their places; and provided they were well enough briefed as to what they would find inside, thieves did not necessarily give up the convenience of the front door because they could not arrange to be let in. Servants who could not be seduced could still be evaded. Some experts with the 'twirls' would boldly force a front door in full view of the street, having first perhaps got a rough impression of the lock from a preliminary try with a wax-coated blank key. Entry had to be made at a fairly early hour before the bolts and chain were put up for the night. Well dressed, bulky in his surtout and tall hat, the thief might look like a resident fumbling with his keys in the bad light or, with a cigar in his mouth, a smoker stooping to light up in the shelter of a doorway. Probably an idling scout kept watch at a little distance while his back was turned to the road.

There were also various tricks and excuses for getting the door unfastened from inside and then dodging the servant, some of which have already been described. One ingenious manoeuvre would save the thief from showing his face and leave the household in doubt as to how the robbery occurred. A servant answering an evening ring sees in the feeble street light a closed cab drawn up at the kerb. From it a lady's voice demands if this is Mr So-and-so's. No servant with a vestige of training is going to stand at the top of the steps and shout, least of all the dignified and tip-conscious porter of a rich household. He goes down, and while he answers inexplicit questions with his head in the cab window the housebreaker slips behind him to the open door.

The vital thing, with this trick as with others, was to know what to expect once one was inside the house. However it was obtained, inside information was the essence of efficient burglary.

Plainly there was no hard and fast distinction between these front-door robberies and some of the activities of the 'area divers' and sneak thieves in the last chapter. As usual when one attempts to scrutinise the underworld, categories merge and differences become matters of degree. It is easy to be over-definite even about distinguishing between cracksmen and (as zoologists say) their allies on the one hand, and pickpockets and theirs on the other. Pickpockets took to housebreaking and housebreakers joined gangs of street thieves; cracksmen's mistresses were often toolers and shoplifters. It is impossible to read very much about professional thieves without getting a strong impression that the great majority of them belonged to a common thief society. Nevertheless, if we ignore the more casual, indiscriminate sort of criminals, there are comparisons worth drawing between what can be called the two main schools of thieving—those who broke into premises and those who stole in public.

For one thing house-robbers did not endure the pickpocket's constant nervous stretch; generally they laid low and relaxed after a successful job and they often spent months surveying and preparing a big robbery. There is no reason to suppose that the most efficient of them were particularly young, as pickpockets were, or that by middle life they would be broken by strain and imprisonment. Most pickpockets were careful about drinking but cracksmen were not. On the contrary they seem to have been apt to steady themselves at work with a pull of spirits. Swell mobsmen travelled miles to race meetings and sometimes migrated from one town to another (some even trying their luck abroad) but on the whole they seem to have been far less willing to make permanent changes of territory than prudence demanded. Cracksmen with the means to travel were often remarkably mobile. Detectives sometimes followed their trails back and forth across the country and experts were now and then invited to come from long distances (as guest artists, so to speak) to carry out robberies set up by local criminals. Unfamiliar to local police and informers, they could arrive unnoticed, do the job—or the trickiest part of it—and be away before anyone got scent of their presence.

Like the swellest mobsmen, the most successful cracksmen tended to live in more or less respectable districts and sometimes in a style that the most prosperous pickpocket could hardly rise to. According to Binny, these masters of the craft kept servants, ate and drank luxuriously, enjoying the 'choicest wines', and adorned their women extravagantly. But they were discreet, and from their manner and dress they were more likely to be taken for 'sharp business men' than burglars. Some saved and invested their savings (perhaps banked in a mistress's name) in a legitimate or almost legitimate business and in time became comfortable publicans or cab proprietors. (These were trades in which an underworld connection could be profitable.) A number are said to have become receivers; others abandoned crime altogether.

These men lived very different lives from the housebreaker in greasy corduroys and an oilskin cap (to hide his jailcrop) toasting his dinner at a nethersken fireside. Yet no gap separated even the topmost minority of cracksmen from the common runways of crime. Indeed the more ambitious the scale on which a cracksman worked, the bigger and more elaborately planned a burglary, the more probable it was that he would need a whole range of criminal connections, major and minor. From first conception to final disposal of the booty, a big robbery could be a complex enterprise, a pie in which many strange hands had a finger.[1]

Since they had to rely on each other for their safety and freedom, one would expect housebreakers to have preferred working with the same associates. Within limits they did, but most of them do not seem to have formed stable close-knit teams after the fashion of the swell mob. Instead one finds criminals banding together in gangs to carry out a series of robberies, or sometimes just a single coup. Each gang would contain men of various kinds, some of them no more cracksmen than a stall was a picker

---

[1] Then as now, reports of such crimes are apt to give an over-simplified impression because they refer only to those who are prosecuted or whose activities are obvious. Frequently, little of the organisational understructure comes to light. This is a common source of weakness in books about criminals, including this one.

of pockets. An obvious reason for flexible, *ad hoc* associations was that different jobs demanded different combinations. Thieves often preferred to stick to one style of burglary, but even so each job presented particular problems. Some gangs, for instance, specialised in working country houses, but if they found themselves confronted with a Bramah-locked plate room, they might call in an expert safe-cutter who normally tackled city offices.

In many ways, the techniques of housebreaking were much like those that are still in use today. As has been said, information was the first essential. If there was no reliable inside accomplice, much could be learnt from goings in and out, lights in windows, and so on. Even keeping track of a pet dog's regular run could be vital. It was obviously important to study the constables on the beat (in London a fifteen or twenty minute patrol), the times they relieved one another, and any foibles, such as stopping for a quick draw at a pipe, that affected an officer's movements. This sort of reconnaissance, however, was a delicate business. A persistently loitering stranger was always in danger of attracting attention, no matter how discreet his appearance; and a known cracksman who was spotted watching a place was courting disaster. Sometimes a watcher hung round under colour of begging or hawking, but that sort of thing was often associated with minor thieving and might in itself rouse suspicion. Crossing sweepers could be a danger, since they often laid claim to a fixed pitch and depended on the police to help them keep it. It only needed one of a gang to be picked up in the locality for plans on which weeks, even months of work had been spent to be hopelessly compromised.

It was also important to keep a watch while the job was going on. In most organised raids an important part was played by the 'crow', or look-out, who lurked outside, ready to warn his colleagues of any threatened interruption from the street. Sometimes, too, he could see danger coming inside the building by watching the windows. He had to be on the scene before the break-in was attempted and it was often his job to give a starting signal. At the finish he would also give the all-clear for departure—particularly important when cumbersome loot had to be brought out at a street door. Sometimes a series of signals would be kept up between the crow and those in a deserted office or warehouse: the men inside would time their work, lying low or pressing on with their lock smashing, according to his instructions. Crows resorted to all sorts of calls—whistles, bird and cat noises, coughings and hawkings and so on—as well as visual signs like flourishing a handkerchief or striking a match. A small house-breaking gang seems quite often to have consisted of a crow and two burglars.

When he could not get in by the door, the burglar looked for a weak spot, usually giving the house as thorough a daytime survey as he dared. A barred but unshuttered window in the basement or at the back of the ground floor was often a good place to break in. One traditional device for dealing with bars consisted of a length of rope and a strong metal rod. The thief passed a doubled loop round two bars, inserted the rod between the strands and turned it end over end, twisting up the rope and drawing the bars together. With luck the bars would be bent or loosened in their sockets enough for an adult housebreaker or a snakesman to slip between. However, this simple method did not always work well (perhaps because the winding rod had to be short and was tricky to manipulate so as to clear the window behind) and advanced thieves preferred to use a small jack worked with a ratchet and pinion, rather like a simple motorcar wheel jack.

Thieves seem to have avoided shutters as much as possible. There were no great technical difficulties in getting through a set of ordinary wooden shutter-leaves, but it took time. The tool used was a kind of brace and bit fitted with a large, adjustable cutting-head, and with this the thief made a circular hole big enough for him to put his hand inside and raise the bar. Win-

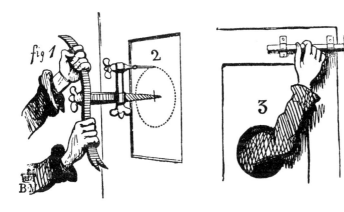

dows were either cut with a glass-cutter's stone or 'star-glazed':
a competent professional is said to have been able to remove a
piece of pane, release the catch and open a sash in fifteen seconds
flat. Where they had to force a shutter in a conspicuous place,
careful thieves pasted a piece of dark paper over the damage.

Housebreaking tools were made in London, Manchester and
Sheffield, but probably the largest source was Birmingham,
where suppliers of all sorts of criminals' equipment could be
found among the innumerable small workshops. The following

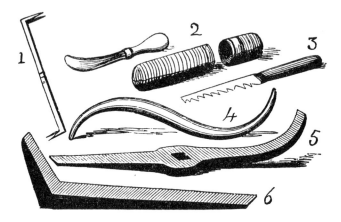

list of standard housebreaking kit is taken from Binny: a very
strong sheath knife or chisel; a jemmy; an 'American auger'
(brace and bit) with various blades and drills; a length of rope;
a jack; a dark lantern capable of throwing a spot of light
no bigger than a shilling from an oil-fed wick (a device that
became atrociously hot and could not be lit without showing
a diffused light); a set of 'bettys' or picklocks; an 'outsider'

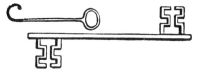

(fine pliers with modified jaws for grasping the butt end
of a key in a lock, or alternatively an instrument of strong
hooked steel for the same purpose); and a 'petter-cutter' for
safes. This last was very much a specialist's tool. It was a drill
that could be clamped to the keyhole of a safe, allowing powerful leverage to be applied to the cutter; this was made of hard

steel and bit a small opening over the lock through which the wards could be manipulated. Considerable experience was needed to use a petter-cutter quietly and effectively, and it was also expensive to buy. None of the other items were very costly, taken one by one (the American auger could be bought for a pound or less) but it must have been a serious matter to buy a whole set, especially as cracksmen were apt to be fussy about their tools. However lack of funds or loss of equipment were not necessarily fatal: one could hire what one needed by the night.

The equipment used for different jobs naturally varied enormously. For some, the thief wanted little more than something to hold the swag, but where really serious obstacles had to be forced, housebreakers were liable to need an outfit too elaborate to be hidden under their clothes. Apart from that, if they were stopped on the way and found to be loaded with the appliances listed in the last paragraph, the law would hardly need further evidence. So at this point another auxiliary to an organised housebreak trudges onto the stage, carpet-bag in hand. Whenever he could avoid it, the high-grade cracksman did not carry his own kit; it was taken along another route by someone unlikely to attract notice. This was usually a woman known as a 'canary', and her other important job was to relieve the cracksman of his load as soon as possible after the crime, and carry it off in a different direction. Sometimes the parts of crow and canary were doubled, but in many robberies this can hardly have been feasible, and in any case it was important for the canary to spend as little time as possible on the scene of the crime.

Except when they were actually in use, a careful professional's tools were kept scrupulously swaddled, not only to avoid clinking but so that, if he was interrupted and had to run, he could in the last resort jettison the bagful without a crash that telegraphed his position to everyone in the neighbourhood.

Besides being bulky and compromising, the Victorian burglar's equipment was somewhat in arrears in technical development. By the beginning of the sixties no cracksman's drill could penetrate the modern steel products of the leading safe-makers. (Nobel was only at the threshold of his career and many years elapsed before the benefits of nitro-glycerine were widespread enough for 'soup' to be regularly used for safe-cracking.) The petter-cutter was slow and so could be defeated by a series of locks. From many points of view, with business premises as with private houses, treachery and corruption were better than drills and jemmies for tackling a stiff job. No instrument in the cracksman's arsenal could compare for speed and safety with a well-fitting key.

The difficulty, of course, lay in getting the help of someone who had access to the necessary keys, such as a clerk, messenger or cleaner. This meant delicate negotiations and perhaps the outlay of so much time and money that it would only be justified by very good takings. The accomplice might well have to be a person of some sense and adroitness, especially in an office or warehouse—and it was with such buildings, left locked from outside, that a key most often offered the ideal solution.

A careful wax impression was perhaps the best method, since it did not mean removing the key from the premises. Thieves are reported to have been willing to pay five pounds apiece for these impressions and no doubt they spent far more than that where the prize was big. However, it was sometimes very tricky to get hold of the original key to make the impression and another method was to take a blank key, coat it in wax and insert it in the lock so that the wards would leave marks from which a key could be cut. This was work for an expert and once again it probably meant bribing an employee to let him in.

Sometimes an astonishing number of keys had to be obtained. At a raid on a city business house, said to have required four months' preparation, the robbers first unlocked an outer door into a yard, then a triple-locked door requiring three separate keys, then the iron door securing the counting house. Here there was a safe which they opened in the same way and inside it a further locked recess for which they also had a key. This particular raid was obviously worth taking some pains over. Besides lesser valuables the thieves lifted bonds, negotiable bills and other scrip worth £13,000.

With some robberies, especially raids on warehouses, the main difficulty was breaking out rather than breaking in. When the gang had selected a suitable place and had got some knowledge of the layout and procedure, a respectable-looking man would visit it with an equally plausible companion not long before closing time. While his companion was engaged with the clerk or salesman, he would choose his moment, pretend to leave, and slip into some hiding-place behind bales or in a cupboard. When the staff had all left he could come out, but he might now have to negotiate several locked barriers to reach the others who, at a fixed time, would be waiting outside. Or again, burglars might force a back entry into a store but be unable to remove their booty without opening a way to the street. In either case similar problems were likely to arise: accomplices would have to be punctually admitted and awkward parcels got safely away at the right moment. If a vehicle was being used, its movements had to be arranged in advance to fit the schedule of the constable on the beat, and it had to be loaded and driven away quickly. Everything, in fact, depended on timing and on precise coordination between those in the building and those outside.

A raid on a draper's in Westminster Road points to the sort of trouble that could occur, and also throws a little light on police problems in the fifties. Two thieves got onto the top of some latrines near the back of the premises, climbed up a drain pipe onto the roof, and walked some way in the dark along a coping about nine inches wide. When they reached a skylight they were able to lower themselves into the shop by a rope ladder they had carried with them. At first all went well and they had picked up about thirty pounds worth of assorted silks when—either in a desperate attempt to alert them or through negligence—the crow outside the shop front gave a signal within earshot of a constable. The constable saw what was up and started twirling his rattle. The din must have thoroughly alarmed the burglars, but for some reason they did not retreat by the route they had come. Instead, they made their way over the roof to where an eight foot space separated them from the next housetop. They leapt over and hid behind a chimney stack.

Several officers came up onto the roof of the draper's but the thieves were invisible from that side and the police, unsurprisingly, were not eager to pursue a search (with bullseye lanterns) across a gap some fifty feet deep. However, the inspector who was now in charge came to the conclusion that the men who had been parcelling up the silk were somewhere among the roofs and posted a couple of plainclothes men to keep watch. At about eight a.m. the thieves came swarming down a rain spout that led into a water butt in a back yard, where a man called Fitzgerald was washing himself. Evidently he did not see them, for one of them landed on his back, at which he managed to cry out 'Murder and police!' Before they could get much farther they were both seized by the plainclothes men.

Even then the thieves were not at the end of their resources. While they were waiting trial someone had a talk with Fitzgerald—that recurring figure the thief's woman is said to have bribed him—and when the case came up he refused to identify either of the men. They had to be acquitted, though both were later transported for other crimes.

When they had secured their way out into the street, thieves still had to load up their loot and carry it away. This could be the riskiest part of the whole business. It only needed one passerby at the wrong moment, or a neighbour who happened to be lying awake, to ruin everything. Various things could make the getaway more difficult. It might be the nature of the load: quantities of textiles and furs were stolen, and though they were not particularly heavy they were bulky and awkward. There were also enterprising thieves who lifted ponderous spoil like sheet lead and copper from empty premises. Again, difficulties could arise from the site of the robbery. Some city cracksmen specialised in raiding country mansions and this might mean getting a helper from the neighbourhood with a fast horse and trap who was familiar with the local routes. Any problems of this sort not only made the actual departure more dangerous: they were likely to add to the number of people involved and so increase the chance of a leak.

Few things more sharply point the difference between conditions now and a hundred years ago than the fact that the commonest getaway vehicle from a town robbery was a one horse fly. It was relatively slow but no form of transport was less conspicuous. The cabman had to be fully party to the crime, briefed and prepared beforehand and often paid a proportion of the share-out. He waited at some distance till the moment arrived, sometimes with false licence plates fixed on his cab; then he drove up and, in response to a signal or message from the crow, brought the fly as close as feasible to the site of the burglary, preferably up to the very door. The booty was rushed out, packed in and rolled away; one member of the gang went with it and the rest dispersed. Even if the nature of the load did not absolutely demand it, this could still be the safest and most convenient method. A closed carriage rattling through the streets in the small hours was less likely to be stopped than a man lugging a bag or a covered coster cart.

Once the thieves were clear, the chief danger lay at the other end of the journey. The goods were often taken direct to the receiver, and receivers' premises were liable to be under observation. Even if a constable merely happened to see the cab being unloaded or disappearing into the yard of a public house, it could easily make him suspicious. In well managed schemes, therefore, another lookout was waiting by the destination, and if he did not signal the all-clear the cabby drove on.

One part of the cracksman's outfit was not mentioned in the list of tools quoted earlier. He often carried a cosh. The patterns were similar to those favoured by footpads, including the metal ball on a length of cord or gut, and the purpose was the same: to cut short outcry and disable resistance. Occasionally a burglar deliberately showed himself to a victim, creeping into a bedroom and terrorising the occupant into producing cash or jewellery by 'swinging the stick'; but that was only for the cruder sort of criminal who gratified (and also frustrated) himself by these displays of ferocity.

House robbers are the only sort of thieves, except poachers, who are commonly reported as carrying firearms, and on the whole it seems it was the more skilled and sophisticated ones who were likeliest to have a pistol. Revolvers (though they became popular with army officers in the fifties) were unfamiliar, clumsy, pocket-bulging things. Small single- and double-barrelled pistols were common articles, bought and sold without hindrance and easily hidden; the general introduction of percussion caps had made them reliable and at short range a marble-sized ball had great stopping power.

Householders and their servants quite often used firearms when confronted with dangerous intruders: this appears to have been especially so on farms, but the urban housebreaker, too, ran a fair risk of stopping a charge. It was not uncommon for a responsible manservant to sleep armed in the pantry or wherever the household silver was kept. Two cases that occurred in 1850, both referred to in some detail by Binny, show firearms in use.

In the first, two men named Edgar and Blackwell were involved in a scheme to burgle the shop of a Regent Street furrier who lived on the premises. They were apparently smart, practised criminals but had become over-confident; both were prosperous-looking and Edgar is said to have cut an elegant figure with a frilled shirt and considerable display of jewellery. Next to the furrier's was a public house, and they went there late one evening with a third man who was to act as crow. Edgar and Blackwell soon drifted out into the yard, where there was a lavatory, and no one noticed that they had not returned when the place shut at midnight. However, instead of remaining quietly in the yard until the crow had seen that everything was clear and signalled them to start, they became impatient and went up a fire escape on to the roof of the house they meant to enter. Close above the parapet was an attic window from which they removed two panes and the frame in between. It was while they were doing this that the results of their impatience caught up with them: a maid coming up to bed without a light discovered what was happening, crept silently downstairs and told her employer. Soon enough the furrier appeared like a jack-in-a-box at the window with a barker in each hand and told them he would shoot them unless they gave themselves up. Blackwell was so disconcerted by this that he toppled off the parapet, fell three storeys, and was instantly killed. Edgar scrambled for safety, managed by a 'desperate leap' to reach another roof, and went down by a trap door into a house that fronted on a side street. The people living there woke up, and in trying to escape them he made another desperate jump, this time from an upstairs bedroom into the road. He dislocated his ankle. Late passers-by saw him come down and he was soon in the hands of the police, who economically pushed him into a cab with Blackwell's corpse and carried them off to Vine Street station.

The second case concerned three ex-convicts who, at two o'clock on an October morning, broke into a house by Regent's Park belonging to a rich American. They climbed a wall into the garden behind the house and got into a back parlour where the butler was asleep, a loaded sporting gun at hand. The point of entry was dangerous but in one way it was well chosen, for they were able to open the window and the shutter behind it with only a knife and jemmy, and so quietly as not to disturb the sleeping servant. They could easily have unprimed his gun but apparently they did not see it. They simply opened the door of the room, which was locked on the inside, and began making their way upstairs. On the stairs one of them stumbled noisily enough to wake the butler, who got up—not much alarmed, since he did not take his weapon. He found two of the thieves and grappled with them, meantime trying to rouse the household, till he was floored by a blow from a cosh. In a panic, the three now bolted back into the garden through the window they had forced, but found it hard to get over the walls. The butler got to his feet, took hold of the gun, which was loaded with game-shot, and called to them to stop. One of them, named Mitchell, was just getting over the wall when the butler fired. Part of the charge caught him in the upper back, but he struggled on, got to the top and escaped. The other two had still failed to get away when the police, hearing the gunshot, arrived and collared them.

From 'an anonymous correspondent' the police south of the Thames learned that a man who had been wounded in an attempted burglary near Regent's Park was in bed in a house in an unsavoury district off Blackfriars Road, where he lay dressed in a woman's nightgown and cap. The inspector who followed this up cannot have had much difficulty in seeing through Mitchell's disguise—he is described as a stout pug-faced blackguard of about forty—and the unfortunate man, dressed in his cotton-stuff coat pocked with shot-holes, was carried off to Marylebone police court.

Despite the skill with which they broke in, Mitchell and his companions must have been men with very poor professional standards. It is easy to understand how, in the darkness, they missed the gun, but not why they made no effort to immobilise the butler. They could easily have fastened the door of his room behind them, and this was so common a trick that the police went out of their way to warn citizens of the danger of being locked in their bedrooms by burglars. It is hardly conceivable that they meant to leave the house by going back past the butler, loaded with their plunder, and over the awkward garden wall. The usual way was to leave by the front door, but these thieves seem to have made no effort to secure any line of retreat. They were all jail birds, known to the police (one, aged 34, had served ten years transportation) and it is very likely that capable and careful criminals were unwilling to work with them: men who had done a lot of time were often unstable and devitalised. As a result of this bungled attempt, they were all sentenced to transportation for life.

That sort of encounter suggests a state of armed warfare between criminals and society, but in fact the most efficient thieves tried hard to avoid violence. Those who carried pistols were more likely to use them when they were cornered in some rookery hideout than at the site of a robbery: in a world without internal combustion engines, a shot at night set sashes opening and policemen running. The limitations of road transport also

discouraged violence in another way. In the horse and railway age it was not easy for anyone to get safely away after committing an act of open brigandry in a well populated country where most men's hands were against the thief. Horses were slow and to use the railway a robber had to pass through a station where he would be seen by various people: a train could be a trap. Really ambitious robberies were almost invariably clandestine, designed to remain totally unsuspected until all was over; the last thing an expert cracksman wanted was the uproar of a gunfight.

Perhaps the most sensational theft of the mid-century was the removal of £12,000 in gold coin and ingots from a train. Round the time of the Crimean War, shipments of gold from London and Paris were regular enough to attract the attention of criminals and allow careful plans to be laid, and this particular gang took full advantage of the opportunities. So far as was ever revealed, the prime mover was a man called Pierce. He had a criminal record and had been employed in a betting shop—a common hang-out for disreputable characters. Pierce brought into the scheme two vital accomplices; a clerk in the South Eastern Railway's traffic department by the name of Tester and a skilled screwsman, Agar. There must also have been other helping hands, perhaps unaware of the full scope of the plan.

The routine with the bullion was to pack each consignment in sealed iron-bound boxes which were placed inside steel safes. These were loaded on a London-Folkestone passenger train and at Folkestone harbour transferred to the Boulogne steam packet. The railway officials, who were responsible for the gold in transit, evidently felt such confidence in the heavy modern safes that no other special precautions were taken; the consignments travelled in the guard's custody in his van with other luggage. (The guard did not, of course, leave his van while the train was moving.) The safes had similar double locks and needed two keys to open them; and there were two sets of these keys in the railway company's possession, one with the traffic superintendent in London, the other at Folkestone.

The conspirators spent more than a year preparing for the big pull, during which time they achieved two essential and tricky objectives. They succeeded in corrupting a guard called Burgess who was sometimes employed on the run; and they got duplicates of the safe keys. This last task was complicated by the fact that the two keys comprising a set were not kept together and regulations at the London office were fairly stringent. However, when the safes were temporarily withdrawn from service for overhaul by Chubb's, the makers, a chance presented itself. Tester, the traffic clerk, was able to get hold of a single key for long enough to show it to Agar who took a wax impression. Then slackness at the traffic department at Folkestone provided another opportunity. Pierce, who had been keeping the place under observation and was lurking ready, found a moment when there was no clerk in the place and slipped in. There, in an unlocked cuboard, was the key they wanted, and he was able to remove it, get another quick impression taken by Agar, and put it back in its place without anyone apparently being the wiser.

The safes were finely made affairs and could not be expected to yield to keys rough-copied in this way, even by an adept. However, though it was irregular, it was not very unusual for a passenger to travel in the van (for instance if a valuable animal had to be looked after) and Agar boldly accompanied Burgess when he had a gold consignment on board and tried out his new keys on the safes, filing and adjusting them until the locks responded perfectly. All was now ready.

One day in May 1855 Agar and Pierce, equipped with several couriers' bags took first class tickets to Folkestone. The porters who put the bags in the guard's van must have found them particularly heavy for their size, as they contained a large quantity of small-shot sewn in pockets. Pierce took a seat in a carriage but Agar, waiting till the train was just moving out, hopped into the van at the end of the train, an action that evidently excited no particular notice. Their information was correct; Burgess was in charge and three safes on board. Agar unlocked one, carefully opened a bullion box, removed the gold, substituted lead shot, refastened and resealed the box, locked up the safe again, and put the gold in his courier bag in place of the lead. At Redhill Tester met the train and collected the bag with the gold, while Pierce walked down the platform and managed to join Agar in the van. During the rest of the journey they took part of the contents of the other two safes, substituting lead, resealing and relocking as before. At Folkestone, while the safes were being unloaded, they hid in a dark corner of the van; then when all was clear they got out with their heavy bags. Instead of returning direct to London they went first to Dover. They had previously got hold of tickets for the Ostend-Dover crossing, and gave the impression of being travellers from the continent.

The theft was not discovered until the safes were eventually opened in France, when a discrepancy was noticed in the weight of the box. Reports of the case roused great excitement: the substitution of the lead, the sealed bullion boxes and the locked, undamaged safes made a dramatic newspaper story, and of course immediately directed attention to the officials responsible for packing up the gold in the first place. It was not until after endless enquiry and many abortive arrests that, eighteen months later, the authorities got a firm line. And then, seemingly, it was only through a stroke of luck. Agar was arrested over an affair involving a cheque forgery. He had a mistress by whom he had had a child, and now, in a desperate situation, he wanted her to be given some money from his share of the proceeds of the train robbery. But Pierce, who was actually holding the funds, seems to have decided either that this was a good opportunity to cheat his partner or that it would be dangerous to let the woman handle the money. Either way, his reluctance to disgorge had fatal results. Agar's woman knew something about how the robbery had been carried out, and when she was convinced that Pierce meant to cheat her, she turned informer. Agar, in Newgate and facing transportation, followed suit. Pierce, Tester and Burgess were all caught and sentenced, on Agar's evidence, to long terms.

The fate of the train robbers points up the great deterrent that faced all cracksmen. Without proper preparation and organisation, robbery was likely to be both risky and miserably unprofitable. Yet, by an obvious paradox, the more elaborate the arrangements for a burglary, the greater the chance of some blunder or betrayal. To each associate everyone else involved—inside accomplice, screwsman, buck cabby, crow, canary, negotiator of stolen property—was another hostage to fortune.

The police, like their enemies, relied on inside information, and the surprise encounters, anonymous denunciations, betrayals by jealous mistresses and similar lucky strokes constantly cited at this period to explain their successes are too numerous to be convincing. It is worth recalling that detectives and informers were, politically, a highly sensitive topic, and when the new police were found using undercover methods it aroused widespread hostility. Much of this was rather illogical, considering the traditional importance of informers and the record of the London magistrates' runners who were still active up to 1839; but there was a widespread fear that the new police would become an instrument of state authority like the foreign gendarmeries. These misgivings were encouraged by scandals over plainclothes constables who had gone beyond their proper role and acted as *agents provocateurs*. The authorities were therefore at pains to emphasise that the British peeler's prime function was to *prevent* crime occurring by his conspicuous presence, rather than to gather in wrongdoers. Emphatically he was not, like the agents of continental autocrats, to cultivate a jail-harvest. The use of plainclothes policemen at all was suspect and played down by police authorities: at the end of the sixties the official detective force at Scotland Yard was less than twenty officers, a tiny appendage to a total establishment some nine thousand strong. (This was certainly only a fraction of the men actually engaged in detective duties.)

But, whatever the public might feel, 'criminal officers' in London and elsewhere had to get convictions if they were to keep their enemies in check, and they could only do that by getting to know the underworld those enemies inhabited and in some ways coming to terms with it. It is an axiom of criminal investigation that a detective's efficiency depends on criminal contacts whom he must cultivate and safeguard—and with whom his relations are necessarily personal and confidential. Unquestionably, the connection between police and underworld was far more intimate and complex than most contemporary accounts would ever lead one to suppose.

There was one type of house-robber who was much less menaced than most by this network of police contacts. This was the 'snoozer'. It was a misleading name, for his habits were notably wakeful: the snoozer was a well dressed, apparently well behaved man who worked hotels. This type of thieving went on even in modest board-and-lodging places, but the skilled snoozer's proper place of work was an inn or hotel of some standing, catering for a transient clientele. He belonged to the aristocracy of the criminal underworld, and his craft called for a presentable manner, quick observation, cool nerves, and a delicate touch with one or two small pieces of screwsman's equipment.

A typical snoozer gave the impression of being on some sort of business. He arrived at the hotel, booked a room, and quietly began to study his fellow guests and the layout of the place. His manner with servants and strangers was easy and encouraging. He dined, for choice, at 'the ordinary', perhaps sharing a bottle with a neighbour, and afterwards smoked a companionable cigar with his fellow travellers or lounged, chatting, where he could see people collecting their bedroom keys. After retiring for the night in the ordinary way, he waited until all was quiet and then came out wearing slippers to visit the rooms of those he had marked down as best worth attention. Guests who snored loud enough to be heard in the passage were a particular boon. The locks of hotel bedrooms were not usually complex and it was a common practice to leave the key in after turning it. The thief only had to take an 'outsider' and gently turn it back. If the door was fastened but the lock empty he tried a skeleton. Either way, he worked very fast.

When he had made as large a collection as seemed wise the snoozer returned to his room, packed up his takings, and left very early next morning. Unless he was unlucky he was away before his victims had woken and discovered their loss. Hotels at railway stations were convenient, for an early train provided both the means and the explanation of an early departure. Also these hotels were used by commercial travellers, and it says a lot for the snoozer's coolness and resource that he not only preyed on that alert and knowing fraternity but now and then passed himself off as one of them, joining in the elaborate ritual of the commercial room.

The coming of steam had certainly made travelling cheaper, but by modern standards it could still be an expensive business. Apart from rail fares, it might cost a great deal to hire horses to take one on beyond where the railway reached. Hotel food was dear and the traveller seems never to have stopped tipping. For all these reasons a good supply of ready money might be needed on a journey, so that hotel thieving could be highly profitable. At an hotel near King's Cross a snoozer is reported to have lifted more than £700 at a single sweep. On the other hand the risks of the game were plainly very great and must have increased as the thief, continually on the move, became known to an increasing number of regular travellers. It is hard to think that anyone can have worked the lay successfully over a long period, unless he moved from country to country.

Certainly one strikingly bold snoozer either was or passed himself off as a visitor from the States, since he was known as American Jack. This man had the misfortune to be caught, brought before the recorder of Chester, and sent to prison. He managed to escape, and as he had connections who were ready to set him quickly on his feet, he turned up almost at once at Bacon's Hotel in London, a highly respectable haven for members of the ruling class. Here, as luck would have it, he ran into the recorder who had sentenced him and engaged him in casual conversation without being recognised. Undeterred by this, he then broke into sixteen rooms and successfuly decamped with the spoil. This outrage stimulated the lawyer's memory; he recalled where he had seen his hotel acquaintance before and—feeling perhaps a bit sheepish—went to Bow Street station and reported what had happened.

As Mayhew's collaborator Hemyng remarks in his account of the case, it was common knowledge that where 'no reward is offered for the apprehension of an eminent criminal the police are not so active as when they have a monetary inducement to incite them'. On this occasion American Jack's effrontery served him well. The management of a very superior private hotel were naturally *not* anxious to advertise the fact that they had welcomed a notorious burglar who had robbed their clients right and left without hindrance. They not only offered no reward: they must have exerted themselves to pacify the victims and persuade them not to do so. At any rate no offer was made. American Jack disappeared into hiding, it was believed among the purlieus of the vice trade in the alleys off Haymarket. Despite the double offence of jailbreak and robbery he was not arrested. And here we get an unusual glimpse of the plain bread-and-butter aspects of thief taking. A waiter who had worked in one of the nighthouses of the quarter told a police sergeant that the finger could be put on the wanted man for only twenty pounds. No one would put up the money and the snoozer quickly got away to France, where he became mixed up in a big jewel robbery, was caught and sent to the galleys.

Women sometimes went in for hotel thieving, normally in partnership with a man, but apart from such liaisons the snoozer

seems to have been a lone operator. Of course, like every professional thief, he needed contacts and a refuge, and it would
have been out of keeping with underworld usage if he had not
sometimes made a deal with a boots or a chambermaid. But for
the most part he was on his own, free from the risks of betrayal
and the need to share the takings involved in a big break-in.
Further, while he stole watches, pins, dressing-case fittings and
of course bank-notes, all of which would probably go to the
receiver, a large part of what he took was hard coin. This was a
great advantage, and not merely because of the receiver's heavy
profit: ready cash gave the thief independence, lack of it was apt
to make him the receiver's creature.

No aspect of crime lends itself less to pat description than
receiving. Between fence and thief all sorts of relationship were
possible.

At one extreme, a fence might be the real boss of a gang, the
moving spirit in its activity. Behind many crimes was an obscure
figure known as the 'putter-up', the man who conceived the
design and got others to carry it out, while he himself remained
in the background. He might be the keeper of a pub or lodging
house which was a centre for criminal contacts; or he might be
in some trade such as plumbing or decorating which had no
obvious associations with crime but offered good opportunities
for choosing projects. In London a number of putters-up were
perfectly well known to the police, but were so shrewd and careful that they carried on for years with impunity. These shadowy
entrepreneurs must always have been fences, or at least closely
concerned in handling the stuff stolen on their initiative; otherwise they would have had great difficulty getting hold of their
share of the profits.

At the other extreme, the receiver might merely be a shop-
keeper who occasionally bought goods about whose origin he
took care not to enquire. The word covers alike the promoter
of big robberies, a kidsman such as Larry of the Adelphi, and any
unscrupulous retailer prepared to buy a chunk of pilfered bacon.

The essential function of the receiver is to get stolen property
back into legitimate circulation. A business of this sort is by
nature two-faced, and the receiver's tendency to hunt with the
hounds and run with the hare—the intimate connection between
receiving and informing—is as clear in the underworld of the

nineteenth century as in that of the seventeenth (and for that matter the twentieth). This association with treachery is obviously the reason why the fence has traditionally been portrayed with such distaste.

It is not difficult to appreciate the position in which a receiver could find himself. His stake in some legitimate business—at once the cover for his criminal activities and a source of regular earnings—kept him tethered and vulnerable. Publicans, loan-shop keepers and people of that sort in poor areas were very exposed to criminals, and the fence was all the time dealing with dangerous men against whom he often could not openly invoke the law. At the same time, once the police were on to him (and it was enough for one cornered client to blab) he and his premises were forever after liable to be under scrutiny. He was forced to play off the forces menacing him, and without supposing every fence an informer, far less a monster of gratuitous treachery, it is easy to imagine circumstances in which it was almost impossible for a known receiver to avoid becoming a double agent.

No one can know how often such situations arose. It seems clear that the big receivers were good at steering clear of trouble, since there were not many convictions for large-scale deals. (Though that is not a final argument. A big receiver might well be convicted only on one quite trifling offence, and convictions for small-scale receiving were very common.) So far as the police were concerned one must remember that the trade was hydra-headed. There was no chance of extirpating it, and there was little to be gained by cutting off every known (and so partly controllable) intake simply for the sake of directing the flow down fresh, undiscovered channels.

There is a natural affinity between receiving and second-hand trading. A typical place for a cracksman to take his haul might be a small business licensed to deal in gold and silver, where trinkets and second-hand watches, pieces of lace and ormolu chimney ornaments were displayed in the window and precious scrap could be handled in the back workroom. It was not merely a matter of passing the goods on. Watches had to be 'christened' (that is, the identifying marks had to be deleted and others substituted) and this was a tricky, time-consuming business. Jewels had to be reset and perhaps recut. Anyone caught at these jobs was as good as convicted, and the small second-hand shop gave him the cover he needed.

Taken as a whole, the second-hand business was a catholic sort of commerce that traded in a wide variety of things. Along Petticoat Lane, on the boundary of the City, goods were on sale ranging from steam engine parts to fancy buttons, from coffins to shoe buckles. A stone's throw from the southern end was a rectangular enclosure of about an acre of damp ground surrounded by a high plank wall: lit at dusk by reddish oil flares, it was an animated and noisy scene. Shouting hawkers offered sheep's trotters and other delicacies while from a raised stand in the centre a Jew cried glasses of hot wine; but most of the hubbub rose from the throng of traders. Sellers sat on benches before reeking mounds of clothes, boots, skins, whalebone, umbrellas, whips and articles of every description, watching and chaffering with the rummaging buyers. In a corner there was a kind of refreshment room where more confidential negotiations could be carried out over drinks and games of draughts. This place, in every sense unsavoury, was the Houndsditch Clothes Exchange. To the south the trade continued patchily down to the swarming alleys and pavements of Rag Fair (Rosemary Lane). In fact there stretched in a disjointed line down the eastern flank of the City, bordering a series of criminal rookeries, a sort of flea market zone where the activities of the innumerable backstreet dealers who dotted every low urban district in the country, were reflected on a greatly magnified scale. Swept into this market's currents, a stolen article soon became (or could be made) untraceable.

Of all trades, it was probably the one in second-hand clothes that handled the most stolen stuff. Stealing clothes is the most frequently mentioned crime of the period and there must have been a very large number of articles to dispose of. Most poor people seem to have despised 'translated' garments but many of them could not avoid using them. Genteel men and women would not wait for their clothes to wear out before discarding them (they were almost morbidly conscious of a worn nap) and second-hand woollen cloth in decent condition was better wear than the damp-retaining cotton stuff which was the best new material most of the labouring class could afford. (The musty odour of damp cotton fustian was held, like the smell of toasted herring, to be characteristic of the lower orders.)

Some expensive items—for instance top-boots—were bought second hand by people ready to pay a fair price for a dressy article, while the wretchedest slops found a market among those whose poverty made them accept whatever covered them cheapest, often with grotesque results. There was a whole sweat-shop industry engaged in renovating garments for resale; turning, patching, faking, working up one pair of shoes out of two, and so forth. Rags beyond hope were baled for paper or sold to manufacturers of shoddy (to be picked apart in infernos of filth and fluff, cleaned and rewoven into poor-quality cloth).

In the second-hand and reach-me-down slop trade, the shopman who wanted to stay solvent can sometimes have had little choice about handling stolen goods. It was a highly competitive business, with rival traders often concentrated together so that customers were encouraged to compare every price. Alleys were lined with almost identical little open-fronted shops, and markets crowded with stalls carrying exactly similar stock. Plainly no class of goods offers more scope for flexible pricing than what has never been paid for in the first place, and the trader whose scruples gave that advantage away to his rivals would not have lasted long in a line where any sort of qualms were out of place. There was no secret about it; in places shop after shop would flaunt great variegated bunches of silk kingsmen whose origin was perfectly well understood by everyone in the place, including the policeman on his beat.

'Ou' clo',' the plaintive yell of the barrow buyer, was a synonym for the Jew. In conventional minds there was also a strong connection between the Jew and the fence, and from Fagin downwards the stereotype of the dealer in shady goods has a Semitic nose. It is worth digressing to see how far this idea corresponded with the facts.

In the first place Jews undoubtedly played a large part in second-hand trading as a whole, especially in old clothes. They organised and controlled the Houndsditch Exchange and some of them ran businesses there whose size was out of all keeping with their own dilapidated appearance. Wholesale and retail, every part of the trade in cheap or second-hand clothes was Jewish territory, though they had no monopoly of it. A poor immigrant who wanted to start a business had to find one that needed almost no capital outlay, and that was certainly true of street trading in cast-off goods which at its lowest merged with straightforward scavenging. (For this reason it also appealed to

the Irish, the only other group of nineteenth-century immigrants that mattered in the underworld.) Further, prejudice against Jews was widespread and there were many occupations which it was difficult for them to enter. They were also hindered by the restrictions their own religion imposed. In the cheap clothing business, with its various ramifications, they found a trade that was open to them, and all the more freely because it tended to be despised by native Englishmen.

There is, however, no evidence that it was the Jews who were responsible for its connection with crime. The whole business was permeated with stolen goods and the belief that the Jews handled them out of proportion to their numbers can be put down to prejudice.

The same thing is true of the notorious exploitation that went on in the cheap garment-making trade. The very fact that it was so accessible to immigrants, who were desperate to secure a toe-hold and ready to submit to atrocious conditions, naturally kept down standards and increased its fertility as a breeding ground of prostitution and delinquency. But again there is no reason to suppose that the Jews as a body gained. Far more of them were sweated than sweaters, and no inborn shrewdness and resilience saved thousands of them from literally murderous exploitation.

Another occupation which had connections with stolen property and in which Jews played an important part was money-lending. The dread phrase 'in the hands of the Jews' meant being entangled with the discounters of extortionate bills and promissory documents which, with the aid of a good deal of lawful chicanery, were made the instruments of a staggering usury. Spendthrift young gentlemen with prospects were popularly supposed to be the favourite victims (heroes in novels often got into trouble by backing a friend's bill) though in reality it was perhaps more often the desperate clerk or small businessman whose bones were picked clean. This disreputable trade was at the centre of a shadowy half-world of finance, and on its fringes it connected with many different sorts of crime. Jews were by no means the only people involved in it. Very likely they were not even the most important ones, but it is clear that they provided enough of its front-men, the cajolers, sharks and bullies, to attract most of the odium.

Jews were also traditionally connected with another form of money-lending—pawnbroking. It has become hard to realise what an important place in urban life the pawnbroker used to fill, but without him the lives of many poor people would have been even more precarious.[1] It is a travesty of his position to suppose that he merely pandered to the lower classes' inclination to turn everything they possessed into alcohol: he also acted, in effect, as their banker. For instance, a working man would buy

---

[1] It was not only among the poor that the three balls were an important sign. There are endless literary references to the way in which middle class people resorted to this shaming expedient and the very prosperity of the trade shows that it must have been used by more than one class. (Between 1851 and 1871 the number of registered pawnshops increased by 130 per cent.) It was not unknown for a housewife afraid of being seen visiting the place herself to send a servant round the corner to uncle with the teaspoons.

something relatively expensive, say a good greatcoat, by giving practically all the cash he had for it; then he pawned it for food and rent, redeemed it on a payday for a Sunday's wear, re-pledged it again for a smaller loan, and so on until, if no disaster occurred, it became his whole-time property. This arrangement was less costly than the tallyman's hire purchase terms: pawn-brokers' rates were controlled by statute, and though they found ways to bend the law, their greed was checked by fear of losing the licence they needed to carry on their business.

It is hard to guess quite how far pawnbrokers justified their reputation for shady dealings. Despite all the opportunities it provided, the pawnbroker's was not an ideal place for handing over a really valuable piece of stolen property. Not only were his premises more open to investigation than an ordinary trader's, but if he was prosecuted he was unlikely to get the benefit of a magistrate's doubts and was in danger of forfeiting his precious licence. One experienced police officer put it on record that he found the trade's bad reputation largely unjustified.

Below the regular pawnbrokers, however, were the un-licensed 'dollyshops'. To these squalid back street dens the very poor brought their trumpery (but perhaps essential) posses-sions—an iron frying pan, a blanket, a set of worn tools. The security was chancy, the transaction technically illegal, and to secure a tiny loan one might have to pay twopence or threepence for a week's use of a shilling. The dollyshop keeper was a creature of the social depths and there can be no question that stolen goods often passed through his hands. His den was a natural resort of beggars and sneak thieves with something to dispose of.

In all these trades the Jews played a large part and in many of them they tended to rise to the top. As a group, poor Jews appear to have been more self-disciplined than their non-Jewish fellows and, though they were often wretchedly ignorant, they were also more commercially sophisticated. Their frugality, the strength of their family ties and the confidence they often put in one another helped to make them prominent in any activity in which they took a large share: and as we have seen, social forces pushed many of them into trades which had close connections with crime. Jews, like their neighbours, could take easily enough to thieving and trickery, but on the whole their strong family-based culture made them less subject to the despairing reckless-

ness and resentment that drove so many poor people into delinquency. The truth seems to be that in various ways the Jews
were noticeably superior to the general run of the slum population among whom circumstances had forced them to live. Their
chief importance to the underworld was that a number of the
more unscrupulous ones took to crime (and notably receiving)
with more intelligence and vigour than was usual among their
gentile neighbours. In a word, Jews in slums raised the mental
average—including that of the professional criminals.

Despite the strong connection between receiving and second-
hand trading, there were other trades that provided even more
convenient cover for the fence. He needed to be in a position
where he could be easily contacted without being compromised,
and what could be better than a public house, open from dawn to
midnight, where no visitor's presence need mean anything more
than a wish for a drink? Except for the modern gin palaces, pubs
in working class districts usually carried on their trade in poky
little apartments that lent themselves to confidential meetings.
Pubs in towns were often on corner sites with entrances on different streets; often, too, there was a high-gated yard where a trap
could be loaded or unloaded in comparative privacy. In many
low districts there were pubs well known as criminal 'lumbers',
patronised by thieves and sometimes dangerous for a stranger
to wander into. But one may suspect that it was at more discreet
rendezvous (like the Hole in the Wall, described by Arthur
Morrison in his documentary novel of that name) that most
publican-receivers carried on business. The celebrated flash
pubs were too much frequented by detectives and informers.

More, even, than publicans, it is lodging house keepers and
deputies who are most often mentioned as receivers, though
improved policing, and perhaps better living standards, reduced
their share of the trade in the second half of the century. For the
most part they dealt in clothes and other things of low value, and
it is not difficult to see why netherskens were bad places for
dealing in highly priced swag. Privacy was almost unknown in
them, and among all the people who drifted in and out there was
very likely to be someone happy to inform about anything
valuable enough for a reward to be offered. However, if the
individual items in which he dealt were of little value, it did not
follow that in the aggregate a lodging house receiver might not

carry on a considerable business. Men like the celebrated Taff Hughes probably made good livings. He had a place conveniently near Petticoat Lane and he was supplied by a number of young thieves to whom he would pay a shilling for a pair of new leather Wellingtons (worth at least ten times as much). If any of his smaller clients came in empty handed this grotesque kidsman removed the strap that held on his wooden leg and flogged them unmercifully.

London was the centre of the receiving trade, and a large part of the more valuable goods stolen throughout the country eventually reached the London market. There were customers here for every sort of commodity, and goods that might have been dangerous to put on sale locally, even in a great provincial centre, could emerge into the commercial daylight. For shipment overseas, the vast port provided ideal facilities, including innumerable small craft that plied day and night on every sort of errand among the shipping in the fog-infested river. (Some, with little braziers amidships, peddled hot grog from waterside pubs to the night watches.) Little short-voyaging vessels, especially from the Low Countries, were forever shuttling back and forth from the Continent and never entered the dock enclosures.

It was just this pattern of small enterprises making up a vast and complex whole that made London such a suitable place for the receiver. Despite a number of great firms, and the Thamesside heavy industry, east London was an area of countless small businesses, and in this it echoed the organisation of the underworld. There were some big criminal entrepreneurs, but on the whole the criminal underworld was not organised, or even much influenced, by its leading citizens: fortunately for the rest of society it remained essentially a community of small operators.

To all appearances, this was as true of receiving as of other crimes. The man who refurbished the coat, christened the watch, melted the plate, cracked the diamond or hung out the demonogrammed kingsman in his doorway—he, rather than the mere taker-in of loot, was the key, indispensable fence: and he, so far as the record goes, was typically a man in a small way of business up a side street.

CHAPTER SEVEN

Beggars

In the morning, when the residents were getting themselves ready for the day's work, the kitchen of a beggars' lodging house must have presented a grotesque scene. Many 'gegors', or professional beggars, made their way by exhibiting wounds and sores, and faking them realistically was a traditional art always open to fresh variations. It was known as the 'scaldrum dodge'.

One simple trick was to cover a patch of skin with a layer of soap and apply strong vinegar, so that what appeared to be large, yellow, matter-filled blisters formed; another was to hide a lump of raw meat under an elaborate clotted dressing. Even beggars with genuine mutilations found that a bit of artifice helped, and before starting work they would touch up the stumps of healed amputations so that they looked inflamed and purulent. Other poor wretches went to the lengths of searing and discolouring parts of themselves with gunpowder, or used vitriol to raise fresh sores and aggravate old ones. In the end they must often have produced a real injury by the means they used to fake one.

A common site for an artificial sore was the shin, where it justified a limp and could easily be shown without offending even a lady's modesty; but sometimes an eye or ear was inflamed and made to produce the effect of a discharge. The standard procedure was to cover the focus of interest with a coil of filthy bandage. When the gegor had waylaid someone suitable, he slowly unravelled the bandage as he talked, all the while urging closer inspection—which the revolting appearance of the dressing effectively discouraged.

'Working the shallow' was another common way of playing on physical distress. The typical 'shallow cove' was a man who called at houses in a half naked state asking for money and clothes. Some who followed the lay became expert wheezers and shakers, with graveyard coughs and an ability to fall into ghastly shivering fits that greatly increased their appeal. (A too-persistent shaker was in danger of acquiring an involuntary palsy so that he started vibrating at any time, in season and out.) The shallow was best worked in bad weather, and many of those who followed it had little need of pretence: they were already ill-clad and if they took off any of their few clothes in the hope of filling their bellies they must have suffered greatly for meagre gains.

The advantage of the system was that old clothes were easier to get than other forms of charity, while the importance Victorians attached to ample body covering (on grounds of health as well as propriety) no doubt made them all the readier to respond. If sixpences were rare, old shirts and waistcoats (known professionally as 'mittings' and 'bends') were fairly common and, according to the wear left in them, they are said to have fetched from three-halfpence to fourpence apiece from the barrow man or dollyshop. Barefoot 'limpers' specialised in collecting boots and shoes which, even when badly worn, still realised a copper or two: second-hand boot vampers could work temporary miracles with glue, heelball and varnish.

Since cast-offs were only to be got at people's homes, each begging expedition had to cover a fresh house-to-house round. This did not mean that shallow coves were continually on the pad: that would have been an inconvenient way of life for anyone who needed all the time to be within reach of a market for old clothes. Probably, like other house-to-house beggars, they often gave the impression of being tramps when in fact they were working from a fixed centre, usually a big town, and covering different sectors of the surrounding area in turn. An important advantage of this plan was that, except in London, there were likely to be different police authorities for the middle of the town, where the beggar lodged, and the residential areas outside it, where house-begging was most profitable. Experienced cadgers would make their way out to the edge of a great city and then, towards evening, come limping dustily back through the better-class suburbs, ready to explain that they were tramping artisans without means of a night's shelter. A favourite 'blob'[1] was to say one had trekked through England because there was work nearby for men trained in such-and-such a speciality, but it was

---

[1] A hard luck story (the same word as *blab*.) Those who begged by telling stories in this way were said to be 'on the blob'.

useless applying in rags or without some particular item of craftsman's kit. (If a beggar found his hands getting too soft to suit this story he could keep them horny by regular treatment with irons heated at paddingken fires and passed across the palms.) The most nearly ideal begging conditions are said to have been in prosperous residential suburbs on fine Sunday evenings when people could be caught returning from evensong or taking a quiet after-tea stroll, at peace with the world. (Where the servants went to evening service too, or had the afternoon off, suburban Sunday twilights also meant excellent opportunities for a quick break-in.)

Some beggars practised a form of the shallow by hanging about the streets in scanty tatters asking for alms; but the beggar who exposed too much of himself in a busy, respectable street risked attracting altogether too much notice and landing up in the House of Correction. On the whole, static begging was best practised by decorous-looking women and children, and of course by those (genuine or bogus) who were obviously crippled. Many beggars carried a card, slung round their necks or fixed to a tray of snells (hawkers' trifles) on which the way they had been crippled and their claims to charity were set out, sometimes at astonishing length. This procedure was known as 'standing pad on a fakement' and, compared with accosting, it was less likely to get one taken up or moved on as a nuisance. The trouble with standing pad was that the beggar had not only to face the chance of being moved on by the police, but also to get and hold his pitch against a great deal of competition: a good site was valuable. Many street beggars spent half their waking lives on the run, scuffling and pleading with passers-by or furtively dodging from one brief stand to another.

Among the stationaries, blind beggars were prominent. Untreated gonorrhoea, smallpox, industrial accidents and diseases, all increased the incidence of blindness among the poor; and for many of those who lost their sight, begging can have been the only hope of not disappearing for ever into the workhouse. Not all blind beggars, naturally, stood pad; some worked regular beats and at least a few managed to survive wandering about the country. Beggars were the only regular exponents (and presumably had been the originators) of the guide dog system—the dog not only leading the man but adding to his appeal. Beggars' dogs were taught to bring their master to a halt whenever a suitable passer showed interest, and we hear one poor old mid-Victorian mourning a dead guide most feelingly and remarking that his new one, not yet properly trained, would pull up to 'have a word' with other dogs so that his proprietor wasted his patter on empty air.

Sham blindness seems to have been a good deal less usual than one might at first suppose. It is not an easy thing to feign consistently over a long period; and though the police were inclined to be easy-going on genuine blind beggars, they were watchful and suspicious until satisfied of their bona fides. A blind man was liable to rough treatment in the brutish society of the streets, especially from the young, and a fake had to put up with a fair degree of ill-usage or give himself away. In his *Secrets of the Prison House* Arthur Griffiths cites an Irish blind beggar who had a dodge for turning this sort of persecution to account. He frequented country fairs where he would now and again latch on to some good-natured person to whom, in a most pitiful state of fear, he described the cruel baitings he suffered. He begged to be escorted clear of the crowd and set on his road. After being led some way he used to ask if there was anyone else in sight, and on being assured there was not, treacherously sprang on his companion, mauled him, picked his pockets and made off. The way he questioned his victims on whether the road was deserted was of a piece with the extraordinary consistency he showed in maintaining that he was, in truth, blind. Caught and sent to jail, he stuck firmly to his story, and in the face of persistent— and no doubt none too delicate-handed—efforts by the prison staff to prove him a sham, he betrayed no sign of being able to see anything. His patience was remarkable, but in the end he gave himself away by an uncontrollable thirst for revenge. A magistrate had ordered him to be birched for his crimes, blind or not, and he acknowledged the debt by later waylaying the man and furiously assaulting him in a way that made it perfectly plain he had the use of his eyes.

Finally one must mention a specialised and sometimes highly skilled faker—the professional fit-thrower or bogus epileptic. There were poor ragged alcoholics who would fall down in the street or tumble into roadside ponds, simply in hopes of being revived with a measure of spirits (it always happened close to a public house) but the proper bogus epileptic was a decent looking character, a neat, threadbare, hollow-eyed man whose favourite opportunity was a congregation coming out of church or chapel. At the right moment, before the good people dispersed, he collapsed on the ground in convulsions, limbs threshing, foam and cries escaping from his lips. On coming round he would confide something of his tragic circumstances to those who were helping him and produce a paper signed by a clergyman. This usually described the bearer as a man of excellent character, pious and industrious, but prone to seizures that had reduced him to undeserved penury, and it earnestly commended him to Christian charity. With luck a collection was taken up on the spot. The foam was produced by soap shavings under the tongue, and occasionally an examination by a doctor or some other suspicious witness led to the fake being exposed.

The scaldrum dodge exploited the miseries of the beggar's own body. Another kind of begging took advantage of the miseries of society. Troubles and slumps in industry, for example, not only added to the number of vagrants; they also provided opportunities for versatile gegors quick to exploit their topical appeal. A well publicised accident at a coal pit might produce a crop of sham survivors, hobbling about blackened and bandaged, usually in areas well away from the site of the disaster. Beggars on this sort of lay went in for quite elaborate histrionics. Sometimes a knot turned up at a house supporting in their midst a tottering sufferer, apparently *in extremis*, on whose behalf they modestly asked for a glass of water. It was unwise to let them in, however, for once inside they would change their manner and become hard to dislodge until bought off with silver. In good times, working class districts could be profitable, since the people who lived there knew all about the insecurities of a wage earner's life. In these places it could be useful to pass oneself off as having lost one's job through a lock-out or having been blacklisted as a striker, but that kind of pretence could be dangerous. Miners, iron workers and the like were often very open-handed but they were also notoriously rough customers, and a charlatan caught imposing on the feelings of a colliery village ran a real risk of a lynching.

The distress among handcraft workers ousted by technical development inspired a whole line of gegors. A favourite dodge was to represent oneself as a decayed lace maker, for here the appeal to charity could be doubled with a modest swindle.

Miserable, decent-looking characters tramped the streets armed with testimonials and pieces of cheap machine-made lace, offered as their own fine threadwork. Only desperation, they said, induced them to sell it in this way, and pity was helped by the prospect of acquiring the expensive stuff at a fraction of its normal price. Profits were good—collars at sixpence each were made from Brummagem strip lace at a ha'penny a yard—and the game worked so well that quite elaborately organised bands took it up. One band, working in London, had a long printed announcement supposed to be issued on behalf of fifteen Nottingham families. Ruined but courageous, they were engaged in raising funds to emigrate to Australia (the fashionable recipe for relieving unemployment). This document and a couple of lace samples were left at selected households by scouts who went on ahead spying out the land and, in regular mendicant fashion, marking the houses they visited with tell-tale signs. Guided by these, a strong follow-up party soon presented themselves, loaded with imitation lace and all ready to launch out in an affecting spiel. The purpose of the unsolicited samples, left without payment, was of course to blackmail scrupulous people into giving the followers-up a hearing.

About the mid-century, many who practised the scaldrum dodge swore their sores had been acquired in the Arctic, on one of the rescue parties sent after Franklin. Literary influences, too, had an effect. Hood's famous *Song of the Shirt* (published by 'Punch' in 1843) encouraged beggarwomen to pose as broken-down seamstresses, while ten years later the excitement roused by *Uncle Tom's Cabin* set off a minor boom in destitute negroes from the slave states. An exceptionally successful beggar of this sort is described as scrupulously clean-looking and dreadfully scarred, with a board on which the atrocities he had undergone were set out in some detail. However, whatever he had suffered, it had not been on American plantations: on investigation he proved to have come from Africa and to have been chosen and carefully coached for the part by his backers. No doubt he was a first-class investment, for despite their topical appeal genuine negro beggars seem to have stayed fairly rare. At the height of the boom, a number of optimistic Europeans corked their faces like Christy Minstrels in hopes of imposing on the public; but their careers soon ended in the police court.

As with thieves, the beggar's most important contacts were

the people from whom he collected information. From exchanges with other beggars, from paddingken keepers (who would expect to be paid for the service), from all sorts of hints and signs (including the marks left by forerunners on the outside of premises) he tried to learn who was worth approaching and how to tackle them. Ignorance of a neighbourhood's potential meant not only lost opportunities but blunders.

In general, ministers of religion were considered excellent prospects, and for many gegors with a line of pious cant 'gulling a choker' was a favourite exercise. But there were plenty of justices of the peace among the beneficed clergy, and a call at the wrong rectory could result in an encounter with an old-fashioned port-and-pepper incumbent and committal to the lock-up.

The whereabouts of retired naval and military officers were also well worth knowing, for they were often a soft touch for applicants who put up a convincing show of being ex-servicemen deserving better of a neglectful country (some of them, of course, actually were). Here again, inadequate briefing could easily lead to trouble.

People of almost any profession and opinion could be played on, if only their bents were known in advance, and knowing the servants could be as useful as knowing their employers. An archdeacon in Kensington, who was a perfect goldmine to mendicants, had to be laid up for and intercepted at the right moment; cadgers at the parsonage met his formidable butler— feelingly described by one old hand as 'a bugger and a half, *good weight*'. In short, nothing could make up for lack of knowledge, and the more ambitious the monkry the greater the need to be primed beforehand.

The most abominable feature of beggardom was the systematic employment of young children, who were often initiated into the business almost before they could walk.

Vagrant beggar families were a common sight, and infants must often have been painfully humped along simply because their parents had nowhere to leave them. But they could also greatly enhance an adult's appeal. Women going from house to house on the blob were sometimes accompanied by two or three little creatures, pale and woebegone but dressed with a neatness that contrasted touchingly with the mother's tattered appearance. They were taught to lisp out pathetic confirmations of her story. Blind beggars sometimes used a small child in the same way as a guide dog. A woman noticed by a chronicler of the Metropolitan Society for the Suppression of Mendicity, about thirty-four years old and paralysed in both legs, used to sit on a board with an infant propped in front of her, propelling herself with her hands. The pair roused a great deal of compassion, 'whereby she not only supports herself and child, but also maintains a strong, healthy man with whom she cohabits'.

But primarily 'grafting with chavies' meant setting children to beg on their own. Markets, passenger docks, big railway stations and similar places were often infested with tiny, pestering urchins ready to pick up anything eatable or saleable, plucking at the sleeves and scuffling under the feet of passersby with offers of pins and matches they had no intention of selling.

They would persist until they were discouraged by a blow or bought off with a penny. Constantly referred to as ownerless waifs, most of them seem in fact to have been useful pieces of property.

Standing by the terminus of the North London Railway, for instance you may witness the periodical visits of slinking and bedraggled women—weedy as to their apparel, and with the attenuation and pallid hue of much gin on their faces— who come to take of one or other of these poor little wretches the money they have 'picked up' during the day. Any one of these women may be the mother of one or more of the children, or may merely employ them to do her cadging. Sometimes she brings them slices of coarse bread and butter wrapped in a dingy handkerchief; occasionally a heavy-eyed sodden-looking man will wait for her at the street corner, or, in her absence may himself secure the few coppers which he extorts from the child, with an anxious glance round him lest he be observed. Both he and the woman, should they catch the eye of a passenger during their operations, will assume an expression of demure, poverty-stricken resignation, and affect to wipe away a tear as they contrive to display, by well-affected accident, the bread and butter they have 'gone without themselves'. . . . Mostly, however, they will avoid observation by stealthily pushing the child before them into some bye-place where there is nobody to interrupt them. What wonder that these miserable juveniles soon try to 'go on their own hook', and when they cannot start with a box or two of vesuvians take to pilfering.[1]

Beyond this crude extortion from ragged little outlaws, there were more scientific methods based on the complex contemporary attitudes to children. It is notorious that the taste of the period included an extraordinary relish for literary scenes in which a good-looking, fatally ill child, often of humble status, is released from suffering by an edifying death. However, Little Nell, the Little Match Girl, and all the countless others were ideal creations: between the prosperous bourgeois and the actual wild, verminous starveling in the gutter there was a gulf that inhibited any immediate warmth and charity. If he was moved to action, the obvious course for a level-headed citizen

---

[1] Thomas Archer *The Pauper, the Thief and the Convict*, p. 95.

was to send a guinea to the Mendicity Society. But nothing could be better calculated to touch a sluggish imagination and evoke a pre-conditioned response than a tranquil, wanly-pretty beggar child, wasted with misery yet as neat and almost as nicely dressed as one brought down to the drawing room from a respectable nursery.

This was known and traded on. Skilful manipulators of child beggars got them up with care in clean pinafores and collars and well-combed locks. Sometimes false ringlets were added, and where the child's face was not sufficiently spiritual-looking and suggestive of mortality, the eyes could be shadowed, or made to look hollower by a spotless bandage about the forehead. Several children might be stationed within a short walking distance of each other; they could then be conveniently intimidated into staying put and their takings could be regularly collected by a supervisor. It seems to have been quite a profitable style of begging even with very mediocre stands. Near Pentonville Hill, which was by no means an affluent place, four girls aged from five to twelve were reported to have kept an unmarried couple in idleness. (Two were claimed by the man as his own children, two by the woman.) Even in the savage mid-winter frost of 1853–4 when canals were ice-bound, these four little wretches were callously sent out and 'nearly frozen to death'—though one may question whether they were much better off when they were later shut up in the St Giles Union.

To profit from begging children, it was not necessary to breed them up from babyhood. Small boys and girls could be hired for a copper or two a day (though perhaps not very accomplished ones) and sometimes they changed hands permanently for a few shillings. No doubt it was partly by such trading that the master beggars who made a regular speciality of training and organising youngsters got hold of their human material. Their method of instruction remains obscure, but plainly some of them were exceedingly adept at teaching their pupils how best to exploit their childish pathos, for according to a contemporary report, children so schooled 'when turned out of hand by their tutors are generally the most successful impostors in the metropolis on account of their age'.[1]

In 1853 the Mendicity Society's records showed that children accounted for eleven per cent of registered cases, many of them

[1] Society for the Suppression of Mendicity. Report for 1852–3.

being the sole subsistence of people 'of the worst description'. This figure is almost certainly an underestimate. The Society was chiefly concerned with confirmed professional beggars in London (especially in the respectable districts where they were most obvious to the Society's subscribers) so its interest was in the children regularly trained and manipulated by professionals. But in fact parts of every large commercial town were alive with half-savage brats scratching a living by every means under the sun. To them cadging—like pilfering—was simply a matter of opportunity, and as natural as breathing. If they are included, child beggars probably outnumbered adults.

The police, hard put to it to keep juvenile thieving in bounds, were more or less defeated by the incessant street-arab mendicancy. Many urchins who lived by begging put up some sort of camouflage. Perhaps, like the tiny wretches who swarmed around King's Cross, they flourished a few damp lucifers under pretence of sale; or those who were a little older hung about by the gutter and rushed forward in squads offering to hold the horse's head whenever a carriage showed signs of stopping. The little make-believe roadsweeper who could 'only splash the mud from side to side with the stump of an old broom,' like the boy who turned cartwheels among the traffic or 'curled up his tiny body as closely as a woodlouse' and trundled himself along the pavement 'wabbling like an egg', was looked on by the public with a kind of favour: at least he was trying to earn a living rather than steal one. In the eyes of the law it might aggravate the offence to hawk without a licence or obstruct the highway; but a six foot officer cut a poor figure chivying a half-starved urchin and hauling him off to the tune of the crowd's ironical congratulations. Moreover he was likely to get no thanks for producing his capture. Magistrates were simply at a loss how to deal with these children, and unless one of them had already been before them on a more serious charge they were apt to let him go with a futile warning. In general the only place they could rationally send them to was the workhouse, which was where children usually were consigned when their parents were imprisoned for setting them to beg or when there was no one who would take responsibility for them. But parish authorities were often almost as reluctant to take in children as the children were to be taken, and many city poorhouses would certainly have been flooded out if every loose beggar child had been admitted. All the same, terror of the workhouse must have kept many an exploited little beggar—like many a little pickpocket —loyal to his master.

Leaving aside their tendency to turn into professional criminals, the hordes of juvenile beggars and half-beggars were a fertile source of nuisance. Where they were not kept severely in check, they might literally mob anyone unwise enough to get a reputation for generosity; they even chased down the road in howling throngs after cabs and buses in which they had spotted a favourite mark. If a victim was mobbed in this way in a narrow footpath and was not robust enough to scatter his (or her) pursuers, things might take an unpleasant turn. In London, many child beggars hung about the night resorts—prostitutes were well known to be free handed—and became involved in a great deal of mischief. Young sparks on a drunken 'frolic', tired of chasing little beggars and lashing out at them with their sticks, sometimes bribed them to cut all sorts of offensive capers. 'The drunken gentleman is always either jolly or spiteful,' some boys observed to Mayhew, who tells of small crossing sweepers encouraged by tipsy army officers to knock down a drunk passerby, sweep filth over a woman and set off an uproar at a pastrycook's by dancing on the tables.

Also, child beggars naturally lent themselves to the needs of sexual deviants. Little girls would hopefully pursue provincial visitors, foreigners and sailors, sometimes waiting about the entrances of city offices for a likely prospect to emerge. Their downward path was 'expedited by old debauchees . . . to whom their indecent language and abandoned indifference to modesty have been a fresh stimulus and a piquant gratification'.[1] No one remotely acquainted with the subject will doubt that small boys were active in the same way.

Until the seventies there were no means by which, even in theory, children could be required to attend school, outside certain institutions and occupations;[2] and though, by the fifties,

---

[1] Thomas Archer *The Pauper, the Thief and the Convict*, p. 98. Archer cites such corruption as an argument for state education.

[2] In 1858 a parliamentary commission reckoned that less than five per cent of children were receiving *no* elementary schooling. Granted the figure has been considered too low by competent historians, and that much of the instruction was admittedly wretched, it is still remarkable that such an estimate was feasible considering the miserable provision made for 'popular education' and the number of adult illiterates in circulation. The development from 1870 onwards of a national system of compulsory education was a powerful agency in altering the character of the juvenile (and so of the whole) underworld. The school attendance officer is, of course, a key figure in the social history of the last hundred years.

even some of the poorest were acquiring the rudiments of literacy (thanks partly to ragged schools and Sunday teaching) most juvenile beggars must have grown up wholly unlettered. Apart from anything else, many of them led vagrant or semi-vagrant lives, while those who lived by exploiting child beggars would not willingly put them in contact with the teachers, clergy and other welfare-working busybodies who concerned themselves with charitable education. Here workhouses and reformatories really could confer a benefit on the children who fell into their hands; for in a fast evolving industrial society, the analphabetic was at an ever graver disadvantage, whether he followed an honest or a criminal way of life. More and more jobs demanded an elementary education, and the unemployed workman who could not read or write was doubly likely to be reduced to beggary. Mendicancy was both a result and a cause of illiteracy.

If beggars of all ages were often illiterate, literary compositions of various sorts played an important part in their lives. Those who stood pad needed clear, tellingly worded notices to display, and there can have been very few beggars whose chances were not bettered if they could produce a testimonial or letter of introduction. Some grafts were entirely built up round ingenious documentary evidence, and for many professional beggars, whether they could read or not, it was vitally important to be in touch with a reliable screever.

Forging credentials and drawing up hard-luck petitions were the staples of the screever's trade. Satisfactory screeves must have been pretty hard to come by, at least outside the great centres, for cadgers would send many miles to London for the product of a skilled hand. (The man was usually to be found at some nethersken or pothouse.) Considering everything, fees do not seem to have been excessive. For a straightforward letter of recommendation the screever is said to have charged from sixpence to ninepence, and for certificates, petitions, etc., from one to three shillings according to length and the trickiness of the imposture. A 'ream monnicker' (the genuine signature of a ruined clergyman or some other person of standing reduced to screeving) might cost eighteen pence; while 'gammy monnickers' (forged signatures of well known and reputable people) were supplied at half a crown apiece. The beggars who bought this sort of thing tucked it carefully away: they liked to keep the papers in a condition neither so virgin as to excite suspicion nor worn enough to suggest countless previous inspections.

Gegors with experience of the sea or dockwork sometimes used to pose as shipwrecked survivors. A band would set out on tour together from a port town, tramping through country places in ragged but unmistakably nautical slops, scrounging their living from kind hearted farmwives and at the same time taking up subscriptions. Here is the major part of a screeve prepared for such an expedition:

THESE ARE TO CERTIFY, to all whom it may concern, that the THUNDERER, Captain Johnson, was returning from China on her homeward bound passage laden with tea, fruit, etc. . . . That the said vessel encountered a tremendous gale off the banks of Newfoundland, and was dismasted, and finally wrecked [time, date, latitude and other particulars]. That the above-named vessel speedily foundered and only the second mate and four of the crew (the bearers of this certificate) escaped a watery grave. These, after floating several days on pieces of the ship, were providentially discovered, and humanely picked up by the brig INVINCIBLE, Capt. Smith, and landed at this town and harbour of Portsmouth, in the county of Hants. That we, the Masters of Customs, and two of Her Majesty's Justices of the Peace for the said harbour and county, do hereby grant and afford to the said . . . this our vouchment of the truth of the said wreck, and their connection therewith, and do empower them to present and use this certificate for twenty-eight days from the date hereof, to enable them to get such temporal aid as may be adequate to reaching their respective homes, or any sea-port where they may be re-engaged. And this certificate further sheweth, that they may not be interrupted in the said journey by any constabulary or other official authority, provided, that is to say, that no breach of the peace or other cognisable offence be committed by the said Petitioners.

As witness our hands,

John Harris, M.C.	£1—0—0.
James Flood, J.P.	£1—0—0.
Capt. W. Hope, R.N., J.P.	£1–10—0.

Given at Portsmouth, this 10th day of October, 1850

GOD SAVE THE QUEEN

Underneath was appended:

Rev. W. Williams	£1—0—0.
An officer's widow	10—0.
An old sailor	5—0.
A friend	2—6.[1]

Though perhaps less than perfectly convincing, this seems a workmanlike document for two and six, quite good enough to fox rural parish officers. One may suspect that it was composed by a one-time attorney's clerk. Broken down lawyers and lawyers' clerks were held, for obvious reasons, to make particularly good screevers and 'gag-makers'.

Gag-making meant contriving new tales and wheezes (usually fresh variations on time-worn themes). It was often part-and-parcel of the screever's function, and aside from any penwork that might be needed it is easy to see how useful a man of some education and professional experience could be in working up a convincing deception. This did not mean that those who, from better things, sank into the company of cadgers and vagrants, always found a niche where they could survive by becoming, as it were, consultants in mendicancy. Many—perhaps most—of these exiles from respectability were derelicts too broken by hardship, drink, age or self-hatred to turn their abilities to account: rare though they may have been, there were ex-officers and masters of arts who had fallen even below the level of screeving and who were to be found rotting in the lowest crannies of the beggar's underworld.

The most important of the literate beggars were not the screevers but the professional writers of begging letters. These men were helped by the improvement and cheapening of the postal services, but they did not rely exclusively on the Post Office. Often they chose to deliver letters by hand, having found out something about their quarry by earlier visits to his habitat. There was nothing diffident or retiring about the typical Victorian begging-letter writer. As a rule his letters were simply the means of opening a connection (or keeping it alive) and he quickly followed them up in the flesh, trusting to a dramatic appeal for the actual touch. Once a connection was firmly established, the same victim might be milked over and over again by a talented operator, and for increasing sums.

[1] See Mayhew, Vol. I, p. 340. The charges for screeving are from the same source: no doubt, like those for other services, they went up during the fifties and sixties.

Sometimes a begging-letter writer turned out to be a man of some means—one occupied an entire house, in the attic of which he faked up touching tableaux for his visitors—and many were indefatigable travellers, working one provincial town after another in a way that must have cost them a great deal in fares. It was, however, a highly competitive business, and to win a living from it required not only nerve and talent but unflagging industry.

Anyone who became a focus of attention for these men could be driven half-wild. Dickens, well-off, famous and with a reputation for philanthropy, was an obvious target. (Perhaps he was made the angrier by the uneasy knowledge that his post contained almost indistinguishable appeals from poor wretches who were *not* professional mendicants.)

I ought to know something of the Begging-Letter-Writer, [he wrote in an article[1] that did something to diminish his earlier popularity with the underworld]. He has beseiged my door, at all hours of the day and night; he has fought my servant; he has lain in ambush for me, going out and coming in; he has followed me out of town into the country; he has appeared at provincial hotels, where I have been staying for only a few hours; he has written to me from immense distances. He has fallen sick; he has died, and been buried; he has come to life again, and again departed from this transitory scene; he has wanted a great coat to go to India in; a pound to set him up in life for ever; a pair of boots, to take him to the coast of China; a hat, to get him a permanent situation under Government. He has frequently been exactly seven-and-sixpence short of independence. He has had such openings at Liverpool—posts of great trust and confidence in merchants' houses, which nothing but seven-and-sixpence was wanting to him to secure—that I wonder he is not Mayor of that flourishing town at the present moment.

The natural phenomena of which he has been the victim, are of a most astounding nature. He has had two children, who have never grown up; who have never had anything to cover them at night; who have been continually driving him mad, by asking in vain for food; who have never come out of fevers and measles; who have never changed in the least

---

[1] *Household Words*, April 1850. The extract that follows has been truncated.

degree, through fourteen long revolving years. As to his wife, what that suffering woman has undergone, nobody knows. She has always been in an interesting situation through the same long period, and has never been confined yet. His devotion to her has been unceasing. He has never cared for himself; he could have perished—he would rather—in short —but was it not his Christian duty as a man, a husband, and a father, to write begging letters when he looked at her?

What his brother has done to him would have broken anybody else's heart. His brother went into business with him, and ran away with the money; his brother got him to be security for an immense sum, and left him to pay it; his brother would have given him employment to the tune of hundreds a year, if he would have consented to write letters on a Sunday.

He has been attached to every conceivable pursuit. He has been in the army, in the navy, in the church, in the law; connected with the press, the fine arts, public institutions, every description and grade of business. He has been brought up as a gentleman: he has been at every college in Oxford and Cambridge.

Sometimes he has never written such a letter before. He blushes with shame. Don't answer it, and let it be understood that, then, he will kill himself quietly. Sometimes (and more frequently) he has written a few such letters. Then he encloses the answers, with an intimation that they are of inestimable value to him, and a request that they may be carefully returned. He is fond of enclosing something—verses, letters, pawnbroker's duplicates, anything to necessitate an answer.

Sometimes, he writes to inform me that I have got rid of him at last. He has enlisted into the Company's service, and is off directly—but he wants a cheese. He is informed by the serjeant that it is essential to his prospects in the regiment that he should take out a single-Gloucester cheese, weighing from twelve to fifteen pounds. Eight or nine shillings would buy it. He does not ask for money, after what has passed; but if he calls at nine tomorrow morning, may he hope to find a cheese? And is there anything he can do to show his gratitude in Bengal?

Once, he wrote me rather a special letter. He had got into a little trouble by leaving parcels of mud done up in brown paper, at people's houses, on pretence of being a railway porter, in which character he received carriage money. This sportive fancy he expiated in the House of Correction.

At another time, my friend (I am describing actual experiences) introduced himself as a literary gentleman in the last extremity of distress. He had had a play accepted in a certain Theatre—which was really open; its representation was delayed by the indisposition of a leading actor—who was really ill; and he and his were in a state of absolute starvation. Well! we got over that difficulty to our mutual satisfaction. A little while afterwards he was in some other strait. And we adjusted that point too. A little while afterwards, he had taken a new house, and was going headlong to ruin for want of a water-butt. I had my misgivings about the water-butt, and did not reply to that epistle. But, a little while afterwards, I had reason to feel penitent for my neglect. He wrote me a few broken-hearted lines, informing me that the dear partner of his sorrows died in his arms last night at nine o'clock!

I dispatched a trusty messenger to comfort the bereaved mourner: but the messenger went so soon, my friend was not at home, and his wife was in a most delightful state of health. He was taken up by the Mendicity Society and I presented myself at a London Police-Office. The Magistrate was wonderfully struck by his educational acquirements, deeply impressed by the excellence of his letters, exceedingly sorry to see a man of his attainments there, and quite charmed to have the agreeable duty of discharging him. A collection was made for the 'poor fellow' and I left court with a comfortable sense of being universally regarded as a sort of monster.

Next morning, an Irish gentleman, a member of the same fraternity, who was very well persuaded I should be chary of going to that Police-Office again, positively refused to leave my door for less than a sovereign, and, literally 'sat down' before it for ten mortal hours. The garrison being well provisioned, I remained within the walls; and he raised the siege at midnight, with a prodigious alarum on the bell.

The Begging-Letter-Writer often has an extensive circle of acquaintance. Whole pages of the Court Guide are ready to be references for him. Noblemen and gentlemen write to say there never was such a man for probity and virtue.

He always belongs to a Corresponding-Society. Anyone

who will, may ascertain this fact. Give money today, in recognition of a begging-letter and for the next fortnight you will have a rush of such communications. Steadily refuse to give; and the begging-letters become Angels' visits, until the Society is from some cause or other in a dull way of business, and may as well try you as anybody else.

That the calling is a successful one, and that large sums of money are gained by it, must be evident to anybody who reads the Police Reports of such cases. But, prosecutions are of rare occurrence, relatively to the extent to which the trade is carried on.

In a way the begging-letter writers did keep up a kind of corresponding society. There were lists in circulation which gave the names of rich, generous people who had responded to appeals in the past, and which, like the rolls kept for gegors at paddingkens, could be obtained for a fee. The cool and discerning Sir Robert Peel features prominently in one of them.

The most sensible writers were methodical and avoided the sort of blunders Dickens mentions by entering particulars of each dupe in a register. One busy, highly mobile impostor who fell into the hands of the law, kept a record from which his activities could be reconstructed in fair detail. Some of the entries run:

Cheltenham   May 14, 1852

Rev. John Furby—Springwood Villa. Low Church—Fond of architecture—Dugdale's Monastica—Son of architect—Lost his life in the 'Charon', S.S. packet—£2 and suit of clothes—Got reference.

Mrs Branxholme—Clematis Cottage—Widow—Through Rev. Furby, £3 and prayer-book.

Gloucester   May 30

Andrew Taggart— . . . Street—Gentleman—Great abolitionist of slave trade—As tradesman from U.S. who lost his custom by aiding slope of fugitive female slave—by name Naomi Brown £5—N.B.: To work him again for he is good.

Grantham   July 1.

Halliday (from whom the above is taken) was quite fascinated by these lively and versatile cadgers. He reviles them as energetically as Dickens, but does them the justice to remark the 'unfaltering courage' their methods demanded, along with 'tears and hysterics at immediate command' and an eye for costume. By his account, many must have looked rather like poor clergymen, for he describes an archetypal figure in a high collar, white choker, well-brushed bare-seamed coat, darned black gloves, 'pudgy gaiters', umbrella, macassared hair and shaven cheeks. In his investigations he came across whole families devoted to the business, one of which included a girl of real ability.

In worn black silk, neat, sad, quiet and proud, every inch the reduced gentlewoman, this talented girl would call at grand London houses, attended by an elderly manservant of respectable appearance with a small basket. Leaving her companion on the pavement and taking the basket she would ring the bell and ask to see the lady of the house. If she was refused she would call for pen and paper and write an elegant little note, reserved yet touching, indicating that she sought the honour of including the lady's name among certain patronesses who were 'kindly aiding her in disposing of a few necessaries for the toilette'. This deftly worded appeal was likely to get her an interview a few days later, and then her prospective benefactress was allowed to draw out the harrowing tale of her poor father. This man (in reality a swindling ex-butler who had run off with his employer's daughter) doubled the roles of loyal old retainer and bedridden military veteran, ruined by a disastrous lawsuit. Inveigled to the cheats' nest, the new patroness found the aged Peninsular hero in a garret 'made as clean and uncomfortable as possible' and surrounded by all the trappings of a devoted, well bred family struggling to preserve decency amid terrible want. Stroke by stroke, the agony was piled up (two wan children, supposed to be orphan relatives whom the good folk in their own distress were tenderly nurturing, provided the crowning touch) and soon the visitor was not merely ready but straining to pour out her bounty on the gallant little household.

Begging-letter writers did not always confine themselves to victims they could tackle in person. Some of them were better writers than actors, and there were times when a visit was impracticable. Also, to avoid personal contact meant avoiding the ever-present risk of walking into a trap. But as in other fields of begging, there was fierce competition, and an unsupported letter made a feeble impact compared to a direct confrontation— unless quite exceptional ingenuity could be brought to bear.

One clever idea was to approach not a living but a dead subject. The newly-bereaved family of a gentleman of some standing would be pained to open a letter addressed to him by a fallen creature with whom, evidently, he had once kept up an illicit liaison. Until recently he had been supporting her, and now this woman was in extremity—cast off by her own people, totally without means, about to become the mother of an unwelcome little kinsman. No doubt in her desperation she would be capable of actions that would publicise the whole affair. Few approaches could be better calculated to set a solid upper-class household buzzing, or to take advantage of the fact that, directly after a man's death, his heirs were prepared for heavy outlay on his behalf (as the exuberance of mourning displays shows).

On the other hand, where there was a wealthy estate there were also likely to be executors and lawyers ready to investigate claims. Presumably it was for this reason that the game was so often worked across the Atlantic. English papers carried obituary notices of Americans with close connections in England, and vice versa, so that the selection of targets was not difficult from either side of the ocean. Moreover there were plenty of connections between crooks in England and the United States (including the movement of individuals in both directions) so that letters sent from one country could be based on close information from the other. Probably they most often came eastwards and from recent immigrants: what could be more in keeping than a poor betrayed girl trying to start afresh in a new world?

These cruel post-mortem appeals had to make an immediate emotional impact, unsupported by a visit, and their style was sometimes unusually spirited, even for professional begging-letters. 'For God's sake,' one runs, 'send without an instant's delay and pay the postage of your letter to me, or I shall be unable to obtain it, for I am selling everything to live. On my knees I beg of you, and for your dying son's sake, send to me immediately or I shall go mad. God bless you and yours. May you be supremely happy. Bless you. In mercy send soon; and so farewell. May God Bless you is the fervent prayer of your unhappy but true friend.'[1]

There were plenty of begging lays in which the writing of

---

[1] Society for the Suppression of Mendicity. Report for 1859–60.

letters was, so to speak, optional. One imposture of this kind, well attuned to the boom-and-slump conditions of the mid-century decades, was acting the ruined businessman or shop-keeper. A typical exponent of the school was a middle-aged or elderly man dressed in the relics of sober, clerkly garments; everything about him, from his napless tall hat to the well polished rags of leather on his feet, was designed to show how he was hanging on to the vestiges of his old respectability by the last threadbare stitch. His present state was ascribed to fire, bank-failure or some other common trouble that would raise uneasy echoes in the minds of men of the class he claimed to come from; and he would go round to a number of houses leaving petitions describing his misfortunes. In the evenings he might visit pubs, where, in bad times, his sudden, lamentable appearance among a collection of tradesmen in the snug bar parlour, must have had the effect of a death's-head at a banquet. On these occasions the old hand, satisfied that his entry had attracted attention, often remained mute; then, too humiliated to utter, with a jerky, painfully inept and diffident gesture, he would proffer a single box of matches. Properly executed before the right company, the manoeuvre was infallible.

This public house routine was good enough for the less ambitious beggars working the lay, and some of them were not above trying it on working class housewives—best caught on Saturday evenings, taking a glass with their weekend shopping money still on them. But the higher-flying ruined trader went after altogether bigger game, using far more elaborate methods. Besides a selection of references from bankers, churchwardens and others, he would have ready a formidable set of account books to impress any gull he could interest, and he probably made his first approaches by correspondence. Halliday gives a memorable sketch of one specimen in his gallery of begging-letter virtuosos: a mock-pious character, whose patter like his letters, was a 'jumble of arithmetic and scripture', furnished with a 'dazzling display' of accounts showing that he was an unpaid creditor.

He has a wife whose appearance is in itself a small income. She folds the hardest-working-looking hands across the cleanest of aprons and curtseys with the humility of a pew opener. The clothes of the worthy couple are shabby, but their persons and linen are rigorously clean. Their cheeks shine with yellow soap as if they were rasped and beeswaxed every morning. The male impostor, when fleecing a victim, has a habit of washing his hands 'with invisible soap and imperceptible water', as though he were waiting on a customer.

A rascal of this type was likely to shape well as a 'prater' or bogus preacher—another rather sophisticated lay that was taken up by beggars with varying degrees of education. Ordinarily, praters seem to have worked in small travelling parties. The leader, sombrely dressed after the style of a non-conforming minister and nearly always, for some reason, wearing spectacles, would do the actual preaching: his associates stirred up preliminary interest in the meeting and acted as a sort of claque when things were under way. Since it was neither prudent nor paying to loiter in one place, praters were mostly confirmed wanderers who would make short stops at small towns and rural centres. (Perhaps in response to the revival movements that swelled up again in the second half of the century, there was also some working of fugitive street-corner stands in big cities.) It has to be remembered that, for many poor people, an open-air religious meeting was likely to be a welcome diversion from everyday monotony, and more especially from the stupefying uneventfulness of Sabbath afternoons. A preaching and hymn-singing could be an excitement, and not just in remote farming districts.

On a fine evening a gang would form the nucleus of a congregation on a convenient open space, borrow a cart or wheelbarrow as an extempore pulpit, perhaps unroll a banner, and put down a conspicuous receptacle for the offertory. Then, trusting to the range of his voice to gather a crowd, the preacher would rise and launch into his discourse, varied perhaps with an interval or two of hymn-singing, to which the gang gave an energetic lead. A favoured text was Psalm xxxvii, verse 25: 'I have been young, and now am old; yet have I not seen the righteous forsaken nor his seed begging bread.'

Perhaps one should include among the praters those who attended genuine religious meetings, preferably of the more ecstatic sort, and took the chance of testifying to their conversion and spiritual regeneration while indicating a need for temporal assistance. A sensational variant of the gag, demanding above everything *fervour*, was a refinement of the fit-throwing routine already mentioned. The prating fit-thrower staged his paroxysm so that it appeared to be brought on by the preacher's exhortations and, on reviving, enthusiastically attributed it to his power—perhaps to the casting out of an unclean spirit. Provided the seizure was well-timed, capping rather than interrupting his eloquence, the preacher might well be gratified by the tribute, and amid general edification the new vessel of grace was unlikely to be sent empty away.

The great interest in overseas missions was a boon to praters. A versatile character known as Chelsea George had a particularly dark complexion, possibly from having left the country for several years. Returning home, he lived by various dishonest shifts till, falling foul of the law, he was sentenced to a short term in Winchester jail. At this time—it was probably during the later forties—the silent system was not strictly enforced in the prison and George was able to make plans with two other inmates: Russia Bob, an Irishman so named because he had been to Russia, and a fluent impostor called Jew Jim. All three were freed at about the same time and soon afterwards quitted the unfriendly south and made their way northward. They were attracted by the news that a missionary from Sierra Leone had recently held a series of highly successful meetings in large towns round Staffordshire, but had not visited the villages and smaller centres. They equipped themselves with suitable clothes and handbills, secured the services of some minor assistants and were soon ready to go to work. Their performance at the little town of Torryburn was evidently either witnessed by Mayhew himself or described to him by an eye witness.

The chief part was taken by Jew Jim who declared himself a Jewish convert to Christianity who had subsequently become a minister and missionary, carrying the Gospel light to the South Seas, the coasts of Africa and all over India. Russia Bob was then presented

as his worthy and self-denying colleague, and Chelsea George as the first fruits of their ministry—as one who had left houses and land, wife and children, and taken a long and hazardous voyage to show Christians in England that their sable brethren, children of one common Parent, were beginning to cast their idols to the moles and bats. . . . As argument always gains by illustration the orator pulled out a tremendous black doll dressed up in Oriental style. This, Jew Jim assured his audience, was an idol brought from Murat in Hindostan. He presented it to Chelsea George for his worship and embraces. The convert indignantly repelled the insinuation, pushed the idol from him, spat in its face, and cut as many capers as a dancing bear. The trio at this stage began 'puckering' [talking privately] to each other in murdered French dashed with a little Irish; after which the missionaries said that their convert (who had only a few words of English) would now profess his faith. All was attention as Chelsea George came forward. He stroked his beard, put his hand in his breast to keep down his dickey, and turning his eyes upwards said: 'I believe in Desus Tist—dlory to 'is 'oly Name!'

This elicited some loud 'amens' from an assemblage of nearly 1000 persons, and catching the favourable opportunity, a 'school of pals', appointed for the purpose, went round and made the collection. Out of the abundance of their credulity and piety the populace contributed sixteen pounds. The whole scene was enacted out of doors, and presented to the stranger very pleasing impressions. . . . One verse of a hymn, and the blessing pronounced was the signal for separation. A little shaking of hands concluded the exhibition, and 'every man went to his own house'.

After this, the whole party, including the pals, caught a train for Manchester—presumably their operational base for the time being. No doubt they would have had many more successes had not Jim's arrest for an earlier crime—beating up and robbing a woman—broken up the gifted trio.

Among the gags that needed a respectable appearance one more deserves mention: 'playing the noble'. This was not a specific routine so much as a style of approach, and its essence lay in a display of disinterested virtue. For instance, a poor fellow—a self-respecting, down-at-heel artisan, by the looks of him—collapses in a public place. Soon a man with a certain air of authority pushes through the bystanders and kneels by the prostrate figure. In an unflurried, professional way he loosens the man's neckcloth, feels his pulse, turns up an eyelid, produces smelling-salts, and as the man gradually returns to consciousness, fires a question or two at him. Then, brushing off his trouser knees, he announces grimly that there is nothing wrong here but plain hunger. Stooping, he up-ends the fellow's hat, empties into it all the change in his pocket, and turning on his heel marches off. The fact that this medical Samaritan himself looks far from prosperous strengthens the example. If the act has been well played and the site well chosen, one bystander after another will follow suit, glad to discharge their consciences with so little inconvenience.

A different sort of noble conduct was shown when a lady, walking alone, was followed and annoyed by a coarse brute of a tramp—until a well-spoken shabby young chap appeared on the scene, quickly drove off the cowardly lout and escorted her to the safety of her garden gate in a most respectful fashion. He even reluctantly waited, cap in hand, while she darted indoors for a reward. Here, as in many other chivalrous gags, nice judgement must have been necessary to appear superior enough to make a really substantial tip unavoidable, without running the risk of putting off the dupe by seeming too high-minded to be tippable.

Reading through the long catalogue of mendicant types in *London Labour and the London Poor*, or turning the pages of the Mendicity Society's annals, one seems to be looking at an endless, infinitely varied parade. Here are beggars who were products of industrialisation and beggars who belonged to Tudor England; sinister beggars skulking in lonely lanes and bland beggars advertising in newspapers; beggars who survived by creeping into middens on frosty nights and plump beggars warming themselves at their own hearths; exotic beggars of every degree, from refugee noblemen to escaped plantation slaves— negroes, Teutons, Slavs, Latins, Arabs and Hindus.

How many people supported themselves by mendicancy at any one time, nobody could tell. Both the numbers and the types of beggars changed incessantly; sometimes (as with the huge post-famine flood of Irish) on a nation-wide scale and for obvious causes; sometimes (as with the influx and waning of Asiatic crossing-sweepers in London) local and mysterious. Vagrant beggars often changed their lay according to the season, and many of them varied begging with all kinds of other activities, from passing dud coin to hop harvesting.

What is plain enough is that, at least during the first four decades of the Queen's reign, beggars of one kind and another were always active and numerous enough to be a serious nuisance, and were felt to be a grave scandal. Nothing is more striking about most contemporary references than the way in which they emphasise the annoyance and viciousness of beggary, rather than the misery it implied. Nearly every commentator (though he may make some brief references to genuine hardship) is strongly hostile both to casual charity and to the people who received it.[1] Yet most of these writers were far from callous. What disturbed them was that beggars lived on lying and imposture and used those means to get hold of the money that ought to have been spent on projects for helping the deserving poor. Giving to them was thus not only mistaken but morally wrong, rewarding chicanery at the expense of well-doing.

The philanthropic Sir Walter Besant remarked at the end of the century that if only everyone could be persuaded always, in all circumstances, to rebuff any personal appeal for alms, then the whole incubus of mendicancy would vanish at once. He was only putting in unusually strong terms what men of different sorts had been suggesting for generations. Furthermore the premise was undeniable: nobody begged for pleasure.

Some efforts were made to keep it all within bounds. The police authorities no longer allowed aggressive throngs of beggars to cluster round profitable sites; but they had, as ever, to control what they could not abolish, and in places large numbers of beggars were in fact tolerated. Their pitches were often under the control of some local official, such as a constable or beadle, who in effect had a patronage over begging stands, and it is impossible to believe that the goodwill of these officials was not sometimes bought, especially since many of them were badly under-paid. It was not only the paddingken keepers and other such underworld characters who had a hand in the elaborate arrangements of Victorian beggary. The very authorities who were supposed to be putting it down often played their part.

On the face of it, it seems surprising that the community should have supported such a large and irritating body of parasites when there was such strong feeling against both begging and alms-giving. Victorians were, of course, as capable as ourselves of holding discordant opinions simultaneously. Believers

---

[1] The observation applies to a greater or less degree to every writer but one quoted in this chapter, and their opinions are paralleled by the evidence in government reports. Mayhew himself (not Halliday) is the exception; he delights in stories of beggars' rascality, but the writing published under his own name is touched by a compensating pity.

in the paramount rights of property advocated forcing railways through private land by Act of Parliament: Malthusians supported the health-of-towns movement. In the same way, the popularisation of laissez-faire ideas went hand in hand with a sharpening social conscience, and for many mid-century Englishmen the condition of the destitute was a standing reproach to the most progressive and affluent Christian society ever to exist. The charitable impulse was there, and though after 1850 the condition of the poor generally improved, the impulse went on growing. In the bitter winter of 1860–1 the London police courts were so embarrassed by the flood of cash offerings pouring in that magistrates rebelled against the practice of using them as large-scale almoners: a few months later, the suffering caused by the American Civil War in the Lancashire cotton towns evoked an unparalleled response.

People were ready to give. But what were they to give to? There was a great deal of organised charitable activity but much of it had a very restricted appeal. Most organisations were denominational, and therefore subject to fierce sectarian feelings. Old-established foundations were suspected of being nests of Hanoverian torpor and jobbery; new enterprises of not being bona fide. Above all, most fund-raisers aimed at a relatively wealthy public: they thought in terms of published contribution lists, subscription dinners and so on. It was not until late in the century that a number of big societies came into being which collected widows' mites as well as rich men's donations and which provided generally acceptable channels for most kinds of charity. Meantime the obvious outlet for the impulse to give remained the beggar on the door-step.

Again, largesse in one form and another was a vital part of the social machinery. The revolution in money values and living habits makes it hard to realise how important the tipping habit used to be, but a century ago it was one of the great supports of a ruling-class status.[1] The better-off were conditioned to handing out gratuities, and just where tipping ended and alms-giving began was not at all clear. It was mean not to throw something to the poor fellow who darted into the gutter to hold one's horse's head; stingy to ignore the sweeper at the crossing; natural to spare an occasional trifle for the respectful wretch who

[1] With regard to the value of tips it is odd to reflect that Thackeray, neither very wealthy nor a show-off, thought it appropriate to tip schoolboys a sovereign—more than the weekly income of *two* Devonshire labourers with families to support.

only shivered and pulled off his hat. And what was a trifle to the giver might be salvation to someone who had learnt how to stay alive on a few coppers a day.

But first and last, the real strength of the beggar's claim was that it was unanswerable. The poverty and suffering on which the claim was based were matters of common knowledge, and the fact that any particular beggar might be a fraud did not dispose of them. Of course there were rich beggars. One spectacularly filthy man who came before a magistrate turned out to have over £300 in a savings account. Another, who put up a stiff struggle when the police tried to search him, had £64 in gold sewn up in his tattered clothes.[1] But neither that sort of case nor anything else could alter the stark, terrible fact that a large part of the population was all the time under the menace of total destitution.

It is not easily overestimated. The long files Mayhew saw

[1] Both cases were reported in the Proceedings of the Society for the Suppression of Mendicity, 1846.

turned away on freezing nights from packed charity shelters illustrate part of the story, but a great deal of the worst distress never showed in public. If the landlord was merciful, people starved behind doors. Now and again a death from famine came before a coroner and was reported in the press, often briefly. A case that evidently attracted some attention concerned a man known as Williams who died in February 1849 (the cholera seems to have stimulated a crusading spirit that winter, though it was not a particularly evil one for the poor). For ten weeks Williams had occupied a room in a poor quarter of Westminster with a woman and their four children. The rent was half-a-crown a week, though in fact only three weeks rent had been paid. The family had tried to survive by the sale of lettered window cards (Williams was described as an artist) and by hawking knitted articles in the streets; but they had little success, though the children were out on it all day—and no doubt, in effect, begging. They had very little food and the father could not bring himself to take any of the scraps that the others procured. Latterly he had spent most of his time lying on a straw palliasse. The family had no blankets or other bed-covering.

When Williams died the poor law surgeon was sent for, and attended very promptly, arriving long before dawn. When he had examined the corpse and satisfied himself that life was extinct he had a look at the children, remarked they would be the better for a dose of castor oil and went. About three hours later the landlord, finding the children still lying uncovered on the floor beside the dead man, set off after the doctor, who told him that he would submit his report in due course but otherwise had no immediate concern in the business. The landlord then went to the relieving officer's, but he found the outer door of the office locked and no one answered his knocks. Next he went to the workhouse gate, where the porter told him it was no use coming blustering there, he must go to the relieving officer: without his authority no one could be admitted. The relieving office, however, remained firmly shut and the officer inaccessible. Finally the landlord, taking a daughter of the dead man by the hand, went to the local police court and applied to the magistrate. It was a fortunate move.[1]

[1] This was a likelier resource in London, where the stipendiary magistrates were constantly in court and more or less divorced from the poor law organisation. In the provinces justices of the peace might be hard to find and were *ex officio* guardians responsible for the management of the workhouse.

Three days later the coroner's court sat at a local public house. A doctor (not the parish surgeon) deposed that he had carried out a post mortem. The stomach of the deceased had contained a small quantity of opaque fluid; 'no trace of any food' could be discovered in his bowels. Death was the result of debility from lack of nourishment. Witness had also examined the deceased's wife, whom he found to be in a deplorable state from want of food. The landlord also told his story. The coroner asked if the poor law authority had seen fit to send a representative to the court and was told they had not. However a gentleman got up and volunteered the information that the landlord had since been 'examined before the Board of Guardians' in front of which impressive body he had sung a rather different tune. Later another gentleman, a member of the board but present only in a private capacity, said that the workhouse porter was the man at fault, and added that everything that could in reason be done for the poor in Westminster was in fact done. The coroner remarked that no one was to blame for the death, and the jury found it had occurred as a result of the deceased's wants being 'concealed from the parish'. Williams, however, had not died altogether in vain, for as a result of the publicity the case attracted, eighty pounds was received in two days at the magistrate's court for the use of the family.[1]

This was at a time when the scandals of the Tooting infant pauper asylum were being ventilated (though in fact Westminster did not ship off its workhouse children to that lethal establishment) and it was perhaps particularly easy for the public to sympathise with parents who preferred to starve rather than hand over their children to the mercies of the guardians of the poor. But the full terrors of destitution were not confined to those with a suicidal horror of the workhouse. Even those who would have been ready to accept its help could not always get it. In the last resort, probably even the harshest board of guardians would take in someone who was clearly resident in the area, or give him out-relief, even if it was not his parish of settlement. But vagrants, outsiders drawn by false hopes of work, the many drifting citizens of nowhere, were in a different case. Union authorities were reluctant to take on responsibility for these immigrants into their parishes; it added to the pressure on accommodation that was already often inadequate, and it let

[1] See *The Times*, 19 February 1849.

them in for expenses which it could be hard to shift from their ratepayers' shoulders. At the same time, parochial officers were pastmasters in the arts of obstruction, brow-beating and pro-crastination: they abused regulations even to defeat the ends for which those regulations were made. Moreover pauper 'casuals' —people on the move and entitled to at least one night's shelter and something to eat—were, as we have seen, the most trouble-some and lawless class that workhouses had to deal with. Officials were naturally inclined to ignore their obligations to-wards them. After the celebrated Poor Law Board minute of August 1848, pointing out in strong terms the bad effects of indiscriminate hospitality (while skilfully leaving the Commis-sioners uncommitted) many Unions—probably the great major-ity—took the hint and gave up taking in casuals at all.

According to Lloyd Baker, this worked to the advantage of case-hardened gegors. For though deaths by starvation were, Baker argued, very unusual, the mere fact that such deaths could occur encouraged people to give money to beggars when they knew that the authorities to whom a man should have been able to turn were dodging their obligations. Though they really knew better, people still had disquieting doubts 'lest each applicant for charity *might possibly* be an honest traveller' and they were reluctant to think of him starving for lack of a trivial sum. Lloyd Baker adds that at the time of writing (1865) all the Unions in Gloucestershire, where he was himself an influential magistrate, had come to accept the need for casual relief, though some had only recently seen the light. By then, in fact, the Poor Law Board had changed its tune and was once more urging boards of guardians to carry out their legal duties; by then, too, institutional charity for various classes of destitutes was growing —and went on doing so throughout the century. Nevertheless it is doubtful whether there was ever a time in the nineteenth century when an Englishman could reasonably calm his con-science on the score that none of his countrymen need die of hunger.

Clearly it was hard for charitable people to avoid encouraging the undeserving. Not only were professional beggars often remarkably clever impostors, but the distinction between the genuine out-of-work and the professional might be almost metaphysically fine. Every paddingken was an academy where novices could pick up the arts of monkry; and because a man honestly and desperately wanted work, it was no reason why, once he was reduced to begging, he should spoil his chances by neglecting the tricks of the trade. The process of corruption was almost inevitable. Merely to be alive without legitimate means of support was criminal, and the act of begging made a man a self-acknowledged delinquent with a weather eye permanently cocked for the constable. Beggars frequented the company of beggars; the more successful often worked in groups; to become an accomplished cheat and impostor was to achieve a certain standing. Chicanery demands a degree of spirit, and the skilled mendicant was something better than a defeated down-and-out: in his way he fought back.

Intelligent people who still gave money to beggars knew all this. Sir Robert Peel and others who figured high on the professional cadger's list of good touches were not naive, sentimental gulls. If such people responded to such appeals it can only have been because they knew that some of them were likely to be true and they had imagination enough to realise what that implied. The liberality of the poor to beggars was often noticed and it points the same moral. It was not just ignorance that supported the army of professional beggars. It was understanding.

CHAPTER EIGHT

Magsmen, macers and shofulmen

A great many classic, time-proved swindles were based on the greed of the victim and his willingness to take part in a shady deal.

Among the crowd at a fair or race-course a smock-clad countryman suddenly stoops and picks a ring out of the mud. Looking at it with a round-eyed, simple-minded air, he naively enquires of a passer if it could be gold and what is its value? With luck the worthless pinchbeck then changes hands for a pocketful of silver and of course the buyer has no redress. This little stratagem was known as 'fawney dropping'.

In towns a tidy, seedy looking creature (of much the same stamp as the ruined-tradesman beggar) might sometimes be seen in front of a pawnbroker's, clutching a watch or some other personal valuable and apparently screwing up his resolution. In he would go, and soon come trailing despondently out, contemplating a pawn ticket for six or seven shillings which, with a sudden impulsive gesture of despair, he would offer to any interested stander-by at its face value. Pressed, he might even accept a shade less. The ticket was of course a sham, and as soon as the man who had bought it turned into the pawnshop the vendor scuttled away as fast as his legs would carry him.

Among early Victorians 'duffer' commonly meant not a dull witted man but one who exploited dull-wits—and, more particularly, tricked them by selling them 'duff' things in a way that made them think they were being exceptionally fly. The fiddle-duffer visited saloons and bar-parlours at night, playing the part of a drunken musician. Grasping his violin case he would stagger about the room, bumping into furniture, full of tipsy conviviality. He would order drinks and then, discovering that he had spent his money and his pockets were empty, show himself recklessly set on keeping up the spree. 'Here, I must have money.... For'—breaking into song—'I won't go home till morning, till morning, I won't go home till morning, till daylight doth appear.' And staring round he would take out the violin and swear to sell his valuable Cremona rather than go short. Whoever took him up on the offer and bought the violin for a sovereign or two soon found that he had got hold of an instrument that was useless for any purpose except fiddle-duffing.

Cigar-duffing was a seaport lay. Fitted out in nautical rig, suggesting perhaps a merchant petty officer returned from a long passage, the duffer haunted quaysides and shipping hotels. He would roll up to what looked a promising 'flat', get into conversation and work round to intimating that he knew of a parcel of weeds going duty-free at far below market prices. In fact, he admitted in a burst of confidence, he had himself brought back a few pounds of the choicest Manillas or Cubas as a little personal speculation, and was anxious to dispose of them before a suspicious customs officer got any closer on his tail. An agreement was made, the customer being given a specimen or two to try before completing the deal. The specimens, naturally, were excellent—and the rest the vilest Stinko-D'Oros procurable. Some who worked this kind of swindle were worse than mere sharps and, under pretence of taking the dupe to collect the goods, would lure him into a trap where he was beaten helpless and stripped.

These were a few of the countless methods of cheating worked up by the underworld; but for the great majority of people (especially country folk) much the most familiar type of sharp was the 'magsman'. Originally this meant a man who ran a pitch-and-toss game[1] but it came to be used for almost any small professional swindler and above all for the travelling gambling-game operator. Innumerable men of this kind collected at every event where they had a chance of enticing the holiday-making flat's money out of his pocket, from the remotest rural fair to Epsom races.

Some of these types and their skills can still be studied in action, others are long extinct. Among the most prominent were the thimble-rigger with his three tiny cups and the dried pea he picked up under his horny thumbnail; the knob or under-and-over man inviting passers to drop stakes on his patterned sheet; the broadsman or three-card trickster with cuffs turned back at the elbows and little baize covered table; the dumplin operator with his two skittles and biased ball; the lounging keeper of the

---

[1] Known as 'magflying' from the mags (halfpennies) used in it.

E.O. stand with its bouncing pill and lettered slots (a little like a cross between roulette and a pin-table); and the charley-pitcher with his cogged dice.

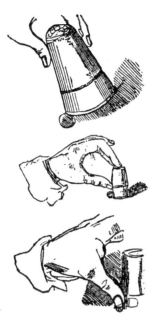

Not one of these arts could be profitably worked by a single man. The simplest required some cooperation by undercover assistants—known as 'sweeteners', 'nobblers', 'jolliers' and 'buttoners'—both to attract attention to the game and to protect the magsman and his takings if anyone became aggressive about his losses. Pedantically speaking, sweetening meant encouraging spectators by playing and appearing to win heavily, whilst buttoning and nobbling meant mingling in the crowd and enticing flats to have a go. In some games the fraudulent manipulation was best left to one of these helpers: for instance the hidden undercloth on the E.O. table, which by a touch stopped the little ball dropping into an unprofitable hole, could be worked by a stooge who pretended to be an excited player and pressed up close while the proprietor stood clear till the coup was finished.

Itinerant magsmen of this type seem on the whole to have enjoyed a good deal of licence. Probably they usually paid for the right to take up a stand. (In the early forties the lessee of Epsom race course charged them five to ten shillings a time, for

which they were given a permit which they stuck in their hats.)
However in some places they were chivied by the law and must
have needed look-outs to save them being arrested as vagabonds.
(A thimble-rigger or three-card man can pack up and vanish in
seconds.) Further, there were numbers of hard characters around
fairs and sporting meetings who made money out of intimidation
and extortion. No doubt it was not always easy to draw the
distinction between hiring buttoners and look-outs and paying
protection money.

Dickens draws a vignette of some assorted types at a smart
suburban race course.

Here a little knot gathered round a pea and thimble table
to watch the plucking of some unhappy greenhorn and there,
another proprietor with his confederates in various disguises
—one man in spectacles, another in an eye-glass and stylish
hat; a third dressed as a farmer well to do in the world, with
his top-coat over his arm and his flash notes in a large leathern
pocket book; and all with heavy handled whips to represent
most innocent country fellows who had trotted there on
horseback—sought by loud and noisy talk and pretended play
to entrap some unwary customer, while the gentlemen
confederates (of more villainous aspect still, in clean linen

and good clothes) betrayed their close interest in the concern by the anxious furtive glance they cast on all new comers.[1]

These were a far dressier set of blackguards than most of the magsmen one would expect to see at the common run of provincial gatherings, where a smock-frock and hobnails (reassuring to rustic victims) long remained a favourite get-up for minor sharps and ruffians. On the other hand, during the next few years new railways and new race meetings greatly extended the field open to the bigger rogues Dickens is describing.

In fact fairground and race-course sharping covered a wide range of types. Some of them were mere tramps who doubled sharping with footpadding: others were prosperous operators, as artistically rigged out as the swellest mobsman, who could afford to swoop down for a day or two at profitable meetings and who were soon able to reach Bath or Cheltenham as easily as Hampton. Some of them used apparatus which represented a fair little capital and needed a covered cart to carry it; and these necessarily followed the pattern of other show folk, methodically working a seasonal tour from site to site. Others carried their traps in their pockets or a carpet bag and could set up where they pleased, in a street market or on a seaside esplanade, so long as they could escape the constable's attentions.

As has been remarked earlier, gipsies, Jews and foreigners made up a large proportion of the travelling fairground population (and they certainly included plenty of doubtful characters) but most regular magsmen were solidly British. Indeed, with one exception, it looks as if the native British predominated in every type of professional sharping. A reason is not hard to find. It was a competitive trade in which a downright English voice and appearance were invaluable assets. Allied to a solid, round-faced, beef-eating physique and a healthy open-air complexion they gave their owner an overwhelming advantage. Every simpleton knew that a dark skin and foreign-sounding speech were not to be trusted.

To survive, a magsman must have had a flexible mind and the ability to adapt himself to different sorts of 'pull'. Fairground work was largely seasonal and for months at a stretch the roving thimble-rigger had to make a living away from the road; while city-sharping meant frequent shifts of hunting ground and so at

[1] *Nicholas Nickleby*, Chapter 50.

least minor changes of method. (Binny believed that the London magsmen had some sort of arrangement for swopping territories, so as to avoid becoming too well known in one area.) It has to be remembered that, unlike the thief, the sharper could not act swiftly and secretly; on the fairground or in city streets he had always to get the attention of his quarry, so that his proceedings were inevitably conspicuous. He needed, too, more than any other sort of criminal, a good supply of fresh, inexperienced and preferably idle victims; and it was no doubt for this reason that spas and seaside resorts were, with London, the magsman's favourite places. Given this supply, however, a skilful man was able to carry on with remarkable freedom. In the sharp-haunted districts round the railway terminuses at King's Cross and Waterloo, along Oxford Street and High Holborn, by St Paul's and the Abbey, the same types (if not the same individuals) could be seen all the time, watching for visitors to fleece. Presumably they owed this latitude largely to the fact they could only be brought to book on their victim's initiative; and the victim— left in an uncertain state of mind, and feeling that he had little prospect, whatever happened, of seeing his money again—was often reluctant to start proceedings that were bound to advertise his own gullibility. (Financially this was a mistake; when sharps were prosecuted they often sent someone, very likely a woman, to buy off the person bringing the charge.)

In the city, the magsman often turned his hand to confidence-tricks that took the form of quite elaborate charades. One play may, for want of a better name, be called 'The Provincial Stranger'. Let us imagine some skittle sharps at work, using this well tried, indeed hackneyed, gambit. Like most such schemes, the routine will need at least three men working in smooth, practised partnership.

The prime mover—the Provincial Stranger himself is a solid-looking fellow not unlike the pseudo-farmer Dickens pictures at Hampton. In thick country-cut coat and low-crowned hat he walks down the street by himself, well ahead of his two colleagues, gawping curiously as he goes. Seeing a likely victim he accosts him, and establishes his provinciality at a stroke by pointing at Westminster Hall and asking what it is. The overture succeeds. As it turns out the young man in painfully smart new clothes and an 'illustrated' shirt front can tell him and is happy to do so. They exchange some remark about the lawyers passing in and out, fall into conversation, and turn into a bar for a glass of beer.

The Provincial Stranger is surprised to find that his companion is, like himself, a visitor to London. Apparently drawn to him by the discovery, he mentions in his blunt way that he's a midland grazier, in town on business but taking the chance of a little pleasure and sight-seeing. He is friendly but not effusive; his clothes, his gold hunter, his confident manner proclaim a man of sense and substance. Everything about him encourages trust, and as he by no means monopolises the conversation there is soon quite an exchange of information. By an interesting coincidence it turns out that he has old links with the young man's home. He was actually born nearby and has even thought of making a bequest to a place of which he cherishes happy memories. Only, having left it in infancy, he knows little of affairs there, nothing of the local poor; perhaps his new friend might be willing to supply information as to how a legacy of that sort could best be used? Perhaps he could find time to write him a letter when he gets home? From a well-stuffed wallet he produces a card, which leads to the new friend opening *his* pocket book to put the card safely away.

Meantime one of the other magsmen has followed them in and takes a place at the bar alongside. He is clearly unknown to the grazier, but a chance observation and the latter's forthright ways quickly lead to his being included in the conversation; though it is evident that the grazier does not take quite so kindly to this newcomer.

The talk veers to celebrated feats of skill and strength, and then takes a more personal and competitive turn. To illustrate some point the grazier recalls a cast he made with a ten pound shot; the others seem a trifle sceptical, and a trial of prowess is suggested. Why not stroll over to a sporting public house on the other side of the river where the matter can easily be put to the test? The dupe, of course, has not been left out of these exchanges and is a firm partisan of the grazier's. Off they go to the testing place where there is a skittle ground that ought to have served their purpose very well, but unfortunately on being paced out it proves too cramped for a fair trial. However it's a capital skittle alley and the grazier challenges his rival to a throw or two. Without any great brilliance being displayed on either side, he shows himself the better man, and the dupe who has been tempted into backing him finds himself pocketing a handful of silver.

By this time the third member of the gang has arrived on the scene. He turns out to be a nodding acquaintance of Magsman Number 2 (who treats him rather off-handedly) and a rather indifferent skittles player. When, after a little casual practice, a regular game is suggested—the two provincials against the others—Number 3 is tempted but reluctant, insists on low stakes, and finally joins in only to avoid the charge of being a spoilsport. Another round of drinks and the match is on. The dupe is now hooked, and it only remains to play him safe into the landing net. First the dupe and the grazier win comfortably, then lose a little, then triumph: excitement quickens, the pot-boy is busy, stakes are raised and variations introduced. But success is again followed by reverses. After a bad turn the grazier makes a reckoning, discovers that he and his partner are more heavily down than might have been expected, and wants to stop. The others are sportingly reluctant to leave off as heavy winners and suggest breaking up the pairs. Magsman Number 3, now tipsy and cock-a-hoop with undeserved victory, challenges the grazier, who is obviously the stronger player, to a solo match. The grazier demurs. Thick-voiced and arrogant, brushing aside his worried companion, Number 3 insists, suicidally offering to back himself to any amount. Cool and a trifle grim the grazier rolls up his sleeves for the massacre, and winks to the dupe, who plunges deeply, certain of recouping. Disaster. The chagrined grazier confesses he could have done better blindfold. But there is still hope: what price double or quits all round? Agreed. A coin flickers. But once again the provincials are unlucky. In a few moments the frantic dupe has doubled, then quadrupled his debt.

'Short reckonings make long friends,' says the grazier calmly, and with the aid of the flash wad in his pocket book speedily pays his own heavy losses. Clapping on his hat he tells his friend to hurry and do likewise, and come to a chophouse. But the dupe can't pay up—not in full—he hasn't the wherewithal: and all at once the social atmosphere freezes. Now, abruptly, it's three to one; outraged sportsmen against a shamefaced welsher. No one cares what he might be able to do when he gets home, or to-morrow, or next year. What does he take them for, babes unborn? The alley door is poked shut with a knobbed walking stick: someone suggests that the little yard at the back would be a suitable place for gents to discuss private business. But in the end moderation prevails. For the time being at least, the winners will settle for whatever's immediately available—and they take it, down to the silver-gilt stud in the poor wretch's shirt.

Nothing about the whole business of sharping is more striking than the simplicity of many successful tricks. The skittle-playing charade would have seemed crude to a first-class card sharp, but compared to many of the methods in use at the time it was highly sophisticated. Some of the tricks, indeed, seem more like music hall knockabouts than serious efforts to cheat sane people. Sometimes the victim would be drawn into a group of magsmen who were betting on which of them had most money in his pockets; he would bring out his own cash for inspection and hand it over to be counted. Or he might take on a bet that he could not get hold of such-and-such a sum within, say, a couple of hours; and would dash off to collect it, returning inside the time to slap it down triumphantly in front of the expectant criminals. Or again, challenged to a bet he was morally certain of winning, he might be inveigled into letting one of the gang act as neutral stake-holder and take charge of pretty well every penny he had with him. Sometimes these manoeuvres ended with one of the magsmen simply bolting with the money, his confederates distracting the victim's attention at the crucial moment and then disappearing in pretended pursuit. On other and better organised occasions, sharps would get their victim to leave his money behind while he went out of the room. Things might be so arranged, for instance, that the dupe's stake formed part of a pool to which others in the party had contributed, making it awkward for him to insist on subtracting his share when he only had to leave the room for a minute; anyway, one of the other contributors would set a good example by coming out at the same time. Since these maggings usually took place in pubs[1] with everyone drinking beer, calls of nature must often have served the magsmen's turn; but the ability to make them move about as they wish is a striking feature of the sharps' ascendancy over their victims.

The amounts involved in this sort of blatant magging were frequently small, even trifling. But not always. In a case cited by Binny, a young master baker was picked up by a couple of

[1] Many of the tricks would have been impossible without the connivance of the landlord, who must have been perfectly able to recognise sharps when he saw them at work. Probably many publicans took a cut.

London sharps in a country road somewhere near Croydon. One of them attached himself to the young man and took him to a railway hotel for a drink, where he was introduced to another man who was apparently prepared to make substantial loans, spot cash, at moderate interest to recommended persons. The baker was presented as a friend by the amiable sharp who had brought him, and on the strength of the introduction was soon offered the cheap use of £100. The only stipulation was that he should first produce an equal sum of his own to demonstrate his worth as a solid citizen. Somewhat slow-witted even to be a convenient gull, the baker trotted off home and hopefully returned with a ten pound note. Nothing doing. So leaving the ten pounds—presumably as proof he meant business and was coming back—he again went home and this time reappeared with £100 in gold and notes. The lender was satisfied and ready to advance his £100 in exchange for a formal receipt. For this, however, a stamp was needed, and no one had a stamp. So the baker had to go and buy one, which he did, leaving the money on the table covered with his handkerchief—with the inevitable result.

Accounts of the mechanics of sharping, and especially of simple confidence tricks, often seem absurd because they fail to convey the psychological adroitness that is the real core of the business. Granted he needed naive and inexperienced subjects to work on, there is no reason to suppose the Victorian sharp enjoyed a supply of particularly stupid victims or that those who fell even for the crudest ploys were necessarily fools. The key to nearly all these tricks (the principle is as old as the hills and still as valid as ever) lies in the bond established between cheat and victim. If it is skilfully managed, a chance acquaintanceship only an hour or two old can become—*relative to the strangers the two new acquaintances encounter*—a confirmed and dependable friendship. Often, as in the cases we have been considering, the strangers were members of the sharp's gang, whose job was to promote the friendship by every means available. Some magsmen would go to the length of staging stand-up fights among themselves and knock one another about in convincing fashion to foster the idea that the dupe and his betrayer were allies in a hostile world. Once that was established all the rest followed. One may believe, in fact, that dupes of this sort were caught less by hopes of gain than by that potent lure, a sense of being liked and valued 'for oneself'. What the sharp most hoped to see in his prey's face was not stupidity but loneliness.

One celebrated case shows this force at work with startling power, though the chief character can hardly be classed with ordinary magsmen.

Sarah Rachael Leverson came from the dregs of society. She never troubled to acquire the rudiments of literacy and her wheedling pretensions easily gave way to gutter ferocity; yet for all that there was a touch of genius in her. When, around 1859–60, 'Madame Rachael' (as she called herself) began to attract the attention of the world at large, she was already a coarse-featured, middle-aged woman with an insinuating manner. Her past is murky, but she had come to London from Lancashire a number of years before and since then had engaged at various times in the old clothes, fried fish and fortune telling lines. Before the move south she is said to have been married to an apothecary's assistant, from whom she may have gained a knowledge of dispensing that later served her in the preparation of cosmetics (then often made from such tricky ingredients as arsenic, white lead and antimony).

Somehow she launched out in what would now be called a beauty salon catering for the fashionable Mayfair market, and her flair for publicity soon made her name familiar to the up-to-date and worldly. But something went wrong (her project was highly ambitious and probably under-capitalised) and by 1862 she was out of business and in a debtor's prison. The following year, however, saw her re-established and mistress of the handsomely appointed little business in New Bond Street that was to be the scene of her meteoric success. Perhaps the means were provided by the shadowy Mr Leverson (to whom she was married at about this time) or perhaps an attorney named Haynes, who was associated with her affairs, had by now spotted her potentialities and decided to back her. What is clear is that she had valuable and anonymous assistance in promoting her business—the more so in that she is reported to have been incapable of even writing her name.

The slogan *Beautiful for Ever* that glittered above her shop-front was also the title of a publication, price two-and-six, in which Madame Rachael's message to womankind was set forth —a clever blend of titillation and claptrap. Later it was claimed that one of her two daughters who helped in the shop prepared her advertising copy; but though the girl may have acted as secretary to her mother it is exceedingly unlikely that such effective publicity was the work of a near-child with so restricted a background. Everything points to a lively, but not over-cultivated, literary talent at Mrs Leverson's disposal.

Among the innumerable powders, oils, washes, soaps and so on offered for sale, 'oriental' products were much to the fore; and the allusive reference to the usages of the harem proved a telling attraction. An especially well-promoted line was Magnetic Rock Dew Water, at once exotic, stimulating and hygienic. By the inspired adoption of some balderdash culled from a periodical the Dew's amazing qualities were made clear:

> In the interior of the Sahara, or the Great Desert, is a magnetic rock, from which water distils sparingly in the form of dew, which is possessed of an extraordinary property. Whether a latent electricity is imparted by magnetism, or an additional quantity of oxygen enters into its composition, it is not easy to say. But it appears to have the property of increasing the vital energies, as it restores the colour to grey hair apparently by renewing the circulation in its capillary tubes, the cessation of which causes greyness; and it gives the appearance of youth to *persons of considerable antiquity*. This water is brought to Morocco *on swift dromedaries* for the use of the Court, and its virtues are much extolled by their physicians. It might be called the antipodes of the Lethean Styx of ancient times.

Considering the 'enormous outlay' Madame Rachael incurred in bringing this stuff to Bond Street, two guineas a bottle was hardly excessive, and in fact it was among the cheapest of her wares. Those who wished to be more completely equipped could have a 'Bridal Toilet Cabinet' costing from twenty-five to two hundred guineas, or even invest in a Royal Bridal Toilet Cabinet, as supplied to the Sultaness of Turkey, at a thousand. A similar scale of charges was made for the treatments taken in adjacent premises, including the celebrated Arabian Baths (an infusion of bran in hot water) and ablutions with precious Jordan Water (from which the bran was omitted). By 1867 Mrs Leverson had a handsome coach and pair, a house in nearby Maddox Street, and could afford a box at the Opera at £400 for the season.

But this enterprising woman was much more than a seller of paint and powder and ridiculous nostrums: it could be that her preposterously priced cosmetics were not even the main source of her wealth. It must be remembered that at this period the very notion of make-up carried a flavour of impropriety. If it was used at all, it was supposed to be invisible—purely a means of improving nature—and if worldly society allowed older women a certain latitude, any detectable artificialities on a girl's face were indecent. The legitimate side of Madame Rachael's business was therefore directed mostly towards free-spending women, fairly senior and not too straitlaced. No doubt there were also gentlemen customers who bought the sort of presents that could only be given to women with whom they were very intimate. The more discreditable side of the business harmonised very conveniently with a trade of this kind.

The 'house of assignation', where lovers can meet in secret, is an immemorial feature of London life, and it flourished in an age when, though women were enjoying new freedom, even demi-mondaines often had to be very discreet. The *Beautiful for Ever* enterprise, with its premises for bathing and treatment, provided admirable cover, and in fact it had something of the character of an eighteenth century *bagnio*. Probably business of all kinds boomed precisely because its reputation *was* literally questionable—there was a risqué, enticing quality to the luxurious little shop, yet the place was not so unambiguously disreputable as to frighten off every customer with a regard for her good name. A touch of naughtiness went well with the sale of cosmetics.

The opportunities for blackmail must have been splendid, and from what is known of Mrs Leverson, they were well exploited. But again the scope of her activities can only be guessed from a few facts that later came out. One customer, the wife of a City broker, left her diamond rings and earrings in a dressing room while undergoing treatment and found they had disappeared. When she insisted on their return Madame Rachael dropped her pretences and ran up her true colours. The victim was harshly told not to 'give herself airs'—she had already been watched and followed, it was known where she lived, and if she gave trouble her husband would learn that she had been coming to meet a lover. The woman went home without her jewels and told her husband what had happened. He believed she was innocent and took legal advice. Counsel's reluctant opinion was that they would be ill advised to proceed with the matter: a prosecution in the circumstances must inevitably expose them to such an orgy of mud-slinging in open court that, win or lose, the lady's reputation would be destroyed.

The incident shows the strength of Mrs Leverson's position, how perfectly suited her set-up was for safe and easy extortion. But it also shows her weakness. She was too vulgarly rapacious, too ready to grab every immediate chance, to be a completely successful swindler.

In 1867, the year she spent £400 on a box at the opera, a middle-aged woman called Mary Tucker Borrodaile, the widow of an army officer, presented herself at the shop in New Bond Street. Whatever looks she may have possessed had wholly withered under tropical suns, but she was devoured by a thirst for glamour and romance. She was very far from bright and endowed with a limitless capacity for self-deception: she was, though not rich, an almost ideal subject. She had a modest property in real-estate and about £5,000 invested.

Having quickly sold Mrs Borrodaile £170 of cosmetics, Madame Rachael soon had her measure. It fell out that, when she was on the premises, the widow once or twice encountered Lord Ranelagh, a sporting bachelor. Whatever led the fashionable old buck to haunt Madame Rachael's establishment, it was not the prospect of meeting people like Mrs Borrodaile and the contact (if the word is not too emphatic) was brief and uneventful. But it supplied a germ of reality round which was woven a great cocoon of fantasy. Mrs Borrodaile was given to understand that the nobleman was wildly attracted. He had actually taken the ungentlemanly liberty of peeping at her through a spyhole (apparently one of the facilities of the establishment) while she was having a rejuvenating Arabian Bath and had fallen deeply in love. He was determined to make her Lady Ranelagh, but unfortunately it was essential for family reasons to keep the connection completely secret till the wedding day. Any open recognition between them was out of the question; they must communicate only through Madame Rachael. Thus the wooing was carried out by love letters which Mrs Borrodaile received from 'Granny'—as she was now taught to call Madame Rachael —and by answers which she composed, prompted by Granny, in the parlour behind the scented boutique.

The curious thing is that the two women seem to have mutually intoxicated each other: Mrs Borrodaile was robbed of every vestige of sense by the letters she was given, and Mrs Leverson thrown into a sort of delirium of avarice by the discovery of an ascendancy so complete that there was nothing she could not make her victim believe. By Lord Ranelagh's express wish his betrothed embarked on a further thousand pounds' worth of treatment, but this was a mere preliminary. Her old jewels being unworthy of her prospective station she gave them over to Granny and with her help bought new ones, including a diamond tiara, of which Granny took charge. She invested in quantities of expensive lace and a handsome carriage, likewise entrusted to Granny. Lord Ranelagh, it transpired, was in temporary financial embarrassment over the volunteer corps he commanded and which he had to accompany to Belgium. Mrs Borrodaile was proud to help. Granny introduced Mr Haynes, the lawyer, who advised her as to the disposal of her capital, and in three brief months they had stripped their prey to the bone.

The supposed lover's letters, though crude enough, show facility and insight. Mrs Borrodaile, as might be expected, treasured and preserved them. In one she learnt that Lord Ranelagh slept with her letters and likeness against his heart. With another she received a vinaigrette and pencil case, his father's first gifts to his worshipped mother who died with them in her hand; at the same time she was told that her peeress' coronet had been made and bidden to keep Granny sweet. . . . 'My dearest one, what is the matter with the old woman? She seems out of sorts. We must manage to keep her in a good temper for our own sakes.' Feeble attempts at resistance were overcome by reproaches. One letter, evidently fairly late in the series, goes:

May, my heart's love,—Is it your wish to drive me mad? Granny has my instructions. Do as she tells you. Four letters, and not one reply. What is the meaning of this delay at the eleventh hour? Granny lent me the money. You shall pay her, my own sweet one. Get the lace today and fear nothing. . . . Your sister and her husband have behaved very badly towards you if you knew all. I tell you, love, if you are not careful they will divide us for ever. To the Strand to-day. Leave all to me, my own love and fear nothing. If you have lost all love and confidence in your ugly old donkey, tell me; but this suspense is terrible. I receive letters every day, telling me that you only laugh at, and show, my letters. Mary beloved one of my heart, do not trifle with me; I love once, I love for ever. Leave all to me. I guard your honour with my life.—With fond and devoted love, I am your devoted William.

There was a crowning effrontery about these letters: many of them were actually written in different hands. Mrs Borrodaile was told that her lover had injured his arm and had to dictate to a confidential servant, which also explained occasional slips in spelling. Further, Lord Ranelagh was called Thomas, not William; but the signature was accounted for on the ground that correspondence signed 'Thomas' might, if discovered, fatally compromise the romantic design. So precious was her fantasy to the poor woman that she swallowed all these excuses, and in fact Mrs. Leverson and her letter writer were not so stupid as might appear: these absurdities were among the most sensible precautions embodied in the fraud.

Besides her property Mrs Borrodaile had a widow's pension of some £300 a year. Having got hold of everything else, Madame Rachael determined to make a clean sweep and take this too. Armed with a bond that one of the love letters had induced her victim to sign, she now had her committed to jail until the pension was made over. It was an act of folly. Ruined, and faced with God knows what torments of disillusion, Mrs Borrodaile could no longer evade the relatives she had previously fended off. At such a pass they were not to be deterred by scandal, and in due course Mrs Leverson appeared before the Recorder of London.

In the witness box at the Old Bailey, Mrs Borrodaile, 'spare, thin, scraggy-looking', her face heavily rouged and her hair dyed vivid yellow, did not make a good impression. The fantastic inconsistencies in the correspondence told strongly for the defence. How could anyone have been deceived week after week, by such manifest rubbish? Was it not plain that the woman had deliberately used the facilities of Madame Rachael's establishment for her own convenience, and poured away her money buying gratification for her lewd appetites? The case caused a good deal of scandalised entertainment. Mrs Borrodaile, described by the press as a 'senescent Sappho', became a regular figure of fun, and there was loud laughter in court at her expense. It is a comment on the conventions of the time that Lord Ranelagh, sitting in a place of honour by the Recorder, joined heartily in the merriment. A puzzled jury could reach no decision; but the prosecution did not let Madame Rachael escape them. A month later, at a fresh trial, they secured a verdict of guilty and heard her sentenced to penal servitude.

There is a curious continuation to the story. On her release in 1872, the brazen old cheat was still full of spirit—she is said to have called on the governor of the penitentiary, swaggering in her finest feathers—and actually set up in the beauty business again, in less fashionable quarters but not far from her old premises. Her custom and opportunities must have been very small compared to the old days, but apparently she found the game worth keeping up for another six years. Then she got into trouble over a young woman who had deposited a couple of necklaces worth about fifty pounds with her as security for a course of treatments and wanted them back. The necklaces were no longer in Madame Rachael's possession. Considering her past triumphs the amount involved was a bagatelle; but her day was done. The trial that followed was her last public appearance, for she died before her sentence expired.

But for the greed shown in her treatment of Mrs Borrodaile, Rachael Leverson might have died in more or less reputable prosperity and passed into oblivion.[1] In a sense she was not a unique figure, only an unusually well publicised and exposed one. It is, after all, the charlatans who over-reached themselves and came to grief that we hear of—and then often in terms that give only the cloudiest idea of how the game was really played. Our knowledge of the way Mrs Leverson devoured Mrs Borrodaile is largely a matter of chance: how many more flourished in security, protected by the laws of libel and the frightened silence of their dupes?

In any civilised society, there are plenty of people ready to exploit the vanity and ignorance of well-off victims, often with the aid of half-veiled erotic appeals. The magnetic waters, electric beds, 'ether frolics', fraudulent seances and quack

[1] As it is, Mme Rachael seems destined for immortality. The most recently published description of her I have come on was in a child's comic paper with a national circulation. Here my chief sources have been W. Roughead's essay in *The Bad Companions* (1930) and Montagu Williams, Q.C., *Leaves of a Life* (1890).

mesmerists of Victorian charlatanry have their counterparts in every age. But beyond question the times were good and, particularly where there was any question of sexual irregularity, the prospects of blackmail were excellent. For many people in the growing leisured class, and most notably for women, it was an era of idleness, limited diversions, and passionate preoccupation with social status and proprieties. And if Victorians were no more ill-natured than those who came before and after them, they were certainly much more severe on those who betrayed their station by allowing themselves to be involved in open scandal. Moreover they enforced their code not only with contempt but derision. A mid-nineteenth-century gentlewoman who publicly compromised her honour—and above all compromised it through the agency of some squalid charlatan or pander—faced a nightmare of ostracism and ridicule we can scarcely imagine.

On the whole the social and technical changes of the nineteenth century tended to favour the higher grades of fraud rather than the magsman. It is true that, at first, the coming of steam transport was a boon to him. It not only allowed him to travel quickly and cheaply to his quarry: it brought his quarry to him in vast numbers. Thousands of green[1] provincials, whose parents would have thought a twenty-five mile journey a major enterprise, came flocking cheerfully into the great cities and resorts on business and pleasure. The magsmen reaped the harvest, but in the long run the transport revolution worked against them by helping to form a more sophisticated, town-centred society. In the same way the spread of literacy, the stopping of public lotteries, the outlawing of betting shops, stricter control on places of entertainment and the extension of public prosecution all helped to put an end to many age-old systems of conycatching.

In exchange, the revolution offered a host of new opportunities to the sharp who was equipped to take advantage of them. The cheap, prepaid mail, which was introduced in 1840, opened up a new world for the literate swindler. A well drafted letter in an educated hand still carried a strong presumption that the writer must be a respectable man, and it was a fine way of obtaining things on false pretences. One enterprising lot of

[1] The word 'green', used in this sense, was about the most over-worked adjective of the period. Its vogue among all classes seems to coincide with the revolution in transport between the forties and the sixties.

cheats got away with a herd of cattle, having arranged by correspondence to collect them and graze them in a gentleman's park.

Newspapers, too, were reaching a wider and wider public,
and their advertisement columns provided a way of tapping the
ambitious, self-improving type of workman who was not easily
tempted by the magsman. The bogus employment bureau was
a good line and large profits could be made even when the
individual fees were small. One man found it worthwhile to
advertise non-existent work in the booming Australian gold-
fields to the Cornish tin miners for a registration fee of a shilling.
Another rented an empty house in Chorlton-upon-Medlock
where the police found floods of letters arriving with five shilling
remittances inside. They were from candidates for the post of
bailiff on an imaginary farm, and a woman had been collecting
them twice daily. She was caught with eleven pounds' worth of
letters in her basket but the chief swindler got away untraced.
It was reckoned that he had raked in £700 before the police cut
things short, in return for a very modest outlay in advertising,
postage and a quarter's rent.

Most of these tricks worked best with people of little education. Higher up the social scale, the best of all means of extorting
money was the bill of exchange. This was still a very common
way of raising money and it lent itself to a whole catalogue of
abuses, lawful as well as unlawful. Indeed the extortion that
went on became so notorious that there were sharps who traded
on it by getting some dunce to invest in a worthless bill, per-
suading him that he was a shrewd and ruthless man of affairs
about to screw large profits out of a fictitious victim.

If the gambling sharps described earlier had been on a higher
level—gentlemanly 'macers'[1] plucking a carefully chosen pigeon
over cards and dice, punch and anchovy toast—they would have
ended, not by taking his shirt studs, but by getting him to put
his name to a piece of stamped and negotiable 'stiff'. Of course
they would ease things by pointing out, in their genial men-of-
the-world way, that the paper was only a formal memorandum
for the winner to hold until another evening's play liquidated
the debt. In fact, however, they would dispose of it to a contact
in the shark-haunted underwaters of the city and it would soon

---

[1] Macing (or maceing) chiefly meant cheating by obtaining credit, especially in connection with gambling debts. It could be stretched to cover various rackets based on false
pretences and at its lower end overlapped with magging. In general, however, the macer
worked at a higher social level than the magsman.

reappear in the victim's life, surfacing perhaps through a bank in his home town. If that happened, he had better settle promptly, at whatever sacrifice, if he wanted to keep any local credit for himself and his family.

Given a suitable pigeon, it might be more profitable if the debt was not discharged on time. If he succumbed to the bullying and cajoling of the men who dogged his life, he could find himself enmeshed in such a tangle of renewals, liens, and other 'accommodations' that he might in the end have paid his original debt several times over before he was thrown into jail in the hope of stimulating his friends and relations to further efforts. Moreover, there was the prospect that a hard driven victim would get friends to help him out by putting their own names to his paper, so bringing fresh grist to the usurer's mill: like the victim of a vampire he might himself be transformed into a predator. Indeed, the middle or upper-class macer, part victim, part accomplice of the sharks he supplied with new custom, seems to have been an accepted hazard of fast-living circles. A standard item of parental advice to the freshman going up to a university or the newly commissioned subaltern was: *Never* back a friend's bill.

All these forms of deception together did not add up to so serious a nuisance as one single species of fraud—forgery.

Forgery of one sort or another was a commonplace. Beggars and hucksters had their faked testimonials, the cracksman's inside accomplice got the job by a bogus 'character', the false-pretences cheat depended on references, the stolen dog fancier forged pedigrees and the resetter of stolen watches 'christened' them with fake marking. But forgery in the narrower sense of making false coins, bank-notes, cheques and bills, was the work of a small number of highly skilled criminals, protected by a whole series of intermediaries who had a vested interest in keeping them safe. Each one of them might be the centre of a web of criminal activities which, unless he himself was convicted, could always be rewoven by new criminals ready to profit from his skill. Behind it, the master forger could work quietly away at the mysteries of his craft.

Those who took part in the bad coin industry were known as shofulmen and, looking at them, one is once again struck by the complexity of underworld enterprise. Crudely, the trade could be divided into three sections: the coiners, the agents or bulk-dealers who distributed the forged coin from fixed rendezvous, and the 'smashers' or utterers who passed it into circulation. A great many disreputable people up and down the country took a part in smashing, and probably one coin would pass through the hands of several of them before it reached the public. The essential need was to prevent the flow of 'snide' coins being traced backwards, and the more tenuous the connection between the smashers and the original source of supply, the better.

Passing bad coin was not a full time job. It was something a tout, sharp, moucher or whatever added to his repertoire of tricks when opportunity offered, so that the stuff had to be distributed among a large circle of customers, many of whom could be expected to get into trouble. For obvious reasons, a wandering way of life lent itself to 'snide pitching', and its prevalence at fairs, race meetings and country markets was one reason for the hostility of magistrates towards travelling show people—though the showmen themselves were often victimised. As is mentioned in Chapter 2, there was a trade in small counterfeit silver pieces supplied in an unfinished state to gipsies and tinkers who prepared them for circulation.

As might be expected, the chief distribution points seem to have been slumland pubs and other low places of public entertainment (although Binny declares that some counterfeit dealers actually sold in the open street). A pothouse in Christopher Street, Bethnal Green, run by a certain Cokey Hogan who was also a fighting-dog fancier was at one time a well known centre for the trade. So was the Clock House in Seven Dials, and indeed Seven Dials remained for a long time such a notorious mart for false currency that it is hard to resist the idea that the police looked on smashing rather as they did the stolen goods trade—preferring, sometimes, to leave ill alone where they could keep their eye on it, and being more concerned with tracing the fountain heads than with blocking the outlets of a traffic that would always find new channels.

One curious fact about forgers of this period is that they seldom applied themselves to the most valuable coinage—gold. Binny, who is full of information about coining, gives no account of gold counterfeiting. Several reasons present themselves. In the eighteenth century makers of false guineas had received up to fourteen shillings apiece for their carefully fashioned hand-stamped products; but changed techniques now seem to have favoured larger production and lower profit margins among coiners, and for such a trade silver currency was better. Bad gold pieces, unless they contained a high percentage of gold, were never easy to pass. The weight of even a small gold coin gives it a characteristic feel, and a lead filling was quickly betrayed by a bite or by sounding on a hard surface. Valuable coins are likely to be carefully scrutinised so that a particularly high standard of finish was needed and the calling in of short-weight gold specie by the government made over-worn pieces suspect. Perhaps the best way to dispose of a dud sovereign was by 'ringing the changes'. A good sovereign was tendered for a small purchase, rung on the counter, then taken back by the cheat who fumbled with some small change—'Hi, wait, I've enough . . . no, won't do'—and then handed over the dud.

At the other extreme, forging coppers cannot have been a paying game, and what bad pence there were about may have been chiefly relics of an earlier age, or amateurish 'plain goods' (smooth thin discs of base metal treated to look like very worn coins). But bad silver money was a plague, especially for the poor among whom even a sixpence could be a matter of anxiety. By 1850 the total in circulation was perhaps diminishing rather than increasing, but the two mid-century decades were clearly a very active time in the 'bit-faking' industry.

Under the old traditional system, counterfeits were cut out of metal plates or 'flats' and impressed with a hammer and die. Flats for good imitation silver were made of a mixture of silver and blanched copper, the stamped coins being treated with nitric acid which brought up a convincing silvery surface. A cruder alternative was to strike coins from pewter—a fairly easy thing to lift from public houses. The pewter pieces were then polished and most of their face darkened, leaving bright patches, so that they passed as dirty sterling silver. Technological advance brought a two-fold improvement: in the first place it became usual to mould instead of strike counterfeit coins, and in the second they could be electrically plated. Since Victorian forgers used both pewter and 'Britannia Metal' (an alloy from which cheap spoons and forks were made) it is probable they sometimes moulded them into counterfeits that could be made passable by buffing and staining; but obviously these products cannot have been as good as pieces coated with real silver, and must have been far more dangerous to handle.

Though it was on the whole a humble job, carried on in slums by proletarian criminals, silver coining was an elaborate and skilled business. It needed a certain amount of working capital and also, for a decent output, a team of trained workers. Often it seems to have been run as a family enterprise, and women normally took an active part: in effect, it was a kind of cottage industry.

Silver plated coins were made from bronze medallions—a good alloy could be made with a high proportion of tin to copper and a small quantity of antimony. They were cast in plaster of Paris moulds, and making one of these moulds by pressing a genuine coin into wet plaster was expert work. Each mould was made in separate halves for the obverse and reverse faces, and a series of matrices might be impressed in the same pieces of plaster so that several coins could be cast simultaneously. The halves of the compound mould had to fit with precision, leaving clear the little channels through which the molten metal (sometimes poured down a clay pipestem) flowed into the forms. Making these fine necks was a delicate and crucial operation on which the accuracy of the reproduction largely depended. When the metal had cooled and hardened, the medallions were taken from the opened mould, the 'gats' or tails that marked the necks of the matrices snipped off. Then the two halves of the mould were reunited and the forms refilled.

During the next stage, the prepared castings were attached to the negative lead from a galvanic battery and hung in a cyanide solution in which a piece of silver, connected to the pile's positive terminal, was also immersed. When they had taken a thick enough coating of silver they were removed, washed, and 'slummed'—that is, treated with a compound of oil and lampblack to tone down their brightness. The amount of silver used cannot have been very great in relation to the output, and glazed earthenware pie dishes could be used for the electro-plating baths. But the ponderous electric batteries were far from being everyday articles, and it must have been expensive and tricky to get hold of them without attracting inconvenient interest.

The combined moulding and plating process (a good deal more complex, of course, than this sketchy account indicates) was widely used during the forties, if not earlier, and implies a rather surprising technical sophistication. One cannot be certain, but it seems likely that coiners got their knowledge of these skills through contacts with the type-founding and printing trades. There were many connections between coining and note forgery—necessarily the work of men well trained in printing techniques—and the use of electro-plating in certain printing processes was among its earliest industrial applications.

Coining was essentially an urban trade. It was probably practised in all the great industrial towns, at any rate sporadically, though it was certainly not confined to them: Wantage, of all places, long enjoyed an evil reputation as an important centre. Birmingham had a long tradition that included the half-legendary exploits of a man named Booth, something of an underworld folk hero. He was said to have inhabited a sort of stronghold on a patch of open ground across which he could see his enemies coming. Inside there were no stairs but only ladders which, when threatened, he drew up after him, so that by the time an assault party gained the upper floor where he carried on his craft it was always too late to catch him with his forgeries undestroyed. Finally he was out-manoeuvred by a party of cavalry, who galloped breakneck across the open space before he could put his defences in order, and in due course he was hanged.[1]

In Victorian times it was the dense-packed rookery that provided the typical locale for counterfeiting, and though Birmingham remained a prominent centre of the business, it was the London criminals who seem to have dominated it. Old St Giles, Bethnal Green, the maze between Whitechapel and Spitalfields, the slums of Southwark and the stinking purlieus that bordered on the precincts of Westminster Abbey—all the worst criminal slums in the capital, outside the port district, notoriously harboured nests of coiners.

The traditional notion of a coiners' den in a cellar harks back to days when a din of hammering and a brazier to melt metal were best kept below stairs. Nineteenth-century coiners, whose firing was done with an old saucepan on a domestic grate, liked working near the roof. Good window lighting was no doubt important, but there was another vital point: if they were detected a great deal depended on the degree to which they were caught red-handed. In prosecutions for counterfeiting it was always highly desirable, if not essential, for the Crown to produce concrete evidence of the crime. What the police wanted

[1] Counterfeiting money ceased to be a capital offence in 1832 but the death penalty was retained (though not inflicted) for certain classes of document forgery. The last hanging for forgery in England was in 1829.

were specimens of the forged coins to produce in court, and they did their utmost to get them. A few minutes grace was enough for the destruction of this damning material in fire and crucible, so that a top-storey room approached by a single, easily defended stairway, and offering a chance of escape over neighbouring roofs, made a far more desirable coining shop than any basement.

Often coiners' premises were guarded by a dog or two, chained by the door, and a watchful 'crow' lounging near the courtyard entry, while the stairs might be booby-trapped. Police raids were usually based on fairly detailed information and they had to be planned as surprise irruptions. Plainclothes officers drifted quietly into the vicinity and then, without warning, made a sudden assault, smashing through doors and rushing up to the coining-shop as fast as they could go. They could expect a warm reception, for cornered coiners were rough customers, quite ready to use their molten metal and acid as weapons. Since the raiding party had to be kept small, so as not to be too conspicuous, even the most modest counterfeiting outfit could give a good deal of trouble.

In 1845 three men, a police sergeant, a constable and a special officer called Brennan, visited a court in Shoreditch where there was a small two-room dwelling, 'one up, one down', occupied by a coiner. Leaving the constable on guard at the end of the court, the other two approached the house. One of them produced a sledge hammer (hidden, presumably, under a loose coat) and they stove in the door. Inside there was a lively fracas. Brennan rushed upstairs and ran into the coiner, who tried to get back into the upper room but was prevented by Brennan grabbing his leather apron. Together they pitched down the staircase, Brennan never relaxing his hold though the coiner's knee was in his belly and his head was injured by the fall. Meantime the coiner's wife, a tall masculine-looking woman, and his daughter, an active girl of thirteen, and a bulldog had all set about the sergeant. The constable from outside joined the battle and the little household was finally overcome, though the bulldog kept his grip on the sergeant's trousers for nearly half an hour. Brennan, victorious but badly knocked about, went back upstairs and found 'four galvanic batteries in full play' besides some five hundred pieces, from crowns to sixpences, 'in various stages of manufacture'. By modern standards the sentences passed on the wife and daughter seem odd. The woman, who was held to

have been only obeying her husband, was let off, while the child
got two years imprisonment. The coiner was condemned to
fifteen years transportation.

(Brennan was the bane of the counterfeiters during the forties
and fifties. He was an agent of the Royal Mint, not one of the
new Detective Police, but his enquiries were responsible for
many police raids in which he seems usually to have taken a
leading part, and according to Binny (in 1861) the hunting down
of coiners in London was under his management. In later years
his son worked with him and the two were involved in a number
of battles with forgers.)

It was impossible for the police to post enough men in a dense
and hostile slum district to cordon off the area where a raid was
planned without giving the game away, so it is easy to see how
some of a gang might escape even the best managed coup. The
raiding party had both to take the coining shop with its contents
more or less intact and simultaneously capture the coiners.
Seeing that, from the coiners' point of view, everything depended
on holding up the attackers, it seems less remarkable that they
sometimes arranged traps than that any gang should have
neglected to do so.

Brennan was once rushing upstairs in an assault on a master
counterfeiter called Morris when his hat crashed into a spiked
obstruction: the dark stairwell had been closed by letting down
a flap studded with sharp iron prongs two or three inches long
and about as far apart. Thanks to this device, which was very
hard to shift, Morris escaped over the roofs, and although he
hurt himself badly jumping down twenty-five feet onto an out-
building, reached friends who got him away to Birmingham,
where he was able to go into hospital till he recovered.

Two years later he was back in London and had set up in
Southwark, where the dogged Brennan, accompanied by a police
detail, 'paid him a visit at 7 o'clock on a winter's evening'.
Discovering his danger, Morris, who had been busy on some
half-crowns, threw himself from a first floor window onto an
officer standing guard below and then tore off coatless through
the streets with Brennan after him. Unable to shake off his
pursuer, the coiner dived through a doorway, down a step into
a room where a man and woman were by the fire and their
children lying on a bed. Brennan missed his footing on the step
and stumbled across the bed; but he managed to recover himself,

warn off the householder whose child he had narrowly missed injuring, and trip and pinion Morris before he could dodge out of the room. A crowd gathered from the tenement and stoned the officers while they were removing their handcuffed prisoner. Morris tried to kill himself under the wheels of a passing waggon before he was safely brought in a cab to the police station. At his trial he was sentenced to thirty years transportation.

On another occasion, Brennan broke into a house in Westminster where a man called Bob Cummings carried on his counterfeiting. They reached the coining-shop and arrested several of Cummings' gang, but when they came down to the bottom of a flight of stairs they found a gaping pit: the flooring had been opened to expose a kind of oubliette in which the leaders of the party could have come to a very unpleasant end.

Cummings, who was caught soon afterwards, was a fly, resourceful character who had a long and varied criminal career and seems to have been a man of consequence in counterfeiting circles. He had started life as an engraver but as a young man took successfully to the highly competitive 'resurrection' trade —lifting fresh-buried corpses, usually with the sexton's connivance, for peddling to medical schools. (Once he brought a suburban stiff through Camberwell turnpike, propped up as a passenger in his cart.) When the Anatomy Act ruined the body-snatchers' market in the thirties he turned his attention to counterfeiting. He was also involved in bank note forgery—in which capacity we shall meet him again.

Coiners worked hard for a living. London smashers are reported to have paid a distributor 2d apiece for forged shillings, 3d for florins, 3½d for half-crowns and 4d for 'bulls' or five shilling bits. Where the distributor was an independent dealer he might make a middleman's profit of up to a hundred per cent, so that the forger himself would then get only half these wholesale prices. It looks as if competition was reducing coining almost to the status of a sweated industry.

If the rewards were low, the penalties for being caught were high, and even when the death penalty had been abolished for counterfeiting, the courts continued to pass particularly severe sentences on forgers. Coining was no life for the ambitious crook: for him, the medium to work in was paper and the cream of the counterfeit money trade was in forged banknotes. The work demanded a very high standard of trained expertise in an exacting and slowly-learned craft and appears to have been confined to a limited number of craftsmen who were carefully safe-guarded by the accomplices who profited from them. It may be for this reason that, while contemporary allusions make it clear that false paper money was no great rarity and 'doing a bit of soft' a common resource among slick and well set-up sharpers, references to the forgers themselves are relatively meagre.

The trade certainly had its difficulties. Since the temporary withdrawal of gold caused by the French wars paper money had been in free use, but the lowest note left in common circulation was for five pounds—quite valuable enough to invite close inspection, especially when tendered in payment for a few shillings, and moreover a form of currency there was no obliga-tion to accept.[1] Where coiners needed no more than a room with a chimney and some equipment that could be quickly and easily moved, the efficient production of forged notes required a ton or more of expensive plant, some of it extremely cumbersome and practically impossible to instal secretly.

In fact, though the key expert, the 'scratcher' or engraver, might do most of his work in secret and keep his plates securely hidden away when not in use, many of the best forged notes were run off in the little back-alley workrooms of small indepen-dent printers who also carried out normal above-board work. It was possible to go a fair way towards reproducing a counter-feit note without exposing oneself to prosecution. The reader may have noticed various allusions to the 'flash' money used by magsmen and confidence tricksters. This consisted of notes that were not exact reproductions but merely imitations of the genuine thing which the cheat handled in a sheaf, generally with a few real notes on top, and did not allow his victim to examine. Instead of 'Bank of England' a flash bill might have 'Bank of Engraving' printed on it, and paper of this sort was not illegal: it had a legitimate use in the theatre, for example. Its significance for the forger was that, while it had to be clearly distinguished in some way from real money, that did not prevent it from being in many respects a faithful copy. The forger could complete all sorts of processes without anyone being able to prove that he intended to produce not flash notes but counterfeit.

---

[1] The mid-century gold strikes in California and Australia increased the amount of gold in circulation, and so tended to make paper money less common, and more suspect, in small transactions.

'Turn him out!' A characteristic scene
off the Ratcliffe Highway. Gustave Doré

Second-hand
shoe dealers
in Dudley
Street,
Seven Dials,
a notorious
centre for the
counterfeit
coin trade.
Gustave
Doré

Forgers occasionally copied the notes put out by provincial banks, but these often involved colour printing and other technical complications and were also less widely acceptable than the regular Bank of England five and ten pound issues. The more 'long-tailed' denominations must have been much trickier to handle, and probably, as with stolen money, were negotiated at a proportionately heavy discount.

The chief centre of production was Birmingham, that hive of small workshops still keeping her old supremacy in this section of the bad money industry. Notes printed in Birmingham were brought in bulk to London, and no doubt to other centres, passing through agents to utterers who, it need hardly be said, were kept ignorant of its origins. Like false silver, 'soft' was often passed on to the public by transients, though by spryer and more prosperous rascals than the poor smasher who risked months at the treadmill for passing a few bad shillings. A passer of soft might visit a provincial town at a busy season, perhaps while a fair or market was in progress, posing as a horse dealer. This was a trade in which quick and heavy transactions in well-used notes were common and he could quickly unload his forgeries about the market and at inns and shops. He would then get out of the area before they began to reach the local banks—though a first-class forged note might be accepted by a bank teller and remain undetected till it eventually found its way to Threadneedle Street.

It seems that highly skilled engravers and printers, given enough time and the right equipment, could print so good a facsimile of a Bank of England note that the difference in the impression was undiscernible to the expert, unless he subjected it to extraordinary scrutiny. Ink and design could be almost exactly reproduced: what kept the forgers' activities within bounds (and explains their occasional resort to the troublesome copies of provincial bank issues) was the impossibility of duplicating the Bank of England's bill-paper. Sheets of the likeliest papers were damped and ironed, doctored with bicarbonate of soda and chloride of lime to impart the right hue, stamped to reproduce the watermark, and subjected to all kinds of ingenious treatment. But no matter how well the work was done and how carefully the note was dirtied and creased to conceal its deficiencies, the result could not deceive an alert cashier. Furthermore, if anyone was suspicious enough he did not need to be an expert; if he sponged a forged note and then, as it dried, held it up to the light, the watermark disappeared, since it was only stamped on the paper, not formed into it while it was being made.

It was a supply of paper that started the greatest note-forging conspiracy of the mid-century. In the spring of 1861 a couple called Burnett came and put up at the Three Horseshoes at Whitchurch in Hampshire. Nearby was the Laverstoke paper mill where Messrs Portal, an immensely reputable firm, had been manufacturing special papers for the Bank of England for over a century. The couple, who seemed in no hurry to leave Whitchurch, were not the modestly respectable young people their appearance suggested. Burnett had just been released on ticket of leave from a stiff sentence of imprisonment for dealing in stolen goods: his 'wife' (who was in fact not married to him) had been an accomplice. Her real name was probably Ellen Mills.

The first move was that 'Mrs Burnett' got to know a youth called Brown who worked at Laverstoke. His father was a carpenter, responsible for keeping parts of the plant in repair, and this gave the son the opportunity to go into different parts of the mill. Ellen Mills was a not unattractive woman of about thirty and soon she had so worked on young Brown that he was ready to steal paper intended for bank note printing. He found an opportunity in the drying-room, where the sized paper was dried off before glazing, and began removing sheets which he brought to the Burnetts. However he was not clever enough to carry on this game without being spotted, and before long a workman by the name of Brewer tumbled to what was happening. But Brewer was not over-eager to report his suspicions. No doubt he realised that the discovery could be turned to profit, and he threatened Brown without, apparently, confiding in anyone else.

The Burnetts proved themselves capable of dealing with this. Brown was given an extra three pounds to hand over to Brewer as a temporary mouth-stopper, and Brewer himself was then cultivated so successfully that before long he was up to his neck in the business. In the end he stole more than Brown. The paper the two were able to remove was not absolutely finished, but it was fully watermarked and very well suited to the forger's needs. It was either brought to Burnett or sometimes (perhaps after the Burnetts had left Whitchurch) taken on a train to London by Brewer. Following instructions, he transferred it to a woman in black who met him at Waterloo Station and whom he recognised by a preconcerted signal.

Security measures at Laverstoke mill plainly left something to be desired. (One has the impression of a quiet-running business where standards of workmanship were the chief pre-occupation and the familiar local employees were not subject to suspicion.) It was not until the following year that Portal's discovered discrepancies in their stocks of bill paper and informed the Bank of England. The Bank was alarmed and in August 1862 decided to make the news public through its solicitor, causing considerable public concern. Meantime, of course, officials were on the lookout for spurious notes printed on genuine paper, and a number were identified which had been previously accepted as authentic. The situation was unquestionably serious. Brown alone, the lesser thief, had managed to take away between three and four hundred sheets, from each of which two notes could be made; moreover if the forgers should prove ambitious a good deal of the missing paper was appropriate for high denomination notes of up to £1,000. The forgeries were virtually undetectable in ordinary circumstances, and the prospect of hundreds of them floating about the world to the detriment of business and the discredit of the Bank called for energetic steps. The City police chief, Captain Hogan, was put in charge of the investigation and a reward of £1,500 was offered.

The police must have found themselves on a very cold scent. By the time the theft of the paper was verified, the Burnetts had long left Whitchurch, and so had Brown. On the other hand the standard of policing throughout the country had recently much improved, and there are signs that in this case the different police forces involved cooperated closely with each other. The prosecution of offenders was initially to be directed by the Bank's highly intelligent solicitor, and the detectives were obviously allowed a good deal of freedom in coming to terms with criminals who could help them. The Bank would certainly have been ready to buy information, over and above the published reward. Most importantly, the investigators resisted the temptation to stop the spread of forgeries by swooping on anyone known to be holding stocks: they held their hand till they were in a position to sweep all the principal criminals into their net.

The police evidently began by investigating events at Laverstoke. They probably got hold of Brewer at a fairly early stage and secured a certain amount of useful information from him; but he was not on close terms with the Burnetts and can have known little about what they did when they were not in Whitchurch. His mysterious contact at Waterloo was never identified.

Brown was another matter. He had thrown up his job at the time of the robberies and had now completely vanished. He was an obvious focus of suspicion and soon the object of a hunt. As it happened the police could not have found a better target for their energies.

After leaving the mill in the summer of the previous year Brown had moved about in a desultory way, staying for a time at Portsmouth and even returning briefly to the Whitchurch neighbourhood (where there was as yet no alarm). But more and more he attached himself to the Burnetts, in London: they may have thought it best to keep an eye on him and they certainly used him as a messenger and go-between on various errands connected with the bank-note project. When the Bank of England's warning, and the announcement of the £1,500 reward, made it plain that the hunt had started, Burnett decided that Brown must be 'put in lavender' before he was spotted. He installed the youth in a hideaway by Seven Dials.

This proved to be a disastrous move. Either Brown did not lie low enough or he was betrayed by someone in the house where he was hiding. In a few days he was in the hands of the police. He was not, however, brought before a magistrate and remanded to jail: on the contrary, a detective quietly took him into his home and not only provided him with board and lodging but stood him treats in the form of visits to the Crystal Palace and other popular resorts. In return, no doubt, Brown was expected to keep his eyes open and tell his host if he recognised anyone.

Under this genial treatment Brown confided in the police. Above all he put the finger on a man who now became the centre of the whole investigation. Burnett had been careless enough to let Brown see him going into the shop of a Westminster butcher called George Buncher. Brown was not supposed to know about this man but he was able to pick up enough to make him think that he was deeply involved in the bank-note affair. Buncher was in fact a principal partner in the scheme, and very probably the original putter-up. Although the police were now almost certainly in a position to collar the Burnetts they left them alone and concentrated on Buncher.

They found that he was visiting a couple in New Cross, Mr and Mrs Campbell. The Campbells were outwardly respectable but in fact they had connections that were very useful to anyone wanting to dispose of 'gammy stiff'. They were also in a position where they found it advisable to comply when the police urged them to cooperate. About five o'clock one morning in September three detectives arrived at the Campbells' and made their preparations. The house had adjacent front and back parlours, and by removing a couple of bricks from the thin dividing wall and screening the hole on the front parlour side with a 'light picture', they made the back room into a convenient listening post. Here the policemen were waiting when Buncher, accompanied by a friend, turned up later in the morning and was received in the front parlour. The friend seems to have spent a good deal of the time outside the house, keeping a useless watch.

Buncher was a robust character. (His more vigorous expressions were unfortunately expunged from the published evidence.) Getting down to business he demanded £200 for a consignment of forged notes he had ready,[1] 'as promised on Wednesday'. Mrs Campbell refused and suggested £50. This naturally started an argument, in which Mr Campbell proposed they should have a look at the counterfeits. Buncher replied that it was 'not —— likely' he would part with the stuff until he had the money. 'You take me for a —— fool, but you're mistaken. In fact you never was more mistaken in your life, you little ——. Once for all, you know there's fifteen hundred pounds reward for me. I am the —— that's got the bank paper. I've thirty thousand now, and the —— Bank of England can't stop it.'

Campbell insisted that he must be allowed to inspect the notes before buying them. Buncher made it plain he expected to be entirely trusted and would run no unnecessary risk. Under his rage he seems to have become increasingly wary. 'May I be —— well paralysed,' he said, 'may God strike me —— blind, if you put the money in my hand, you shall have the goods within quarter of an hour.' Unable to strike a bargain on these terms he demanded two pounds for his expenses, saying he had had to bring his companion 'up from the country', and had lost three or four pounds worth of business by neglecting his shop to come to New Cross. In the end he became so enraged that he shouted at

---

[1] From the evidence, this appears to have either consisted of, or included, ten fifty pound notes.

Campbell 'I'll smash your —— face and break every —— thing in the place.' At this point the other man came in and calmed him down enough to get him to leave.

Buncher, circumspect but quite unaware of his danger, was kept under watch and seen to make several trips to Birmingham. This tied in with information about another criminal to whom Brown had also pointed—Bob Cummings, the coiner. Cummings (the one whose house had been equipped with an oubliette) was now an elderly, sour-faced and notoriously dodgy ex-convict.

It seems that Burnett and Buncher did not set about making arrangements for getting the bank-note paper turned into forged money until all or part of it had already been stolen and removed from Whitchurch. Then Burnett, making cautious enquiries for a 'scratcher' worthy of the opportunity, was put in touch with Cummings, to whom a specimen of the stolen paper was entrusted. As a result, Cummings, who knew the shoful trade from end to end, got into contact with an exceptionally skilful engraver and copper plate printer in Birmingham called James Griffiths who had for years been a successful forger. Griffiths had a living place and workshop in the city, and also a farm or small holding on its outskirts where he had at least two conferences with Cummings and Buncher.

Fired by the prospects opened up by a supply of genuine Bank of England paper, Griffiths went ahead with preparations to print notes in a number of denominations and by the summer of 1862 had already produced some masterly forgeries. He worked on a small scale and in privacy—there is no mention of his employing any assistant—but he was preparing to increase his output by getting hold of copper plates ready engraved by another hand for printing certain parts of the complex process. Altogether the only necessary limitation to a flood of perfect forgeries was the final exhaustion of the stocks of stolen paper.

At the end of October 1862 the police made a sudden, concerted sweep. On the 27th, detectives with warrants called on Buncher in Westminster and Griffiths in Birmingham and arrested them both: Cummings was picked up in a street off the Strand. The wisdom of not interfering with the rest of the gang until the forger had been tracked down was now proved. A meticulous search of Buncher's butchery and living quarters yielded nothing of consequence. Cummings, when seized, said calmly 'You needn't hold me, I've nothing about me but a neddy'—which a search of his pockets at Bow Street proved to be true. But the Birmingham officers who had been watching Griffiths, and who now descended on his dingy premises, had very different results to report. The engraver was taken completely off guard. On a press in the corner of his work room were twenty-one part finished Bank of England notes, and on a bed twenty completed ones. Plates for reproducing various parts of the design lay about. Caught without hope of evasion, Griffiths led a party of his captors out to his farm property where, under a field bank, a number of other plates had been buried, carefully done up in waterproof wrappings.

The complete success of this coup perhaps owed something to Griffiths' habit of relying entirely on his own secretive habits, so that once marked down he was liable to be caught without warning or protection; but the system seems to have served him well up to this point for he confessed to having been engaged in successful counterfeiting for the past seventeen years. Burnett, who escaped the round-up on the 27th, was caught next day near Birmingham by an inspector of the London City police. In less than three months the whole complex conspiracy had been unravelled and all the principal actors laid by the heels.

Griffiths' wholesale confessions—he inculpated Buncher to the hilt—did him no good at all. The prosecution (that is the Bank) had already made its bargains and was determined to put his talents out of harm's way. At the Old Bailey the following January he was sentenced to penal servitude for life. Of the others who stood beside him in the dock, Buncher got twenty-five years, and Burnett twenty; an engraver who had supplied Griffiths with a plate got away with four. Brown was not among the accused. Brewer and Cummings were brought to trial but discharged on the grounds that the prosecution had offered inadequate evidence, the judge instructing the jury that it was a 'proper rule of our law that no person should be convicted on the testimony of an accomplice without it is corroborated'.

The slippery old coiner may have been very lucky and very adroit; but the fact that the police failed to produce the necessary evidence is no proof that they could not have done so. In the circumstances it was hardly possible to avoid charging him, and not bringing forward enough corroboration would have been the only way to reward him for betraying his associates. It seems clear that Brown was not the only source of the inside information that led to the ruin of the great bank-note conspiracy.

The man who made a profession of faking signatures on cheques and negotiable bonds belonged, as a rule, to a higher level of the underworld than the 'soft money' forger.

Compared to the complex business of reproducing a bank-note, cheque forgery was a straightforward exercise in calligraphy. Technically it was child's play, and for the expert professional the problem was as much a matter of smooth stage management as skilful counterfeiting. A mid-century burglar who left a cheque book behind when he was rifling a desk was clearly not up to his job, for there was a strong demand for these forms. Bank accounts were confined to a smaller section of society than now and were less often used for small payments; moreover, banks did not always take very effective precautions against honouring cheques taken from stolen books.

Once he had got a virgin cheque blank, the criminal needed to find a customer with a big, active account at the bank in question and get a specimen of his signature. The man from whom the cheque book had been stolen was not a good subject, since his bankers were likely to know of his loss and have his name in mind. A business-like way of setting to work was to identify an attorney who had constant dealings at the bank (a watch on the clerks calling at the premises might supply the clue) and then, posing as a frustrated creditor, to approach him for help in recovering a debt of a few pounds. As the debt was a put-up job, the lawyer would be able to collect it without delay and would then, almost certainly, send his client the sum due by cheque. By this means the sharper got a model from which he could copy (or get copied) not only an account holder's signature but the whole way in which his cheques were made out. With this before him, and enough blanks to allow a few discards, it would be hard if a competent forger could not prepare a convincing document.

Even with the best craftsmanship, however, there was always the chance of things going wrong. Banks were not an easy prey and those who made a practice of stealing from them had to be wary of traps. Cheque sharps usually seem to have worked in partnerships so that the same faces did not become too well known, but this had its own dangers. If one of them was caught inside a counting house in the act of cashing a fake cheque he had little scope for evasion of any kind, and since the penalties of

conviction were very severe the risk of his reaching an agreement with the prosecution to betray his associates was especially
serious. The way round this was to employ a stooge who knew
nothing about the sharpers or their intentions.

There were several variations on the system but they were all
based on the same principle. A good start was to put a notice in
a newspaper offering a vacancy for a junior clerk at an attractive
salary, applications to be addressed to a box number or accommodation address. A candidate whose letter suggested he would
make a suitable dupe got an answer instructing him to present
himself punctually for interview, perhaps at an office in a
building shared by several businesses, perhaps at a coffee room
—a reasonable rendezvous if the job was supposed to be out of
town. If the interview was to be at an office, the applicant's
entry into the building was probably forestalled by a bustling
man who appeared in the doorway as he arrived and announced
himself as the prospective employer, called out on unexpected
business. In any event, if the lad seemed up to expectation he was
handed a paper and told to take it to a bank not far away, collect
so much cash, and return directly by the same route. After
walking a little way the stooge was likely to notice that he was
being followed—possibly by the bustling businessman himself
—and conclude that he was being subjected to a test. Shortly
after coming out of the bank he was stopped by his smiling employer, who took over the cash, congratulated him on having got
the job, wished him goodbye till Monday week, and vanished.

The really skilful forger could grow rich at his trade, especially
if he dealt in cheques and fraudulent bills of exchange. Above all,
he needed to make himself the centre of other men's activities:
as in other fields, it was not the craftsman but the organiser who
made the big profits.

There was, for example, a remarkable forger known as Jem
the Penman[1] who varied counterfeiting with all kinds of other
criminal shifts. He may have been the putter-up behind the great
bullion robbery described in Chapter 6, though this was never
brought into the open, and clearly he was the centre of a whole
web of criminal contacts. For years he remained a shadowy

[1] His real name was James Townshend Saward. He was a well educated man who had
originally been called to the bar, and seems to have taken to crime as an act of deliberate
preference. He had perhaps that kind of romantic temperament that is attracted to out-
lawry for its own sake. See Arthur Griffiths, *Chronicle, of Newgate*, Chapter 8.

menace to the banks and business houses on which he preyed, and though in the end he was caught and given a life sentence, in his heyday he made several thousand pounds a year from his crimes. It was as good an income as many a highly successful professional man's.

Even this was not to be compared with the earnings of those who rose above counterfeiting and took advantage of the opportunities that business practice offered to the really ambitious swindler. For such men the possibilities were almost endless. The issue of limited liability shares was greatly increasing, and since it was often inadequately controlled, it gave scope for a variety of crimes, from peddling imitation certificates to fraud on the most majestic scale. Again, the tendency to larger commercial units and less intimate methods of control strained accounting systems and stimulated large-scale embezzlement. In 1850 considerable interest was created by the trial of Walter Watts, a clerk in an insurance office, who had succeeded in misappropriating over £70,000. A curious feature of the case was that, before his wealth aroused suspicion, Watts had become (in his spare time as it were) lessee of the Olympic Theatre and a prominent figure in London theatrical circles. A more careful man would have taken advantage of the ease and speed with which it was now possible to disappear overseas beyond fear of repatriation.

Even Watts' £70,000 did not put him among the very top swindlers of his time. Between 1840 and 1860 there were, for example, Leopold Redpath's £150,000 forgeries on the Great Northern Railway Company, R. F. Pries' manipulation of falsified lading bills and corn warrants on a scale that affected the international market, and Beaumont Smith's production of £350,000 of dud exchequer bonds. (This last set off a scandal that involved the reputations of many prominent people including Louis Napoleon, soon to be Emperor.)

This type of crime, however, leads into territory far beyond the range of this book. Apart from a few professional forgers and their associates, financial swindling was characteristically the crime of business and professional men. A man who commanded the resources to shake the money market could hardly be considered a member of 'the dangerous classes' and it is almost axiomatic that the biggest and most profitable crimes were beyond the reach of what is here called the underworld.

CHAPTER NINE

The sporting underworld

On the ninth day of September,
Eighteen hundred and forty five,
From London down to Nottingham
The roads were all alive;
Oh! such a sight was never seen,
Believe me it is so,
Tens of thousands went to see the fight,
With Ben Caunt and Bendigo.

And near to Newport Pagnell,
Those men did strip so fine,
Ben Caunt stood six foot two and an half,
And Bendigo five foot nine;
Ben Caunt a giant did appear,
And made the claret flow,
And he seemed fully determined
Soon to conquer Bendigo.

Chorus   *With their hit away and slash away,*
So manfully you see,
Ben Caunt has lost and Bendigo
Has gained the victory.

So begins the broadsheet ballad, probably sold within a day or two of the fight by hawkers and street patterers all over England. What remains of its spun-out account (these broadsheets were often sold by the foot) is too generalised to be worth following: a good deal of it was no doubt composed before the fight, so as to catch the market while interest was still hot, with alternative versions prepared for different upshots. However, the story of the fight itself is worth telling, for it marks a stage in the history of the old bare-knuckle prize-ring.

'The fancy' or P.R., as everyone interested called it, was *par excellence* the underworld's favourite sport; and the underworld ruined it. Since prize-meetings were illegal they could not be officially policed, and though they were popular with men from every level of society, the increasing concern for respectability made it difficult for people in authority to attend them. In the forties plenty of old prize-fighters remembered the Regent and his courtiers at the ringside; the patronage of Prince Albert was inconceivable. If a local notable was seen riding over with two or three attendants, it was now likelier to be a 'maw-worm'[1] magistrate come to put a stop to the whole thing than a sporting squire prepared to lay a bet and see the fun. The railways brought crowds from distant towns to the big fights and whirled them away again, beyond risk of pursuit. Prize-meetings had always been rowdy affairs, beloved by roughs and pickpockets: now they were becoming chaotic. Apologists for the prize-ring—and they were many and vocal[2]—found its practice harder and harder to defend. The lower the ring fell, the less it was patronised by those who might have reformed it, and the more it passed into openly disreputable hands.

Though it was illegal, there was little secrecy about the Caunt–Bendigo fight. It was for the championship belt, rather dubiously held by Caunt who had taken it from Bendigo in 1841. The match was announced in April 1845, five months before it took place, and the fighters' backers put up £200 a side. This was a small sum for such an occasion but as time passed (and trade improved) interest grew and a lot of money was staked: by September excitement in sporting circles was approaching fever point. As usual with championship fights, thousands who had no intention of going near the ring were betting on the outcome and both contestants had prospects of winning a great deal more than the official purse.

By modern standards the two old rivals were an oddly matched couple. Caunt was the more reputable and substantial character. (His father had been a servant and sparring partner of Byron's.) He was now thirty years old and landlord of the Coach and Horses in St Martin's Lane, a giant of a man who, when presiding in his own tap-room, normally weighed over 17 stone. After arduous training at Barnet he had got down to just under 14 for the fight, but was still reckoned more than thirty pounds heavier than his opponent. 'Bendigo' (his real name was William Thompson) was the nineteenth child of a poor (and reputedly ferocious) Nottingham woman, a close coupled, cocky fellow,

---

[1] Enemies of the fancy were still coarsely called maw-worms (gut-worms).

[2] They included influential noblemen and others whose support was not based merely on sporting considerations. It was widely held that fist-fighting was a strong influence for moral good, encouraging manly virtues and preserving society from the knifings, shootings and clubbings common among foreigners. Certainly it provided young men of the upper classes with a substitute for duelling. There was also an idiotic theory that by promoting strong arms it enhanced British prowess with the bayonet.

a splendid boxer and fighter and a thorough ruffian. In the words
of a sporting journalist, he was 'as game and as active as a
tarantula spider'.[1] He was four years Caunt's senior.

Caunt's manager and principal supporter was the great Tom
Spring, an ex-champion and one of the most esteemed figures of
the prize-ring; a man of whose acquaintance young Corinthians
loved to boast. Bendigo was managed by another celebrated
pugilist, Jem Ward (who had taken Spring's belt 20 years
earlier) and he had trained under him at Crosby near Liverpool.
Bendigo was the darling of the North and Midlands, where his
following was enormous, and Caunt was popular in London,
though Bendigo's supporters included Jem Burns, the proprietor
of the Queen's Head off Windmill Street, a flash public house
famous for its sparring matches, and Hannan, the famous St
Giles light-weight, better known as 'the Pink of the Holy Land'.

Following the usual practice, representatives of the two
parties met to choose the ground which, in accordance with the
original 'articles', had to be roughly half-way between London
and Nottingham. It was decided that a suitable place would be
Newport Pagnell in Buckinghamshire and that the fight should
be held at the nearest 'safe locality'. This would put it within
reach of three county boundaries, so that if there was trouble
with one set of magistrates it would be easy to move into
another jurisdiction.

On Sunday (the ninth of September was a Tuesday) Bendigo
and his party arrived ostentatiously at Newport Pagnell—a
stupid thing to do, for the local authorities there were of course
perfectly well aware of what was going on. The high constable
of the little town soon turned up and told Bendigo he had a
warrant and orders to arrest anyone attempting a breach of the
peace within the hundred. After this Bendigo's friends took him
to a farmhouse where he stayed till the morning of the fight.

Caunt had dined on Sunday with a party of his followers at
Spring's pub in Holborn and distributed quantities of the customary coloured handkerchiefs as favours (the men who took
them would be expected to pay him a guinea apiece if he won).
Next day he travelled down by train and put up at the Cock in
Stony Stratford, a few miles from Newport and close to Wolverton railway station. He and his immediate supporters were not
the only followers of the fancy to descend at Wolverton station

---

[1] *Bell's Life in London*, 14 Sept. 1845, from which this account has been largely taken.

that day; a horde of excursionists from the north also arrived, most of whom tramped towards Newport Pagnell. The roads, as the song says, were all alive with vehicles and walkers, and more crowds from north and south came in by rail early on Tuesday. It is not hard to see why, despite the disorders and blackguardry, many people welcomed a prize-fight in their neighbourhood. Not only roughs but free-spending sportsmen rolled up by the score, from counting-house 'half-swells' to fashionable bloods from the clubs and universities. Between Newport and Stratford any miserable dossing place in a barn could be let at exorbitant prices, innkeepers and food sellers could do half a year's business in a few hours, while places 'on the wretchedest rattletraps' offering transport to the fight could only be 'obtained with difficulty at a sovereign a head'.

Some witnesses of all this were disturbed by the appearance of part of the northern mob. It was not overwhelmingly from Nottingham, as seems to have been supposed at the time (it included parties from Liverpool, Manchester, Sheffield, Leicester and other centres) but the Nottinghamshire men seem to have been the most disconcerting group. What was alarming was less the common disorderliness than the discipline of a strong contingent who, arriving in good time, spent Monday night billeted about Newport Pagnell. Bunches of them were seen answering to their leaders' roll calls 'like so many policemen going on night duty'. The long cudgels known as 'Nottingham twigs' were much in evidence.

On Monday evening Tom Spring came over to the Swan at Newport and proposed to Bendigo's people that the ring should be set up at Whaddon, outside the Newport hundred. Then, if necessary, they could move right away into Oxfordshire where there was little chance of interference. Bendigo's party objected to this plan, which they said favoured Caunt's friends at Stony Stratford at the expense of the folk in Newport. They suggested a site in Bedfordshire. There was a good deal of ill-feeling but evidently Spring had his way, for early next day the commissary's cart with the necessary equipment led a procession out of Newport to Whaddon.

The prize-ring commissary, on this occasion an experienced old scapegrace called Oliver, was a crucially important man. He was responsible for bringing up and erecting the ring; and his cart, loaded with ropes, posts, canvas and other impedimenta, was the mark that every fight-goer tried to follow, though for obvious reasons he often preferred bye-ways and field lanes. So on Tuesday morning off went what was called in sporting circles 'the prad-move and toddle' (that is the followers with horses and those afoot). Some five thousand strong, they streamed over to Whaddon in pursuit of Oliver. Here the Nottingham lads and their allies quickly got to work establishing an enclosure from which, with the aid of their 'twigs', they forced back anyone unwilling to pay for a close view. Bendigo was present and apparently did nothing to control his followers, who demanded from one to five shillings—presumably depending on how they estimated the customer's purse. It was clearly going to be an unusually lively occasion, with plenty of broken heads. All was more or less ready when, instead of the champion, an emissary from Spring arrived to say the site would have to be changed.

What had happened (typically enough) was that an officer had arrived at the inn in Stony Stratford. He was very polite—perhaps because of the well-to-do patrons present—but he told Caunt's party that 'however reluctant he might be he had no other alternative' but to arrest both fighters if any attempt was made to hold the match anywhere in the county. The Buckingham magistrates were now determined to prevent it. Bendigo's partisans, some of whom had tramped ten miles and who found themselves very well satisfied with things as they were, refused to allow the messenger to approach Oliver, tore up the letter he had brought from Spring, and swore there should be no move. However, since the fight plainly could not take place without Caunt, certain 'influential parties' went back with Spring's man and, finding that he was telling the truth, agreed that the ring should be moved across the border to Lillington Lovel. This was a well known site, the scene of a previous championship match, which spectators could be expected to find without much difficulty. Oliver packed up and prads and toddlers were soon on the move again along the hot dusty roads, heavily reinforced as they went by fresh arrivals from Wolverton. Bendigo, coming close to his rival's party in his trap, shook his fist at Caunt and swore to punish him for causing so much trouble.

The gist of the matter was that both sides had good reason to suspect each other of manoeuvring so as to have the advantage in getting their own supporters established on the ground.

Bendigo had no cause to worry: though the crowd had doubled
by the time it gathered at Lillington his adherents soon established their supremacy, cheering him wildly and continuing to
wield their twigs and collect money. As preparations went
ahead disorder increased, and the arrangements that Oliver and
his assistants made were swept aside. Round the twenty-four
foot square of the prize ring was an area twelve yards wide,
known as the 'inner ring' where by tradition only privileged
spectators were allowed. This cordoned-off zone was necessary
to keep the throng away from the umpires, referee and seconds
and allow free movement around the ring. (There were two
umpires—one chosen by each side—and a single referee
appointed by common agreement.) Now a number of the mob
began to infiltrate into the inner ring, jostling against the prize-
ring ropes and shouting for Bendigo. The prize-fighters standing
near made little effort to stop them. At the last minute an
acrimonious disagreement arose about the referee and a prominent
local sportsman whose carriage was drawn up nearby was asked
to officiate. With some reluctance he agreed, and afterwards
wrote in a letter to the press: 'I shall always consider it one of
the greatest acts of folly I ever was guilty of in my life.' It was
about half-past three on a blazing afternoon by the time all was
ready. The betting was six to four on Caunt.

As the two fighters, in knee breeches and stripped to the
waist, stood ready to come up to scratch—that is to the line
across the middle of the ring—the contrast between them was
dramatic. Caunt, his ugly scarred features impassive, looked
greyhound thin with the bones of his great ribcage gauntly
prominent and pads of muscle standing out on his arms and torso.
Bendigo, all compact strength and bouncing vitality, plainly in
the pink of condition, answered his supporters' cheers with
boasts and lively obscenities. Both men's features were darkened
by the astringent 'pickle' with which prize fighters' hands and
faces were systematically treated during training to toughen
the skin and minimise bleeding. Behind Caunt were Tom Spring,
the renowned negro prize fighter Molyneux, and two other
experienced seconds; behind Bendigo were his trainer Jem
Ward, Nick Ward (whom Caunt had defeated four years before),
Jem Burns, and the wicked little Holy Land Pink.

From the start the two fighters' methods were as distinct as
those of a pair of diversely armed Roman gladiators: Bendigo,

The
notorious
Sayers–
Heenan
championship
fight of 1860.
From a print
based on a
photograph by
G. Bonier,
evidently
posed before
the match
started.
The meagre
crowd is more
respectable–
looking
than might be
expected at a
prize fight at
this date.
(Mansell
Collection)

Rat pit at the Blue Anchor, Bunhill Row. The minute dog. 'Tiny the Wonder', twice killed two hundred rats in less than an hour. From an oil painting about 1850. (London Museum. This note is based on John Hayes' *Catalogue of Oil Paintings in the London Museum*)

infinitely the better boxer, weaving and feinting, then coming in to punish Caunt and frequently dropping quickly on one knee to prevent a continued exchange; Caunt remorsely following his nimble opponent, trying to exploit his superior size and power, always seeking the opportunity to close in a grapple. Given their different physiques and capacities, the prize ring code virtually forced the men to fight in this way. With a long struggle before him the bare-fist fighter could not afford, and was not trained, to strike often with his full strength: as it was the last rounds of a match were usually fought with the contestants' hands in a ghastly condition. 'Quick, sharp knocks cutting open a cheek or lip, and ornamenting the ribs with aching bruises' were what the experts looked to. These blows would be delivered from an upright position and without the full weight of the body behind them, for 'slogging' meant prematurely shattered knuckles and dislocated forearms.[1] Moreover, as soon as they became swollen, the pickle-hardened fists lost their valuable cutting power.

Between first-class men the chances of a quick decision were negligible. Even flooring an opponent before he was severely damaged, though it pleased the mob and various side-betters, was unlikely to be worth much: unless his seconds were unable to restore him it usually decided merely the round, not the match. What the followers of the fancy wanted were protracted exhibitions of skill, speed, bloodshed and aggressive bravery under suffering, and its laws and conventions were admirably designed to provide them. Nine fairly won fights out of ten were decided by the loser's total exhaustion. The prize-fighter's prime duty was to his backers and (like the fighting cock he was often compared to) 'gameness' was his indispensable virtue. Not till their man was deaf and blind with blood and contusions, his broken hands and wrists swollen like sponges, half moribund with shock and fatigue, with no faintest hope of staggering on till his similarly crippled opponent collapsed—or in his confusion committed a disqualifying foul—did his seconds dare 'throw up the castor'.[2]

---

[1] 'Hammer' Lane, a pugilist famous for his phenomenally hard fists and hitting, once survived for thirteen rounds against Molyneux with his right hand hopelessly injured. He had disabled himself in the sixth round of the match. Despite his gifts and courage Lane never reached the top of his profession.

[2] Hat—in the prize ring traditionally a low-crowned beaver. Although the prize fighter risked his life, and of course the dire consequences of infected injuries, he seems, as one might expect, to have been less liable to brain damage than professional glove boxers.

A round—which might last for anything from a few moments to more than a quarter of an hour—commonly ended with the clinch and fall. The prize-fighter was forbidden to use his legs against his opponent, but he could still clasp him above the waist and wrestle him to the ground, the man who fell underneath normally losing the round. This was Caunt's great resource; not because winning the round was likely to count for much but because by repeatedly hurling his weight on Bendigo he hoped to injure his breathing apparatus, and so either totally incapacitate him or at least seriously slow him down. If he were slowed before Caunt himself became groggy, Bendigo was lost: his survival depended on his agility.

But Bendigo's chest, like everything else about him, was a tough nut to crack. He was lissom as an eel, and innumerable falls—the rounds came in quick succession—seemed to leave him undamaged. Bendigo's method of dealing with Caunt largely depended on the rule that it was a foul to hit a boxer who had one hand and one knee (or both knees) on the ground; his opponent had to let him rise. Bendigo would attack energetically, drop, and then—saved from being pinned against the ropes or grappled to a fall—leap up and continue the fluid, quick-shifting battle on his own terms. Also he often caught the slower Caunt a serviceable blow as he sprang up. It was, naturally, a foul to fall deliberately without being hit; in theory the privileged kneeling posture was meant to be involuntary, the result of a blow. In fact in a bout of rapid 'fibbing' it was very hard for the judges to see just what was the consequence of what, and a quick and skilful man who dropped on his knee after such a flurry had almost always taken a knock that could be used as an excuse. Caunt's crucial tactic, if not in the highest traditions of the game, was perfectly legitimate; Bendigo's meant continually sailing very close to the wind.

As the fight went on, the disturbance around it became outrageous. More and more blackguards flourishing staves and whip handles packed the inner ring; Spring was thwacked with a Nottingham twig and on one occasion Bendigo himself received a blow from a spectator—said, of course, by Caunt's supporters to have been aimed at the champion. The ringside officials became frightened and distracted. Time keeping was highly inaccurate. Under a reformed regulation (merciful because it tended to shorten fights) the interval between rounds was supposed to be only thirty seconds, but now, despite the protests of Caunt's party, a full minute or more was constantly allowed. This pleased the Nottingham men, for the late afternoon had brought no relief from the sweltering heat and Bendigo's leaping and dodging made every second's respite invaluable to him.

At about half-past five, after the eighty-third round, Caunt's backers were cheered by a flow of fresh blood from Bendigo's mouth, apparently brought from his lungs by the last fall. This seems to have roused Bendigo's followers to even greater excitement. During the eighty-fifth round, the wretched referee, whose post was outside the ring, was driven to climb through the ropes and take refuge inside until Jem Ward, who had some influence on the mob, succeeded in getting him back in his place. The confusion was now terrific, and the better class spectators hemmed in on foot about the ring were in an unenviable situation. Cudgel blows rained in all directions, and yells and threats drowned every appeal for fair play and order.

During the ninety-second round, Bendigo, ducking low to avoid a return from Caunt, hit him well below the waistband. Caunt let his hands drop and fell, while Bendigo, a master of prize-fight stagecraft, continued his stoop and collapsed also, eventually rolling right over. It is probable that the gross foul was unintentional. Caunt was not in fact hit in the genitals; a later examination by a surgeon showed he had received a blow over the pubic bone that could hardly, even at that stage in the fight, have had much effect on such a man. Almost certainly his dramatic fall was designed to call attention to a foul which should, unquestionably, have given him the match. But the umpires disagreed and the referee, amid frightful turmoil, declared he had not seen the blow.

In the next round Caunt knocked Bendigo off his feet and then returned towards his own corner, as if the round were over. Bendigo got up and made after him; and seeing this, Caunt, before he could be attacked, abruptly sat down. He seems to have thought that Bendigo was so clearly in the wrong that this was the simplest way of stopping him. Immediately Jem Ward and the Holy Land Pink shouted foul and appealed to the referee. The referee, perhaps influenced by the fact that he was in unmistakable danger of being murdered, gave the match to Bendigo, who left the ring the victor to the roaring huzzas and brandished clubs of the mob.

A subsidiary fight had been arranged to follow the championship, but a good part of the crowd began to drift away towards Wolverton. Since this part included virtually all the less blackguardly people there, the level of the remaining mob sank still lower, and the less popular of the two pugilists now due to fight very sensibly refused to court lynching. At Wolverton the railway officials closed the station gates against their disorderly passengers until their trains arrived.

The result of the championship set the sporting world in an uproar. The referee's decision, which he refused to go back on, was endlessly and bitterly attacked. Apart from anything else—and the whole story of the last two rounds bristled with debatable points—the manner of the decision itself was highly irregular; for the appeal should have been addressed in the first place to the umpires, and the referee should only have been asked for a decision if they differed. Mazed with the din and threats he had overlooked this, and in his agitation given an immediate verdict. Caunt, or friends acting in his name, threatened the parties holding the prize money with legal proceedings if they paid over to Bendigo, and as it was a cardinal prize-ring principle that 'bets go with the battle money', this added notably to the universal ill-feeling.

In a day or two it was generally realised that the referee's decision must be accepted, but nothing could efface the extreme disreputableness of what had happened. *Bell's Life*, the dominant sporting weekly, earnestly studied in clubs, colleges, messes, commercial rooms and almost every kind of masculine meeting-place, was not alone in its fury. But coming from such a source so close to the prize-ring, an attack not only on the 'disgraceful and disgusting exhibition' at Lillington but on the fancy as a whole, was indeed a sign of the times. 'A blow has been given to the boxing school from which it can never recover,' it declared and went on to tell the school's 'professors' that henceforth 'the fingers of all honest and honourable men will be raised against them and . . . we shall be slow to cry "shame" on those magistrates who use their utmost exertions to prevent the repetision of such enormities.'

From this time on it was obvious, even to its most simple-minded patrons, that the prize-ring was conducted by and for delinquents. An authoritative amateur, who so loved the old bare-knuckle game that he still considered all else 'mere travesties' of boxing, admitted after its death that prize-matches were attended 'by some of the most dangerous ruffians in the world, and no man of respectability dared to appear except under the protection of some well known member of the confraternity.'[1] As we have seen, their protection could be a flimsy shield.

For as long as it lasted,[2] the prize-ring remained a financial prop of the underworld. Never a full time occupation, it was closely linked with the public house business, gambling and the vice trades. The society of prize-fighters appealed strongly to sporty young men of all classes and, paradoxically enough, this was largely because of the same passion for sparring that contributed to the prize-ring's eclipse. In some pot-houses gloves

could be hired for a penny or twopence a night, and a scarfaced old bruiser would offer all comers a run for their money. At Jem Burns' notorious Queen's Head, lounging Corinthians watched the bouts in company with sharps and shofulmen. Sometimes sparring was combined with 'flash chaunting' (singing and reciting) and comic turns. At the low-fashionable Black Lion

[1] E. B. Mitchell 'The Prize Ring' in *Boxing*, Badminton Library.
[2] It is impossible to give a firm date for the P.R.'s extinction. One strong influence was the growth of 'out-and-out sparring' (with gloves) as a sport in its own right. Gentlemen could assist at these matches without risk of being beaten-up, and the most high-minded amateurs could fight in this style with easy consciences. In the sixties the Queensberry Rules and the founding of the Amateur Athletic Club gave glove boxing a firm code and jurisdiction such as the P.R. had always lacked. During the same decade the authorities' attitude to the professional ring greatly stiffened, and in 1868 the running of fight-trains became illegal. Thenceforth the United States, where the law was easier and the set-up could hardly have been dirtier, was the chief theatre for prize-fights and fighters.

off Drury Lane, the evening's entertainment was for a time under the direction of Sambo Sutton, a versatile black boxer who enlivened things by dancing a hornpipe upside down, his feet beating on a board hung from the ceiling. Often the failing pugilist became nothing better than a blackguard layabout, and a high proportion of prostitutes' fancymen, footpadding 'bearers up', brothel bullies and the like were decayed bruisers.

So the prize-ring sank into total disrepute. Perhaps the last time it roused any general national interest was the match in 1860 between the huge American Heenan (the Benecia Boy) and Sayers, the small native champion—a vicious fight that was only broken off when both men were in an appalling condition. (Heenan continued to fight in England, until, treacherously doped before a match, he was so injured that his health never recovered.) The national championship of 1862 was held in a hole-and-corner fashion at Thames Haven on the line of the Tilbury Railway. Many who turned up to catch the 5 a.m. special had their tickets grabbed before they could use them by the gangs of rampsmen and pickpockets milling and scuffling about the station. (The tickets cost two pounds each including the train fare: the game could still be profitable, even in its last decay.) According to the correspondent sent by the *Sporting Life*, no one could hope to get on the train without first 'having the rule run over them' by professional fingers. Rather surprisingly, the police seem to have washed their hands of the business, for when the 'managers of the trip'—presumably the railway people—desperate at the chaos and delay, 'sent to the nearest police station . . . and offered a couple of sovereigns a head for twenty constables for an enforcement of those already on duty,' they met with a 'positive refusal'. And this was a championship match: minor matches had become so entirely dingy and corrupt that they can have offered little entertainment to any but the dullest of the criminal classes.

(Among all this it is pleasant to be able to report one triumph of virtue. Bendigo, after twenty-eight convictions for assault and misconduct, became a mission preacher with a special vocation to London cabmen.)

There were many links between the prize-ring and the turf. By the mid-century it was perhaps no longer possible to have a career like Jack Gully's, who is said to have been brought from

Newgate for his famous fight with the Game Chicken in 1808, but later did so well as a bookie that he became an MP and the owner of three Derby winners. All the same, for shrewd ex-pugilists as for other sporting professionals, laying the odds in one form or another remained the royal road to fortune.

In the thirties and forties the two sports had enough in common for it to look as if racing might fall into the same disrepute as prize-fighting. Scandal followed scandal. The Derby of 1844 was distinguished by the exposure of two fraudulent runners—four-year-olds masquerading as three-year-olds. One of them, supposed to be a colt called Running Rein, won the event at odds very satisfactory to the organisers of the coup and became the subject of a long and colourful enquiry. The identity of the other and less successful ringer, entered under the name Lysander, seems always to have remained something of a mystery. His owners apparently lost their heads, destroyed him with suspicious speed directly after the race on the ground that he had injured himself, and buried him. A little later the remains were dug up and the lower jaw was found to be missing; however, the rest of the skull was submitted to veterinary experts, who pronounced that the animal could not have been eligible for the Derby.

Much of the tangled story of the Running Rein swindle was laid bare in a public mud-slinging match, involving several of the topmost racing men and rousing great excitement. Egged on by Lord George Bentinck, the so-called 'Dictator of the Turf' to whom the Jockey Club had not very wisely delegated most of its limited power, the owner of the horse that had come in second denounced the imposture and claimed the race. A Mr Wood, who owned the pseudo Running Rein but seems to have been the dupe of a master cheat called Goodman, went to law in an attempt to silence his accusers and vindicate his position.

In the Exchequer Court, Wood's eminent and high-feed counsel took an aggressive line. By raising the question of the origin of heavy wagers against Running Rein he suggested the blackest motives for the attacks on his client and did all he could to make Bentinck and the Jockey Club appear in an odious light. Indeed he openly identified them as the real defendants in the case. But all his spirited efforts at defamation were not enough. Under examination by the Solicitor General, who appeared for the other side, Wood's witnesses gave a poor account of themselves. A breaker-in of young horses who had—so the defence sought to show—been first flogged and later bribed by one of Goodman's creatures to keep his mouth shut, denied the story in a way that confirmed its truth. Goodman himself, an un-prepossessing villain, inspired no confidence. Finally, when the judge proposed that he and the jury should inspect Running Rein for themselves, it suddenly transpired that the valuable Derby winner could not be produced. Presumably it had been overtaken by the same fate—rather more discreetly managed—as the unfortunate Lysander.

Bit by bit the curious, complex tale came out. Briefly, the so-called Running Rein had been a quite well known horse called Maccabeus which was supposed to have attracted wide attention at Newmarket the previous year. Supposed, because this race too had been the subject of trickery. Goodman, in fact, had been engaged in a double-banked imposture. He had run an (in-eligible) Irish horse under Maccabeus' name at Newmarket while the real Maccabeus, masquerading as Running Rein and lodged with a corrupt trainer, was being openly got ready for the Derby. As Goodman was already so notorious that his ownership of a horse was virtually a guarantee of malpractice, he had transferred Maccabeus to Wood before he was due to be officially entered for the Derby.

The jury were never called on for a verdict. When this much of the story had been elicited by the Solicitor General, Wood threw in the sponge and withdrew, declaring—and his words carried conviction—that he had been made a fool of. If the judge betrayed a certain class-bias in his concluding remarks, he never-theless put the turf's trouble in a nutshell: 'Since the opening of this case a most atrocious fraud has been proved to have been practised; and I have seen with great regret, gentlemen associat-ing themselves with persons much below them in station. If gentleman would associate with gentlemen, and race with gentlemen, we should have no such practices. But if gentlemen will condescend to race with blackguards, they must expect to be cheated.'[1]

The learned Exchequer Baron overstated the case: needless to say gentlemen sometimes swindled other gentlemen. Never-theless, it was just this mingling of the rich with the criminal classes that made racing so corrupt. The vast amount of easy-

[1] *Annual Register* 1844, Chronicle, p. 352.

circulating money about the turf attracted innumerable rascals, while the generally louche character of sporting life allowed them to penetrate every branch of the game until it became something like a criminal industry. At the same time, the wealth involved and the prestige of horse-breeding patrons enabled

racing to survive the underworld's embrace and remain not only popular but fashionable.

It was indeed uniquely privileged. Race courses were often the scenes of disorder, brutality and lewdness: yet, only a few feet away, ladies brought up to display on ordinary occasions an almost pathological delicacy sat in their carriages twirling their parasols and picnicking. (Taine, who was used to the less squeamish conventions of France and who saw the Derby when a more orderly spirit had begun to prevail, was still astounded at the contrasts and blatant indecencies.) Nowhere could one see so much of the genteel part of society cheek by jowl with its dregs as at race meetings. On the other hand, strait-laced people of all sorts looked on racing with horror, and many solid upper-class folk who gambled at cards and hunted foxes had come to feel an increasing distaste for the turf and 'turfites'.

Even the Running Rein scandal did not lead to immediate reform. During the next few years the corruption worsened, while meetings, stimulated by the railways, grew bigger, more numerous and more disorderly. But then the prevailing spirit of the age, the urge towards respectability, asserted itself. For all the sport's popularity, money was being lost. Gradually, urged on by pressure from outside, the turf began to set its house in order. The redoubtable Admiral Rous, Lord George Bentinck's successor, imposed a more effective control on both betting and horse management; the influence of bookies was curtailed; many courses were partially enclosed; police uniforms became more in evidence at meetings and the legion of touts, sharps, bullies, and pickpockets less flagrantly obstreperous. At least in major events recognised by the regular turf authorities, fair racing became the rule. By the sixties the sport's reputation was on the up-grade.

There was, however, one kind of crime that increased. As professional bookmaking expanded, the race-gangs preying on the bookies became more and more of a menace, though they scarcely affected the ordinary racegoer. In 1892 a number of bookmakers approached the Jockey Club for protection against the gangsters who were active on every course and who levied a toll even on the privileged rings. Funds for the 'raising and maintenance of a body of detective police' to control the 'desperadoes' were offered; but in the end the scheme collapsed.[1]

---

[1] See *Racing* by Lord Suffolk and W. G. Craven in the Badminton Library.

In the early years of the century, the true professional book-maker, ready (like the celebrated Gully) to 'hold a bag against all comers' was still something of a novelty; and even during the forties a vast amount of regular backing evidently remained a matter of private transactions between acquaintances. It was common form for ordinary racing men to open books on particu-lar events, and in club rooms and at racing breakfasts and other sporting gatherings, punters and layers seem to have sought one another out rather like brokers on an exchange floor. Even at Tattersall's—much the greatest centre of off-the-course betting in the country[1]—most of the dealings were personal contacts between people well known to each other, whether it was bet-ting with bookies or between private individuals. The world of serious horse gambling was in fact fairly small, and one where (however bad his record in other ways) a man's reputation for settling-up was precious. To that extent, the gambling was easy to discipline. At Tattersall's, Newmarket, Doncaster and else-where, defaulters' names were punctually posted, and the news travelled fast. The bookmaking trade was largely concerned with credit transactions with a limited, often heavy-wagering public, and the successful bookie prospered according to his standing among them. The most prominent—men such as the great 'Leviathan' Davis—could reasonably be considered as safe as many a contemporary bank.

But with changing times another style of bookmaking was coming to the fore, catering for a far broader and less discriminat-ing clientele. Popular interest in horse racing was giving rise to an urban betting public whose shillings and crowns cumulatively represented a river of wealth for enterprising professionals to tap. And once the potentialities of the game became clear they were not slow in tapping it to the full. During the forties a species of off-course cash bookmaker, organised to appeal to the new public and unconcerned with the views of the Jockey Club and its allies, sprang into prominence. By the end of the decade he had become an important feature of sporting life.

Most often the business started in a tobacconist's. Men idled about these places, smoking, ogling the girl behind the counter, chatting. Sometimes there was an ottoman and copies of sporting

[1] The famous sale-ring and 'high-change of horseflesh' by Hyde Park Corner. Settling day for bets contracted under the committee's rules was Monday, when all outstanding debts incurred during the previous week had to be discharged. The establishment—though long known as 'the Corner'—shifted to Brompton in 1865.

newspapers, in which case the premises might qualify as a cigar divan. The proprietor was often of a sporting turn and ready to enhance a leisurely trade by accepting occasional bets with customers. As the taste for backing horses spread and quickened, a change overtook many gossipy little shops. A dull room might suddenly blossom with ornate lights and richly papered walls: instead of a few dinner-time clerks and casual loungers puffing their weeds, there would be a constant and very varied crowd of people. Sometimes the tobacco jars and cigar bundles disappeared altogether, and a head-high partition, pierced with pigeon holes and surmounted by a stout brass rail, replaced the old counter. But even with new establishments, designed from the start for betting, there was a strong tendency to evoke the comfortable divan atmosphere, carpeted and upholstered, tempting the customer (like the glittering gin palace) by contrast to the harsh workaday world outside. Always there were lists of runners hanging from the walls, marked-up with the latest odds. Hence these betting shops were known as 'list shops' or, more vulgarly, 'listers'.

As the boom grew, the control of a promising little business was apt to change hands, though the name of the original trader might be preserved and the shop itself kept unchanged. Dealing in hard cash, uncontrolled by any organisation, demanding relatively small outlay on premises, readily organised so as to allow the proprietors to decamp and set up elsewhere under another front, the list shop was almost ideally suited to grafters. The famous racing correspondent, The Druid, calculated that at the peak of the boom in the early fifties there were about four hundred betting shops in London alone, of which perhaps four per cent were genuinely solvent. So great was the success of the listers that one or two of the most ambitious were able to reach beyond their original market and begin to encroach on the established big-money bookies. Since the betting shop proprietor had to be ready to welsh if luck ran too decisively against him, he was able to offer competitive prices.

The best known of all the shops was Dwyer's in St Martin's Lane (they still sold cheroots). By a policy of fair, punctual settlement, and by quoting rather better odds than could be got at Tattersall's, Dwyer's had built up a large custom that included a number of heavy-weight punters. At that period the Chester Cup was the foremost handicap in the betting man's calendar, and in 1851, when the favourite won, something like a million pounds is believed to have changed hands. Dwyer's was known to have accepted a fair amount of money on the favourite, but apparently no particular suspicion was aroused. However on receiving the news from Chester they made speedy dispositions at St Martin's Lane. During the night following the race every piece of movable property was whipped out of the premises, and in the morning Dwyer and Co. were found to have vanished, leaving the mere shell of an old cigar shop and twenty-five thousand pounds owing.

"BOLTED!"

No doubt the failure discouraged regular racing men from risking part of their stakes in such places. Nevertheless, despite this resounding piece of welshing (and countless lesser ones) the demand among small betters was so strong that listers continued to multiply. In the eyes of authority they were a scandalous nuisance, actively encouraging disorder and lack of thrift among the lower classes. Furthermore, they were notorious refuges for any kind of bad hat who could do simple arithmetic. 'Employed in a betting shop' was about as unfavourable a description as a man could give himself, short of admitting he was an outright criminal. Finally, at the end of 1853, legislation was passed to put a stop to the scandal. Unfortunately the framers of the act were frightened about the political consequences of meddling with 'the legitimate species of betting' (i.e. the betting habits of the ruling class) and instead of making an effort to regulate the trade as a whole, they simply banned off-course cash bookmaking entirely. The result was the appearance of an illegal cash bookmaking industry and a brand new underworld occupation—bookie's runner.[1] This inevitably set up new connections between bookmaking and crime and proved a boon to street corner delinquents and corrupt policemen for a century.

Besides the betting shops, the growing popularity of horse racing had also led to a large increase in the number of race course bookmakers, and so to new opportunities for race course blackguards. With the banning of the shops, the attraction of legal on-the-course cash betting naturally became still stronger among the vast multitude who, if they wanted to back a horse, had to bet with ready money. Race going was becoming a mass recreation.

Apart from the famous meetings to which excursion trains brought crowds from far away, dozens of lesser ones were springing up about the country, many of them close to the great centres of population. Some of these minor meetings, ignored by sporting authority and under indifferent management, were perfectly suited to the sort of crooked operators whose activities were being curtailed at more important fixtures.

But it was not a game at which to make mistakes. To fall under suspicion of being involved in a racing swindle could have very unpleasant consequences. The bookie who found himself double-crossed over a fixed race, and unable to pay his cash debts, faced an enemy more implacable than any race gang. The law's protection against betting frauds was very uncertain, so that people were the more inclined to take matters into their own hands; and an apparently good natured racing crowd would quickly

[1] In places however street bookmakers were so little chivied by the law that they hardly needed runners. In the sixties they stood in Fleet Lane by Newgate with bags and boards openly taking bets from passers-by.

show how thin was the skin over the old mob ferocity. Caught on the race course—even a well policed race course—a welshing bookie was in desperate peril.

In the autumn of 1868 James Greenwood, a journalist who specialised in social reporting,[1] was at a meeting at the newly opened Alexandra Park course at Muswell Hill. He heard a shout, pitched like a cry of *Fire*, go up inside the railed enclosure, and saw a rush being made 'towards a man in a black wide-awake cap, with the regular betting-man's pouch slung at his side'.

As he watched, the man went down, but he was a powerful fellow and quickly got back on his legs, only to be pulled down once more and savagely booted. 'He was up again, however, without his hat and his face a hideous patch of crimson, but hustled towards the gate, plunging like a madman to escape the fury of his pursuers; but the policeman blocked his way and they caught him again, and some punched his face while others tore his clothes.'

Half the man's clothes had been ripped away and flung to the raving crowd behind before the constable at the enclosure gate let him through. Beyond the barrier he was set on and dragged to the ground by fresh attackers, but struggled up and broke free of them—only to be floored by another bookie who flung his high stool at him and so 'brought him to earth again for the twentieth time'. Rising and falling among the flailing mob, he finally managed to fight to where an empty hansom cab was standing, and scrambled in. Some were trying to pull him out, while others poked and lunged at him with their sticks and umbrellas, when a mounted policeman spurred forward and succeeded in interposing himself and his horse. The crowd turned on him with such fury that only great courage and energy saved him from being unhorsed and subjected to the same treatment.

Other police now came up in force and rallied round the hansom, clearing a space. Then 'the poor tattered wretch, ghastly, white and streaming with blood, was hauled out and dragged away insensible, with his head hanging and his legs trailing in the dust, amid the howling and horrible execrations of five thousand Englishmen.'

The police carried him to the grandstand. They were in a quandary; there was a quarter of a mile of open ground to be

[1] He was chiefly known for an account of a night spent disguised as a tramp in a workhouse. The following story and quotations are taken from Chapter VI of his *Seven Curses of London*.

crossed before the gates of the race course could be reached, and they dared not risk an attempt to get the welsher away before the crowd dispersed. Their first duty was to prevent a riot. Moreover at Alexandra Park there was no defensible police post and lock-up such as by now existed at Epsom and other great courses. Nothing remained but to hide him. Accordingly the battered wreck of a man was hastily lowered through a trap-door in the stand and taken by underground ways to a cellar, used as a dump for empty bottles, there to await the end of the day's racing.

What medical help, if any, the man received in the cellar Greenwood never discovered, but he was eventually got home under cover of dark. A few days later a newspaper report noted that 'The unfortunate man, who so rashly roused the fury of the sporting fraternity at Alexandra races, is dead.' No one seems to have suffered for his part in this murder. Provided enough sportsmen acted in concert there was probably little risk in lynching a welsher.

The first two or three years of Victoria's reign belong to the golden age of English gaming houses. They were all in fact illegal, from the palatial Crockford's where the Duke of Wellington and Talleyrand were members and the cook (Monsieur Ude) reckoned the best in the world, down to the lowest back-alley hell with its raw gas jets and unshaven strong-arm men, pipes in their mouths and neddies in their sleeves. But the law was virtually a dead letter, and even after 1839, when it was strengthened and attempts made to enforce it, it remained remarkably ineffective. The favourite play was hazard, a dice-game, which was highly profitable when honestly managed and not difficult to make more so by sharp practice.[1] It had the further advantage that its apparatus could be quickly swept away in emergency. (The mere presence of a marked-out hazard table was evidently not good enough evidence of gaming.) In the circumstances it is inconceivable that the police were not sometimes offered large bribes. Moreover, the most zealous officers were likely to think twice before tackling one of the richer houses. The procedure for securing a conviction was long and chancy, and a policeman who made a false step could be prosecuted for trespass: if he lost the

---

[1] The impeccable Crockford is said to have spent £2,000 annually on new dice to make unfair play impossible.

case he could be ruined. According to one metropolitan superintendent, a gaming house keeper who expected a raid might have his rooms in a blaze of light as if play were going on, and instruct his staff so that any unwary policemen who marched in found themselves in a carefully set legal trap.

As for the inferior houses, largely run by 'prize fighters and other desperate characters,' they took refuge behind narrow guarded entries, Judas-slitted doors and padded shutters that neither light nor sound penetrated. They were most unsavoury and sometimes very unsafe places. At the upper-class establishments a highish standard of decorum was insisted on, but a (perhaps rather excitable) contemporary declared that 'an assembly of the most horrible demons could not exhibit a more appalling sight'[1] than the company at play in a low gaming room. These dens supported an army of touts and blackguards, and the money that flowed into them was virtually a subsidy for crime.

In 1845 a new Gaming Act, following the report of a Select Committee, transformed the situation. It became a lot easier for the police to do their duty and, in the face of public policy, almost impossible for them to neglect it. In London, where the commissioners were determined enemies of gaming, hundreds of houses of every grade were shut down, and for many years commercial gaming on any but the smallest hole-and-corner scale appears to have been no more than a memory.

The oldest popular sporting tradition in England had already suffered a severe decline by the mid-century   baiting animals and setting them to fight.

Bull and bear-baiting were finally outlawed in 1835. 'Ox-driving' (chivying a bullock mad with fear and pain till it collapsed) came under the same ban but persisted for some years in places where it was an established part of holiday festivities. On at least one occasion it had to be suppressed by calling out troops. Legislation was perhaps less a cause than a symptom of the improvement. It might be difficult to believe, after contemplating the public atrocities at Smithfield and many another fatstock market, but humane sentiment towards animals was growing fast. Many cruel practices had almost ended before they were effectively controlled by laws which, anyway, were often supported by very mild penalties.

---

[1] See John Ashton *A History of Gambling*, p. 137.

In general, the baiting-sports that survived were those that could be cheaply staged in the stable yard or back room of a public house, and which appealed especially to the lower classes. This makes it all the more surprising that cock-fighting, once the most widespread of them all, should have decayed as it did. It was marvellously adapted for betting and not easy to prevent, and certainly the legislation of 1849, making it an unquestionable offence even on private premises, cannot account for its lack of appeal. Some cock-fighting did continue (and survives to this day) but it had already lost much of its old popularity when the public cock-pits were closed early in the century. In 1830 one of the greatest cocking matches ever fought was held at Lincoln between Lord Derby and the great game fowl breeder Gilliver, with seven birds a side, a thousand guineas on each main (separate fight) and five thousand on the match. Yet the sport continued to decline. It also, and not very logically, roused particular indignation among humanitarians.[1] At all events it seems to have become more and more a discreetly followed pastime among farmers, landowners and a section of country society, and of decreasing interest and profit to the underworld.

The odious sport of dog-fighting, on the other hand, flourished. In London it was a favourite recreation among costermongers and the like, and much practised round Southwark Mint, Spitalfields and, of course, St Giles—where in Great St Andrew's Street one could pass dozens of dog fanciers' notices for sporting trims (an operation that could include slicing off most of the vulnerable earflaps) and offers of sale. According to Mayhew it was a common enough sight to see a coster lad 'walking with the trembling legs of a dog shivering under a bloody handkerchief covering the bitten and wounded body' in his arms. But the sport was probably even more popular in parts of the midlands and north, especially among the expert dog breeders and handlers of the coal towns.

Raising a really first-class fighting dog was a skilled business, demanding care, patience and a certain expenditure; it may have been chiefly the work of publicans, livery stable keepers, sporting butchers and others with means and premises. Though the

---

[1] Cocking was rather less black than it is often painted: it was a lesser cause of suffering than large game-shoots and less corrupt than prize-fighting. Cock-pits were sometimes equipped with a cage, rather like a large lobster pot, attached by a pulley to a roof beam. Anyone contracting cash bets he could not discharge was forced by the management to enter this contraption and hoisted to the ceiling, where he remained for the rest of the proceedings—a penalty preferable to the lynch law of the race course.

trainer might get a useful fighter from a dog thief who knew his trade, sound breeding was normally looked on as essential. Proper fighting dogs were of the old English bull breed, evolved for baiting and fighting, often shown in sporting prints. (The only surviving strain seems to be that rare, ugly and delightful

beast the Staffordshire bull terrier.) Since they were matched by weight—often more stringently than prize-fighters—too large an animal was not desirable, and about forty to fifty pounds was probably the maximum for a top class fighter. Larger animals were apt to be somewhat loose coupled and either slow or too rangy for a narrow arena. The ears, but not the tail, were close docked.

The best bred dog could 'turn felon' as the phrase went and prove useless, and young animals had to be carefully entered to the game. Careful feeding and judicious exercising were considered vital—trotting untethered under a quiet-jogging trap or coster cart was good hardening as the young dog reached full strength. Two sorts of practice encounter introduced the learner to his profession. In the first, he would be set to fight with an 'old gummer', an elderly and rather decrepit fighting dog who had either lost his eye teeth from senility or had had them extracted by his owner. The old dog, though relatively feeble, was skilful and taught the young one to move quickly and not expose himself. These worries were usually just sparring bouts, and not allowed to go very far. The next stage was the use of 'taste dogs'—poor curs fed up to give them a bit of strength and spirit on whom the apprentice acquired the habits of a killer. Before being put in the pit a taste dog had the most vulnerable parts of his body shaved so that his opponent learnt to attack these places. Often the young fighting dog needed much urging and egging on before he would keep at it and rip the other to pieces; but after he had been given one or two 'real mouthfuls' of this sort of butchery he was, as trainers said, 'made'.

Like human athletes, dogs were brought to a pitch of efficiency before a match, which might take place in a special boarded pit or simply in any convenient private spot where backers and enthusiasts could gather. The terms were arranged beforehand and naturally varied, but matches were not generally, and perhaps only very seldom, deliberately fought to the death. Each animal had a second who encouraged him with noises, and as in a human prize-fight the second might throw up the beaver when his principal was plainly going under without chance of victory. His broad, shortish, very powerful muzzle gave a good fighting dog a fearful grip and, once he had a vital hold, his bred-in instinct led him to hang on heroically. However, if other means failed and the terms of the match allowed it, dogs could usually be separated by a liberal application of flour: without injuring the eyes or mouth it caked up their air passages, so that they had to relax their grip to breathe and could be prised apart.

Fighting dogs were also used for badger baiting, though it is likely that the most promising were not readily risked at this amusement. It consisted simply of setting one or several dogs to worry a captured badger, shut into a small closed space or secured with a chain. The badger's tough hide, punishing bite, and reluctance to die have long made it a favourite victim of loutish sadism.

No nervous and intelligent creature excites less pity than the rat, and the keen vogue for ratting as an elaborately organised indoor urban amusement may, paradoxically enough, have owed something to the general decrease in brutality. It was competitive, it lent itself to betting, and it was well suited to the more modest sort of dog fancier and a rough, poor public. The authorities did little to interfere, so that meetings could be freely advertised. Public house rat-pits were not new attractions but in the middle years of the nineteenth century they seem to have been exceptionally popular (partly perhaps because of the suppression of cocking).

Winter was the great season and at this time of year streets like Great St Andrew's were liberally studded with notices for 'Rats Wanted' and 'Rats Bought and Sold', while the proprietors of the major rat-pits literally dealt in cartloads. Jimmy Shaw, a publican prize-fighter who ran a well known ratting house, boasted to Mayhew that he took delivery of between three and seven hundred rats a week, and on occasion had as many as two thousand alive on his premises. Some twenty families were engaged in supplying him. A more modest establishment, kept by another retired pugilist in Bunhill, received between two and five hundred weekly. A strong demand made for good prices, at least for the pit keepers, who sold retail to competitors. In times of scarcity the best quality rats reached a shilling apiece, though inferior ones were sometimes obtainable at half-a-crown the dozen. Country-caught barn rats were the most esteemed; sewer rats (easily identified by their odour) were considered inferior and liable to infect a dog's mouth.

Animals were backed to kill a given number of rats within a set time. At properly conducted meetings rules were strict: the terrier or ferret was weighed (weight in relation to performance was crucial) and proceedings checked by stop watch. Frequently there was a trophy for the best dog. A notice of a meeting at a pub in Compton Street, Soho, was headed 'RATTING FOR THE MILLION. A SPORTING GENTLEMAN who is a Staunch Supporter of the destruction of these Vermin WILL GIVE A GOLD REPEATER WATCH TO BE KILLED FOR BY DOGS under 13¾ pounds weight.' The rats were to be killed 'in a Large Wire Pit' with 'a chalk Circle to be drawn in the centre for the Second. Any man touching dogs or rats, or acting in any way unfair, his dog will be disqualified.' Competitors were 'to go to scale at half-past 7', an hour before the entertainment began. Beneath ran the legend 'Rats always on hand for the accommodation of Gentlemen to try their dogs'.[1]

Mayhew, with his wonderful eye for off-colour humanity, was plainly fascinated by this sleezy pastime, and his account of a meeting perfectly catches the setting and atmosphere of one kind of sporting pub.

The front of the long bar was crowded with men of every grade of society, all smoking, drinking and talking about dogs. Many had brought with them their 'fancy' animals, so that a kind of canine exhibition was going on; some carried under their arms small bull-dogs, whose flat pink noses rubbed against my arm as I passed; others had Skye terriers curled up like balls of hair and sleeping like children, as they were nursed by their owners. The only animals that seemed awake and under continual excitement were the little brown English terriers,[2] who, despite the neat black leathern collars by which they were held struggled to get loose, as if they smelt the rats in the room above.

There is a business-like look about the tavern which is a low roofed room without any adornments generally considered necessary to render a public house attractive. The tubs where the spirits are kept are blistered with the heat of the gas, and so dirty that the once brilliant gilt hoops are now quite black.

Sleeping in an old hall-chair lay an enormous white bull-dog with a head as round and smooth as a clenched boxing glove. When this animal, which was the admiration of all beholders, rose up, its legs were as bowed as a tailor's, leaving a peculiar pear-shaped opening between them. It was a white dog, with a sore look from its being peculiarly pink round the eyes, nose and indeed all the edges of its body. On the other side of the fireplace was a white bull-terrier with a black patch over the eye, which gave him a rather disreputable look. This animal was watching the movements of the customers and occasionally, when the entrance door swung back, would give a growl of enquiry. About the walls were many clusters of black leather collars, and pre-eminent was a silver dog-collar, which,

[1] Mayhew, Vol. I, p. 503.
[2] More properly black-and-brown: the breed was the one now known as the Welsh terrier.

I learnt, was to be the prize in a rat-match in a fortnight's time.

As the visitors poured in, they, at the request of the proprietor 'not to block-up the bar' took their seats in the parlour; and accompanied by a waiter who kept shouting 'Give your orders, gentlemen,' I entered the room. Sporting pictures hung against the dingy walls. Over the fireplace were square glazed boxes in which were the stuffed forms of dogs famous in their day. Pre-eminent among the prints was that representing the 'wonder' Tiny, 'five pounds and a half in weight' as he appeared killing two hundred rats. Tiny used to wear a lady's bracelet as a collar.

Among the stuffed heads was one of a white bull-dog with tremendous glass eyes sticking out, as if it had died of strangulation. The proprietor's son was kind enough to explain to me the qualities that had once belonged to this favourite. 'They've spoilt her in the stuffing, sir,' he said. 'That there *is* a dog,' he continued, pointing to one represented with a rat in its mouth, 'it was as good as any in England, though it's so small. I've seen her kill a dozen rats almost as big as herself, though they killed *her* at the last; for sewer rats are dreadful for giving dogs canker, and she wore herself out with continually killing them, though we always rinsed her mouth out well with peppermint and water.'

The company assembled in the parlour consisted of sporting men, or those, who from curiosity, had come to witness what a rat match was like. Seated at the same table, talking together, were those dressed in the costermonger's corduroy, soldiers with their uniforms carelessly unbuttoned, coachmen in livery, and tradesmen who had slipped on their evening frock-coats and run out from the shop.

The dogs belonging to the company were standing on the different tables, or tied to the legs of the forms, or sleeping in their owners' arms, and were in turn minutely criticised—their limbs being stretched out as if they were being felt for fractures, and their mouths looked into, as if a dentist were examining their teeth. Nearly all the animals were marked with scars from bites. 'Pity to bring him up to rat-killing,' said one, who had been admiring a fierce looking bull-terrier, although he did not mention at the same time what line in life the animal ought to pursue.

There were among the visitors some French gentlemen,

who had evidently witnessed nothing of the kind before; and whilst they endeavoured to drink their hot gin and water, they made their interpreter translate to them the contents of a large placard hung from a hatpeg and headed

EVERY MAN HAS HIS FANCY
RATTING SPORTS IN REALITY

About nine o'clock the proprietor took the chair in the parlour, at the same time giving the order to 'shut up the shutter in the room above and light up the pit.' This announcement seemed to rouse the spirits of the assembly, and even the dogs tied to the legs of the tables ran out to the length of their leathern thongs, and their tails curled like eels, as if they understood the meaning of the words.

The performances of the evening were somewhat hurried on by the entering of a young gentleman whom the waiters called 'Cap'an'.

'Now, Jem, when is this match coming off?' the Captain asked impatiently; and despite the assurance that they were getting ready, he threatened to leave the place if they were kept waiting much longer. This young officer seemed to be a great fancier of dogs, for he made the round of the room, handling each animal in turn, feeling and squeezing its feet and scrutinising its eyes with such minuteness, that the French gentlemen were forced to enquire who he was.

There was no announcement that the room above was ready, though everybody seemed to understand it; for all rose at once, and mounting the broad wooden staircase, which led to what was once the drawing room, dropped their shillings into the hand of the proprietor, and entered the rat-killing apartment.

'The pit,' as it is called, consists of a small circus, some six feet in diameter, fitted with a high wooden rim that reaches to elbow height. Over it the branches of a gas lamp are arranged, which light up the white painted floor and every corner of the little arena. On one side of the room is a recess, which the proprietor calls his 'private box', and this apartment the Captain and his friends took possession of, whilst the audience generally clambered upon the tables and forms, or hung over the sides of the pit itself.

All the little dogs which the visitors had brought up with

them were now squalling and barking and struggling in their
masters' arms; and when a rusty wire cage of rats was brought
forward the proprietor was obliged to shout out—'Now you
that have dogs, *do* make 'em shut up.'

The Captain was the first to jump into the pit. A man
wanted to sell him a bull-terrier spotted like a fancy rabbit,
and a dozen of rats was the consequent order.

The Captain preferred pulling the rats out of the cage himself, laying hold of them by their tails and jerking them into
the arena. He was cautioned by one of the men not to let them
bite him, for 'believe me' were the words 'you'll never forget
Cap'an; these 'ere are none of the cleanest.' Whilst the rats
were being counted out, some of those that had been taken
from the cage ran about the panelled floor and climbed up
the young officer's legs, making him shake them off and
exclaim, 'Get out, you varmint!'

'Chuck him in,' said the Captain, and over went the dog;
and in a second the rats were running round the circus, or
trying to hide themselves between the small openings in the
boards round the pit. Although the proprietor of the dog
endeavoured to speak up for it, still it was evidently not worth
much in a rat-killing sense; and if it had not been for its
'second' we doubt if the terrier would not have preferred
leaving the rats to enjoy their lives. We cannot say whether
the dog eventually was bought, but we fancy no dealings took
place.

The Captain seemed anxious to see as much sport as he
could, for he frequently asked those who carried dogs whether
'his little 'un would kill' and appeared sorry when such
answers were given as 'My dog's mouth's a little out of
order, Cap'an', or 'I've only tried him at very little 'uns.'

Preparations now began for the grand match of the evening,
in which fifty rats were to be killed. The 'dead 'uns' were
gathered up by their tails and flung into a corner. The floor
was swept, and a big flat basket produced, like those in which
chickens were brought to market, and under whose iron top
could be seen small mounds of closely packed rats. This match
seemed to be between the proprietor and his son, and the
stake to be gained was only a bottle of lemonade. It was
strange to observe the daring manner in which the lad introduced his hand into the rat cage as he fumbled about and

stirred up with his fingers the living mass, picking up, as he had been requested, 'only the big 'uns'.

When the fifty animals had been flung into the pit, they gathered themselves into a mound which reached one-third up the sides, and which reminded one of the heap of hair-sweepings in a barber's shop after a heavy day's cuttings. These were all sewer and water-ditch rats, and the smell that rose from them was like that from a hot drain.

The Captain amused himself by flicking at them with his pocket handkerchief and offering them the lighted end of his cigar, which the little creatures tamely sniffed and drew back from, as they singed their noses. It was also a favourite amusement to blow on the mound of rats, for they seemed to dislike the cold wind, which sent them fluttering about like so many feathers; indeed whilst the match was going on when-ever the little animals collected together formed a barricade as it were to the dog, the cry of 'Blow on 'em! blow on 'em!' was given by the spectators, and the dog's second puffed at them as if extinguishing a fire.

The company was kept waiting so long for the match to begin that the impatient Captain again threatened to leave the house, and was only quieted by the proprietor's reply of 'My dear friend, be easy; the boy's on the stairs with the dog'; and true enough we shortly heard a wheezing and a screaming in the passage without as if some strong-winded animal was being strangled, and presently a boy entered, carrying in his arms a bull-terrier in a perfect fit of excitement. 'Lay hold a little closer up to the head or he'll turn round and nip yer', said the proprietor.

When all the arrangements had been made the second and the dog jumped into the pit. The moment the terrier was loose he became quiet in a most business-like manner and rushed at the rats, burying his nose in the mound till he brought out one in his mouth. In a short time a dozen rats with wetted necks were lying bleeding on the floor, and the white paint of the pit became grained with blood. In a little time the terrier had a rat hanging to his nose which, despite his tossing, still held on. He dashed up against the sides, leaving a patch of blood as if a strawberry had been smashed there.

'Hi, Butcher! hi, Butcher!' shouted the second, 'good dog, bur-r-r-r-h!' and he beat the sides of the pit like a drum, till the dog flew about with new life. 'Dead 'un! Drop it!' he cried when the terrier nosed a rat kicking on its side, as it slowly expired of its broken neck.

'Time!' said the proprietor, and the dog was caught up and held panting, his neck stretched out like a serpent's, staring intently at the rats that still kept crawling about. The poor little wretches in the brief interval, as if forgetting their danger, again commenced cleaning themselves, some nibbling the ends of their tails, others hopping about, going now to the legs of the lad in the pit and sniffing at his trousers, or, strange to say, advancing smelling to within a few paces of their enemy the dog.

The dog lost the match, and the proprietor, we presume honourably paid the bottle of lemonade to his son. But he was evidently displeased with the dog's behaviour, for he said, 'He won't do for me. He's not my sort! Here, Jim, tell Mr G. he may have him if he likes; I won't give him house room.'

A plentiful shower of half-pence was thrown into the pit as a reward for the second.

A slight pause now took place in the proceedings, during which the landlord requested that the gentlemen 'would give their minds up to drinking. You know the love I have of you', he added jocularly, 'and that I don't care for any of you'; whilst the waiter accompanied the invitation with a cry of 'Give your orders gentlemen,' and the lad with the rats asked if 'any gentlemen would like any rats?'

Several other dogs were tried, and amongst them one who, from the size of his stomach, had evidently been accustomed to large dinners, and looked on rat-killing as a sport and not as a business. The appearance of this fat animal was greeted with remarks such as 'Why don't you feed that dog?' and 'Shouldn't give him more than five meals a day.'

Another impatient bull-terrier was thrown into the midst of a dozen rats. He did his duty so well, that the admiration of the spectators was focused upon him. 'Ah', said one, '*he'd* do better at a hundred than twelve'; while the landlord himself said, 'He's a very pretty creetur, and I'd back him to kill against anybody's dog at eight and a half or nine.'

It was nearly twelve o'clock before the evening's performance concluded. At last the landlord, finding that 'no gentlemen would like a few rats', and that his exhortations to 'give their minds up to drinking' produced no effect, spoke the epilogue of the rat tragedy:—

'Gentlemen, I give you a very handsome silver collar to be killed for next Tuesday. Open to all the world, only they must be novice dogs, or at least such as is not ph*ee*nomenons. We shall have plenty of sport gentlemen, and there will be loads of rat killing. I hope to see all my kind friends, not forgetting your dogs likewise. . . . Gentlemen, there is a good parlour downstairs, where we meets for harmony and entertainment.'[1]

Surprisingly, Mayhew says nothing here about the betting that was a vital feature of ratting matches and must have been going on all around; presumably he did not wish to expose the place to anti-gaming penalties, and for the same reason the odds may not have been openly cried. From the quality of both dogs and rats, and the absence of prize money or trophy, it is clear that this was a distinctly second-rate occasion. A better-found meeting would probably have produced competition for the egregious Captain. Jimmy Shaw the prize fighter, who used only country rats, was well accustomed to genteel patronage. 'Bless you,' he told Mayhew confidentially, 'I've had noble ladies and titled ladies come here to see the sport—on the quiet you know. When my wife was here they would come regular, but now she's away they don't come so often.'

A curious feature of the ratting craze was a cult of expertise about rats and their catching and handling. An odd, elderly man called Jack Black who wore a sort of surcoat with V.R. embroidered on it and described himself—apparently with justification —as 'Rat and Mole Destroyer to Her Majesty' was quite a well known figure. He sometimes sold rat poison in the streets but his cottage in Battersea was a regular depot for rats, ferrets and other small game. His familiarity with rats was remarkable and he would often have several clambering about inside his clothes and squatting on his shoulders.

Black was also a leading exponent of another popular fancy— the caging and training of song birds. Here again was a petty industry with ancillary trades such as cage making and the hawking of the fresh turf divots which were considered essential for captive wild birds. Starlings, blackbirds, thrushes, finches—

---

[1] Mayhew, Vol. III, p. 7 et seq. The quotation has been shortened.

especially the common linnet—and occasional much-prized nightingales were taken with nets or limed twigs on forays into the countryside, put into tiny cages and sold. Club Row in Bethnal Green and parts of St Giles were among the best known London markets. Roughly speaking, training consisted of darkening the cage and whistling or playing a pipe nearby until the captive learned to imitate a constantly repeated air or 'toy': some wretches blinded their birds in the belief that it made them better singers. Even in this unlikely field the national propensity asserted itself. 'Julking' or bird singing competitions were sporting events, the birds being set to sing toys against each other for bets. It was a very humble little sport, yet sometimes as much as a couple of sovereigns might depend on the outcome of a match.

If one surveys the whole field of sporting life at this period it is hard to find a dozen sports of any importance in which the most disreputable people did not play a significant part. Indeed it is obvious that a good deal of the attraction for members of the upper classes lay in a coarse, even scoundrelly, bohemianism that was a welcome contrast to the protocol and tongue-guarding of their own drawing rooms. Popular football (outside certain schools and colleges) was largely a brutish mob pastime, almost on a par with bullock-baiting; the horse-coping connected with fox hunting was wide open to criminals; game-preserving nourished urban poaching gangs. It is impossible to give anything like an exhaustive account of the links between sport and the underworld, for it would have to be a review of almost the entire sporting scene.

But there was one popular diversion which, if it can hardly by the wildest stretch of definition be called a sport, had so much the character of a sporting event that it must be mentioned. Until the passing of the Capital Punishment Amendment Act of 1868 executions were heavily attended spectacles. The spirit in which spectators gathered is happily expressed in the traditional expression—'a hanging match'.

The attraction of hangings varied according to the place and the notoriety of the condemned man. At some lesser assize towns, such as Dorchester, there might be only a few hundred reasonably well-behaved people; but where a famous criminal was to be turned off within reach of a dense population, enormous crowds collected. Some jail sites lent themselves admirably to this. In September 1849 John Gleeson, a murderer of some note, was hanged outside Kirkdale Jail in Liverpool, before a gathering estimated at 100,000 strong, many of whom had been brought by special trains. 'All the vacant ground in front of the prison and spreading down to the canal presented much the same appearance with respect to numbers as Aintree or Epsom on the Cup or Derby Day.' And it was not merely in numbers that these turn-outs resembled race meetings, for like any other open air festivity, executions were marked by high spirits and hearty appetites. Sellers of fried fish, hot pies, fruit and ginger beer commonly drove a humming trade, as did hawkers of mournful ballads and fake condemned-cell confessions—known in the business as 'lamentations'.

Popular gallows literature, indeed, seems only to have reached its full flowering in Victorian times. In the old days when, as a hawker explained to Mayhew, it might be 'sentence o' Friday and scragging o' Monday,' there had not usually been time to prepare a flood of broadsheets and spurious biographies; but with the coming of at least a week's grace for the condemned, printers began to discover a great new field for exploitation.

Although it was not well suited for a large crowd of spectators, Newgate was much the most famous execution place. Offenders were hanged there from the combined City and Middlesex shrievalties, so that it was better supplied than other sites as well as being in the centre of the metropolis. Workers in and around the City could conveniently take in a hanging at the cost of being a little late for work. Sometimes more than thirty thousand people would jam the streets outside the prison, the slope of Snow Hill and the approaches from Newgate Market. With capital cases virtually confined to murder, executions were sometimes infrequent even at Newgate, and this must have enhanced the appeal of those that did take place.[1] The lowering, heavily-rusticated frontage of the prison—a sinister work of art if ever there was one—made a grimly appropriate setting.

There was a certain amount of variety in the hanging appliances used at different jails. At some the death-trap was little more than a sort of hinged flap, supported against the prison wall, with a beam above to carry the rope. At Newgate, how-

---

[1] In fact there were no Newgate hangings in the years 1849 and 1851. In the boom year 1864, however, there were eight out of a national total of nineteen.

ever, the apparatus was quite elaborate and very substantial. It consisted of a black-covered scaffold 'about the size of a large [showman's] caravan' surmounted by the stout uprights and crossbeam of the gallows, from the middle of which a short chain hung down. Under the cross-beam was the trap, worked by a lever 'similar to a common pump handle' which released a draw bar under the leaves.

The scaffold was not a permanent structure. Executions usually took place on a Monday, and soon after midnight on Sunday a heavy waggon loaded with poles and boarding would pull out of the main gate and come to a halt by the famous black-painted side door a few yards away. There a gang of workmen would set about unloading and assembling the scaffold. But long before then, perhaps as early as eight or nine on Sunday evening, the forerunners of the crowd would have begun to appear so as to get the best places. By about half-past four in the morning, the gathering along Old Bailey was beginning to thicken and acquire a corporate personality. Refreshment pedlars were already active and the neighbouring coffee shops busy and ablaze with gas—including the one directly across the road from the prison, from which the condemned man's breakfast would shortly be carried over on a tray. A low barrier was erected to keep the crowd back from the scaffold and soon a strong squad of frock-coated constables marched up to man it—the first sign, apart from the scaffold, that authority was stirring.

Like most mobs, a Newgate crowd was full of unpredictable vagaries. They might protect an abused woman, buffet and brutally misuse a tract-seller, good-humouredly cheer a man climbing a house pipe, amuse themselves by kicking a stray dog to death. Besides the throng in the road, the windows and roofs opposite the jail were packed with paying spectators, from seedy young clerks perched along a coping to the fashionable bucks lolling on the sills of a second floor front close above the scaffold; and between these and those below all sorts of jokes and insults were exchanged.

Between six and seven, especially if it was summer and a well publicised murderer was due to hang, the crowd extended far into surrounding streets: there was difficulty in clearing a way for the Sheriffs' carriages, their windows flickering in the early light. By now work and hammering at the scaffold should have ceased, and experienced execution-goers watched to see the rope 'coiled up like a serpent' laid on the platform from below. 'The human hand that placed it there was only seen for a moment . . . and then again was suddenly withdrawn, as if ashamed of the deed it had done.'

Sometimes the crowd took to chanting, with an ambiguous mixture of sentiment and ribaldry, the lines of the revivalist hymn *Oh, my!—Think I've got to die!* but would quieten as eight o'clock approached. When the clock of St Sepulchre started to chime the hour there would go up a sort of murmurous roar 'awful, bizarre and indescribable' through which could be heard the quick, feeble jingling of a second bell. When this discordant sound stopped, the door in the prison wall opened and a little party emerged and came up onto the scaffold. The condemned man, open-necked and with his wrists pinioned by a broad leather strap, was preceded by the chaplain, book in hand, and immediately followed by Calcraft the City executioner, a whiskered, almost parsonical figure in dingy black. At sight of the prisoner there was a cry of 'Hats off!' and every man and boy uncovered. Then there were shouts of 'Down in front!' from those whose view was still obstructed. While the clergyman read aloud, Calcraft strapped the man's legs together, pulled a nightcap down over his face, adjusted the rope through the chain and about his neck, then returned down the steps and pulled the handle that worked the trap. If need be, he or his assistant would appear, jack-in-a-box-like, at the opening under the hanging man and, grasping his legs, heave on them until strangulation was complete.[1] This last exhibition was only available to those who had secured places above the gallows. The body remained suspended for an hour before it was cut down and lowered into a coffin within the scaffold, after which the mob finally dispersed.

There was something like a cult of execution-going among better-class sensation seekers, especially dashing and would-be dashing young men. The use of a room with a good view at Newgate might cost as much as twenty-five pounds—though at other places it was a lot cheaper—and smart parties would make

---

[1] The drop method, calculated to kill quickly by dislocation, had in theory been generally adopted since 1783. But in practice, with only a rule of thumb knowledge of anatomy to guide them, hangmen easily misjudged the fall. Moreover, although he was the City's official executioner from 1828 to 1871, and in addition undertook much work for other authorities, Calcraft seems not to have been particularly proficient at his trade. According to Major A. Griffiths' *Chronicles of Newgate*, from which a good deal of the information given above is taken, the City paid Calcraft a guinea a week retainer, a guinea for each execution, and half-a-crown a time for floggings, as well as a modest allowance for birches and cats-o'-nine-tails.

Above: Tom Sayers (winner of the British championship belt in 1857) in action at various fights. From a memento card (Mansell Collection)

Below: Preparing for an execution at Newgate, 1848 (Mansell Collection)

Bluegate Fields, St George's-in-the-East.
The ornate houses of a once-prosperous quarter now formed part
of the most dangerous portside slum in England. Gustave Doré

a night of it, regaling themselves like Lord Tomnoddy and his
guests in *The Ingoldsby Legends* with quantities of punch and a
sound supper:

> *Cold fowl and cigars, pickled onions in jars,*
> *Welsh rabbits and kidneys—rare work for the jaws:—*
> *And very large lobsters, with very large claws*
> *And there is M'Fuze, and Lieutenant Tregooze,*
> *And there is Sir Carnaby Jenks, of the Blues,*
> *All come to see a man die in his shoes!*

The Marquis of Waterford, the young and rakish head of the
great sporting clan of Beresford, was so regular a patron that
his absence at the hanging of Courvoisier—a manservant whose
murder of his employer in 1840 made a great stir—was a matter
of surprised comment.

According to Thackeray, who stood for four hours on the
cobbles outside Newgate to see Courvoisier swing, the mob on
that occasion 'was extraordinarily gentle and good humoured'.[1]
On the other hand Dickens (who was also at Courvoisier's
execution and received a rather different impression) wrote to
a foreign friend after witnessing the death of the Mannings,
husband and wife, over the entry of Horsemonger Lane Prison
nine years later: 'The conduct of the people was so indescribably
frightful, that I felt for some time afterwards almost as if I were
living in a city of devils.'[2] By and large, that view seems to
correspond better with contemporary experience, and it was
largely the scandal of the street scenes that at last led to the
scaffold being put behind the privacy of prison walls.

Where all testimony agrees is on the attraction of hangings
for the criminal community and the failure of the spectacle as a
deterrent. Thieves, tarts and cadgers, mostly of the worst sort
and including a high proportion of juveniles, swarmed round the
gallows. A Bristol prison chaplain declared that out of 167
condemned criminals whom he had interviewed during his
career, only three had not witnessed an execution.[3]

---

[1] 'Going to see a Man Hanged' in *Sketches & Travels in London*. Thackeray also noticed
in the windows 'some quiet, fat, family-parties, of simple, honest tradesmen and their wives,
looking on with the greatest imaginable calmness and sipping their tea'. It seems very
unlikely he would have seen them there twenty years later. If, as appears probable, the
behaviour of hanging crowds deteriorated during the last years of public executions it was
perhaps partly because of the withdrawal of respectable people.

[2] Quoted in *Dickens and Crime* by Philip Collins, p. 240.

[3] Collins, p. 229. Even in the days when trivial thieves were hanged, pickpockets were
notoriously active at executions.

But to suppose that the mob at a hanging was likely to draw moral lessons from it was to misread the whole character of the occasion. The people who milled around outside Newgate, eating and drinking and passing the time with songs and horse-play, had not come to be instructed or elevated. They had come to an entertainment. The one real difference between a hanging and a sporting crowd was that no one was interested in betting on the outcome of the event.

CHAPTER TEN

Prostitution

Nothing formed so close a bond between the underworld and respectable society as prostitution. By modern standards the importance of commercial sex in Victorian life seems extraordinary; and what is so striking is not just the number of prostitutes in a society that has come to be a byword for sexual repression, but the blatancy with which they carried on their trade, even in the heart of fashionable London.

The specialised character of 'Babylon' was as obvious by day as by night. At noon, when nearby streets were bustling with life and business, the Haymarket with its half-deserted pavements and many closed shutters had a drowsy, withdrawn, almost sabbatical air; only the omnibuses clattering up and down gave an impression of weekday animation. Leicester Square, despite the hotels and shoppers, was no more than half awake. Where doors and windows were open to air the rooms, women with mops and yawning shirt-sleeved men could be seen at tasks that, in more respectable quarters, had been finished hours before breakfast. During the afternoon, growing numbers of women began to patrol the area and the neighbouring arcades and shopping streets, but it was only when the lights began to flare at the theatre entrances that the place became fully alive. Then there were heavily painted women in droves, all along the street and waiting at the alley corners, smarter lorettes making for their regular resorts, child prostitutes dodging after clients and plucking at their sleeves, bursts of light and snatches of music as doors opened in the dimmer side streets; and everywhere a constant setting down of well dressed men and women from broughams and hansoms.

The porticos of the main theatres, and the neighbouring pavements, were the most celebrated whores' parades in the country, while inside the theatres themselves the saloons and passages were a favourite stamping ground for high-class prostitutes. The tangle of streets and alleys at the upper end of the

Haymarket—and most especially along Windmill Street and the courts opening off it—was the core of the whole complex, where rouge-caked drabs, unshaven bullies and prize-ring touts, bawds, swells in starched fronts and opera hats, and elegant women in yards of watered silk, were to be seen cheek by jowl. Here there were squalid and dangerous criminal taverns like the notorious Black Bull and high class 'night houses' bright with cut glass and staffed with liveried waiters.

A prostitute told Bracebridge Hemyng:[1]

> Why, if I have no letters or visits from any of my friends, I get up about four o'clock, dress and dine: after that I may walk about the streets for an hour or two and pick up anyone I am fortunate enough to meet, that is if I want money; afterwards I go to the Holborn, dance a little, and if anyone likes me I take him home with me. If not I go to the Haymarket, and wander from one café to another, from Sally's to the Carlton, from Barns' to Sams', and if I find no one there I go, if I feel inclined, to the divans. I like the Grand Turkish best, but you don't as a rule find good men at any of the divans.

This girl, who struck Hemyng as intelligent for one of her standing, belonged to an inferior grade of Haymarket prostitute, though very far from the lowest. The cafés she mentions were at that date second or third-rate night houses; not especially squalid, but jostling places where there was a risk of having one's pocket picked and men lounged about lewdly winking at women and expecting to be accosted. Though occasional disturbances might break out, these haunts were hardly dangerous, for the police were strong in this area and went in and out as they pleased. In some there were show cases where gloves and cheap trinkets were displayed at five times the regular price for women to wheedle admirers into buying. Oddly enough the Reverend Baptist Noel, who conducted a mission to prostitutes, was able to hold late night services in one—though apparently not with any useful results.

The most celebrated night house in the fifties and sixties was the Café Royal in Princess Street, Leicester Square, better known as Kate Hamilton's.[2] Its entrance was down a long

---

[1] Author of the long survey of prostitution which forms the first and largest section o Vol. IV of Mayhew's *London Labour and the London Poor*. (See p. 34.)

[2] Not the same as the great brasserie that became famous in the late Victorian epoch.

passage and carefully guarded—probably not from fear of the law but to prevent the premises being cluttered with unprofitable customers and inferior prostitutes. Mrs Hamilton, who presided,[1] was a mountain of a woman, hideously ugly but with one of those mysterious talents for promoting 'atmosphere'. From midnight on she sat swigging champagne, now and then shaking with laughter like a gigantic blancmange.

Mayhew's print of the place shows part of a crowded apartment lit by globed gas brackets with pendant lustres, and panelled with high mirrors framed in ornate moulding. Perhaps half the men are in evening clothes and most of them have their tall hats clamped on their heads. Some of the women are bare-shouldered in daring decolletage; others are shawled and bonneted and hold their muffs as if they proposed to remain only a few moments. At the sides are tables flanked by upholstered benches and dotted with bottles and tall glasses (the standard drink is champagne or moselle at an outrageous twelve shillings a bottle). Across the end of the room, somewhat like a judge's seat, is a sort of raised counter behind which sits Kate herself, flanked by cronies of both sexes. Many are sitting with their backs to the tables, legs crossed, and the only refreshment visible is in the thin glasses. The men's attitudes are noticeably more casual than the women's and nothing better points the character of place and company than the cigars in their mouths; one graceless young gentleman in opera hat and white waistcoat is actually standing, hands in pockets, in the open centre of the room making a proposal to a handsome cocotte without bother ing to remove the short clay pipe that juts from under his curly moustache.

At Kate's and several other high-class night houses, the police were seldom seen. The drinks were the essential source of revenue and in some of these places they were sold in defiance of the licensing regulations.

Many of the night houses' late customers came on from the casinos. These dancing places, a prominent and relatively novel feature of early and mid-Victorian night life, often covered large

---

[1] The place is said by Hemyng to have belonged with several other night houses to a Jewish family combine. He may be referring to David Belasco and his associates, known to have built up wide interests in brothels and night houses, though by the early fifties Belasco himself had gone bankrupt and was reported to be working as a waiter. In 1862 the titular owner was a certain John Fryer. It was common knowledge that background proprietors often controlled groups of night haunts.

sites and perhaps for this reason were much more scattered than most of their rival attractions. The very popular Holborn Casino (patronised by the girl who described her pick-up schedule to Hemyng and properly called the Casino de Venise) was a large, brilliantly lit hall, 'glittering with a myriad prisms,' where a horde of dancers spun about to strenuous polkas and quadrilles. It was frequented by a variety of young men— medical students, apprentice lawyers, young ships' officers, clerks, well off young tradesmen—and by a large number of amateur and professional prostitutes. The floor, the band and the easy pick-ups were the great attractions; for all its shady reputation it was a cheerful, bouncy, sober sort of place where the chief drinks were soda water and bitter beer. There was a policeman on duty in the lobby, but as a rule there was little for him to do.

Every casino had its own atmosphere. At Laurent's Dancing Academy in wicked Windmill Street it was considered rather low to dance; the more stylish clients loitered in the gallery above, overlooking the languid and mildly unsavoury scene below. Close by were the lively Argyll Rooms which had grown in a few decades from a modest tavern to one of the most famous Haymarket resorts. Here the atmosphere was far racier. An acrobatic negro called Kangaroo enlivened things for a time, and Lord Hastings, a well known sportsman, provided a memorable evening by emptying a sack of rats among the whirling crinolines. To dance with the more expensive women of the town, however, it was generally necessary to go to the smaller, luxurious Portland Rooms, familiarly known as Mott's, where for many years gentlemen not in dress coats and white waistcoats were refused admittance.

After the theatre or casino, or both, it was common form to go to a supper place. Evans's in Covent Garden was a kind of small, glittering music hall where smart parties sat in their boxes, eating and drinking, while singers from the opera performed on the stage. Casual picking up by prostitutes was discouraged and women were not allowed to circulate among the grog drinkers in the pit. At Kellner's in Leicester Square a naughty continental atmosphere was fostered; there was a bar with attractive French and German barmaids, and concert turns by artistes whose appearance carefully harmonised with conventional ideas of foreign dress. The Garrick's Head off Bow Street had renowned supper rooms: those who were indiscreet enough could spend a night there and even enjoy the lady's company for breakfast.

As one might expect, there were many circles of men who constantly met for suppers of this kind, where a woman's power to amuse might be as important as her physical attractions. Hemyng mentions an official at the Admiralty who was commonly referred to as 'Suppers' from his well known reluctance to foot the bill at these expensive little entertainments.

At none of these night haunts, smart, low, native or exotic, could one expect to see a respectable woman. From Caudwell's dance hall in Dean Street, almost too humble to be called a casino (though young noblemen could at times be found enjoying the sweaty jostle), to the expensive amenities of Mott's and Evans's, the essential relation between male and female patrons was the same. It is true that men often ate in supper rooms, and sometimes drank in night houses, without feminine company, but it was not for this that the night life of Babylon was organised and financed. Here was a large and lucrative entertainment industry, whose whole prosperity depended on prostitution.

The connection between prostitution and the theatre was not just a matter of both being centred in one part of London. Despite the status achieved by some theatrical families, and despite the care some actresses had always taken of their reputations, prostitutes and actresses were still not in wholly separate categories. Until late Victorian times 'actress' was a disreputable description; and whether or not there really was a secret underground passage linking the rebuilt Lyceum theatre with a brothel, the persisting legend had a symbolic validity.

Many of the best known courtesans of the century were women of the theatre, and the double role was not confined to the fashionable or notorious. The horde of shifting players, who formed the bulk of the theatrical profession, were for the most part rated as dissolute Bohemians, dangerous company for a young man and sometimes no better than the fair-ground folk with whom many of the rougher ones associated. Certainly the harsh, rootless lives most theatre people led did not foster moral scruples.

An actor's work was extraordinarily hard. If houses were good, performances at a cheap suburban or provincial theatre might start in the middle of the morning and end after midnight.

One performer would take several roles in a double or triple bill, including the strenuous pantomime parts, and when they were not on the stage the members of the cast appeared outside in their costumes, cutting capers on the pavement to bring in customers. What with the preliminary chores, a seventeen hour day was by no means out of the question. It is not hard to see how a woman who lived under such conditions could slip into casual prostitution as a means of earning a little extra money.

Among prostitutes in general, there can be little doubt that a great many were driven into the trade by the low wages and harsh conditions of so many of the industries open to women. In the present-day world it is arguable how far prostitution springs from economic rather than psychological roots, but in the nineteenth century those who studied the subject were largely agreed that many women became prostitutes from sheer necessity. More and more of them depended on selling their labour on a highly unstable labour market, and the wages most of them earned were miserable enough to make them want to seize any means of raising cash. The very fact that women were paid so little meant that employers often used them to replace the men who might have supported them.

William Acton, the author of much the most solid account of prostitution in Victorian England, believed firmly that poverty was the chief cause. In this he followed Mayhew, and cites some of his researches, though one cannot read his book[1] and suspect him of being tamely derivative.

Mayhew, who understood the class he was investigating and (by the standards of the time) was at some pains to check his witnesses, interviewed a series of London garment workers. Many of them accepted whoring as an inescapable result of not having a man to help support them. One girl was pregnant by a young artisan who had left her, and she confessed she was 'obliged to go a bad way' to live. In busy times she managed to stitch a dozen pairs of trousers a week at seven or eight pence apiece; but thread and lighting had to be paid for and, since work was irregular, she cleared on average no more than three shillings a week. Yet trouser-making was relatively well paid. 'There isn't,' she said, 'one young girl as can get her living by

---

[1] *Prostitution considered in its Moral, Social and Sanitary Aspects* by William Acton, M.R.C.S. Bracebridge Hemyng in Vol. IV of *London Labour and the London Poor* adduces other evidence to the same end.

slop work': only those whose parents kept them in food and shelter could afford to remain virtuous.

Another much older trousers-hand was better off, in that she earned about the same but lived at her employer's premises. Seven years a widow, she had been left with two small children, one of whom had survived until a few months earlier. She had applied for parish relief and had been told she must go into a workhouse: since that inevitably meant being separated from her child, she had refused to do so, preferring to supplement her wages by picking up men—as, she declared, did hundreds of her

fellows, married and single. A second widow (who had also buried her two children) said that in this respect they 'pretty well all shared one fate'. While her husband was alive she 'never did him wrong'; now she could not even earn the price of her food by sewing.

A more unusual case was a young woman who had become some kind of domestic servant and was given an excellent character by her present employers. For a time she had tried to keep herself and her small child by sewing shirts, 'collars and wristbands stiched, six buttonholes, four rows of stitching down the front,' at a fee of twopence-halfpenny each. She also made small things like pincushions and hawked them about the streets, carrying the child with her. At times they had been without a roof. One night, when she had at last determined to go into the workhouse, the little boy's legs froze to her side as she carried him. A woman, seeing them squatting on a door step, took them in, gave them food, and chafed the child's legs with spirits; but when they reached the workhouse they were turned away as she had no official admittance order. Up to this point, the girl told Mayhew, she had been struggling to give up prostitution because of the child; but now she reverted to it, though only temporarily. 'Had I remained at the shirt-making, I must have been a prostitute to this day.'

Finally, after convening a sort of sweated needlewomen's congress at which each one was interviewed out of sight of the rest, Mayhew reached the conclusion that about a quarter of these women were in fact prostitutes.

Granted that London seamstresses were a notoriously exploited class, their situation was not unique. Many women in other jobs and in other great cities were exposed to similar pressures. Poor Law Unions were naturally very unwilling to give outdoor relief to anyone practising a sweated trade, since the reformed Poor Law aimed to avoid encouraging employers to pay inadequate wages by, in effect, subsidising them from public funds. If a working woman was unmarried but had dependent children her situation was likely to be desperate, since, with a view to discouraging bastardy among the poor, the law laid the support of an illegitimate child virtually on the mother alone. At the best she might hope to claim two and sixpence a week maintenance from the putative father.

Sheer need drove many women towards prostitution, and

there were other social forces that encouraged it. Commercial prostitution is more an urban than a rural institution, and many of the people who were being packed into the industrial and seaport towns had become emancipated from traditional restraints without being subject to new ones. Whatever the barbarisms of agricultural society, the cottager who drew attention to to himself—and more particularly herself—by openly flouting conventional morality was likely to pay for it. If life in the industrial jungle was no harsher than in the countryside, it was chancier, more disorientated, and in important ways a lot freer. The promiscuous woman in Liverpool or Salford, Stepney or Bermondsey, had opportunities and inducements to prostitute herself that were not to be found in a country parish.

Paradoxically, some current social attitudes, explicitly hostile to loose living, actively promoted prostitution. Nothing in the literature of the time is more striking than a tendency to lump all unchaste women into one category. Apart from the innocent —yet forever 'soiled'—victim of a single seducer, any woman contaminated by fornication was put practically on a level with the professional harlot. Such conventional notions, however at odds with reality, can have immense influence on everyday conduct. Under their sway appearances become all-important. When social commentators spoke of a young woman who had mothered a bastard as half-way to the streets, they had good reason; for though these girls were not always thrown onto the world with no resource but prostitution, they did carry with them permanent evidence of a debasement that, by common convention, fitted them for just that fate. Careful women drew away, men were emboldened. The fallen girl from a decent family was less likely to be restrained by social pressures than encouraged to promiscuity and the rewards of prostitution. Like most of us, she was apt to do what was expected of her.

Again, so far as men were concerned, the stress on propriety encouraged casual sexual encounters that could be kept right apart from their ordinary daylight lives. Fast characters in fashionable society might carry on intrigues veiled by little more than formal concessions to decorum; the capitalist might (and quite often did) keep a *poule-de-luxe* in a suburban nest; the bohemian artist cohabited with his model more or less openly; but for the ordinary careful citizen, sexual adventure usually meant an excursion to the brisk market in cash-copulation.

Apart from the specifically sexual inhibitions of ordinary society, its general prudishness and formality produced their own counter-effects. Men often sought the company of disreputable women, rather as they did that of jockeys and prize-fighters, simply for its unbuttoned easiness. For the shy and

socially inept, as well as for the bored and rakish man-of-the-world, it was not just sexual desire that made it enjoyable to share the society of attractive women with whom one could lounge and smoke and joke without constraint.

In Acton's view—and it had strong support—prostitution

owed much of its booming prosperity to the propertied classes' horror of imprudent marriages.[1] Through the middle and upper levels of society, there was a marked reluctance to accept the fall in standards that could result from a young or unsuccessful man marrying. The acceptable image was of a bridegroom older and wiser than his bride, bearing her off to a well upholstered home where they could raise their speedily growing family in a state at least as good as the one they had been accustomed to. Gentlemen of limited means who valued their position in life were inclined to stay single, and now and again, after dining at the club, take a purposeful stroll up the Haymarket.

With all these pressures at work, one may ask why any woman who had once taken the plunge and begun to earn part of her income from prostitution should ever have kept on with a legitimate job that was likely to be atrociously underpaid and laborious. A prostitute had to have reached a very degraded level not to be better rewarded than a sweated piece-worker.

One obvious answer is that many of the women who were forced into prostitution were thoroughly ill-suited to it—were in truth whores only in the last resort, and ready to escape back to another life as soon as they could. Another explanation lies in the very prevalence of prostitution. The competition was fierce. Great though the demand was, the supply was more than equal to it, and the number of women who made a living from prostitution alone can only have been a minority, perhaps a fairly small minority, of all those who hawked themselves.

At the same time, despite its risks and penalties, prostitution was, materially, an attractive trade for a girl who could get on top of the competition. Indeed, with the exception of the stage, it was the only one in which a woman without capital could reasonably hope to earn a substantial living by her own efforts.

Acton and Bracebridge Hemyng are at one in discounting the popular moralising view of the doomed harlot, smiles and paint masking the haggard corruption within, inevitably fated to a premature and edifyingly distressful end. Provided she was shrewd and lucky, a prostitute could enjoy a prosperous retirement. Acton had 'every reason to believe, that by far the larger number of women who have resorted to prostitution, for a

---

[1] See *The Times* 7–9 May 1857, which calls this 'the real cause of most of our social corruptions'. But the theme in one form or other—especially attacks on selfish bachelorhood and mercenary mothers of marriageable daughters—is a Victorian commonplace.

livelihood, return sooner or later to a more or less regular course of life.' Many were on the look out for making 'a dash at respectability' through marriage, and 'to a most surprising, and year by year increasing extent' they succeeded. Now and again prostitutes married men of high social standing (Hemyng cites two notable cases almost at the moment of writing)[1] but perhaps they more usually found husbands to whom a bride with a little working capital did not come amiss. Some, again, set up on their own, or with the backing of clients whose good will they had gained, as milliners, toilet-shop keepers and suchlike. Dubious coffee shops, cigar-divans and other places closely connected with the vice trade—including, of course, out-and-out brothels—were often run by superannuated whores, who sometimes made fortunes.

Acton was bold enough to compare the prostitute's life with the virtuous woman's, to the disadvantage of virtue. The tribute is all the more striking because it comes from a specialist whose clinical experience must have included a great many diseased prostitutes and who was most anxious to emphasise the danger of these women to public health. He wrote: 'If we compare the prostitute at thirty-five with her sister, who perhaps is the married mother of a family, or has been the toiling slave for years in the over-heated laboratories of fashion, we shall seldom find that the constitutional ravages often thought to be a necessary consequence of prostitution exceed those attributable to the cares of a family and the heart-wearing struggles of virtuous labour.'[2]

If prostitution was often better than the miseries of respectable poverty, there remains the hideous side of the picture. Not every tart was a lively girl, dancing in the casinos or joining a party of men for supper. On city pavements there were plenty of wretched beings worn out with age or disease, alcoholics, semi-imbeciles, female jetsam of all kinds, soliciting an almost inconceivable interest in their dishevelled bodies, or offering to cooperate in

---

[1] One prominent prostitute had just married a German nobleman; another, Mr Windham, a Norfolk magnate who had settled a substantial income on her. Windham's indignant relatives instituted a writ *de lunatico inquirendo*, but the action failed. He was admittedly eccentric and liked to appear in the costume of a minor railway official.

[2] Acton, 1857 edition, p. 63. He was trained at the celebrated Female Venereal Hospital in Paris, and later held an appointment at a public clinic in London, so that his experience cannot have been limited to superior prostitutes able to pay specialists' fees. As a witness he has the merit of writing without cant for an educated, masculine readership.

the squalidest perversions for a few coppers. Even in the streets of St James's, the focus of smart and competitive harlotry, a number of these creatures were to be found maundering about after dark (sometimes with veils over their pocked faces), scarecrow warnings to the brightly dressed street-walkers.

Professional whoring, in short, was a flourishing trade that could be lucrative to the tough, attractive and competitive, but a fearful trap to the feeble or unlucky. To follow it successfully required, apart from the necessary temperamental bent, a certain sort of application, not to say dedication.

At the summit of the profession—and an object-lesson to every pretty, underpaid governess and milliner's assistant—were the smart women who paraded their prosperity in fashionable places and were publicly acknowledged by the more daring of their admirers. Bowling through the Park in parasolled carriages or trotting well-mounted down the Ladies' Mile of Rotten Row, they became in the sixties a standing scandal of the London season. 'There is no difficulty,' wrote a pained reporter, 'in guessing the occupation of the dashing *equestrienne* who salutes half-a-dozen men at once with whip or with a wink, and who sometimes varies the monotony of a safe seat by holding her hands behind her back while gracefully swerving over to listen to the compliments of a walking admirer.'[1] A woman of this sort might well be the centrepiece of a lively little household in Brompton or Chelsea, convenient for Tattersall's and frequented by 'turfites'—'jockeys who are no gentlemen and gentlemen who are all jockey'. Sometimes her establishment was paid for by a free-spending man who in that way established a right to monopolise her favours for the time. For women of this sort, the conventional apotheosis was to appear leaning on the velvet ledge of an opera box, glittering with jewels and framed in the goffered shirt-fronts of titled swells.

Another type of prostitute who, sometimes at any rate, made a very good living, took a diametrically opposite tack, avoiding conduct that might draw attention to her calling and keeping well clear of the night-resorts where prostitutes gathered. She relied on a limited clientele who appreciated her tact and discretion. 'Sober, genteely dressed, well-ordered, often elegant in

---

[1] *Pall Mall Gazette*, 16 April 1869. (Quoted by Acton in the 2nd, 1870, edition of his book.) This invasion of Hyde Park by fashionable prostitutes in strength, mounted or in carriages, appears to have been a new phenomenon, perhaps copied from France.

person—such girls have the taste and the power to select their acquaintances from among the most truly eligible men whom the present false state of society debars from marriage,' Acton declared with something approaching enthusiasm. He added that they preferred 'well-bred men of settled character,' though the drunken, the sick and 'the fool's money' were all likely to be safe in their hands.

A world away from these well paid women, but like them catering for a limited market, were the sailors' tarts. On home-bound ships the shantymen sang:

> *And when we get to the London [or Liverpool] docks,*
> *There we shall see the c——t in flocks!*
> *One to another they will say,*
> *'O, welcome Jack with his three years pay!*
> > *For he is homeward bo-ou-ound,*
> > *For he is homeward bound!'*

The most celebrated welcome was along the Ratcliffe Highway towards which, after dusk, when the gas jets and shining windows gave the sordid thoroughfare a kind of attraction, the sailors' women could be seen coming in droves, walking together and calling from group to group, until they split up round knots of men or disappeared into bars and dance-halls. They were mostly boisterous, loud and hoarse-voiced, and buxomness was a great advantage. Except in wet weather, when they would draw a shawl or kingsman over their heads, they were usually bare-headed (an almost infallible mark of their calling) with their hair sometimes caught up in an ornamental net. Their bright, low-cut dresses, lavishly decked out with ribbons and sham flowers, were short enough to reveal pink or white stockinged calves above coloured morocco boots with glistening brass heels.

Amiability, good spirits and tolerance were in demand here, rather than seductiveness: seamen wanted girls who would rollick with them, sing, stamp and whirl in the dance rooms and, if the connection was more than a fleeting pick-up, endure their moods of hangover and depressed post-coital boozing. The dancing places, normally above a public house tap, were pretty well of a pattern: benches and tables at the sides, a stretch of open boards in the middle, and at the end a dais for the little orchestra—perhaps bearded German musicians such as could

The beau-monde and the demi-monde
in Rotten Row, Hyde Park, about 1869. Gustave Doré

Kate Hamilton's night house, about 1860

The Haymarket, midnight, about 1860

Both from Mayhew's *London Labour and the London Poor*

be seen playing in streets and fairs all over the country. Sometimes there were turns and sentimental or salacious songs from a waiter or possibly a dolled-up lisping infant. In the usual way of such places, they seem to have been either unpleasantly torpid, with a scattering of dull soakers and odd couples of glum girls quietly gyrating together, or according to the hour and current vogue, crammed with people. Then shrill, fast music from cornets, fiddles and fifes sent the dancers spinning around in polkas and waltzes—weather-darkened sailors of every nationality in guernseys or coloured blouses, and chalk-and-pink girls in bright flaring dresses.

Partly, perhaps, from fear of provoking one of the sudden, savage fracas for which the Highway was famous, the girls' behaviour on the floor was often surprisingly decorous, in contrast to their generally reckless air. In the taprooms and bars, however, there was a fair bit of horse-play, including well worn practical jokes. Going into the famous 'Paddy's Goose',[1] the best known seamen's pub in London, Thomas Archer was invited by a friendly tart to sniff her nosegay: he declined, and a few moments later noted the effect 'of the plentiful distribution of pepper' on a young sailor. As the lad stood there with his eyes streaming, a girl of about his own age came up and, with a protective air, took possession of him as if he were her strayed property.

In the cheapest style of dockside prostitution, the woman simply retired with her customer down the nearest dark alley, where their perfunctory business was done against a wall. Here, if he strayed too far from his mates, a man certainly risked being knocked down and robbed; but he was in far less danger than if he let himself be led, drunken, into a slum maze and up the dark stairway of an unknown tenement.

A seaman, however, was likely to want not merely a bed but one he could stay in all night. Indeed when he came ashore after a long passage, in a place far from his home (if he had such a thing) he might very well demand steady female companionship—a woman to eat and drink and spend his money with, as well as to enjoy in bed. And, though seamen's wages were shamefully low, they had gold in their belts when they were paid

[1] The White Swan, near the Shadwell end of the Highway, whose landlord had a sinister reputation. During the Crimean War he recruited for the Navy with conspicuous success 'in a small steamer with a band of music and flags' but did not long remain on good terms with authority.

off at the end of a voyage, especially after the long journeys under sail with few stops in harbour. They seldom put their money by, and it was this that gave prostitution in great sea-ports its special character.

Sailors would look out for a woman who suited their tastes, and perhaps spend their whole time ashore with her. Some would return again and again to the same woman, sending her messages and tokens from foreign ports by home-bound friends. Occasionally the connection became so strong that a woman would travel across England to another port on learning that a man's ship was docking there. Hence sailors' prostitutes, like those who went for 'well-bred men of settled character', might find a good reputation useful. It was not unusual for men to hand over their whole pay to a trusted, experienced woman, who then paid for everything until the time came when she presented her companion, reasonably intact and still possessed of his knife and gear, at a reputable shipping firm to sign on anew. By this means a man not only escaped the worst slum sirens, but could get as drunk as he pleased without falling into the much wider-spread danger of being skinned by the lodging-house keepers, publicans and slop-dealers who preyed mercilessly on seamen— above all the crimps who trapped them into signing on vessels that all sensible men kept clear of.

Some port prostitutes—presumably because of the way clients recommended them to their acquaintances—came to specialise in quite a narrow field. Coloured sailors often tended to return to the same women and, in Liverpool at any rate, a clear-cut group of prostitutes arose who confined themselves exclusively to negro customers. An experienced witness des-cribed a prostitutes' lodging house to which black sailors resorted (and apparently used as their temporary home) as 'really very clean, and comfortable, and well furnished'; and he attributed this not to any special fastidiousness among negro seamen in general but to these men's sensible habit of always reverting to the same woman or group of women, among whom they spent most of their wages.[1]

With a police sergeant, supposedly looking for a woman wanted on a felony charge, Hemyng visited some bawdy houses

[1] *Report of the House of Lords Committee on the Law Relating to the Protection of Young Girls.* Part II. Minutes of Evidence. Parl. Papers 1882 XIII. There is every reason to suppose that the same thing was true in the middle of the century.

in Brunswick Street. This was a dockland street, frequented by criminals and known (like several notorious districts elsewhere) as 'Tiger Bay'. He found rooms larger than he had expected, furnished with old fashioned four-posters, some 'surrounded with faded, dirty looking chintz curtains'. Above mantelpieces decorated with cheap crockery ornaments were gilt or rosewood-framed mirrors. The police party—the sergeant had picked up a couple of uniformed constables on the look out for another delinquent—called 'Police!' outside each door and waited for the occupant to open up and clamber back into her bed before entering and making their inspection. The women obeyed the summons quickly, as if they knew the drill; more surprisingly, the sailors sharing their beds also showed no resentment at this 'somewhat unwarrantable intrusion'.

Later, Hemyng penetrated into the dangerous warren around Bluegate Fields, guided by a police inspector who was responsible for supervising lodging houses in the area. (His responsibility did not in fact cover several of the places he took Hemyng into, but in such neighbourhoods the police often assumed an authority beyond what the law gave them.) In the kitchen of one 'tumble-down hovel', from which the outer door had been removed, they came on the landlady who, with a haggard-faced girl, was warming herself at a low fire. According to her account she paid five shillings a week rent for the two-storey house and let out the rooms to women at four shillings weekly; but it was a slack time on the river and business was bad. However there were people on the floor above, so they went upstairs.

In a room without bed or chairs, stinking of opium smoke, was a Lascar seamen lying more or less comatose on a straw mattress. Beside him crouched a woman 'half-idiotically endeavouring to extract some stupefaction from the ashes he had left in his pipe'. She was very dirty and, squatting against the wall, resembled 'an animated bundle of rags'. A closer look showed that she was strongly made and, despite her crinkled features, not yet decrepit, but rather broken down by poverty and in all likelihood ravaged by syphilis. Kicking open a crazy sagging door, they discovered, lying on the bare boards of a sort of closet, totally devoid of furniture, a creature who had reached the bottom of the pit. She was wrapped in rags, her famine-wasted features were marked with disease, her blood-shot eyes looked at them from beneath a tangled mat. Her voice showed she was an Irishwoman. She was allowed to shelter there, she said, without paying, and in return she cleaned out latrines.

This woman was at the end of the road. The girls who were just starting on it made a more cheerful sight. One important source of recruitment for professional prostitution was the large and heterogeneous class known as 'dollymops'. A dollymop might (like a French *midinette*) be a milliner's or dressmaker's assistant who ate and lodged away from the premises, or she might be a nursemaid who spent part of her day airing an infant in the Park; the essential thing was that she was an attractive working girl not under constant supervision who flirted with men and eventually went to bed with them, either for fun or gain or for both at once. She was, of course, likely to lose her job if she kept this up, and might then turn for a regular livelihood to what until then had been chiefly a matter of pleasure and excitement: to use a modern term she was often a 'larval prostitute'. Dollymopping was a recognised sport among medical students, spruce young clerks and the like, who could hope to persuade a dollymop to share a bed in exchange for an evening at a music hall and an oyster supper. The number of girls involved probably grew as more and more women went into non-residential work; by the mid-century they were numerous enough to make prostitutes complain of the competition and plainly, in so far as they cut out professionals or joined their ranks, they contributed to the inflation of an already crowded profession.

Probably the dollymops made up a large proportion of the bogus virgins and 'fresh country girls' who were provided by professional panders for some heavy-spending debauchees. This was a very lucrative form of procuring, but one had to be discreet in approaching clients since most people abominated the practice. Here is a specimen offer:[1]

Feb. 14th 1841

Sir,

When I was at your office, to bring you a letter from Miss Villiers, I promised to let you know when I knew of any lady —*fresh*. I can recommend you a very pretty fair young girl, just come from the country, and I think you will like her

---

[1] From a tract called *Miseries of Prostitution* by J. B. Talbot (1844).

much; and if it is convenient to you to meet her tomorrow at — Lichfield Street, at the bottom of St Martin's Lane, at eight o'clock, she shall be there waiting for you. If it is not convenient, will you have the kindness to send me a note by post, and inform me when it will suit your convenience.

> I remain, Sir, your most obedient
> humble servant,
> S.B.
>> from—South Moulton Street.

In fact, when the sums to be earned made it worthwhile, a virginally intact condition could be repeatedly faked, and often was. But though clients were defrauded in this way all the time, it was unlikely that a confirmed whore would be able to carry the trick off convincingly, and this meant pulling in girls who were still not hardened to commercial promiscuity. So much money was occasionally offered—even a hundred pounds and more— that procurers must have been tempted at times to all sorts of dangerous and illegal lengths; possibly even to providing in reality that staple of criminal romance, the drugged maiden. A most loathsome feature of this trade was the belief that the act of deflowering was a cure for venereal disease.

Still more depraved than the trade in virgins, and indeed one of the vilest features of the whole Victorian scene, was the long-tolerated and flourishing prostitution of young girls. Sexual intercourse with a girl less than twelve years old was illegal;[1] but, as with little beggars and pickpockets, it was often impossible to discover a child prostitute's true age, so that even this inadequate protection went by the board. In London the openness with which the business was carried on was astonishing, and according to Acton, 'the subject of much comment by foreign travellers'. Especially about the Haymarket, but also in parts of the City and elsewhere, little creatures in petticoats could be seen pursuing male pedestrians, plucking at their elbows and trying to excite their interest by all sorts of lewd remarks.

These children were not on the whole brothel-dwellers—a lodging house full of them would have been too obvious a target

---

[1] Until 1875, when the age was raised to 13. There are indications that, on average, female puberty was achieved later than nowadays—though there were, of course, great individual variations and the 1881 Lords' Committee was told of a pregnant nine-year-old. After 1885 girls were protected by law up to the age of 16 (in some circumstances 18) and adults taking advantage of, or promoting, child prostitution became effectively liable to indictment.

for investigation—or even apparently controlled by procurers. Most of them probably lived with their families (some a long way from the area they worked) and brought home as large a share of their earnings as their elders could make them. More than any other class of prostitute, they seem to have been a product of the rookeries, conditioned to depravity before they ever took to hawking themselves on the streets. In fact the degradations, and above all the overcrowding, of the worst slums led to an indiscrimate sexuality that defies comment. One may read of a man convicted of outraging a small child begotten by himself on his own daughter. Born in such an environment, brought up to fight for existence by every means to hand, habituated to pain and brutality, it is no wonder if some of these children were ready to exploit their one readily cashable asset.

It is necessary to distinguish between this sort of juvenile whoring and that which was essentially a response to the demands of sexual deviants. Where women were often almost hags at thirty, and underdeveloped girls were ready to prostitute themselves, it was inevitable that even men who were not particularly drawn to very young girls should have sometimes taken the chance to misuse them—especially since the younger the girl the less the likelihood of her being diseased. Unlike this more or less incidental evil, specific perversion produced a distinctive pattern of prostitution which seems to have spread wider during the third quarter of the century. According to the chaplain of Clerkenwell Jail, the appeal of immaturity had so increased by the early eighties that, where it had once been common for child prostitutes to ape the appearance of adults, it was now grown prostitutes who got themselves up to look like children.

By this time at least, the trade could provide a number of elaborations. A police superintendent described[1] a visit to a house in Windmill Street:

> I went in with my chief inspector, and in each of the rooms in that house I found an elderly gentleman in bed with two of these children. They knew perfectly well that I could not touch them in the house; and they laughed and joked me, and I could not get any direct answer whatever. I questioned them, in the presence of the brothel keeper, as to what they were paid, and so on. They were to receive six shillings each

[1] *Report of the Lords Committee*. Part I. Minutes of Evidence. Parl. Papers 1881 IX.

from the gentleman, two of them; and the gentleman had paid six shillings each for the room. It was four shillings if there was only one girl, but six shillings if there were two girls for the room.

Babylon catered for a variety of perversions including, of course, pederasty. Homosexual male prostitutes were, as ever, a feature of London life, and a man whose manner or reputation marked him as worth approaching could probably reckon on being accosted if he took a roundabout evening stroll from Windmill Street to Covent Garden. It seems that, if they were reasonably discreet, professional inverts could solicit in the street with little fear of the law, certainly without laying themselves open to a serious charge. Sodomy was a grave criminal offence but mere improper intimacies between males were not prosecutable (or only very doubtfully so) and it is easy to see why the police found it hard, and even dangerous, to get evidence of actual criminal intercourse. They might have to follow the prostitute and his client up some sinister court into a house that was guarded against them, and manage it so unobtrusively that they caught the offenders *in flagrante delicto*. For the police, the game was not generally worth the candle; no doubt they kept some control over the more troublesome young perverts who followed the trade by nailing them on other charges.

Rather surprisingly, this permissive situation did not apparently lead to any great profusion of male prostitutes. Even when one makes every allowance for contemporary reluctance to discuss such people, it remains clear that, at least round the mid-century, they cannot have been a pressing scandal. Even in that age of vocal reformers no public outcry was raised. Few people can have been seriously troubled by the weakness of the law or, indeed, considered the question of any particular importance.[1] No doubt homosexuals took good care to be discreet, but it also seems likely that professional 'she-shirts' were not more conspicuous about the theatres and other pleasure resorts simply because there was a poor demand for their services.

It seems that *active* male homosexuality was less socially obtrusive in the middle fifty years of the nineteenth century than

---

[1] The provisions of the Criminal Law Amendment Act, 1885, that did radically change the law, were an almost unconsidered legislative afterthought, hastily and irresponsibly tacked on to a measure Parliament was anxious to finish with.

either before or after. This may partly have been that social forces produced fewer practising homosexuals. Apart from those who are unambiguously inverted, there are always many men whose desires can be directed either to women or to other men, and the intense pressures of mid-Victorian England would certainly have pushed them towards 'normality'.

But, paradoxically, one of the things that made homosexuality unobtrusive was the fact that strong and emotional friendships between men were so easily accepted. Writers could celebrate one man's love for another without any thought of impropriety crossing their own or their readers' minds;[1] and there is a striking contrast between the prurient delicacy in force between respectable men and women and the uninhibited behaviour allowed between males. Adolescent brothers and sisters might be forbidden to enter each other's bedrooms, but no one in their senses thought it improper for men and boys to bathe naked or relieve themselves in company.

Practising homosexuals could therefore shelter behind the conventions of male friendship, and no reputable person would want to contemplate the revolting possibility that anything more was involved. Most people, if they thought about the subject at all, probably felt that homosexuality was so effectively tabooed that it could be safely ignored; and just because there was little chance of police intervention, their suspicions were not sharpened by fear of being involved in some suddenly exposed scandal. One scandal which did break—the celebrated Boulton and Park case of 1870—involved a group of well-off perverts some of whom went in for the most blatant transvestite capers: it is chiefly remarkable for showing how close to the wind it was possible to sail before getting into serious trouble.

It was recognised, however, that life in fo'c's'les and barrack-rooms was apt to corrupt members of the lower orders. Perhaps, as often as not, it was for sailor boys and young soldiers that homosexuals ready to pay cash went looking. Given the disreputable characters to be found in the ranks, the skinflint pay and brutalising conditions of service, it need hardly be doubted that a fair number of private soldiers took part in the casual prostitution

[1] For example, *In Memoriam*, published in 1850, contains some frankly passionate invocations. David-and-Jonathan friendships feature powerfully in biographical novels of the period. In *Tom Brown at Oxford* the reader is conducted through a perfect panorama of youthful temptations, corrupting acquaintanceships, etc. without encountering a hint of unnatural vice. By the end of the century the omission would have been impossible in a work of this kind.

that was a traditional evil among troops quartered in London.

But it was probably in the great ports that most genuinely professional male prostitution was to be found. Here, the male prostitute, like the female, could count on a succession of paid-off seamen as customers, and there was a wide variety of dockland catamites; if some were desperate young blackguards others were far from what one might imagine. Dickens gives a curiously sickening little account that, incidentally, illustrates how so deft a writer could touch on the subject even in a popular work.

He is describing a night tour with the police round sailors' haunts in Liverpool—'traps for Jack' as he calls them. The party visit a villainous crimp's, prostitutes' lodgings, some pub concert rooms and a yard where someone was murdered. They continually dive in and out of black stinking alleys. Late at night, still in the same slum neighbourhood, they enter a room 'very cleanly, neatly, even tastefully, kept' where, among 'a profusion of ornamental crockery,' are a fearsome fat old woman like something out of a Hogarth engraving and a boy—a schoolboy apparently—scratching away with pen and ink in a copybook. 'Why, this is a strange time for this boy to be writing his copy. In the middle of the night!' With fulsome extravagance the old woman explains that, having been to the theatre, the lad is now attending to his school work, for 'he combinates his improvement with entertainment'. Unctuous and beaming, she calls down blessings on the police and Dickens as they depart— leaving the strange couple *waiting for Jack.*[1]

It is improbable that the underworld in general took a lively commercial interest in homosexuality until 1885. In that year the Amendment Act made virtually any sexual impropriety between males, private or public, a serious criminal offence, and with the enforcement of what an eminent lawyer described at the time as the 'Blackmailer's Charter', the situation was transformed. In exchange for the risk of imprisonment (which could often be avoided by informing) a whole new field of extortion was opened; and as the ugly figures who surfaced ten years later at Oscar Wilde's trial made plain, it did not take long for even dull and timid criminal wits to get the hang of the wonderfully enhanced opportunities open to them.

Night-house tarts, expensive courtesans, sailors' whores, dolly-

'Poor Mercantile Jack' in *The Uncommercial Traveller.*

mops, synthetic virgins, children and catamites—these were only some of the many types of prostitute available to the Victorian with money in his pocket. It would be impossible to give a complete account of all of them, for categories shade off indistinctly and almost every kind of taste and vice was catered for in some way. Where one can see something like a clear pattern is in the way prostitutes solved what is always one of the difficulties of the profession—finding a place in which to practise it.

At the top and bottom of the trade this was no problem. The expensive woman of the town had her own house: the slum whore stood up against an alley wall. In between, the way in which a girl got a room to work in was the thing that, along with the means she used to bring in her customers, set the form of her life.

The most sharply defined type of prostitute's lodging is of course the closed, stay-in brothel. These were rare in the middle of the nineteenth century and accommodated only a small part of the whole population of prostitutes. Still, some of them did exist and in the fifties there was at least one large and well known brothel near the south end of Portland Place. (This was a very mixed neighbourhood. It attracted a lot of visitors from out of town and a number of prostitutes had rooms there.) Hemyng describes a discreetly respectable looking building where the blinds lowered over some of the bedroom windows before nightfall suggested that there might be illness in the house. The interior, with its twill-upholstered chairs and sofas, struck him as being well but inexpensively furnished, though there were chandeliers and 'handsome green curtains'. (If he penetrated to the bedrooms above he did not tell his readers.) Here Hemyng was introduced to a woman in her early twenties who, after he had ordered a bottle of wine, gave him a fairly full account of herself, interspersed with sharp back-chat.

According to her story she was a motherless girl from the East End, where her father was a carpenter. One day, in the street, she had met the woman who ran the brothel and trustingly gone home to tea with her. She was kidnapped and kept for some months in a house south of the Thames, where she was abused and her spirit crushed until she had become compliant enough to meet her captors' needs. She had also been made drunk and induced to sign papers which, in some way she did not understand but firmly believed in, put her in their power. Then transferred to a better district, provided with good clothes and well fed, she had gradually become used to the life, which she had now been leading for several years. Among the men who patronised the house she had a number of regulars who always asked for her and were liberal payers, but very little of the money came her way. She lived, in fact, in slavery, and if she had the opportunity would bolt at once—something the management understood so well that she was seldom allowed out of the house, and then only under guard.

Whatever reservations one may have about this story, there is no doubt that there were plenty of blackguards well qualified to enforce such a system of exploitation. Hardly any feature of prostitution is better attested than the crowd of bullies and 'fancy men' it supported. They were often of a sporting turn, and ranged from the smart, hard-faced loungers subsidised by women of the town to the louts who lived off the poorest street drabs. A degenerating tough, usually with a flavour of the prize-ring about him, skulking in slippers somewhere in the background, was evidently pretty well a standard fixture of the brothel-household. Hemyng pictures him as a brute ready to stick at nothing, who spent his day dozing and sucking a cutty and pottering round the corner to the pub or on errands to the pawnshop. Sometimes he was married to the landlady. Occasionally brothels were openly conducted by a man.

Although the closed house clearly gave the brothel keeper great power over the girls and their earnings it had drawbacks which account for its rarity in mid-Victorian England. Wherever prostitutes are uncontrolled by law the women who scoop the custom are those who can best bring themselves to the customer's attention. This gave a huge advantage to the individual prostitute who could boldly advertise herself where the prospects were most promising, while her customers could shop around and see life at half a dozen night houses before taking the plunge. The brothel, on the other hand, had to keep an inconspicuous front, especially if it was a good-class business in a respectable neighbourhood, and this put it at a great disadvantage. It explains why, from the West End to the Ratcliffe Highway, the vested interests of prostitution were mainly concerned with cashing-in on the ranging prostitute.

For the prostitute herself, an independent life was obviously best, but it presented her with the problem of finding her own room. Unless she was a heavy earner it was likely to be a hard problem to solve. Landladies did not like renting their rooms to tarts, and if they did they exacted heavy compensation. Moreover a landlady who was tempted into allowing one prostitute to have a room was likely to find her other tenants leaving. In the end she might have to let the whole house to prostitutes and keep a close eye on them to be sure of her rent, so that the place tended to evolve into a regular lodging-house brothel.

A lodging-house brothel was one where the girls were at least nominally independent; they went out to pick up their men in the streets or elsewhere, bringing them back to the house where they lived. There were many places of this sort, holding anything from three or four girls to a dozen or more, and they ranged from broken-down tenements to places catering for middle-class clients. They were not confined to poor districts but were to be found all over London, though for reasons that will become clear they were scarce in the great national centre of prostitution round Haymarket and Leicester Square.

As the houses varied, so did the women who ran them. In the dockland these brothels were traditionally presided over by alert and unprepossessing hags whose avarice was proverbial, and there were women who were capable of holding down a houseful of lewd, rough, often drunken trollops and extracting the lion's share of what each man paid them. There were also plenty of relatively detached 'mots' who let their rooms at a fixed charge and were only concerned not to be bilked of the rent. Some landladies managed to carry on a legitimate business on the same premises.

Lodging-house tarts generally led a sort of group existence centred round the landlady's kitchen. Even the better houses of this kind provided a quite peculiarly demoralising environment. According to Acton, the lodgers corrupted one another. No woman could expect a moment's privacy in such a place—

> ... her company is sought for novelty's sake when she is a newcomer, and her absence or reserve is considered insulting when she is fairly settled in; so if she had any previous idea of keeping herself to herself, it is very soon dissipated. ... They are usually during the day, unless called upon by their followers, or employed in dressing, to be found dishevelled,

dirty, slipshod and dressing-gowned in this kitchen, where the mistress keeps her table-d'hôte. Stupid from beer, or fractious from gin, they swear and chatter brainless stuff all day, about men and millinery, their own schemes and adventures, and the faults of others of the sisterhood. . . . As a heap of rubbish will ferment, so surely will a number of unvirtuous women deteriorate, whatever their antecedents or good qualities previous to their being herded under the semi-tyranny of a lodging-house-keeper of this kind. In such a household, all the projections of decency, modesty, propriety and conscience must, to preserve harmony and republican equality, be planed down, and the woman hammered out, not by the practice of her profession or the company of men, but by her association with her own sex and class, to the dead level of harlotry.[1]

The women in these places mostly picked up their men on the streets rather than in casinos or other night haunts. Often they worked late, and a man who accepted an invitation from one of them, after the better prostitutes had left, might be taken back to a lodging house that was still very much awake. He might also have some unpleasant surprises. It was not always easy to guess a girl's status in the feebly-lit streets and he could find himself in a brothel that was much lower and more disorderly than he expected. It was not unknown for a visitor who made himself unpopular—perhaps by stinginess or by being aggressively drunk—to be set on by a bunch of excited whores and roughed-up before being pitched out with empty pockets. In the thirties and forties there were brothels in St Giles from which men sometimes emerged without coat or trousers, lucky to stumble away in one piece.

Some prostitutes made arrangements with criminals to rob their clients, but they were in a small minority and violent robbing was rare. Certainly an affluent-looking man who was foolish enough to venture into a Ratcliffe brothel could expect to have his money and valuables stolen; but even here, we are told, he would not be treated with any greater roughness than was 'absolutely requisite'. It was only the most degraded slum and dockside drabs who decoyed their victims into ambush, to be coshed and stripped by a rampsman. All in all, the danger was

[1] Acton 1857 edition pp. 96-8.

not one that anybody need run into if he had a modicum of sense and was ready to spend more than a few shillings. The street-walker who could regularly pick up men rich enough to be worth robbing could earn more out of straight prostitution than as a thief's accomplice. Her whole manner of working, the way she frequented places where her reputation became known, and also her relations with the police, made it against her interest to help anyone to rob or attack her customers. It was almost always the desperate or incompetent whore who looked to theft rather than voluntary payment.

As to the brothel owners, it was clearly against their interest to allow uproar and robbery. A well patronised house was a valuable property, and trouble could only lead to loss of good-will. It could also bring interference from the police, who were often glad of a reason for investigating a brothel (indeed they were not above inventing one) and police visits were bad for business.

In fact, both the bawdy house keeper and her lodger were often more concerned with protecting themselves. They lived in continual and well justified fear of being defrauded. The prostitute tried to secure payment in advance for her favours and as much credit as possible from her landlady. The landlady's position was more complex: on the one hand it was customary and convenient to keep her lodgers in debt, and so maintain a hold over them; on the other hand, if she let any of her lodgers build up too large a debt, it gave them a motive for decamping and starting afresh elsewhere. Prostitutes were not only restless and prone to changing houses, but notoriously given to 'chousing' (debt-bilking).

This was a particular danger with the girls known as 'dress lodgers'. Some houses not only boarded their lodgers but provided them with clothes to go out in. When the time came for her to set to work the dress lodger put on a dress and trimmings supplied by the keeper and sallied out to hunt for customers; when she had said goodbye to the last of them, the borrowed garments were returned to stock. Sometimes clothes were loaned to girls who were not boarders, but who were, naturally, expected to bring back their pick-ups to the premises.

In return the girl had to pay over most of her takings to the owner, and this meant that even if she did not bolt with the dress she was likely to try and steer her customers into other places where she would only have to pay a relatively small charge for the use of a room and bed. Accordingly, such women, and other tied prostitutes, were sometimes shadowed by employees of the brothel keeper. Hemyng noticed a street walker with a beat along the Strand who was regularly trailed by an elderly woman in a dirty cotton dress. He succeeded in getting hold of this custodian and, by priming her with gin, drew out a good deal of information.

She was a superannuated prostitute who had come down in the world; now she was a sort of servant at a brothel, given her food and bed and occasional shillings, and employed at house work and in watching Lizzie the dress lodger. In general Lizzie appealed to shop-people, commercial travellers and the like, but not exclusively; once in a while she even picked up a straying clergyman from nearby Exeter Hall. Medical students (Charing Cross Hospital was close by) were sometimes attracted but were apt to be hard-up. The girl's appearance was too garish for the best class of street trade. Some nights the two tramped their beat in vain; but that night Lizzie had collected three clients in as many hours and been clever enough to secure forty-five shillings 'for herself'—though in the next breath the old woman made it plain that she for one was expecting her cut.

This was a clear case of a girl being put under a guardian who served the brothel owner's interest and whom she would presumably have been glad to evade. However that was not always the way: the women, and more particularly the men, who lived on prostitutes, could be both welcome and useful to them. Apart from the fact that the job did not make a regular lover superfluous, there were a number of ways in which an active man about the place might be a convenience to a prostitute. A woman bringing in more or less anyone she could pick up who looked as if he could pay (including many the worse for drink) was likely to need help now and again with visitors who turned violent or who had tastes she was unwilling to satisfy. Above all, at least in the low street trade, she needed to be sure of getting her money. Casual prostitution cannot by its nature be a safe occupation, and the protection offered by a household of fellow trollops and a pug-ugly in the kitchen was one of the real advantages a lodging house could offer its boarders. Prostitutes who lived independently also often had a fancy man hanging about, making himself scarce at the right moment.

Many prostitutes, rather than work in a residential brothel or prostitutes' lodging, preferred to take their men to an 'accommodation house'. The girls themselves did not live in these places: they simply went there with their pick-ups and hired a room for a few minutes or for several hours, depending on the man's purse and inclinations.

For the prostitute, the arrangement had many advantages. She could divorce her private life from her trade, making it much easier to find somewhere to live, and at the same time preserve her freedom of action. Accommodation house charges added something to the cost of her services, but against that she was free of the need to pay tart's rates for her room even when she was unable to work in it. Further, a regular connection with an accommodation house might offer her some security against being badly treated there; while her customers could reckon, if they went to a reputable house, on not falling into a trap.

Accommodation houses were common in many parts of London, on both sides of the river, in good and bad areas alike. Not surprisingly, the Haymarket–Leicester Square zone abounded in them, and in this area the high rents charged to prostitutes for the sleaziest lodgings made it hard for them to get rooms on any other terms. Indeed there was something like an accommodation-house belt extending all the way from Bond Street to beyond Covent Garden, through the heart of fashionable and raffish west London. (A few paces from the central Strand, for example, stood a renowned and rather expensive establishment. Charges for a room were ten shillings upward, but it enjoyed an excellent reputation for honesty and orderliness and was much patronised by rich shopkeepers and other sensible citizens.) Along the line of the Strand and as far as the neighbourhood of the Haymarket itself, were coffee rooms, cigar divans, chop houses and other masculine resorts well known to have unadvertised bedrooms at their customers' disposal. Prostitutes would drop into some of these, especially perhaps the cigar shops, to pass the time of day and cast an eye round for clients.

Westward, a different style of house seems to have predominated in the good class trade. Dotted about the shopping precincts of St James's and Mayfair were numbers of shops where a couple, who might have entered separately, would be discreetly admitted into the interior and shown upstairs. These places were often little businesses engaged in a de luxe trade, glovers, bonnet makers, perfumers and so on. A 'first-rate milliner in Bond Street', a Jermyn Street ladies' shoemaker—places of that sort, which were outwardly of the utmost respectability, achieved discreetly scandalous reputations and became magnets for idling gentlemen and over-fashionably dressed women. Elegant fronts in the Burlington Arcade were well known to conceal 'Paphian intricacies' into which a man could follow one of the alert-eyed young ladies who sauntered along the gallery in the late afternoon. Shops of this kind lent themselves to the use not only of prostitutes but of reputable married women and their lovers— the facility the blackmailing Madame Rachael turned to such profitable account.

The variety of accommodation houses was as great in the poorer as in the more refined sections of the trade. There were notoriously a number of big low-class houses around St Giles and Seven Dials; they often consisted of several adjoining premises run together, and one of them is mentioned as having thirty-two bedrooms. Soon after the mid-century they seem to have vanished—netted, presumably, by the new lodging house regulations—but there were innumerable retreats of varying degrees of cheapness and squalor in the run-down area north of Leicester Square and throughout much of Soho. Round the Square itself coffee shops dedicated to the trade blatantly advertised beds that no one supposed were meant for a secluded night's rest.

A slum room might be let for a shilling or so over and over again in the course of an evening. The normal charge at a middling sort of accommodation house in the vice-belt was perhaps about five shillings, for the mistress of a highly successful house off the Haymarket who retired to suburban Camberwell is said to have had 'the questionable taste' to christen her new home 'Dollar House' to commemorate the fees that had built her fortune. A visit to a more discreet and luxurious refuge might cost a guinea or two.

The usefulness of these places was enhanced by the fact that single men, particularly young single men, very often lived as lodgers. A comfortably-off bachelor might retain a set of rooms and keep his own manservant; but whatever her tenant's standing, no reputable landlady who cared for the good name of her house would willingly let him bring prostitutes there. For an important section of prostitutes' clients there could be no question of taking their pick-ups home. (In London a major exception to this rule were the residents of the numerous Inns of Court who could do much as they liked in their chambers. But these, according to the old prostitute Hemyng met guarding the dress-lodger, were well known to be dangerous and were shunned by sensible women, who would leap out of a cab rather than be driven off to the Temple—though the Temple was respectable compared with the proprietary Inns.)

Some idea of the importance of accommodation houses can be got from the figures for C Division of the Metropolitan Police. This division took in St James's, Regent Street, Haymarket, Leicester Square and Soho, and the superintendent in charge reckoned that, out of 500 street walkers frequenting the division and classified as usually working a regular beat and 'perfectly well known to the police', only 150 lived within its bounds.[1] From the tenor of contemporary descriptions, those 500 can have been no more than a substantial fraction of the 'circulating harlotry' of the district; but as the figure obviously covered those most constantly seen at work in the division it must have included a higher proportion of local residents than the grand total. It is probably safe to say that the large majority of prostitutes picking up men in the area took them to local accommodation houses.

As for the better class prostitutes, who chiefly picked up their clients in the more expensive night-houses and supper rooms, these too usually lived at a distance. Some took admirers home to Fulham or St John's Wood for the night (the long drive in a hansom cab was perhaps part of the treat) but many who came in from the suburbs must have found accommodation houses a valuable amenity.

One trade that went well with keeping a good accommodation house was the 'introduction' business. In this a procuress, having reached an understanding with a prostitute, would inform some of the men on her list that she had discovered a girl particularly likely to appeal to their taste who could be met by appointment. If the introduction proved successful the procuress collected commission from both parties, and if she kept an accommodation house, no doubt did what she could to ensure that they continued to meet on her premises.

The procurers of real and faked virgins were in the introduc-

[1] Acton, 1857 edition, p. 17.

tion business, and it also made it easy for amateur and part-time prostitutes to enter the market. For those already in, the introducer often performed a useful service by bringing them into contact with free-spending men. For the men themselves the special attraction of using a reputable 'introducing house' was that they enjoyed—or fondly supposed they enjoyed—some security against venereal infection. Introducers would make great play with their personal knowledge of the girls they produced and the precautions they took over them (they were often portrayed as special and exclusive propositions) and they understood how to attract both the timid and the debauchee. Clients and potential clients were energetically circularised by letter— a man's club or office was the appropriate address rather than his home—and this touting must have demanded some tact and knowledge, the more so since a rumour that a woman was being widely canvassed would have cut down her appeal.

Introducers did not always own accommodation houses, but since they needed places to arrange rendezvous the two trades were closely allied, and there were obvious advantages in running an established introducing house where clients' transactions could be kept under some supervision. Once again one is confronted with the fact that, in the whole organisation of mid-century prostitution, the accommodation house in its various forms was the most important single element.

It would be misleading to leave this catalogue of prostitutes' haunts without mentioning some that were much pleasanter than most of those that have so far been described. Besides the playhouse and the opera, there were a number of places of entertainment where both prostitutes and respectable women were to be seen. Appropriately, the Cremorne Gardens in Chelsea, which in the fifties were the last flourishing representative of the old-style London pleasure garden, attracted respectable citizens and smart whores alike. But not, according to Acton, at the same time of day. On a July evening he noticed how 'as calico and merry respectability tailed off eastward by penny steamers, the setting sun brought westward hansoms freighted with demure immorality in silk and fine linen'. By the time dusk had changed to night, the leafy walks, the gas-brilliant 'crystal circle', the fountains and the great raised platform had been surrendered to vice. Yet, in the ordinary way, it remained remarkably orderly vice; he detected little sign of the women

soliciting in the shadows, and 'barely vivacity, much less boisterous disorder' among the well dressed crowd. Immorality,
like everything else, was becoming more decorous.

The same thing was true of the big new places of entertainment that were springing up in the poorer districts. Upper class
opinion (always given to condemning workers' recreations as
causes of idleness and misconduct) dismissed these places as
haunts of vice; but that was a misconception. A few dockside
music halls may have been almost as dedicated to prostitutes and
their followers as a Ratcliffe dance room or Kate Hamilton's;
but in the main the very size of these modern establishments,
and the capital outlays involved, made it essential that they
should attract a very catholic public. The tremendous Eagle in
City Road, Whitechapel,[1] had grown from a pub to a music hall
to a whole complex of diversions: there was a theatre in which
opera could be staged and a garden with fountains, alcoves and
boxes like a miniature Cremorne, where open-air shows and

[1] Up and down the City Road/In and out the Eagle/That's the way the money goes/
Pop! goes the weasel!

firework displays were held. Honest families could come with their own packets of food, buy their beer, and sit munching through the songs and spectacles. Highgate Barn, out beyond the suburbs, presented a similar scene in a more rural setting. There was no lack of prostitutes and half-prostitutes at such places, and at times there were rough and rowdy scenes; but they were a far cry from the concentrated flesh-markets of Babylon.

The whole pattern of prostitution was so much in favour of the mobile prostitute going out to find her own custom that it is hard not to feel sceptical about stories of women held prisoner in brothels. Some of these tales gained their circulation from mission tracts and they usually chime better with the popular mythology of prostitution than with the comments of informed observers. Acton evidently reached the conclusion, while putting his book together in the 1850s, that, at least in west London and the City, prostitutes were far less subject to constraint than he had previously supposed. He roundly dismisses 'nearly all tales of inveiglement, rape, and involuntary detention' in brothels as mere romance.

The evidence given by senior police officers before the strong Lords Committee of 1881–2 on the Protection of Young Girls largely bears out this opinion, though by then public concern about this kind of 'white slavery' had increased. Some of the police testimony covered a quarter of a century of experience and its gist is plain enough: prostitutes were in such ample supply that to hold girls by force was almost pointless.

The most categoric evidence was given by Inspector Morgan, C.I.D., then with the Marylebone and Paddington Division, and Superintendent Dunlap, who had been chief of C Division since 1868 and before that an officer in Southwark, a district almost as notorious for prostitution as Ratcliffe.

> *Lord Salisbury:* Do you know many girls in your district, or in those other districts with which you are acquainted, who are kept in brothels against their will?
> *Morgan:* I do not remember an instance. I speak from an experience in town and country, and from a general knowledge of the whole of London, because I was for several years attached to Scotland Yard, and I never met with an instance

where a girl was kept in a brothel against her will, where she could not get her liberty.

Dunlap also said that in all his service he had never learnt of such a case.

The officers' evidence is the weightier in that it is plain they would have been much happier to find reasons why they should have more authority to enter brothels and control brothel keepers. It is also plain that for them residential brothels were so much in the minority that when they used the word 'brothel' unqualified they normally meant an accommodation house.

First-hand stories, such as the one Hemyng reports hearing from the girl in the brothel in Portland Place, are by no means conclusive; for, as Hemyng himself noted, prostitutes were much given to romancing about their histories. (They seem to have been specially fond of claiming to be clergymen's daughters.) Nor is it very easy to see how the proprietors of such a house could have held the girls if they had really tried to escape. The building was not, apparently, barred-up or noticeably jail-like, and once a girl had got clear it would have been tricky work to re-kidnap her and drag her back. The house was fairly conspicuous and in quite an orderly district; moreover its large clientele cannot all have been brutes indifferent to any plea for help. An established brothel of this kind was vulnerable to publicity: a scandal could well have forced the parish authorities to suppress it, and there were agencies ready enough to seize on a sensational issue to attack commercialised vice. Notable among these were various newspapers, and one may suspect that if Hemyng, or his principal Mayhew, had felt anything like firm ground under his feet, he would have launched a vigorous campaign.

In fact there does not seem to be a single publicised instance of a contemporary brothel keeper being prosecuted for holding girls against their will. Nor is it very difficult to imagine some women preferring the security of a set-up like the Portland Place brothel to the competitive struggle of the streets and night houses, and even counting themselves lucky to find a billet in such a place.

But if one can dismiss the idea of a whole class of prostitutes kept in slavery, there were still many unfortunate victims of bullying and extortion. Some types of poor prostitute were particularly exposed to exploitation—dress lodgers are an obvious example—and in various parts of London, including the Haymarket area, passers would sometimes notice a heavily-made-up creature in a tawdry ball dress being openly cursed and driven on to greater activity either by her attendant hag or by the bawdy house keeper in person, who had come out to oversee the girls on their beats and drum up brisker business.

On the Continent, the situation was very different. In a country where prostitution was police-controlled, a woman in a licensed brothel lived in something very close to complete captivity. In France and Belgium, once a woman had made a statutory declaration, had her papers endorsed and been entered in the police records as an inmate of a particular house she became scarcely more than a chattel. Many brothels had entrance doors that could only be opened on the inside with a key, and prostitutes were forbidden by law to show themselves at a window. Except by watching for an opportunity to bolt, and thereafter dodging the police, the prostitute who still had some use left in her must usually have had little chance of breaking free unless she could find a sponsor ready to settle the debt she owed to the brothel proprietor. (This debt often existed from the moment she arrived in the brothel, for the price paid to the procurer who introduced her was held against the girl herself.)

Sometimes one of these women was bought out and brought to England, probably by one of the cross-Channel traffickers who recruited English girls for the French and Belgian houses. When she reached England, she must at first have been fairly helpless. Conditioned by her existence in a *maison tolérée*, and probably under a signed obligation to whoever had arranged her release, ignorant of English and without funds, she was very much in the hands of the bawd to whom she was consigned. But once she had learnt a bit of English, she would discover from other girls—or from a fancy man who thought she might be better employed supporting *him*—that contracts involving prostitution were legally worthless in England.

Some women brought from the Continent became street-walking dress lodgers, others received callers inside the bawdy house; and it seems more than probable that many of the bold, dressy, apparently independent Frenchwomen who were a particular feature of Regent Street, reached London through the same channel.

In the opposite direction, there was undoubtedly a trade in English girls shipped over the Channel to work in Continental brothels. This suddenly became a matter of burning public interest in 1885 when W. T. Stead, a journalist who combined a non-conformist conscience with ruthless professional flair, ran a series of articles in the *Pall Mall Gazette* called 'The Maiden Tribute of Modern Babylon'. This set off a perfect hurricane of public excitement and the government's hand was forced.

But the fact that these articles did a valuable service, and were attacked with canting hypocrisy, does not make them accurate documentation. They were a bold, rapidly put-together, brilliantly successful stunt, in which the most spectacular coup was Stead's buying a virginal child from her mother and carrying her over to France. This did not prove, as Stead claimed, that such things were a regular part of the trade: all it showed was that there were women who would sell their children to strangers for a few pounds, and that was no secret. (In fact the laws against debauching minors were much stricter in France than in England, and any ordinary brothel keeper who had accepted the child would have been running a most serious risk.)

The traffic had already been investigated, without rousing any violent public reaction, by the Lords Committee of 1881–2. They had the benefit of a report by a special Home Office investigator and the views of many official and unofficial witnesses, as well as the depositions of girls who had been exported and a quantity of miscellaneous information. Many of the opinions they listened to contradicted each other, but the picture that emerges from the committee's report is reasonably clear and probably gives a fair indication of the way the trade had been carried on for many years. The principal police witnesses were senior officers, some of whose experience stretched back at least to the sixties, and the enquiry reveals a well established trade that can hardly have changed much in its essentials since it attracted the attention of Hemyng and others a couple of decades earlier.

The business was in the hands of a number of *placeurs* who had close connections in Belgium, France and Holland. The *placeur* was not at all likely to be looking for chaste virgins to entice. The girls he collected would have to accompany him on a longish journey, and when they arrived they would have to make a formal declaration that they wished to enter the brothel before they could be accepted and paid for. They would also have to undergo an official medical examination, and to minimise the risk of a 'package' proving venereally infected on arrival, it was a common practice to have the girls examined in London by some elderly procuress with a speculum before going to any further trouble and expense. This in itself would have been quite enough to horrify any girl with a particle of modesty—and forewarn any but the simplest-minded trollop. Everything points to the existence of a large supply of loose young women about London, many of them uncertain where their next meals were coming from, admirably suited to the *placeur's* purposes. What he did, obviously, was to misrepresent the conditions the girls would find and the amount they could expect to be paid.

In 1876 a man named Klyberg,[1] who had been for many years a leading agent in the trade, took two girls over to Holland. One of them later made a statement that gives a number of insights into the way the trade worked.

Fanny—her surname is withheld—deposed that in October 1876 she was just 18 and living with her mother in Chelsea, where at six o'clock one evening she met a friend called Jennie at the corner of Langton Street, opposite Cremorne Gardens. Jennie was with a woman she called Mrs Dunner. Mrs Dunner asked to have a look at Fanny's teeth and inquired if she was 'all right'—which Fanny rightly took to mean, was she diseased? The girl said she was all right. Mrs Dunner then wanted to know if she would like to go abroad. Asked in what capacity, she said 'as an actress', and added that the girls would be able to return whenever they wished and 'go to any theatre in London'. Jennie was going and another girl was wanted to go with her. (It is possible that Fanny was deceived by this but, then as later, 'actress' was a common police court euphemism for 'tart' and there is nothing to show that either girl had the slightest qualifications for appearing on the stage. On the other hand, the fact that they were hanging around by Cremorne Gardens in the early evening strongly suggests that they were already prostitutes.)

Fanny went home and, while Jennie and Mrs Dunner waited in the street outside, collected some clean clothes. Then they all

---

[1] Sometimes known as Kleber. He also worked as a shoemaker, and other London *placeurs* often had legitimate jobs. One of them, known as Albert, was a hairdresser in Leicester Square; another, a Jew called Carroty Jack, kept a fishmonger's in Westminster Road.

went to Mrs Dunner's place in Chelsea, where the girls had a wash and change before accompanying her to Klyberg's house in Soho. Here the girls had supper with Klyberg and his wife, who questioned them and discovered that both had sisters over twenty-one. At this point Klyberg is reported to have asked: 'I suppose Mrs Dunner told you what you were going over for?' and when Fanny replied that she had said they were to be actresses, he told her that was 'quite right'.

That night Fanny and Jennie slept with Mrs Klyberg. After breakfast Mr Klyberg announced 'Now girls, business!'—a favourite expression of his—and left the room while his wife subjected them to an intimate examination. Then they went with Mrs Klyberg to a pub conveniently near Somerset House, where the two girls obtained copies of their elder sisters' birth certificates.

The reason for this move was that on the Continent the prostitution of minors was a serious offence. Since the London *placeurs* found it profitable to take over girls who at a pinch could pass as in their early twenties but were in fact several years younger, they had to find some cover-up. One trick was to get a copy of the birth certificate of a woman of the right age, preferably with the same surname as the girl they were handling. This cost only a small fee at the Registrar General's office and the formal-looking document frequently satisfied the Continental police, who took it for an official identity card.

When the two girls came out with their sisters' birth certificates, they handed them over to Mrs Klyberg who was waiting in the pub: some more drinks, and they all walked back to Soho to join Mr Klyberg for dinner.

In the afternoon Klyberg told the girls that he was taking them to Holland. It would be best for them to call him 'Uncle'— 'because,' he explained, 'he did not want anyone to know him, as he had been backwards and forwards so many times with different girls.' The whole party drove off to Liverpool Street, where Klyberg and the girls caught the 7.30 for Harwich.

On landing at Rotterdam next morning Klyberg said: 'Now girls, we mean business; I suppose you know what you came over for?' Fanny answered 'actress'; Klyberg said no, they were to be prostitutes. There was a brief altercation and Fanny, apparently astounded, said she would go back to England. However, by threats and cajolery, Klyberg managed to get her to go with him and Jennie to The Hague, where they were met at the station by a man who took them to a brothel about a mile away. Here, in the dining room, the girls were interviewed by the proprietress and 'a French lady', both of whom spoke English. They were given supper and taken up to sleep in the French lady's room.

About ten next morning a doctor arrived and examined Jennie, and she was later driven away in a brougham, dressed in clothes provided by the management. On her return she told Fanny she had been to a police station to be booked. Fanny's services, however, were not required, and she and Klyberg now returned to the station—Fanny pleading to be allowed to rejoin her friend. They travelled to Amsterdam where they shared a bedroom, but not a bed, in a hotel. Klyberg made advances which Fanny successfully repelled.

Now Klyberg began to make desperate efforts to sell Fanny. At one house they declared English girls were unmanageable and broke things, and at two others they said they already had a couple, which was enough. That night Fanny shared a room at a brothel with three prostitutes, one of whom was an English girl who told her she had been brought over by Klyberg two years before. She advised Fanny to go home, and on her behalf told the proprietress that the newcomer did not want to stay. Accordingly, it was arranged that 'Madame' should tell Klyberg that the twelve pounds he was asking was too much. But when this was put to him, Klyberg said she could have Fanny for eight. Still the woman refused: Fanny had burn scars on her chest and arms and she didn't want her.

Here the story takes a grotesque turn. Klyberg tried to sell Fanny to any brothel that would take her, and even told her she could go where she pleased if only she would leave him alone. But Fanny had now changed her tack, and instead of trying to get away from Klyberg she absolutely refused to leave him. She stuck to him like a burr. Day after day Klyberg went to brothels, dropping his price until he said they could have her for a couple of pounds towards his expenses, but each time she refused to stop. In one place they tried to hold her and, when she ran away, sent a man after her to get her back. He failed, and she was soon back with Klyberg.

Finally, at a private hotel kept by one of Klyberg's contacts, she met 'two English gentlemen and an English lady'. She told the woman that she thought she had seen her face in Chelsea. 'Yes, no doubt you have,' said the woman and asked how she came to be there. (It must have been obvious what sort of person the stranger was, which probably made it easier for Fanny to approach her.) When Fanny told them her story, one of the men offered to take her across to Harwich and send her home to London in the care of the railway guard. The lady added that she was returning at the same time and would let her share her cab to Chelsea.

That night Fanny again slept in Klyberg's room, but in the morning she slipped off alone to her new friends. Klyberg followed her to their hotel and from there to the Harwich steamer. When he asked what she meant by behaving like this, she answered: 'You will see when I get to London; I shall take further proceedings.' After that he was frightened to let her go off without him, and paid both her fare and his own to Liverpool Street. The long journey ended in total anti-climax, with Klyberg travelling tamely back to London with Fanny while the Chelsea courtesan kept an eye on them.

This kind of comedy may not have been very common, but the evidence in front of the Lords Committee does not suggest a highly organised and profitable business. The *placeurs* appear as shoddy scallywags, sometimes with long crime sheets, not over-clever and plainly without the protection one would expect if large profits had been involved. Ten to fifteen pounds seems to have been about the price they could hope to get from a good-class establishment for a healthy young woman, and even when fares were paid this was far from being clear profit; the business was riddled with contact men and go-betweens who had to be given their cuts. There was also the risk of a girl not being immediately accepted and having to be sold at a loss. Continental brothels seem to have imported Englishwomen rather reluctantly, only taking them if they could not get enough girls locally, or for the benefit of English-speaking clients.

Though the *placeur's* trade was not a very profitable one, it was not, until the last quarter of the century, a very risky one either. He was more likely to run foul of the law abroad than in England, where it was hard to find a charge to stick on him. But by the end of the seventies the British authorities, under pressure from anti-vice campaigners, were stirring up trouble for the trade overseas and probably exchanging information with foreign police. Klyberg's hawking of the recalcitrant, under-age Fanny round the Dutch brothels shows that he had not grasped that times were changing: during the next few years he was twice caught and sentenced.

There was one trade in human flesh, closely linked with prostitution, beside which the dealings of the white slave traders seem almost innocuous: the baby farm.

The way in which an illegitimate pregnancy could turn a girl to prostitution has been noticed; but whether she drifted into prostitution or not, the unmarried mother was likely to have stronger reasons for getting rid of her child than can be easily appreciated today. The essence of the official attitude towards bastardy was that the child was a punishment, and ought to be made as exemplary a one as possible. The statutory lowering of the mother's right to sue for maintenance meant that if she did try to bring up her child it might easily lead only to destitution and the pauper ward, where the child would anyway be segregated from her. If there were mothers who hawked themselves to feed their children, it was also true that a child was a serious liability to the girl who made her living from prostitution. Dependent infants were unwelcome to brothel keepers, and a crippling encumbrance to women trying to set up on their own in a competitive trade. Further, the presence of a child made it harder to reach the goal of many a prostitute and semi-prostitute —to be a kept mistress or, best of all, married.

The practice of farming out illegitimate children was widespread—Acton reckoned that an estimate of 30,000 children in baby farmers' hands was 'probably under the mark'. Not all who took on such work, of course, were callous and neglectful; some fostered their charges well, and a number were well paid for doing so. But the trade had a deservedly evil reputation and bore at least some responsibility for the enormously high death-rate among babies born out of wedlock.[1] The real nature of the services offered by many of them was so blatant that it seems strange—even when one remembers the record of public authorities over pauper children—that they were allowed to continue unchecked.

---

[1] Acton (1870 edition, p. 278 et seq.) is illuminating. He remarks that in 1867 the death-rate among illegitimate children under twelve months was *eight* times higher than among legitimate ones. However, illegitimate births were probably commonest among the worst fed and housed sections of the community.

In a single issue of a paper which plainly circulated in the
dollymop belt, the journalist James Greenwood counted no less
than eleven baby farmers' announcements.[1] Considering what
sort of people usually took up the business, one can assume that
the wording reflected the talents of our old friend the screever.
One advertisement read:

> NURSE CHILD WANTED, OR TO ADOPT.—The Adver-
> tiser, A Widow with a little family of her own, and a moderate
> allowance from her late husband's friends, would be glad to
> receive the charge of a young child. Age no object. If sickly
> would receive a parent's care. Terms, Fifteen shillings a
> month; or would adopt entirely if under two months for the
> small sum of Twelve pounds.

Another read:

> A person wishing a lasting and comfortable home for a young
> person of either sex will find this a good opportunity. Adver-
> tisers having no children of their own are about to proceed to
> America. Premium, Fifteen pounds. Respectable references
> given and required. Address F.X.

To the latter Greenwood offers a common-sense gloss: 'Any
person possessed of a child he is anxious to be rid of, here
is a good chance for him. Perhaps F.X. is going to America,
perhaps he is not. That is *his* business. The party having a child
to dispose of, need not trouble itself on that score. For "respectable references" read "mutual confidence". I'll take the child
and ask no questions of me. That will make matters comfortable
for both parties, especially if the meeting is at a coffee house, or
at some public building, for if I don't know the party's address,
of course he can have no fear that I shall turn round on him, and
return the child on his hands. The whole affair might be managed
while an omnibus is waiting to take up a passenger. A simple
matter of handing over a bulky parcel and a little one—the child
and the money—and all's over, without so much as "good
night", if so be the party is a careful party, and wouldn't like even
his voice heard.'

Not all baby farmers were so expensive, and they were sometimes prepared to give a signed undertaking. The following

---

[1] James Greenwood *The Seven Curses of London*, pp. 35 et seq. The advertisements for
millinery workshop hands and similar employees clearly showed the market at which the
paper was aimed.

document was produced at an inquest at Westminster, held on a child who had died four months after passing from her seventeen-year-old mother into the care of a certain Mrs Brown:

> Received of Caroline Williams 5 pounds, for which sum I agree to take and adopt her child Fanny Williams, and to bring it up in a respectable manner; failing to do which I agree to forfeit and pay to the said Caroline Williams the sum of 20 pounds. The said child to be no further trouble or expense to its mother or friends. Ann Brown.

Five pounds, let alone fifteen, was a large sum for a poor girl to find, but she could at least tackle the child's father. He was not obliged to support his bastard (beyond a derisory pittance) but he might well be persuaded to pay up to avoid the scandal of a desperate mother with his child in her arms. To many a young clerk or shopman it was worth a lot to lay, once forever, a spectre that could destroy his respectable standing and prospects. A shrewd trollop might be able to get contributions from more than one admirer by this threat. The fully professional whore could hardly use it, but on the other hand her earning power was often relatively high and no doubt she could sometimes get help from bawds who would themselves profit by the disappearance of an inconvenient baby.

While the lump-sum adopter had every reason for not keep-in a child over-long, straightforward murder was probably the exception rather than the rule. It is true that unaccounted-for child corpses were no rarity: Greenwood claimed that an analysis of London coroners' returns for 1856–60 showed a yearly average of 226 deaths of infants under two by foul play— and how many small corpses were never recovered? Nevertheless, to make a practice of butchering children out of hand would have been to run an unnecessary danger, and seems out of keeping with the general character of the trade. It is reasonable to think that some of the more attractive looking children found their way into the hands of beggars; Greenwood also believed that many a little creature 'especially if it be of that convenient age when it is able to walk but not to talk,' was simply taken to a distant place and left to the mercies of whoever noticed its distress. Yet the willingness of adopters to take very young infants, and their often-expressed readiness to accept ailing ones, suggest a more ghastly solution than mere abandonment. Even so, it could be argued that on the whole the children handed over with a disposal fee, never to be heard of again, were luckier than those whom the baby farmer contracted to keep out of sight for three or four shillings a week, and so had a motive for retaining alive in her clutches.

Even in comfortable middle-class households, it was not unusual for a whole series of young children to die, and among the urban poor infant mortality was far higher. There was no subsidised 'panel' system and it was not economically feasible for a doctor to give proper attention to patients for whom a shilling charge for consultation and medicine was a serious hardship. If a sick child died without a doctor having ever been called in at all, it was nothing to wonder at. Unless a child had plainly died of starvation or been killed by an act of deliberate malice, it was often exceedingly difficult, no matter how sinister the circumstances, to pin down the blame or prevent others following the same fate. Terrible suspicions often attached to the 'accidental' deaths of children whose parents had been making specially large payments on them to the 'burial man' (insurance collector) but they were seldom brought home. The foster mother's trade was legal, she claimed to bring up her charges as if they were her own, and if they lived dirty and diseased and died prematurely it was no more than the common fate of hundreds of their little neighbours who lived with their natural parents.

In short, baby farmers were able to practise as loathsome a system of crime as can well be imagined, with remarkably little risk. All sorts of twists were open to the woman who took over children at a very early age from parents who never proposed to set eyes on them again. If a child was a source of regular payments he might survive so long as this was compatible with profit, but die (insured) when he threatened to become a burden. Sometimes parents continued to pay for children who had died or passed out of the baby farmer's care. Where the business was conducted on a fairly large scale it must often have been easy to substitute one infant for another if the parents did come enquiring. Moreover, a child who reached five or six years might have a commercial value. There were workers who needed more small children than they could easily get—notably chimney sweeps, who continued to employ tiny climbing boys long after it became illegal.

In practice it was no one's business to notice how the baby

farmer treated a fosterling unless, or until, she announced its death. A regimen of 'neglected infections, bad and insufficient food, exposure, castor oil and a mercifully liberal use of such specifics as Godfrey's Cordial' (a compound of opium and molasses, highly effective as a soothing syrup) could run its course unhindered and leave the child's eventual death attributable to 'natural causes'.[1]

Greenwood answered a number of baby farmers' advertisements, but evidently failed to achieve a convincing manner, for many of his enquiries were ignored. However a person signing herself Y.A., and giving a Stepney post office as her only address, wrote back saying she would be happy to take his weakly little girl as companion to her own darling baby; she asked him to suggest a meeting place where they could arrange the transfer. Greenwood replied that he would like to call on her at home, and got no answer. But he was not a reporter for nothing, and soon succeeded in tracing her name and address through the *poste restante*. He calls her 'Mrs Oxleek'.

Her house turned out to be 'of the small four or five-roomed order, and no more or less untidy or squalid than is commonly to be found in the back streets of Stepney or Bethnal Green'. Greenwood's knock on the door was answered by a slut who seemed to be in a great hurry and told him that Mrs Oxleek was out—she had gone 'to the Liver'. Further questioning got from the girl the fact that this was the insurance company 'where you pays in for young 'uns burying and that'. Greenwood got inside by pretending to be a doctor who had been sent for. In an easy chair by a fire sat Mr Oxleek, a stout, very dirty and greasy middle-aged man, exceedingly indolent but with a pair of 'shoulders fit to carry a side of beef'. Only too clearly the Oxleeks were one too many for Greenwood. He saw a baby wrapped in a filthy garment and in due course Mrs Oxleek returned, a short, fat, florid woman with a 'sunny smile'. But if Greenwood hoped to get anything like conclusive evidence of their practices, he failed: the couple gave away nothing.

The ease with which a reasonably careful woman could carry on the business unscathed is shown by an inquest that attracted

---

[1] Greenwood, *The Seven Curses*. The small minority of baby farmers who came to grief seem to have been quite atypically foolhardy. Mrs Waters, convicted of murdering an infant by poison and neglect in 1870, had by then adopted some forty children and destroyed a considerable number of them. The Infant Life Protection Act, 1872, may have done something to temper the farmers' ruthlessness, but much more significant was the founding in 1884 of the National Society for the Prevention of Cruelty to Children.

Greenwood's attention. It was held on the death of a baby named Frederick Wood whose unmarried mother had handed him over ten months before to a Mrs Savill, living in Bow. Out of eleven infants known to have been in Mrs Savill's care five had died, but he was the first to be the subject of an inquiry. The most untoward thing about the case, from Mrs Savill's point of view, was the interest the mother showed in her child's fate and the way she gave her evidence.

The court learnt that, some time before, the child had broken its femur in an accident on the stairs. Despite the fact that his usual cot was a straw-lined egg-box sixteen inches wide, in which he could not turn, his injury had not mended. Mrs Savill deposed that she had never tied the boy's legs together. Dr Atkins, the household's medical adviser, said that the child had suffered from a malformation of the chest. Death had 'arisen from an effusion of serum into the brain from natural causes, and not from neglect'. He had attended the deceased for a broken thigh and believed the bones had failed to unite.

On this evidence the jury felt themselves obliged to return a verdict of death from natural causes; they wished to record an expression of censure as a rider, but this the coroner could not permit. 'Mrs Savill,' remarks Greenwood, 'by this time has doubtless filled up the egg-box the little boy's demise rendered vacant. Why should she not, when she left the coroner's court without a stain on her character?'

It is impossible to gain a sympathetic insight into mid-nineteenth-century ideas about prostitution—or indeed about sexual relations in general—without giving full weight to the significance of venereal disease. It was undoubtedly widespread, though just how common nobody knew. The etiology of both syphilis and gonorrhoea was very little understood (some medical men thought gonorrhoea spontaneously generated by over-indulgence), the diagnosis of the less obvious symptoms was constantly mistaken, and cures were painful, protracted and doubtful, except perhaps with promptly tackled gonorrhoea. Confusion was compounded by the guilt and secrecy attaching to what many people believed to be a dispensation of wrathful providence. Something of the feelings evoked by venereal disease is shown by the fact that, despite its prevalence, many general hospitals made no provision for treating it, and in those which did patients were usually put into a pariah section officially known as 'The Foul Ward'.[1]

All sorts of superstitions proliferated round a subject that was frightening enough in all reality, and it was reasonable for a sufferer to be torn by guilt and anxiety when he had no certainty that he might not be visiting his sins on his wife and children. The word 'pollution', so often used by Victorians in connection with sexual morality, had clinical as well as metaphorical implications. Many men were afraid to confide in their strait-laced family doctors, and fear and ignorance provided a rich harvest for a horde of charlatans and blackmailers.

Acton was very conscious of the miseries caused by venereal disease, and his book was largely designed to ventilate the question. Official indifference to the subject appalled him and he set himself to shake it. London was on the whole a relatively healthy metropolis (strange though that may seem to us) yet 'in no Continental capital could such frightfully aggravated forms and complications of the venereal diseases be found as present themselves, I may say weekly, to the surgeons of St Bartholomew's.' Venereal disease did not kill a large proportion of its victims, but the contagion spread all the more persistently for that reason. Its effects on the children of infected parents were illustrated by the Registrar General's returns, which showed that, out of a total 468 deaths in England and Wales credited to syphilis in 1855, no less than 269 were of babies under a year old and 343 of children under fifteen. (Indirectly, of course, these diseases—and some of the measures used to relieve them—had long-term lethal consequences that no statistics disclosed.)

Prostitutes were the essential agents of infection: therefore, to Acton's pragmatic mind, they must be controlled, since it was futile to think of abolishing them. For this reason he was by no means an enemy to brothel keepers. Without the 'supervision of some crafty and spirit-proof old hag' many prostitutes would, he believed, 'be more uncontrollably dangerous to themselves and society than at present'. Furthermore, since every brothel keeper had an interest in keeping down venereal disease

[1] In 1856 there were less than three hundred beds in London charity hospitals allotted to venereal patients—including, it seems, the two or three smallish foundations specialising in such cases. Yet three major hospitals (Guy's, St Bartholomew's, King's College) treated some 30,000 V.D. cases in the year, and half the surgical out-patients at St Thomas's fell into this category (Acton, 1857 edition, pp. 142–3). V.D. was rife among merchant seamen and London's situation was presumably aggravated by her enormous maritime trade. Syphilis contracted from sailors from East Asia was especially dreaded for its virulence.

among her lodgers, her 'unsleeping cupidity' should ensure her cooperation in a system of compulsory inspection. Holding these views, he obviously considered the growing independence of prostitutes a social misfortune. He did not advocate closed, state-regulated brothels under keepers whose tyranny was supported by the police, after the Continental model; but with his wide knowledge of the subject he foresaw that any system of official control, such as he favoured, would in practice tend to strengthen the whoremonger's influence.

It is not hard to sympathise with those who wanted to see authority take a more positive attitude. As matters stood, everything seemed calculated to encourage the diseased prostitute to keep at her business as long as her strength lasted and she could find customers ignorant of her condition. Unless she could afford to lie up and at the same time pay a large doctor's bill—and prostitutes were not as a rule savers—almost the only thing open to her was the humiliating service provided by the charitable foul wards. Even here the in-patient accommodation was, as a rule, so grotesquely inadequate that she had small chance of being admitted; and if she went as an out-patient she was likely to have to support herself during the treatment. According to Acton, a sick prostitute trying to get temporary out-door relief put poor law officials so much on their mettle that every resource of Bumbledom was deployed against her; if she succeeded eventually in proving her 'settlement' in the parish, one petty obstruction after another would be put in her way until at last she was bullied into giving up. She could apply for admission to the pauper wards, but like everyone else—and perhaps with better reason than most—she looked on them with horror and fear. Poor prostitutes sometimes obtained medical treatment by deliberately getting themselves jailed.

As for the brothel keeper whose lodger became infected, she was often in a dilemma. If she threw the girl out she said goodbye to any chance of recovering the money almost certainly owed to her; if she let her remain she saddled herself with an awkward and unprofitable resident. But it can only have been the very lowest bawd, totally indifferent to the reputation of her premises, who let her go on bringing back men. Since there were bawds and procurers who were reckoned expert examiners—and were sometimes called in to certify a woman's health—it seems probable that some brothel keepers who had enough control over their girls had them periodically inspected. Closed brothels like the one by Portland Place may have survived as long as they did just because, like the introducing house, they were believed to offer a guarantee against infection.

Except at the most degraded levels, the fully fledged professional, inside or outside a brothel, was less of a risk than the promiscuous dollymop or desperate part-timer, in that she was more likely to have the means and knowledge to undertake some sort of prophylaxis.[1] Any measures to control venereal disease by regulating women's activities would have to include the quasi-prostitute and doubtful case, if they were to be at all effective.

Whatever the attitude of the authorities towards venereal disease in general, there was one quarter where they could hardly avoid confronting it. About a fifth of the troops in the home, Mediterranean and American stations were infected, and since the Brigade of Guards had a bad record it can hardly have been a result of overseas garrison duties. In the navy the situation was still worse. The result was inefficiency, weakened units and a serious waste of public money. Acton made great play with all this, and by the early sixties he and those who shared his views were no longer voices in the wilderness. Reform was in the wind.

By the mid-century, earlier regulations designed to control prostitution (some of them brutally savage) had either fallen into disuse or were being largely evaded. Then, in 1851, the Common Lodging House Act was passed, and this certainly made life harder for a number of poor prostitutes. Until then it had been common for several of them to club together and take a room for the night at a nethersken, all piling in with their customers. It had been a matter of merely speculative interest whether some places were to be considered brothels or common lodging houses. The Act changed all that by giving the police an automatic right to inspect any common lodging house, but it did not give them any authority over a house let out room by room to prostitutes who could claim to be private tenants. So, while numbers of brothel netherskens were cleaned up, the Act was far from putting an end to brothel keeping. Where brothels

---

[1] The condom, an ancient invention, was probably in fairly regular use ('French letter' was a term in common currency by the beginning of the forties) but it was still too coarsely made to be satisfactory.

not classifiable as public lodging houses were concerned—and this included the great majority of accommodation houses— the police could not act effectively on their own initiative. Responsibility for action rested on local (usually parochial) authorities; and since an action was likely to be a long, tiresome business that could cost well over a hundred pounds, it is easy to see why many parishes were not at all eager to inflict this burden on their ratepayers, especially since the brothel keeper could often set up again in other premises.

In rich and scandalous St James's the vestry was for a time very vigorous in putting down disorderly houses, and once had sixteen brothel keepers in the dock together; but there was little improvement. 'It closes the houses in one place but they come up in another,' a police superintendent told the Lords Committee in 1881, and his memories stretched back decades. 'I have been at it for years, and I cannot find anything like a diminution.' Nevertheless, because annoyed and influential citizens could, and constantly did, get individual brothels suppressed, entre- preneurs were discouraged from promoting large, blatant and costly houses, and this had its effect on the whole pattern of English prostitution.

The balance swung more and more in favour of the indepen- dent prostitute. In just those parts of London where the trade was at its most lucrative and concentrated, the authority of the brothel keeper was clearly on the wane. The woman 'sailing', as the elegant phrase went, 'on her own bottom' was becoming commoner, while the miserably dependent dress walker gradu- ally faded from streets where she had once been a familiar figure. The stay-in brothels, where the bawd regulated admissions, grew rarer and rarer.

The police had means of controlling women who plied in public streets, and in London a 'known common prostitute' who could be shown to annoy residents or 'passengers' was liable to a fine that could be a serious matter for the poorer sort of street walker. The girl who worked a fixed beat no doubt had to reach some sort of accommodation with the police, just as she did with her competitors. But the constable's formal powers were limited and in practice police authorities were mainly concerned to keep outward order, confine the most flagrant accosting to recognised areas, and break up links between prostitutes and thieves. The attitude of authority towards prostitutes, like that of society as a whole, was often a rather shame-faced acquiescence in a necessary evil.

In many respects this toleration answered reasonably well. State interference in citizens' affairs was kept to a minimum, whereas in France the licensed brothel keeper was a police spy, required to report on clients. At the same time the business stayed more or less in the open, and those who made good livings from it stood to lose if they became involved in real crimes. Despite the disreputable characters and large profits involved, prostitution did not give rise to much gangsterism; in fact public order improved and property became safer during the period when it was most prosperous. On that score there was no call to regret the barbarous ferocity of the old laws.

But venereal disease was another matter, and to many men besides Acton the uncontrolled prostitute was a fearsome menace to public health. It was this which in the 1860s started a train of events that threatened to transform the whole pattern of English prostitution.

In 1864 an Act was passed providing, in certain limited cases, for the inspection of prostitutes reported to be transmitting disease. Two years later this was followed by a measure under which prostitutes plying their trade at a few important naval and military stations became subject to periodic medical checks; and in 1869 further enactments made, in effect, every prostitute liable to a fortnightly examination if she worked within fifteen miles of any of the major garrison towns except London. This had unforeseen consequences. It brought in many of the evils of state licensed prostitution and led to an agitation that produced a reversal of policy and something like a charter of emancipation for the professional whore.

In the areas affected by the new laws, any woman held to be a common prostitute—that is to say denounced as one by the police—was invited to sign a 'voluntary submission' and thereafter present herself for regular inspections. If she did so, she became a self-acknowledged, statutory whore. If she refused, she was likely to have to prove to the magistrates that she led a virtuous life—something a woman far from being a common prostitute might find it hard to do. If she could not prove it and still refused to sign the submission, she was jailed. Metropolitan officers were drafted to garrison towns to act as a special morals police; and if their conduct was not as bad as the enemies of the

Acts made out, it inevitably left something to be desired. It is not hard to see what terror it could inspire in a woman when an officer had only to swear that 'he had cause to believe' she was a prostitute. The work offered endless temptations and, since it involved spying, it could not always be kept under adequate supervision.

'Now to all those who have any practical experience of the subject, it is notorious that the ordinary authority of the regular constable is amply sufficient to enable him to levy blackmail, either in purse or person, on any woman who is on the streets. The Contagious Diseases Acts enabled the special plainclothes constable to extend the area of his arbitrary authority to all poor women and girls who had no powerful protector,' wrote W. T. Stead. He was a harsh critic, but in fact it is unnecessary to assume that the detectives employed were rascals to see how the abuses crept in. If they had merely taken up the obvious, regular street walkers who could be seen accosting every second male pedestrian, they would have left untouched most of the women who were spreading infection. Every garrison had its camp followers and soldiers' wives were often promiscuous, while following the regiment as a more-or-less open prostitute was sometimes the only course left to their pensionless widows. To grapple with these problems, the police had to rely on confidential and often biased information, and it was natural that they should find common ground with the procurers and brothel keepers, who knew the trade in the district and had an interest in controlling venereal disease. It was also natural that the influence of the brothel keepers should increase as a result of the prostitute's new vulnerability.

Hostility to the Contagious Diseases Acts gathered quickly. Some saw them as a sinister departure from accepted constitutional principles. To others it was an outrage that the state should not merely countenance but actively patronise vice: what a commentary on Christian England that duly certified strumpets now called themselves 'Queen's women'! On the other hand to many practical men, impatient of theorising, the Acts were a victory over cant and humbug, and an advance in public hygiene whose benefits should be extended to the whole country. It was obvious that if those who opposed the system were to succeed, they must attack it before it became an accepted part of the administrative apparatus.

Like so many nineteenth century social movements, the opposition owed a great deal to women. Before the passing of the important third Act, the Ladies' National Association had been founded, in which Florence Nightingale and Harriet Martineau were prominent; and in 1870 the Association's remarkable secretary, Mrs George Butler, threw herself neck and crop into the campaign.

If her sex made it exceedingly indelicate for her to engage in a public controversy on such a subject, Josephine Butler also knew how to reap advantage from the fact that it often showed up her opponents in a very unchivalrous light. Three things greatly strengthened her position: she was whole-heartedly supported by her husband, an eminently respectable clergyman; she had charm; and she had been born into the powerful, aristocratic Whig clan of Grey.[1] There was a strong feminist component in her enthusiasm—women's education was among her reforming interests—and she found it intolerable that women should be debauched for men's satisfaction and then treated as the offenders. The cynical inequity of the contagious diseases legislation roused her anger and drew out her impressive gifts as a publicist. In decent but unequivocal language she laid stress on the affront to modesty of compulsory vaginal inspections—a point which struck home powerfully to a Victorian audience. She was a talented pamphleteer, with a turn for a sudden sharp directness that went under the reader's guard, and though her appeal was largely to Christian sentiment she was well primed in politics. She knew how embarrassing it would be for a Liberal government to be seen upholding a law that could be presented as an authoritarian assault on individual liberty.

In 1870 an interesting situation arose at Colchester, a garrison town. The parliamentary seat was vacant and the Liberal candidate was Sir Henry Storks, a distinguished officer and military expert. Gladstone's government was engaged in important military reforms and considered his support in the Commons essential. At the last general election a Liberal had won the seat with about fourteen per cent more votes than his rival.

Storks was an ardent supporter of the Acts and, as a colonial governor, had enforced similar regulations with draconian zeal.

---

[1] Her father, whose favourite she was, was John Grey of Dilston, a connection and intimate of the Reform Bill prime minister.

He was even on record as having suggested that soldiers' wives should be inspected. He had previously come forward as a candidate at Newark, but a repeal-the-Acts faction had raised such a hornets' nest that he had been obliged to stand down. At Colchester, however, he would clearly prove a tougher proposition. In view of this—and seeing that if the election was properly exploited it would provide a splendid opportunity of focusing interest on her cause and embarrassing the Government—Mrs Butler decided to intervene in person.

Oddly enough to modern ideas, she seems to have made most of her public speeches at religious meetings for women—who were not, of course, voters.[1] But she was the driving force behind an agitation that soon began to gnaw away Sir Henry's prospects. Placards were prepared giving extracts from his rasher pronouncements—including the ones about soldiers' wives—and sandwich men toured the streets with them, rousing the indignation of the military and of respectable trades-people alike. For the Conservatives, this stirring up of the chapel-going interest against their opponent was manna from heaven.

The bawdy house and procuring faction, who were ardent supporters of the Contagious Diseases Act, identified their key enemy without difficulty. In effect they mobilised the local underworld against her. A detailed description of her was posted on walls about the town, so that she could be recognised and mobbed, while anyone who gave her lodging was threatened with violence and arson. By wearing different clothes every day and incessantly moving from one address to another she kept a jump ahead of her persecutors, but the law gave her very little protection, even at public gatherings, and she was repeatedly exposed to danger. From a prayer meeting, broken up by a crowd of bullies and street scourings who shouted that she should not leave alive, she managed to slip out by a back way and fled alone through the night streets with the yelling of her hunters in her ears. After a time she took refuge in a deserted sodawater bottle factory, full of broken glass, listening (in her own words) to 'the rising and falling swell of the howling mob, which sounded very grievous'. Later, when the town had become quiet, she met a prostitute with whom she exchanged some

---

[1] Despite the 1867 Reform Act the Colchester electorate was very small. The non-voting population often played an important role in borough elections, partly no doubt because the poll was not secret.

friendly words; and eventually a well-wishing Quakeress took her to the home of a Methodist cheesemonger where she was welcomed.

After about a week's energetic campaigning she was nearly trapped. Her friends had taken a hotel room for her under the name of Grey, and she had come in late wearing a veil and gone quietly up to it. After she was in bed the landlord knocked and, poking his 'pale and distressed' face round the door, taxed her with being Mrs Butler. She admitted it. Then she must get up and leave. She had been traced and a mob was collecting outside the hotel; they had already broken some windows and were threatening to send the place up in flames. He would take care of her luggage, only she must go immediately. While the landlord went back to harangue the crowd and gain her a few moments' grace, she dressed and escaped through a back door. She found her way up a side street to a humble little house where she was given shelter for the night. In due course the mob found that she was not in the hotel and dispersed, leaving nothing worse than damaged doors and windows.

In fact the ungodly overplayed their hand with these rather old-fashioned electioneering tactics. Poor General Storks, no doubt well aware that his allies were doing him no good at all, became anxious to reach some sort of compromise. He had more important matters than venereal inspections to worry about. But Mrs Butler would have no half measures: there must be unconditional surrender over the Contagious Diseases issue—something the General, committed as he was, could not contemplate. His misgivings proved amply justified. When the day came hundreds of respectable Liberal electors stayed away from the hustings; and Josephine Butler and her family were interrupted in the middle of a meal by a triumphant telegram announcing that 'The Bird' (as she and her friends called Storks) had been shot down. The Liberal vote had fallen by more than forty per cent.

The agitators did not stop there, nor did their more uninhibited opponents. Campaigning at Pontefract, Mrs Butler was addressing a meeting in the loft of a barn when an attempt was made to put an end to her interference once and for all by setting light to the straw stored below. Luckily her supporters had foreseen that move and the straw was well wetted, so that although the meeting was disrupted and some of her audience narrowly escaped being thrown out of a window, in the end no one was seriously injured. While all this was going on a force of police turned up; but having taken a look and, presumably, satisfied themselves that there was no danger to property from the smoking straw, they withdrew without extricating Mrs Butler and her companions from a still ugly situation. She was a trouble maker and far from popular with police authorities.

Yet, ironically enough, she was largely responsible for an increase in their powers that they had long wanted. The bawdy house interest was not mistaken in its hatred of the repeal movement. It was not just that the movement brought about the amendment of the Contagious Diseases Acts, which were suspended in 1883 and repealed three years later. During the campaign Mrs Butler and her supporters ventilated a number of other issues and stirred up concern for the fate of fallen women as a class. Their agitation provided much of the impetus behind the Criminal Law Amendment Act of 1885 which made every species of whoremongering illegal.

Under this Act, procuring and brothel-keeping were effectively outlawed. Brothel proprietors and their agents became liable to simple summary proceedings. A £20 fine and three months hard labour could be imposed for a first offence, and £40 and four months for each subsequent conviction. For procuring young girls, for coercing prostitutes, and for inducing or attempting to induce any female to become an inmate of a brothel, much heavier penalties were provided; and the courts interpreted 'brothel' very liberally. The old legal defences behind which bawdy houses had been sheltering were completely dismantled.

It is true that in several important respects the famous Amendment Act did not so much revolutionise the prostitute's situation as accelerate and formalise a process of emancipation that had been under way for a long time, and which the Contagious Diseases Acts merely impeded. Nevertheless 1885 marks the end of a period in the history of prostitution in England. Thereafter the professional bawd had to operate under cover, and became as unquestionably criminal as the thief or forger. In the whole Victorian underworld no other important field of activity underwent so clear-cut a change.

Epilogue

Alone among all the arts and callings of the underworld, prostitution had an obvious social function. No doubt it was an exaggeration to think that, if there had been no whores, chaste women would have been in constant danger of rape; all the same it is impossible to take a long look at Victorian civilisation without realising that Babylon, in its various forms, was an essential part of it, the dark concomitant to the demands of daylight respectability.

Yet, in a broader sense, the whole underworld was a functional part of the Victorian community, in so far as one cannot conceive of that community without it. Its roots ran everywhere through the social sump, the essential cess-pit into which the human refuse of an intensely competitive society drained. In turn, the underworld's unending assault on the rest of the population—the thieving, begging and cheating with which this book has dealt—had a potent effect on society. By making the underdog into a conspicuous threat or nuisance it forced his presence on to the notice of a world apt to overlook the fate of those who suffer in silence.

On the one hand it is impossible not to be impressed by the ramifying interconnections of the underworld. The hotel robber, sentenced and imprisoned in Cheshire, disappears into a Haymarket warren a day or two after breaking jail: the brothel-bully who has become too well known about St James's bobs up in Manchester. Forged currency, rough-struck in city rookeries, is got ready for smashing in wayfarers' camps. Cadgers working the provinces send to London for bogus testimonials. One can understand the complaint from the Liverpool police that their enemies, drawn from far and near, 'seem to belong to one great criminal profession'.

On the other hand it is misleading to think of the underworld as something self-contained and divorced from the general social pattern. At every turn we are confronted with its dependence on social and economic developments and it can only be realistically considered as part and parcel of an evolving society.

But at this point a paradox appears. Even the most cursory reader will have noticed that many of the criminal activities described in this book are far from obsolete today: some, indeed, are organised on a bigger scale than ever they were in Victorian times. Yet the conditions that seem to have engendered the old underworld—wide and despairing poverty, fortress-rookeries, illiteracy, gross social neglect—have been transformed. Why should crime now flourish so conspicuously if it was, in truth, the material environment of the underworld that gave birth to its crimes?

One obvious answer is that, in comparing our present day society with one so profoundly different, one may expect to find like actions rising from unlike causes. Criminals today may be motivated by different reasons from those that drove their great-grandfathers to break the law, but the *sorts* of crime a man can rationally commit are limited. The fact that two societies, a century apart, both produced a sensational train robbery need not imply that the robbers were products of the same social mechanism.

This in itself, however, cannot explain the improvement in public order and safety that took place during the Victorian era, an improvement that is reflected not only in the sometimes arguable statistics of crime but in the whole tenor of contemporary comment and behaviour. Nor can it explain the poorly organised and fractional nature of crime in that period. How was it that, faced with a small and slowly developed detective force, an underworld that stretched from the teeming desperation of the slum warrens to the fleshpots of the Haymarket, whose channels of communication linked city to city and reached out to the migrant population of the countryside, produced no great criminal combines such as have plagued later and apparently less vulnerable communities?

Various causes suggest themselves, ranging from the probity of the courts to the lively hue-and-cry hostility shown to criminals by people of all classes. Many are too trivial or too self-evident to need listing, or would take us too far from our subject. There is, however, an aspect of Victorian society, easily enough overlooked in this connection, that may be worth noting.

In all sorts of important fields of activity, from waging war to building railways, a vital part was played by the ambitious working man. It is hardly possible to study the Crimean War without being astounded at how much was regularly left to sergeants. In iron foundries and construction works, mills and mines, the boss workman often held a postion of quite extraordinary independence and authority, hiring and firing his own assistants. As the century went on authority in industry became more centralised, but at the same time a new series of responsible jobs had been opening up for the intelligent proletarian— notably in dealing with the steam machinery that was the basis of the country's economic life.

In short, for all the misery and social dislocation, an increasingly industrialised community was offering many opportunities for just those pushing, flexible men who might find the thwarting of their native abilities most intolerable. Literacy was growing and the lure of self-improvement was powerful.

Nor, of course, were opportunities confined to England. The growth of emigration was prodigious, and the idea of settlement overseas appealed both to the respectably adventurous and to the most enterprising black sheep of every class. To reach America and even Australia was continually becoming easier for the poor—emigration was subsidised by a variety of agencies —and the outward flow of hard cases who left England of their own volition was a growing flood compared to the rivulet of criminal transportees that dried up in the fifties.

Hence one can think of the underworld as being deprived of its natural leaders, its boldest and most resourceful spirits. The young bully-boy who outraged decent citizens as a navvy becomes, if he is shrewd as well as tough, a foreman overseer, and ends up a respected citizen with polished boots and a silver watchchain. The lad sharpened on the streets into a budding magsman realises that the distant gold rush is likely to provide far fatter pickings than Epsom Downs. The bright foundling learns his letters in the workhouse school and dreams of the power and status driving a locomotive or policing a beat may bring him.

This was one way in which the underworld was influenced by the community at large—kept within bounds by the very expansionism and energy that characterised the age. But in a far broader, more general way that influence made itself felt in the whole character of the underworld, and the manner in which it did so provides a certain concluding irony.

During the years that spanned the mid-century, a change was coming over the personality of the underworld. Despite the proliferation of slums and the degradation of life in those strongholds of crime, the delinquents who sallied out from them were becoming less blatant in their approach to those from whom they begged and stole. The gangs of clamorous scarecrows who had infested Regency London were no more than relics by Mayhew's day; they belonged not only to a worse policed England but to a different climate of life. The successful beggar was now no longer the old-fashioned 'turnpike sailor', the weatherbeaten 'survivor of Trafalgar' flourishing his brass-shod crutch; typically, he was a frayed, diffident character, painfully clean and heartrendingly respectable, the victim of the same kind of mischance as might strike at the shop-keepers and artisans whose pennies and sixpences fell into his hat.

Bill Sikes, too, with his knobbed stick and blackguardly appearance, was on the downgrade—outmoded as an efficient housebreaker by a more sophisticated and unobtrusive criminal who could return from cracking a crib in a second class railway compartment without exciting notice. The swell mob pickpocket had a sober, almost methodist look. The old, riotous, reckless, openly menacing, Hogarthian underworld, so long a part of the English scene, was fast fading away.

Each culture produces the delinquency proper to it, and by 1850, through all the complexities of criminal life, a subtle but persistent drift can be discerned. The manners of society at large are imposing themselves even on those who are most hostile to it. In a word, the underworld itself is becoming Victorian.

Notes on the text illustrations

prosecutions of unlicensed pantomimes, but there was chronic hostility between humble showfolk and the authorities. (*Punch,* 1851)

78 Hanseller's caravan by a remote cottage. The scene apparently refers to 1850–70 but the engraving is not contemporary. (Mansell Collection)

82 'Livett-throwing'. Gustave Doré

94 Rent collector resisted by slum cellar-dwellers. The donkey suggests they are street traders. (*Punch's Almanack for 1850*)

109 'A Court for King Cholera'. Note the stage-Irish spelling 'thravelers'. (*Punch,* 1852)

130 Plain-clothes officer and ragged gonoph, captioned 'A strong attachment'. (*Punch,* 1841)

140 Rampsmen and victim. Detail from 'Fruits of Intemperance' by George Cruikshank, 1854 (British Musuem)

148 A pull from the tail. (*Punch,* 1841)

171 Burglar's apparatus for cutting through a bolted door. Note that the handle is a coarse jemmy similar to item 5 in the drawing on page 172. This and the three following pictures are from a pamphlet by George Cruikshank *Stop Thief or Hints to House-keepers to Prevent Housebreaking.* (British Museum)

172 Various burglar's tools, about 1850. (1) Small steel jemmy with sharp points, made to unscrew into two parts (2) sharp hollow chisel and case (3) small saw made from table knife (4) (5) (6) assorted levers.

172 Cracksman's twirls (skeleton key and picklock).

173 Bit-and-brace technique suitable for cutting through tough materials (including metal sheeting) by means of a line of connected circular holes, as shown at 5 and 6. An aperture like this would be convenient for putting in a little snakesman.

180 Cover to the pamphlet *Stop Thief* by George Cruikshank.

191 Political cartoon from *Punch* (1851) captioned 'The Dealer in old clothes'. The cartoonist depends for his point on the generally accepted notion of the Jewish fence-cum-pawnbroker and the *ingénu* thief.

203 Child beggar. Part of Plate IV in *The Bottle* by George Cruikshank, 1847. (Guildhall Library)

224 Elderly beggar with child. The man may well have hired—or even bought—the infant as a suitable 'property'. Gustave Doré

228 'Asleep under the stars'. Gustave Doré

231 How the thimble-rigger manipulates his pea—actually a bread pill soft enough to be held under a long thumbnail. (*Illustrated London News,* 1842)

232 A thimble-rigger (perhaps the commonest of all fairground and race-course magsmen) with rustic victims. (*Illustrated London News*, 1842)

277 Sparring with gloves. Gustave Doré

281 'The Derby—lunch time'. If the composition is rather fanciful it correctly emphasises the contiguity of rich and poor which made Epsom a magnet for the underworld. Gustave Doré

285 'Bolted!' Scene outside a lister's betting office. (*Punch*, 1852)

291 'Exercising bulldogs'. Gustave Doré

313 Flower girl with baby. Gustave Doré

316 'A spree in a railway carriage'. About 1870 (Mansell Collection)

340 'Visitors from the country'. The blonde's features, vulgarly dressy costume and boldly exposed ankle combine to suggest the prostitute. Also she is reading what can just be discerned in the original as a programme for Cremorne Gardens. From *The Day's Doings* (Mansell Collection)

365 A burlesque trial in a saloon or supper room. Entertainments of this sort were made popular by the famous and disreputable entertainer 'Baron' Renton Nicholson who, however, often preferred males in drag. Sub-titled 'In the neighbourhood of Leicester Square'. About 1870. From *The Day's Doings* (Mansell Collection)

371 'His mark'. A rough or 'leg' who has suffered, presumably, at the hands of a 'mark', i.e. intended victim. (*Punch*, 1841)

Glossary of colloquial and cant words

alderman   half-crown

bacca-pipes   whiskers curled in small, close ringlets
beak-hunting   poultry stealing
bearer up   bully who robs men decoyed by woman accomplice
beef (verb)   raise hue-and-cry (cf. *hot beef!* = stop thief!)
bend   waistcoat
betty   picklock
billy   handkerchief (usually silk handkerchief)
bit faker   coiner
blob (blab), on the   begging by telling hard luck stories
blow   inform
blower   girl (opprobrious)
bludger   footpad
boat, get the   be sentenced to transportation or a severe term of penal
   servitude
bone   good, profitable
bonnet   covert assistant to gambling sharp
broads   playing cards
broadsman   cardsharp
bug hunting   robbing or cheating drunks (especially at night)
bull   five shillings
buor   woman
buttoner   sharper's assistant who entices dupes
buzzing   stealing, especially picking pockets

cant   present, free meal, quantity of some article (*cant of togs* = gift
   of clothes)
cash carrier   prostitute's manager, ponce
chat   louse
chaunting lay   street singing
chavy   child
chiv   knife, blade
choker   clergyman (*gull a choker* = fool a c.)
christen or *church (a watch)*   remove marks of identification
cly faking   pocket picking (esp. of handkerchiefs)

cockchafer   treadmill
cokum (*noun & adjective*)   opportunity, advantage; shrewd, cunning
cool   look, look at
coopered   worn out, useless (*this ken is coopered* = this place is no longer any good)
couter   pound (money)
crabshells   shoes
cracksman   safebreaker
crapped   hanged
crow   look-out man, doctor
crusher   policeman

dab   bed (*dab it up* = cohabit, 'shack up')
dabeno   bad
daffy   small measure (usually of spirits)
deadlurk   empty premises
deaner   shilling
deb (as *dab*)
dewskitch   thrashing
diddiki   gipsies; half-bred gipsies
dillo   old
dimmick   base coin
ding (*verb & noun*)   throw away, pass on; object so treated (*knap the ding* = take what has just been stolen)
dipper   pickpocket
dispatches   loaded dice
dobbin   ribbon
dollymop   midinette, promiscuous servant girl
dollyshop   low, unlicensed loan shop
dookin   palmistry
down   suspicion (*put down on A* = give information as to A's plans: *take the down off a ticker* = make a stolen watch negotiable)
downer   sixpence
downy   cunning, false
drag (*1*)   three month jail sentence
drag (*2*)   street
dragsman   thief who steals from carriages
drum   house, premises (*break a drum* = burgle a house)
dub (*1*)   bad
dub (*2*)   key, picklock
duce   twopence
duce hog   two shillings
duckett   hawker's licence
duffer   cheating vendor, hawker

dumplin   swindling game played with skittles
dumps   buttons and other hawker's small wares
dunnage   clothes

E.O.   fairground gambling game—'in which the appropriation of the
stakes is determined by the falling of the ball into one of several
niches marked E or O' (O.E.D.)
esclop, escop   policeman

fadge   farthing
fakement   device, pretence (esp. a notice or certificate to facilitate
begging)
family, family people   members of the criminal class
fan   feel someone's clothing for money etc.
fawney   ring
fine wirer   highly skilled pickpocket, especially one who steals from
women
finny   five pound note
flag   apron
flam   a lie
flash (verb & adjective)   show, hence show-off; vulgarly smart; criminal
flash house   public house to which criminals resort
flash notes   paper looking, at a casual glance, like banknotes
flat   easily deceived person
flatch   halfpenny
flats   playing cards
flimp   snatch-pickpocket, snatch stealing in crowds etc.
flue faker   chimney sweep
flummut   dangerous
flying the blue pigeon   stealing roof lead
flying the mags   pitch and toss
fogle   silk handkerchief
fushme   five shillings

gaff   show, exhibition, fair (*penny gaff* = low theatre)
gallies   boots
gammon   deceive
gammy   false, undependable, hostile
garret   fob pocket
gatter   beer
gattering   public house
gegor   beggar
gen   shilling

glim (1)   light, fire; a method of begging by representing oneself as ruined by a disastrous fire

glim (2)   venereal disease

glock   half-wit

gonoph   minor thief, inferior pickpocket

granny   understand, recognise

gravney   ring

gray, grey   coin with two identical faces

griddling   begging, peddling, scrounging

hard-up   tobacco

haybag   woman

hoisting   shop lifting

huey, hughey   town, village

hykey   pride

jack   detective

jemmy (1)   smart, of superior class

jemmy (2)   housebreaker's tool

jerry   watch

jerryshop   pawnbroker

joey   fourpenny piece

jolly   disturbance, fracas; one who promotes a fracas

judy   woman, prostitute

jug-loops   locks of hair brought forward over the temples and curled

julking   singing (of caged songbirds)

jump   ground floor window; burglary through such a window

kanurd   drunk

kecks   trousers

ken   house, place (especially a lodging or public house)

kennetseeno   bad, stinking, putrid

kennuck   penny

kidsman   organiser of child thieves

kife   bed

kingsman   coloured or black neckerchief

knap   steal, take, receive

knapped   pregnant

knob   'under and over'—a swindling fairground game

kynchin lay   street stealing from children

lackin   wife

lag (*noun & verb*)   convict, ticket-of-leave man; to sentence to transportation or penal servitude

lavender, in   hidden from police
lay   method, system (usually of crime or mendicancy)
leg (from *blackleg*)   dishonest horsy person, sporting cheat or tout
lill   pocket book
long-tailed (of banknotes)   note of more than five pounds face value
luggers   ear rings
lumber   pawn; go into seclusion (*in lumber* = in jail)
lurk   place of resort and concealment (*servants lurk* = lodging or public house frequented by shady servants); scheme, method
lurker   beggar (especially a hard-luck story teller)
lush   alcoholic drink (*not*, normally, the drinker)
lushington   drunkard

macer   cheat, sharper
mag   halfpenny
magflying   pitch and toss
magsman   cheat, sharper (of lower status than a *macer*)
maltooler   pickpocket who steals in buses (especially from women)
Mary Blaine   railway train; to meet or go by a train
mauley   handwriting, signature
mecks   wine or spirits
milltag   shirt
miltonian   policeman
min   steal
mitting   shirt
mizzle   quit, vanish
monkry   country parts; beggars' tricks and impostures suitable for a vagrant life
monnicker   signature
mot   woman (especially proprietress of lodging or public house)
moucher, moocher   rural vagrant
mouth   blabber, fool
mumper   beggar
mutcher   thief who steals from drunks
muck snipe   one totally down and out

nail   steal
nancy   buttocks
neddy   cosh
nemmo   woman
nethers   lodging charges
nethersken   low lodging house
Newgate knockers   heavily greased side whiskers curling back to, or over, the ears

nibbed arrested
nobbler sharp's confederate
nommus! get away quick!
nose informer, spy
nubbingken sessions courthouse

onion watch seal
out of twig unrecognised, in disguise
outsider instrument for turning key from outside lock

pack night lodging for the very poor
paddingken tramps' lodging house
pall detect
palmer shoplifter
patterer one who earns by recitation or hawker's sales-talk in the
    streets (especially hawkers of broadsheets etc.)
peter box, trunk, safe
pig policeman, detective
pit inside front coat pocket
plant victim
pogue purse
prad horse
prater bogus itinerant preacher
prig (*noun & verb*) thief; steal
puckering speaking in a fashion incomprehensible to spectators
push money

rampsman footpad, 'tearaway'
randy, on the on the spree
rasher waggon frying pan
ray one-and-sixpence
reader pocketbook
ream real, genuine, superior
reeb beer
rook jemmy (burglar's tool)
ruffles handcuffs

saddle loaf
salt box condemned cell
sawney bacon
scaldrum dodge begging with the aid of feigned or self-inflicted
    wounds
scran food

screever   writer of fake testimonials etc.

screw   skeleton key

scroby   flogging in jail

scurf   exploiting employer or gang-leader

shake lurk   begging under pretence of being a shipwrecked sailor

shallow, work the   beg half-naked

shant   pot, tumbler

sheviss   shift (garment)

shinscraper   treadmill

shoful (noun & adjective)   bad money; counterfeit; hansom cab

shofulman   passer of bad money

skipper   one who sleeps in hedges and outhouses

slang (1)   false, sham (especially of weights and measures)

slang (2)   chain, watch-chain, fetters

slang cove   showman

slap-bang   cheap eating house

slum (adjective & verb)   false, sham, a faked document etc.; cheat, pass
bad money

smasher   passer of false money

smatter hauling   stealing handkerchiefs

snakesman   lithe boy thief employed in housebreaking

snells   hawker's small wares

snide   counterfeit, counterfeit money or jewellery

snide pitching   passing bad money

snoozer   specialist hotel thief

snowing   stealing linen etc. put out to dry

soft   paper money (*do some soft* = pass forged notes)

speeler   cheat, gambler

spike   workhouse

sprat   sixpence

spreading the broads   three card trick

square rigged   soberly and respectably dressed

stall   thief's accomplice who impedes pursuit

star glazing   system of removing pane of glass for robbery

stepper   treadmill

stickman   pickpocket's or shoplifter's accomplice to whom articles are
passed

stiff   paper money, bill of exchange, hawker's licence

stir   prison

stock buzzer   handkerchief thief

stretch   twelve months jail sentence

suck-crib   beer shop

swag   goods, stolen property; cheap manufactured articles, pedlar's
and cheap jacks' stock (*swagshop* = warehouse supplying such stores)

tail   prostitute

tatts   dice, false dice

terrier crop   short bristly hair-cut (denoting recent spell in jail or workhouse)

teviss   shilling

thicker   pound (money)

thrummer   threepenny bit

tightener   good meal (*do the tightener* = dine)

toffken   house with well-to-do occupants

toke   bread

tol   lot, share

tooling   skilled pocket-picking

toper   road

topped   hanged

translators   second hand apparel (especially boots)

trasseno   bad, a bad person

twirls   skeleton keys

under and over   swindling fairground game

vamp   steal, pawn (*in for a vamp* = jailed for thieving)

voker   speak, understand (*voker romeny?* = can you speak cant?)

yack   watch

yennap   penny

Bibliography

Acton, William   *Prostitution. Considered in its Moral, Social & Sanitary Aspects*   1857.   Second, much revised edition   1870

Adams, W. E.   *Memoirs of a Social Atom*   1903

Anon   *London in the Sixties*   1908

Anon   *The History & Mystery of the Exchequer Bills Forgery*   1842

Archer, Thomas   *The Pauper, the Thief and the Convict*   1865

Ashton, John   *A History of Gambling*   1898

Baker, T. B. Lloyd   *War with Crime*   1889

Bartlett, D. V. G.   *London by Day and Night*   1852

Beames, T.   *The Rookeries of London*   1850

Bennett, A. R.   *London and Londoners in the Eighteen-Fifties and Sixties*   1924

Bent, James   *Criminal Life: Reminiscences of forty-two years as a Police Officer*   1891

Booth, Charles   *Life and Labour of the People in London*   1891–1903

Borrow, George   *Lavengro*   1851
      The Romany Rye   1857
      ('Definitive Edition' annotated by W. I. Knapp   1905)

Browne, D. G.   *The Rise of Scotland Yard*   1956

Butler, Josephine   *Personal Reminiscences of a Great Crusade*   1896

Carlyle, Thomas   *Chartism*   1839
      Latter-day Pamphlets   1850

Chadwick, Edwin   *On the Dependence of Moral and Criminal on Physical Conditions. (Transactions of the British Association for the Advancement of Science)*   1857

Chesterton, George L.   *Revelations of Prison Life*   1856

Clapham, J. H.   *Economic History of Modern Britain: The Railway Age*   1926

Cobb, Belton   *The First Detectives*   1957

Collins, Philip   *Dickens and Crime*   1962

Craven, W. G. (with Lord Suffolk)   *Racing* (Badminton Library) 1886

'Custos'   *The Police Force of the Metropolis in 1868*   1868

Dicey, A. V.   *Law and Public Opinion in England during the Nineteenth Century* 2nd edition, 1914

Dickens, Charles   *Oliver Twist*   1838
  Bleak House   1853
  The Uncommercial Traveller   1861
  Reprinted Pieces (various collective editions, including the *New Oxford Dickens* 1947–58)
Disraeli, Benjamin   *Sybil*   1845
Du Cane, E. D.   *The Punishment and Prevention of Crime*   1881

Egan, Pierce   *Jerry Hawthorne Esq. and . . . Corinthian Tom* 1820–21
Engels, F.   *The Condition of the Working Classes in England in 1844* 1845 (translated by W. O. Henderson and W. H. Chaloner 1958)

Faucher, Léon   *Etudes sur l'Angleterre*   1845
Fay, C. R.   *Life and Labour in the Nineteenth Century*   1935
Finer, S. E.   *The Life and Times of Sir Edwin Chadwick*   1952

Gavin, Hector   *Sanitary Ramblings*   1848
George, M. D.   *London Coal-heavers*. Economic Journal, History Supplement   May 1927
Glover, Edward   'Victorian Ideas of Sex'   In *Ideas and Beliefs of the Victorians*   1949
Goddard, Henry   *Memoirs of a Bow Street Runner*   1956
Godwin, G.   *London Shadows*   1854
  Town Swamps   1859
Greenwood, James   *Unsentimental Journeys*   1867
  The Seven Curses of London   1869
  The Wilds of London   1874
  Low-life Deeps   1876
Griffiths, Arthur   *Chronicles of Newgate*   1884
  Secrets of the Prison House   1894
  Mysteries of Police and Crime   1898

Haddon, Archibald   *The Story of the Music Hall*   1935
Hammond, J. L. & B.   *The Village Labourer 1760–1832*   1911
  The Town Labourer 1760–1832   1917
  Lord Shaftesbury   1921
  The Age of the Chartists   1930
Harris, E.   *Treatment of Juvenile Delinquents*   1877
Hart, Jenifer M.   *The British Police*   1951
  'The Reform of Borough Police'. *English Historical Review*, July 1955
Hasbach, W.   *A History of the English Agricultural Labourer*. Translated Ruth Kenyon   1908

Havitt, W.   *Rural Life of England*   1838

Hill, Frederick   *Crime*   1853

Hill, M. Davenport   *Suggestions for the Repression of Crime*   1857

Hobsbawm, E. J.   'The Tramping Artisan'. *Economic History Review* 2nd Series Vol. III, No. 3, 1951

House, Humphrey   *The Dickens World*   1942

Hoyle, William   *Crime in England and Wales in the Nineteenth Century*   1876
   Crime and Pauperism (Open letter to W. E. Gladstone)   1881

Hughes, Thomas   *Tom Brown at Oxford*   1861

Jefferies, Richard   *The Gamekeeper at Home*   1877
   The Amateur Poacher   1879

Jephson, H.   *The Sanitary Evolution of London*   1927

Jerrold, Blanchard   *A London Pilgrimage*   1872

Kingsley, Charles   *Yeast*   1848
   Alton Locke   1850

Knight, Charles   *Passages of a Working Life*   1864–5.
   Editor and publisher: *London.* 6 vols, 1841–4
   The Land We Live In   1846

Letchworth, W. P.   *Report on Deprived and Delinquent Children* 1877

Leyland, C. G.   *The English Gipsies*   1873

Logan, W.   *The Great Social Evil*   1871

Lloyd, R.   *Railwayman's Gallery*   1953

Lloyd Baker, T. B.   See Baker

London Society for the Suppression of Mendicity   *Reports*   1846–1862/3

Martineau, Harriet   *History of England during the Thirty Years' Peace*   1849–50

Mather, F. C.   *Public Order in the Age of the Chartists*   1959

Mayhew, Henry   *London Labour and the London Poor*, Vols. I–III 1851–2, Vol. IV (with J. Binny, B. Hemyng and A. Halliday) 1826
   The Great World of London (An uncompleted series of periodical parts)   1856
   The Criminal Prisons of London (with John Binny)   1862
   Mayhew's London (Selections from Vols. I–III of *London Labour and the London Poor*, edited Peter Quennell)   1949
   London's Underworld (Selections from Vol. IV of *London Labour and the London Poor*, edited Peter Quennell)   1950

Miles, W. A.   *Poverty, Mendicity and Crime*   1839

Mitchell, E. B.   'The Prize Ring' in *Boxing* (Badminton Library)
  n.d.   circa 1890
Morrison, Arthur   *A Child of the Jago*   1896
  The Hole in the Wall   1902

Newton, William   *Secrets of Tramp Life Revealed*   1886
Nicholson, Renton   *Autobiography of a Fast Man*   1863
Noel, Baptist W.   *Spiritual Claims of the Metropolis*   1836

Pare, W.   *A plan for the Suppression of the Predatory Classes*   1862
Pike, L. O.   *A History of Crime in England*   1873–6
Plint, T.   *Crime in England*   1851

Radzinowicz, Leon   *A History of English Criminal Law and Adminis-
  tration from 1750*   1948–
Redford, A.   *Labour Migration in England, 1800–1850*   1926
Ritchie, J. Ewing   *The Night Side of London*   1857
Rose, Millicent   *The East End of London*   1951
Roughead, W.   *The Bad Companions*   1930

Sanger, G. ('Lord George Sanger')   *Seventy Years a Showman*   1910
Simon, John   *English Sanitary Institutions*   1890
Sims, G. R.   *How the Poor Live*   1883
Smith, F.   *Life and Works of Sir James Kay-Shuttleworth*   1923
Stead, W. T.   *Josephine Butler*   1887
Stock, E.   *History of the Church Missionary Society*   1899
Suffolk, Earl of   See Craven, W. G.
Surtees, R. S.   *Mr Sponge's Sporting Tour*   1852
  Plain or Ringlets?   1860
Symons, J. C.   *Tactics for the Times*   1849
  On the Reformation of Very Young Offenders   1855

Taine, Hyppolite A.   *Notes sur l'Angleterre*   1872
  Translated W. F. Rae   1872
  New translation by Edward Hyams   1957
Talbot, J. B.   *Miseries of Prostitution*   1844
Taylor, W. C.   *Notes of a Tour in Lancashire*   1842
Thackeray, W. M.   'On Going to See a Man Hanged'. From *Sketches
  and Travels in London,* various collected editions. Originally
  published in *Fraser's Magazine*   1840
Trail, H. D. & Mann, J. S. (editors)   *Social England,* Vol. VI   1898

Webb, Sidney & Beatrice   *English Poor Law History*   1927–9
Williams, Montagu   *Leaves of a Life*   1890

Woodward, E. L. *The Age of Reform* 1946
Wright, Thomas (The Journeyman Engineer) *Habits and Customs of the Working Class* 1867
   The Great Unwashed 1868

Young, G. M. *Early Victorian England* 1934
   Editor: *Victorian England: Portrait of an Age* 1936

Index

Numerals in italic type show the main reference to the subject